The Breakdown of Class Politics

THE BREAKDOWN OF CLASS POLITICS

A Debate on Post-Industrial Stratification

Edited by

Terry Nichols Clark

and

Seymour Martin Lipset

Woodrow Wilson Center Press
Washington, D.C.

The Johns Hopkins University Press
Baltimore and London

EDITORIAL OFFICES

Woodrow Wilson Center Press
One Woodrow Wilson Plaza
1300 Pennsylvania Avenue, N.W.
Washington, D.C. 20004
Telephone (202) 691-4029
www.wilsoncenter.org

Order From

The Johns Hopkins University Press
P.O. Box 50370
Baltimore, Maryland 21211
1 (800) 537-5487
www.press.jhu.edu

2 4 6 8 9 7 5 3 1

Library of Congress Cataloging-in-Publication Data

The breakdown of class politics : a debate on post-industrial
stratification / edited by Terry Nichols Clark and Seymour Martin
Lipset.
      p. cm.
Includes bibliographical references and index.
   ISBN 0-8018-6576-X (pbk. : acid-free paper)
   1. Social classes. 2. Social classes—Political aspects. I. Clark,
Terry N. II. Lipset, Seymour Martin.
   HT611 .B74 2001
   305.5—dc21
                                        00-012604

v

Contents

Figures and Tables

Figures

Tables

The Breakdown of Class Politics

Introduction

TERRY NICHOLS CLARK AND SEYMOUR MARTIN LIPSET

Class and its linkage to politics became a controversial and exciting topic again in the 1990s. In 1991, we published "Are Social Classes Dying?" (Clark and Lipset 1991; see also chapter 2 of this volume). We argue that social class is declining in its importance in some post-industrial societies. The paper identifies key sources of the decline of social class in the changed social relations of the economy, political parties, and family. The key factors are presented in propositions stressing hierarchy, and some suggestive evidence is offered in support. The paper sparked an exchange in the journal *International Sociology* (Pakulski 1993; Hout et al. 1993; Clark et al. 1993) that continued at several annual meetings of the American Sociological Association, in Bielefeld at the International Sociological Association World Congress (e.g., Goldthorpe 1999), a conference at Oxford (organized by Goeff Evans), and several books (e.g., Nieuwbeerta 1995; Lee and Turner 1996; Evans 1999; Manza and Brooks 1999).

Our main critics were at Oxford (John Goldthorpe, Geoff Evans, and others) and the University of California, Berkeley (Michael Hout, Jeff Manza, and Clem Brooks). The Oxford and Berkeley critics both held (initially) that class was more persistent than we suggested. The positions were more sharply opposed at the outset but have grown far more nuanced as further evidence has accumulated, as is elaborated in chapter 1.

This volume emerges from four main conferences organized by us, the coeditors, two in Washington, D.C. and two in Chicago, and several others covering related issues. The conferences joined key protagonists in the lively exchange over class and politics. Sharply contrasting views were forcefully argued: that class is dead, that class has not declined at all, that aspects of class have changed, that class simply needs to be redefined, and more.

Class has long been a core concept in social science. While its importance and use vary by subfield (see chapter 12), it has been central to much work on social stratification, mobility, and political behavior. Even in 1994, David Grusky's introduction and chapters by many contributors in the reader *Social Stratification* suggest that, despite cosmetic changes, stratification is powerful and persistent, even if specific meanings and measures of class have shifted. Work on political parties and voting by sociologists seemed strongly dominated by class a decade or so ago although political scientists seemed less sensitive to class concerns. But through the 1990s, debate reopened these issues for all social scientists.

Contributions from several traditions of work on class and politics, including those in this volume, have made substantial mutual contributions. The field has achieved greater clarity and depth in recent works that have questioned, tested, and thereby extended interrelated assumptions, methods, and results. Class effects persist in more modest and redefined form than in the past. Recent changes into social and political life have been increasingly incorporated in older institutional specifics, such as the British Labour Party's becoming New Labour under Tony Blair. Future work has a stronger foundation upon which to build.

Summary of the Book by Chapter

This volume includes (1) a broad overview and synthesis of the exchange over class politics and voting issues in the last decade, (2) major contributions by leading participants in this exchange, and (3) original social science contributions, in theory and empirical findings. The volume's writing should be accessible to a broad readership, including undergraduate college students.

Technical and statistical issues are sometimes essential to consider, but most are relegated to appendixes and notes. Summaries of the individual chapters follow:

> 1. What Have We Learned in a Decade on Class and Party Politics? by Terry Nichols Clark

This chapter presents background information on the exchange over social class as new work emerged in the 1990s, challenging past findings and generating lively interest. Large disagreements among researchers in the early 1990s are often replaced by convergence in the late 1990s. Topics include: the decline of organized Communism and questioning of Marxist theories; the ideology of "market individualism" and its penetration into political parties; the weakening of classes as a basis of political activity and voting; important differences in these trends across countries; new research on social class; theories of decline; and conflicting evidence from different sources.

2. Are Social Classes Dying? by Terry Nichols Clark and Seymour Martin Lipset

Originally published in *International Sociology*, this contribution helped spark the debate. It suggests that social class is declining in power as an explanation of many phenomena, especially for politics. But in some locations, class persists. The chapter states key propositions about where and when class is important; for example, it declines as income and education rise and as the economy shifts from manufacturing to services, small firms, and higher tech.

3. The Persistence of Classes in Post-Industrial Societies, by Mike Hout, Clem Brooks, and Jeff Manza

This is a spirited defense of the enduring importance of social class. Unlike most later work by these authors, this chapter does not present original empirical research but is wide ranging, drawing on concepts and results from many subfields for evidence of a class dynamic. It is based on a broad reading of materials on politics, post-industrial economic trends, small firms, unions, and the family. It is drafted explicitly as a response to and critique of "Are Social Classes Dying?"

4. The Declining Political Significance of Social Class, by Terry Nichols Clark, Seymour Martin Lipset, and Michael Rempel

As a first response to critics, this chapter points out how many critics simplified our arguments and evidence, a trend that continued over the decade. It shows that we did not simply say "class is in decline" or that the Alford Index is the main evidence. Rather, it stresses the importance of building a more coherent general interpretation, with structured propositions about where and why class is important or not. It extends "Are Social Classes Dying?" by adding several propositions about where and why class is important—involving overlapping membership, occupational diversification, political party dynamics, dual-labor markets, and rise of social value issues. Past literature is synthesized, and original data are presented in support of these propositions.

5. Class and Politics in Advanced Industrial Societies by John H. Goldthorpe

Class persists in voting, according to this contribution. This need not imply no change, but rather changes in the nature of zigzags that show no systematic trend over time. They thus illustrate "trendless fluctuation." This is the main conclusion of Goldthorpe's synthesis of recent empirical work, especially by the Berkeley and Oxford participants (Hout, Brooks, Manza, Goldthorpe, Heath, Evans). It includes a brief, clear summary of key studies in this tradition. He criticizes our interpretation of the decline of social class.

6. The Democratic Class Struggle in Postwar Societies: Traditional Class Voting in Twenty Countries, 1945–1990, by Paul Nieuwbeerta

Substantial differences in levels of relative class voting existed among democratic industrialized countries in the postwar period. Of all countries under investigation, the Scandinavian countries and Britain had the highest levels of class voting; and the United States and Canada, the lowest. In many of the countries substantial declines in levels of class voting occurred in the postwar period. In most of these countries, with the exception of the United States and Switzerland, the fluctuations in class voting, he suggests, can be regarded as part of an overall declining trend, and not as trendless fluctuations. The declines were largest in the Scandinavian countries, followed by Germany and Britain. However, he found no evidence of substantial declines in class voting (measured using the seven-class scheme of Erikson and Goldthorpe) in Canada, Ireland, Luxembourg, Switzerland, and the Netherlands, where data over a considerable time period were available.

7. Class Paradigm and Politics, by Jan Pakulski

The concept of paradigm from Thomas Kuhn is usefully applied to class politics in this chapter. Old theories never die, and their proponents seldom admit they were wrong. But new paradigms emerge that gradually supplant them. Interpretation of politics in class terms as a reflection of class interests, divisions, identities, and conflicts forms a popular paradigm. Advocates of this class paradigm in contemporary analysis of politics in advanced societies face a "cumulation of anomalies": declining class voting; class-party dealignment; the weakening of class organizations, identities, consciousness, and action; the growing tide of "new politics," "issue politics," and "life politics," and the decomposition of class-based ideological polarities. An alternative interpretive paradigm, derived from Max Weber's analytic tradition, is shown to be more relevant and useful in making sense of contemporary political processes and configurations in advanced countries.

8. Class, Culture, and Conservatism: Reassessing Education as a Variable in Political Sociology, by Dick Houtman

Studies over many years on cultural authoritarianism of the working class have assumed a class politics cleavage, which is questioned in this chapter. The empirical adequacy of occupation and class is contrasted in particular with education, using new empirical findings. Education is far more important in explaining attitudes like "authoritarianism," which has long been seen as an explanation for radical right political parties. The logistic regression methods for measuring class as developed by the Oxford group are applied and found to explain the results less adequately than education. This is important, since many past studies have not adequately included education as an alternative to occupational measures of social class.

9. Social Class and Voting: The Case against Decline, by David Weakliem

This chapter summarizes many key findings from the Oxford, Berkeley, and other groups that have reported no decline in class politics. Weakliem spent time at Oxford and has coauthored many papers with Oxford analysts of these issues. His chapter is, first, a broad overview of past work and, second, an insightful commentary on many specific studies, which make this an original contribution that both summarizes past work for the nonspecialist and engages the specialist.

10. Upper-Middle-Class Politics and Policy Outcomes: Does Class Identity Matter? by Herman L. Boschken

This chapter reverses the normal causality of class politics. It does not analyze citizens in elections, but government officials creating policies. It asks why policies differ across localities (specifically public transit decisions in 42 U.S. metro areas). The quite original answer is to probe how some government officials work with an "upper-middle-class" citizenry in mind, while others do so less. The chapter then tests for differences across localities and finds quite distinct patterns. Next the chapter elaborates specific contours of an American upper middle class, in a creative merging of themes from Thorstein Veblen and David Riesman to current work on public policy.

11. The Decline of Class Ideologies: The End of Political Exceptionalism? by Seymour Martin Lipset

American exceptionalism has two meanings. The first, critical for nineteenth-century Marxists, asked, Why is there no socialism in America? But a second meaning of *exceptionalism* stands the first on its head: it suggests that the United States, in its lack of class politics, was paving the way for other countries. This chapter reviews the major shifts in program by many (especially left) parties around the world and finds that they have largely moved toward new appeals, stressing the environment, gender, and lifestyle issues over class conflict. Blair and Schroeder join Clinton in these respects, as do many others worldwide. Still the United States remains distinct on several points, reflecting its particular combination of liberty with egalitarianism.

12. The Debate over "Are Social Classes Dying?" by Terry Nichols Clark

Where is class important? Class has declined dramatically as an influence in some fields but is central to others. This chapter extends the exchange over "Are Social Classes Dying?" which has mainly concerned stratification and politics. The exchange is briefly reviewed, stressing key points that deserve clarification. Three key assumptions used by many class politics advocates are specified. An alternative model, the New Political Culture, is briefly presented. Some new bits of data are analyzed, testing the two competing models. They show: (1) Party ideology changes have varied considerably from 1945 to 1988, some moving toward the New Political Culture. (2) Parties often covary as much with social as with fiscal issues. (3) Class politics is strong in some national contexts but weak or minimal in others. All three demonstrate *variations;* these are what we should focus on to analyze where and why class rises or falls in importance, rather than arguing if it is important or not in general.

Acknowledgments: The German Social Democratic Party and its New Politics

The lively participants in this worldwide exchange on class politics deserve the first acknowledgment for their creativity and civility. Some 40 persons participated in our conferences. The exchange broadened still further as most manuscripts were circulated and actively discussed via email. We thank those who are not included in this volume but who nevertheless sharpened discussion of key issues: David Grusky, Erik Olin Wright, Christopher Jencks, Kristen Ringdal, Ronald Inglehart, Mark Franklin, Ken Newton, Patrick Dunleavy, Anthony Heath, William Julius Wilson, Kazuo Yamaguchi, Edward Laumann, Robert Sampson, Ross Stolzenberg, Orlando Patterson, John Mollenkopf, Stanley Greenberg, Harry Ganzeboom, Ian Budge, Robert Smith, and Yoshiaki Kobayashi. We thank the staff of the Woodrow Wilson International Center for Scholars in Washington, D.C., especially George Wagner, for hosting a major conference joining most participants in the book on April 19–20, 1996. Kathy Hamai helped coordinate from Chicago.

Funding for the Woodrow Wilson Center conference was provided by the Friedrich Ebert Stiftung, which is supported by the German Social Democratic Party (SPD). Dieter Dettke of the Friedrich Ebert Stiftung personally attended the full Woodrow Wilson Center conference. He then returned a year or so later with some 30 top members of the German Social Democratic Party, to monitor the last week of the second election of William Clinton. We continued discussions with them in Washington and Chicago. It was striking that so many issues in this volume were similarly debated by high-level SPD politicians and their advisors. These were of course the years when SPD leaders were in the opposition and discussing how to return to power; a critical concern was, should they appeal in a classlike manner or shift? They finally compromised on Gerhard Schroeder as their candidate and won a majority in the Bundestag. Chapter 11, by Seymour Lipset, discusses how this transformation of the SPD paralleled changes by Tony Blair in Britain and William Clinton in the United States. These discussions with the SPD leadership were particularly engaging for social scientists who have long studied the SPD via Robert Michels' classic *Political Parties*. The SPD visit abroad and the openness of its leaders' discussions clearly demonstrate that Michels' Iron Law of Oligarchy has been abolished in a new age of popular democracy.

Joseph Brinley, director of the Woodrow Wilson Center Press, was particularly helpful in easing the transition from conference papers to a published volume.

References

Clark, Terry Nichols, and Seymour Martin Lipset. 1991. "Are Social Classes Dying?" *International Sociology* 6 (December): 397–410.

Clark, Terry Nichols, Seymour Martin Lipset, and Mike Rempel. 1993. "The Declining Political Significance of Social Class." *International Sociology* 8, no. 3 (September): 293–316.

Evans, Geoffrey. 1999. *The End of Class Politics?* Oxford: Oxford University Press.

Goldthorpe, John H. 1999. "Modelling the Pattern of Class Voting in British Elections, 1964–1992." In G. Evans, ed., *The End of Class Politics?* Oxford: Oxford University Press.

Grusky, David B. 1994. *Social Stratification.* Boulder: Westview Press.

Heath, Anthony, Robert Jowell, and John Curtice. 1985. *How Britain Votes.* Oxford: Pergamon Press.

Hout, M., C. Brooks, and J. Manza. 1993. "The Persistence of Classes in Post-Industrial Societies." *International Sociology* 8, no. 3 (September): 259–277.

Lee, David J., and Brian S. Turner, eds. 1996. *Conflicts about Class.* London: Longman.

Manza, Jeff, and Clem Brooks. 1999. *Social Cleavages and Political Change.* Oxford: Oxford University Press.

Michels, Robert. 1949. *Political Parties.* Glencoe, Ill.: Free Press.

Nieuwbeerta, Paul. 1995. *The Democratic Class Struggle.* Amsterdam: Thesis Publishers.

Pakulski, Jan. 1993. "The Dying of Class or Marxist Class Theory." *International Sociology* 8, no. 3 (September): 279–292.

1

What Have We Learned in a Decade on Class and Party Politics?

TERRY NICHOLS CLARK

One Question Sparked Many Answers in a Lively, and Illuminating, Exchange

"Are Social Classes Dying?" we asked in Clark and Lipset 1991 and in chapter 2 of this volume. The original paper sparked an exchange that continues. As academic exchanges or debates go, this one has been refreshingly progressive. It started as the Berlin Wall tumbled, and feelings spread that a new era was dawning. Globalization undermines national hierarchies and associated social class relations. With self-destruction of the Soviet Union and official Communism, the legacy of Marx also grew slimmer for social scientists. Marxists were not the sole class analysts, but they long defined themselves as official guardians of the concept. Many sociologists build on Marx in multiple ways, although few claim to be Marxists in any strict sense. From Max Weber and Robert Merton, through W. Lloyd Warner and O. D. Duncan, sociologists have undogmatically stressed class and stratification-related issues. Some concept of social ranking or social stratification has long been the core of sociology. Arthur Stinchcombe even opined that sociologists have just one concept: class. If this were even half true, it would imply a paradigmatic revolution to suggest that social classes may be dying—what then would sociologists do? But maybe Stinchcombe was not right.[1]

The Clark and Lipset paper was immediately challenged by Hout, Brooks, and Manza (1993, and chapter 3 of this volume), who invoked a wide-ranging series of criticisms, concluding that class was alive and powerful in contemporary societies. This was the beginning of a controversial exchange which has been presented so far in over a hundred papers and many books.

The death of class metaphor overstates the issues: clearly there have long been many forms of social ranking, and new, albeit subtle, gradations are likely to persist for some time. As a serious research question it is better not to ask, Is class "alive" or "dead"? but rather, What factors encourage more or less class salience? Beyond the title, this was in fact the more specific formulation presented in the Clark and Lipset (1991) paper. Its answers there were in general propositions like "Affluence weakens hierarchies and collectivism, but it heightens individualism." Alas, too many later writers in this exchange ignored the actual formulations and simplified them to questions like:

1. Is class dead?
2. Is there a universal decline of class in all countries and time periods?
3. Are Clark and Lipset wrong because they cite the Alford Index as one bit of evidence?

Clearly these verge on the tautologically wrong. But other excessive simplifications took place, too, in the debate.

The purpose of this volume is to provide an overview of the core issues that have emerged in this exchange over the role of social class in contemporary societies, especially in regard to politics. It leads us to consider change at six levels:

1. *societies* and their makeup, such as the emergence of a new post-industrial economy
2. *values* and attitudes about society, especially social class, *stratification*, and party politics, held by the general public
3. *ideologies* and programs of political leaders, political parties, and their changes
4. *conceptualization* of the above changes by social scientists, in general, theoretical approaches and specific hypotheses (where is class strong or weak?)
5. *evidence and methods* of social scientists to assess or test their hypotheses (Alford Index, logistic regression, etc.)
6. *commentary* and interpretations by social scientists of recent historical events and research results

We move across these six levels throughout this book. Most discussion focuses on the last three levels, but how these in turn are linked to the first three is at the core of the exchange.

This has been an unusually engaging exchange. First, the conceptual implications are central and broad for sociology and related social sciences. Second, the talent drawn to participate has been exceptional; some of the best minds around today have sought to unravel these issues. Third, a great deal of work has been completed in a brief period—dozens and dozens of papers rapidly build on one another, positively or negatively, but almost always creatively. Fourth, the exchange has been largely driven by genuine scientific concern. Despite clear disagreements and conflict over all six levels listed above, the participants' quality of mind and seriousness have made the exchange cumulative: most authors refuse simple rhetorical victories, one-liner comments, and ideological camouflage. Repeatedly, central issues have been posed, confronted, redefined, and researched with remarkable rapidity. The most powerful evidence that scientific commitment and open-mindedness undergird the exchange is that many of us have changed our views and interpretations as compelling new conceptualizations and evidence have been introduced. A pointed yet serious and civil tone of discussion has been evident at many conferences assembling the participants. Disagreements were clearly wider and more marked at the beginning, but over the course of several rounds of exchange, participants have generally come to respect and appreciate each other's contributions.

Disagreement clearly persists, but it is remarkable to see a large and growing common base of knowledge. We have reached a point where many specific results are clear, albeit broader interpretations of them (level #6 above) remain in contention.[2]

General Concepts and Approaches to Analysis

What Precise Question to Ask?

Clark and Lipset (1991) suggested that "class" was declining in several different ways in different contexts as hierarchies in general were flattening down. In their workplaces people were adopting more flexible rules about work roles. In their social lives analogously, tolerance was increasing about gender roles, sexual preference, and more. Similarly, in politics, parties were shifting their programs, and correspondingly many voters were shifting voting patterns, with independent voting and nonvoting rising, especially among the young. The core ideas summarizing the changes were stated in seven propositions generating the New Political Culture (later expanded to 25 in Clark and Hoffmann-Martinot 1998: chap. 2). Elements of similar changes have been identified in related writings (e.g., Bell 1973; Lipset 1981; and Inglehart 1990), such that one can generally label such interpretations as defining a new "post-industrial society and politics."

The immediate critics were at the University of California, Berkeley and Oxford University. The first direct response to Clark and Lipset, by Hout, Brooks, and Manza (1993, and chap. 3 of this volume), was a broad-ranging essay that cited many examples and diverse sources to argue generally that "class was not dead." Our response (Clark et al. 1993, and chap. 4 of this volume) protested that to define the issue as "is class alive or dead?" was a simplification and misinterpretation of our position. But many subsequent papers criticized us in the same way, starting by posing the three simplified questions above: Is class dead? and so forth. It is understandable for debating purposes and for some empirical studies to posit an extreme, radically simple, null hypothesis. But none of us ever argued that class is dead; we identified factors that weakened class, such as increasing income and education. Later work has often avoided such simple questions and gone further.

General Interpretations versus Country-Specific Factors

Another point of disagreement is the claim, especially by Evans (1999: 324–327) and Goldthorpe (in Mair et al. 1999: 322), that "post-industrial society" interpretations are general and not country-specific; many country-specific factors undermine the general interpretation and validate the importance of empirical work on one country at a time. This sort of anti- or nongeneralizing view is usually taken by historical/qualitative writers, so it is surprising here, advocated along with rather narrow quantitative voting data as evidence. Most of the early Oxford-centered critics of Clark and Lipset conducted single-country studies of voting over a short time period and reported few changes in class impact on voting. By contrast, in his main research area, social mobility, Goldthorpe's major studies encompass numerous countries and test worldwide models. Evans, too, in his valuable original work on Eastern Europe and Russia, brings new light on those countries to this exchange by pointing out how, under Communism, "classes" were prohibited, but since 1989 classlike groupings have been growing stronger (e.g., Evans 1999; Mateju et al. 1999; and Evans and Whitefield 1999). This is exactly the sort of interesting system-level result that leads good cross-national research (especially by sociologists on the social context of politics) to contribute to the ongoing exchange. But in the Oxford conference volume (Evans 1999), there is only one large cross-national empirical chapter, of 16 countries by Nieuwbeerta and De Graaf (1999; see also Nieuwbeerta, chap. 6 of this volume). They report that class has generally declined in its voting impact, especially in those countries that had strong class voting, and they test several reasons for cross-national differences. This leads Evans in turn to criticize their methodology; its results contradict the "no change" interpretation he generally advocates. Evans does discuss the decline of class in the Scandinavian countries, which they reported, but his interpretation is "reversion to the mean," that is, a statistical tendency for outliers over time to move back toward "normality." Note that this invokes an implied "general process" and a general "norm" of "a lower level" of class politics. The weakness of such conceptualization is that introducing "reversion to the mean" in this way is a post hoc empiricist approach rather than an a priori theoretical proposition, which is explicitly tested against competing alternatives.

The more general point is that Evans and others suggest that the rise of post-industrial politics is a general interpretation, while the "no change" in class politics is not a general interpretation. Does this logically hold? Why should no change or the persistence of class be considered any less general than post-industrial politics? It is unclear that no change is less general or leads more logically or appropriately to "single-country" or comparative research. Hence this remains an issue in contention among those who have written on the topic.

Conceptions of Class

Why is class sometimes considered important for politics and other times not? How can this difference be clarified? First, by looking at how class is used by different social scientists. Ostensibly competing views can be partly reconciled just by clarifying definitions. These range from

1. Marx's classical definition opposing proletarians and bourgeois in capitalist society on the basis of their different relations to the means of production

2. broader meanings, stretching well beyond work and production as Marx analyzed it. Dahrendorf initially included "conflict groups generated by the differential distribution of authority in imperatively coordinated associations," so that class may not depend on work-related differences at all (Dahrendorf 1959: 204). Anthony Giddens (1980:

108–112) identified a variety of workplace differences but retained the term *class*, as did Erik Wright (1985: 64–104), who even specified a 12-category "typology of class location in capitalist society," which combined ownership, skill level, and managerial responsibility.

3. A third, still broader meaning of class/stratification derives from any differential treatment of a group where the norm of equality is in some sense violated—women and ethnic minorities became salient "classes" in the 1960s and 1970s. In the 1990s, concerns expanded beyond national boundaries to include cross-national and even global violations of equality. Terms like *exploitation* and *capitalism* are retained, but their meanings have been drastically transformed. These broader meanings blend with general "human rights" issues.

If one defines class in these increasingly broad ways, adding new political cleavages as they arise day by day, class can never die! Clark and Lipset basically hold to the first definition and use multiple measures of it. Most of the Oxford and Berkeley researchers use census-type measures of occupation (only) to measure class. Shifting definitions of other key concepts in the recent exchanges (occupation, party, etc.) are pursed below and in chapter 12 (this volume).

Modeling: Does "Class Causes Voting" Suffice?

The Oxford and Berkeley participants in this exchange are sophisticated in their statistical methods. Hence it is rather shocking to find them violating established principles of data analysis in social science. One basic point is that most social phenomena are complex, related to multiple causes and consequences, and seldom explained by any single factor. Political behavior and voting are clearly such phenomena. Yet in key papers the many potential causes of voting are ignored, and only a few factors are analyzed statistically. The extreme case is Goldthorpe's chapter (in Evans 1999), which analyzes only one independent variable, occupation, and one dependent variable, party vote. Evans (1999: 14) explicitly defends this choice by framing it more generally:

> Less consensual is the extent to which models of class voting benefit from multi variate analysis. Readers versed in literature on voting which employs multi variate analysis will notice that in many of the following chapters there are relatively few independent variables—and in some cases (i.e. Chapter 3) just one: class position. Many familiar control variables—party identification, education, gender, po-

litical attitudes, left right self-placement, for example—are not found. Are such models under specified? I think not.

Why not? His basic answer is that we do not have a sharp enough understanding of the causal interrelations among the potential independent variables. For instance,

> if controlling for union membership reduces the effect of class position on vote, it does not necessarily signify the weakness of class—if anything it gives an insight into the mechanisms though which class position affects political orientation. (Evans 1999: 14)

Yet this is essentially the same in most of social science. Surely path analysis, structural equations, and other tools are readily available to measure such sequential processes. This was one of the first, apparently obvious, weaknesses of the largely sophisticated empirical work by the Oxford and Berkeley teams—noted by myself in chapter 12 (this volume) and by Mair et al. (1999: 309): "For instance we miss the whole world of religion in politics, we miss variations in party systems and of political systems." How could they commit what many would label an elementary error? Some leading researchers (Hout and Goldthorpe) are not really versed in the political behavior literature. Some early papers, especially that of Goldthorpe, were explicitly quite exploratory as they moved into a new field. Yet these sophisticated authors were surely conscious that by omitting "controls" they were stacking the cards in favor of the results they sought to demonstrate: that class impacted voting.

Similar to this point is the focus in interpretation on the overall explanatory power of *all* occupational groups—considering their combined total statistical impact, as measured by a single statistic (like an R^2 or bic, which is a measure of the explanatory power of all the independent variables) rather than considering occupations separately (by inspecting coefficients for each variable and separate occupation, which is part of the standard output of the calculations). What this means substantively is that, if some occupations shift in magnitude of impact or even reverse their sign (as for professionals and blue-collar workers in Hout et al. 1995), this is largely ignored—at least this is the prime conclusion of these researchers: "trendless fluctuation."

Later work by the Oxford and Berkeley participants responds to this point by adding more variables and clarifying more key elements than just trendless fluctuation (e.g., Brooks and Manza 1997), and of course Heath et al. did so earlier (e.g., 1985; 1991).

One Method and Data Source versus Multiple Methods and Data Sources

Yet another major point passed over in silence by most Oxford and Berkeley writers, especially in their early work, is that they have focused largely on explaining one thing: party voting by average citizens over a relatively short time period in one country. This narrow empiricist focus again stacks the cards toward finding little variation, which they indeed report. By contrast Clark and Lipset synthesize more general literature, not just voting, thus deliberately considering a longer time period and wider range of both independent and dependent variables, like education, income, religion, age, and gender, as well as attitudes of many sorts, and how these link to parties and voting. This more comprehensive look at political behavior is also found in the best work by the Oxford team (esp. Heath et al. 1985 and 1991, volumes on British elections, which probe many subtle points in some depth). It was sensitivity to this broader literature and the declining impact of class-related phenomena in many fields of research that led Clark and Lipset to their interpretation. It was not just a single table with the Alford Index, as several critics claimed.

It is heartening to see progress and convergence: we tend to find in the continuing work by some of these same researchers that their later work incorporates more and diverse variables and interrelations (work by Heath, Evans, Manza, and Brooks, albeit generally not work by Goldthorpe or Hout, who each did just one main empirical analysis). Implications for results are pursued below.

Political Parties: A Pandora's Box for This Exchange

As a "first cut" it is perfectly understandable for empirical studies of class politics to use simple models; the core elements were simply:

Occupation → Party Voting

which was studied in this starkly simple model by Goldthorpe (1999, based on a paper early in the decade), although others added a few controls. The main finding of the "first generation" of empirical work by Oxford and Berkeley researchers, "trendless fluctuation," meant literally that they found no change over time in the magnitude of impact of occupation on party voting. They focused mainly on Britain or the United States (Hout et al., Goldthorpe, Weakliem) in roughly the 1960–1990 period, using surveys of national samples of individual citizens. The authors concluded that class politics had not declined.

The immediate reaction of some readers was that this ignored changes in the parties, their programs, their candidates, and thus the patterns of mobilization of different subgroups within the electorate. The Labour Party of 1960 was not the same in the 1990s, most dramatically after Tony Blair and others rebaptized it New Labour, abandoning the socialist legacy and pledging to continue Margaret Thatcher's basic fiscal and economic policies. The Blair revolution even led Goldthorpe (1999: 81,82) to update his analysis and to find:

> So far as Labour's success in 1997 is concerned, it is evident that this was overwhelmingly the result of a very marked increase in its "non-class" appeal relative to that of the other parties....
>
> Second, there are clear indications also that between 1992 and 1997 class voting declined . . . to a lower level than that found in any other election since 1970—and quite possibly since the 1930s—[this decline] would appear open to different interpretations. One would be that it represents the start of a new era in British electoral politics in which the diminished importance of class as a basis of party support—for so long asserted—is at last empirically demonstrable....
>
> The alternative interpretation is a far less portentous one. It would be that the decline in class voting from 1992 to 1997 is simply another "leg" in the zigzag pattern....

He concludes judiciously:

> Which of these two interpretations has the more merit will only be ascertained through the study of electoral behaviour in the twenty-first century.

The emergence of Blair and New Labour illustrates the more general point that has been made repeatedly in this exchange: to analyze the impact of occupation on party over time assumes that "party" means the same thing in each time period. But in many countries there were drastic changes in party appeals over these years. A few were idiosyncratic: these are the perturbations assumed to operate as "random noise" in the "trendless fluctuation" interpretation. Alternatively, they may represent movement toward, or away from, more general patterns, like "post-industrial politics." How can one tell? Below (in chap. 12), I analyze data complementing that used by the Oxford and Berkeley researchers, but critical for interpretation: the national political party programs of 250 parties in 28 countries from 1945 through 1988, classifying them in relative emphasis on "class politics" themes (labor groups, welfare) versus "post-industrial politics" themes (ecology, government efficiency, etc.). The results showed a general movement toward the post-industrial politics themes, leading to the interpretation that, even if the voters did not change their party choices, their votes (e.g, for New Labour), instead of indicating trendless fluctuation, in fact represent increased voting for post-industrial politics.[3]

Outside Britain, changes like Blair's New Labour were underway years earlier (documented as starting in 1974 in the United States, for instance, in Clark and Ferguson 1983: viii, 95ff.). Indeed Britain, like Scandinavia, had some of the strongest class voting in all the countries surveyed comparatively and some of the most intransigent political parties (see Dennis Merritt 1999). Nevertheless, even British citizens were shifting in these new politics directions years before Blair, as Heath et al.'s (1985, 1991) studies show (stressed in Clark, chap. 12 of this volume). With Clinton, Blair, and soon thereafter the victory by Gerhard Schroeder in the new (albeit embattled) German Social Democratic Party (SPD), the observer seeking to document change need no longer invoke just mayors and citizen surveys but can point to national party programs and leaders who explicitly embrace major elements of the new political culture. Researchers in all camps seem more generally willing to accept this point than a half decade or so earlier, although only a few have sought to measure it and build it into a coherent interpretation. The party program changes represent a major illustration of their theories to myself, Lipset, Inglehart, and most post-industrial politics analysts (as well as even the general British public—see *The Economist* story entitled "Class Is Dead"—and even most British social scientists who have studied these issues, cited in chap. 12). Yet this interpretative conclusion (the last of the levels introduced above) is generally resisted by analysts who actively supported a class politics view in the early 1990s.

Results? Models and Their Interpretation(s)

To test and then interpret these alternative views about class impacts involves strategic choices of methods, since the methods dramatically shift results. One clear contribution of the Oxford and Berkeley participants is to heighten sensitivity to methodology. They wrote in detail (especially in the early 1990s) of the limits of others' methods. Yet they largely pursue a broadly similar method and offer minimal, self-conscious discussion of their own methodological choices and interpretations—and the critical impacts on their results. Consider a central issue: how to measure class politics. Before the Berkeley and Oxford intervention, a variety of methods were used in different subliteratures: self-identifying class labels from surveys, residential location in cities, styles of dress and spending, many scales of attitudes and lifestyle including even living room decoration patterns, and holistic assessments such as the Lloyd Warner studies that defined separate classes in U.S. cities.

The Alford Index and Logistic Regression

Clark and Lipset drew on these multiples sources but also cited a student of Lipset, Robert Alford (1963), who developed the "Alford Index" as a simple measure of class politics. It built on the loosely Marxist idea that class politics could be measured by the degree to which blue-collar workers voted for different parties from white-collar workers. It is generally calculated with survey data from national samples of citizens, asking them about voting and occupation. This became the subject of considerable and repeated criticisms by the Oxford and Berkeley participants, with the implication that if Alford's methods could be demonstrated as flawed, then the Clark and Lipset general views and findings about class were refuted. But look more closely.

New statistical methods were introduced in the 1980s, first applied to social mobility by Robert Mare (Shavit and Blossfeld 1993) and then to class politics by the Berkeley and Oxford teams (a technical discussion is in the chapter 12 appendix 2 in this volume). The Mare-inspired methods use variations of "logistic regression." In studies of social mobility, the method is commonly applied to specific "transitions"—from grade school to high school, and from high school to college—to see how much these transitions are affected by father's occupation and other factors. The main result has been "trendless fluctuation": over much of the twentieth century, little change has been found in the impact of father's occupation on son's education, according to these studies. But generally ignored by advocates of logistic regression is the final result that most nonspecialists stress: the total years of education completed by a student. Or, what proportion of persons in a country are high school or college graduates? This sounds like a very simple point, but by changing the focus from *transitions* to *years of completed education*, results dramatically change over time. If the focus is not transitions, but years of education, what happens differently? Studies of the causes affecting total years of education using a variety of methods (like classic rather than logistic regression) find quite different results—specifically *an increase* in the number of years of education completed by the populations in many countries and a *decline* in impact of father's occupation over time. Indeed, these democratic, equalizing trends seem to reflect the "laypersons'" common wisdom of what happened over the twentieth century. By contrast, maintaining the opposite—no change, or trendless fluctuation—leads to immediate surprise. The seriousness and rigor of most analyses reporting the opposite often seem compelling. Methods in this case are thus critically important to clarify for their limits and to apply very self-consciously.

The methodological debates around logistic regression are equally central to interpreting work on class politics. Social mobility—like methods were applied to class politics by Anthony Heath et al. (1985), Mike Hout et al. (1995), and John Goldthorpe (1994). We can label these the "first generation" of logistic studies of class politics. They and others adapt the logistic methods using perhaps seven occupational categories (that is, more than just white and blue collar) as independent variables to explain party vote. Most studies are of one or two countries over the last 20 years or so, using national sample surveys of individual citizens. They generally report similar conclusions to the social mobility studies, which they also label "trendless fluctuation." That is, they suggest class has not declined in its impact on party voting, especially in Britain and the United States, where most empirical work has been done.

First and Second-Generation Logistic Studies

A second generation of logistic studies followed, with important differences, not in statistical methodology, but in the types of data and refinement of interpretation. We may use the term *second generation* for those studies published in the late 1990s (e.g., Weakliem and Heath 1999a,b; and Brooks and Manza 1997). Between the first and second generations of studies were many dozens of papers and debates at multiple conferences and informal meetings, leading the active participants to add refinements that responded to criticisms and results from others. What changed, specifically?

Longer Historical Trends Lead to Major Shifts in Interpretation

Perhaps the most important single change in the second generation of work is the splicing of data from new time periods, backward and forward.

The results generally add substantial evidence supporting the conclusion that the importance of class is declining. Some of these new studies were by the same authors who in their first-generation studies had been strong advocates of trendless fluctuation. (We can expect that the data and methods were double- and triple-checked for errors, because the new studies largely contradict their own previously published conclusions.) The same results emerge not in one country or from one team, but repeatedly.

It was a clear limit of the first-generation studies that they covered shorter time periods (usually the 1960s–1980s) for which data were more readily available. It was also clear that the theoretical work implied the importance of longer-term change, whether in the class theories from Marx and Weber or the more recent post-industrial politics theories from Lipset, Inglehart, myself, and others. That is, to contrast an "industrial society" with a "post-industrial society" using data only from a historical era when industry had already substantially declined was clearly a bit like looking under the street lamp for one's lost glasses. What emerged as more history was introduced?

Weakliem and Heath (1999a,b) in two important chapters in the Evans 1999 book made several important additions. They spliced on data for all British general elections from 1935 to 1992, for all U.S. presidential elections from 1936 to 1992, and for all French legislative elections from 1946 to 1993, thus more than doubling the number of years covered compared with most first-generation studies. They even introduced more than one data source in each country if available. They then analyzed these data, adding several new twists, to assess competing interpretations. They presented their powerful results in their ever cautious and understated manner. Again applying the same sorts of logistical methods that they and others used in the first-generation studies, they find that in Britain and the United States class politics declined substantially over the longer period (specifically rising from the 1930s to the 1940s, then declining). For France their results vary with several alternative methods but do not generally show such a clear picture of decline. These results, finally, are consistent with the Clark and Lipset interpretations (and the Clark, Lipset, and Rempel 1993 findings, contrasting strong class politics in France and weak class politics in the United States using surveys of mayors). They then offer an interpretation for these shifts:

> We suggest that the decline in class voting in the last few decades may reflect declining general confidence in government.... [driven in part by] the increasing cost of the welfare state and slower economic

growth [which] are similar in both nations. [Yet] the decline in class
voting is much more pronounced in the United States. The difference may reflect the fact that anti-government sentiments have traditionally been stronger in the United States. (Weakliem and Heath
1999b: 306)

This interpretation is very close to that of my New Political Culture (e.g.,
Clark and Hoffmann-Martinot 1998) and Lipset's (1996, and chap. 11 in
this volume) American exceptionalism discussions. The Blair election of
1997, which Goldthorpe (1999) included, was not in the Weakliem and
Heath study, but adding it would strengthen their results of a decline in
class voting in Britain.

Manza and Brooks (1997, 1999) completed several creative analyses extending far beyond their initial papers. Indeed, several added refinements
of precisely the sort for which I (Clark 1995, and chap. 12 of this volume)
have called, such as looking at professionals and other individual occupational groups separately and examining factors explaining their change.
They found, in introducing measures of social background as well as attitudes, that in the United States the shift of professionals from voting Republican in the 1950s to voting Democrat in the 1990s was largely driven
by attitudes on social liberalism items, like the role of women—precisely as
the New Political Culture interpretation suggests (Clark and Hoffman-
Martinot 1998). Their second-generation book (Manza and Brooks 1999)
added a chapter on the last presidential election, the second Clinton election of 1996, to update their analysis, as Weakliem and Heath (1996) and
Goldthorpe (1999) did. They conclude:

This chapter's analyses have unearthed two developments that represent dramatic extensions of past trends. [First] The deepening of the
gender cleavage. . . . Second, there was a sharp decline in the class
cleavage between 1992 and 1996. This is a result of non-skilled
workers' partisan dealignment in this election. [Additional analyses
of attitudinal data] are thus grounds for expecting that this development will continue into the foreseeable future. (Manza and Brooks
1999: 216)

Even Michael Hout, who did not continue working so actively on class
politics as his former students Manza and Brooks, noted:

To consider . . . the question asked rhetorically by Terry Clarke [I am
honored that Mike Hout adds an *e* to *Clark*, making me properly
Irish—TNC] and Marty Lipset some years ago "are social classes dy-

ing?" ... in this book we continue to find strong evidence of classes in our data.[in Mair et al. 1999: 317]

But he qualifies this in his next sentence, asking, "Is *traditional* class voting declining?" and answering simply, "Yes." And most important, he adds his proposed method for incorporating changes in party programs in future work.

The trend in second-generation studies from both Oxford and Berkeley teams and their associates thus show convergence with Clark and Lipset's original formulation. That is, class politics is not simply trendless or dead but varies cross-nationally and over time in ways that are becoming interpretable. The *rise* in class voting in Eastern Europe, *persistent but weakening* class voting in Scandinavia, and *declines* in class voting in the United States and Britain look suspiciously more than trendless. Still the small numbers of cases represented by these countries encourage other cross-national efforts (reviewed below) to generalize.

The Alford Index versus (or Is It "and?") Logistic Regression

Many first-generation writers forcefully attacked the Alford Index. But then several of these same persons examined empirically whether results differed by method. All of the comparisons I have found report very similar results when both the Alford Index and logistic regression are applied to the same data and time period. Again, Weakliem and Heath are particularly thorough, reporting results using many variations in methods, such as different numbers of occupational classes (2, 4, 7, and 18), different statistical procedures (UNIDIFF, kappa, betas), and deleting missing cases (listwise and pairwise), reported for multiple time periods. They examine, for instance, the strength of British Labour and Conservative class voting estimated under different class schemes for 1964–1992. They find that the 2-class manual/nonmanual (Alford-type) index correlates very highly with class schemes proposed by others. The correlation of the Alford 2-class measure with a 4-class measure is .994; with the Goldthorpe 7-class measure, is .965; and with the SEG 18-class measure, is .816. And these measures all show a declining impact over this period on party voting: –.633, –.635, –.573, and –.226—all very close except the last (Weakliem and Heath 1999b: 301).

Nieuwbeerta and De Graaf also report numerous comparisons of the Alford Index with others for different countries and time periods. They write: "Although we regard the Thompson indices as a better measure of class voting than the Alford index, it is of interest to examine to what extent use of one or another indices yields different results....the two indices produce very much the same conclusions: in the aggregated country data set the Pearson correlation between the Alford and Thompson indices is.97" (Nieuwbeerta and De Graaf 1999: 30). Similar results hold for the Erikson-Goldthorpe indexes compared with the two other methods (Nieuwbeerta and De Graaf 1999: 35).

Yet again, Ringdal and Hines (1999:190) compare the Alford and log-odds-ratio for Norwegian class voting from 1957 to 1989 and show two very close lines in their figure 7.2, commenting. "The slope for the log odds ratio is almost identical to the one for Alford's index" (189–190).

Comparison of the Alford Index and logistic regression using our Fiscal Austerity and Urban Innovation (FAUI) Project data again showed essentially identical results, first with dichotomous logistic regression (Munson 1995) and second with multivariate logistic regression (Merritt 1999).

These methodological issues should no longer divide researchers. Strong substantive results are consistent across methods. This convergence parallels that in the earlier community power debate.

The Size of the Working Class and Political System Effects

A major factor, I suggest, driving the decline of class voting is the declining size of the manual labor force. It has been a key element transforming the political system of many countries. The decline is similar in most of Western Europe and the United States, where "blue-collar workers" as a proportion of the electorate dropped by about half from the 1960s to the 1990s—albeit not in Japan. Service workers increased everywhere (Clark and Hoffman-Martinot 1998: 128ff.). This drastic erosion of the classic Labour and Social Democratic party base led the traditional left-labor parties in most of these countries to look for ways to find new voters. Most of them acted like the Clinton Democrats, Blair Labourites, and Schroeder Social Democrats: they embraced more market-oriented fiscally conservative policies, while stressing or adopting more liberal social policies (for ecology, women, gays, animal rights, etc.). Lipset pursues this in detail in chapter 11 in this volume. Tracing quantitatively the causal shifts outlined here takes multiple data sources (in particular party programs, which are not included in the survey data used by most of the Oxford and Berkeley researchers). Yet a simple measure that can be included in logistic regressions and analyzed with the sort of survey data these researchers have readily available is the size of the manual workforce. For a variety of reasons, this tradition of class politics work follows the logistic regression tradition of social mobility, which similarly eschews analysis of the changing level of education of entire populations.

One modeling problem is that shifts in size of occupational groups, more than individual behavior or attitudes, are often critical in driving system-level and party-level change. Longer time periods or cross-national comparisons among countries varying in occupations and other characteristics are helpful for modeling such political system effects. Similarly, if regional and local areas differ in these key characteristics, they may help explain the broader dynamics of change. Particularly appropriate here are comparisons of older industrial regions and cities with more working-class citizens against more service, high-tech, and post-industrial economic bases. This comparison is pursued for U.S. cities in Clark 1994 (chaps. 2 and 4) and for 20 countries in Clark and Hoffmann-Martinot 1998 (esp. chap. 4), discussed just below, which document precisely the dynamics driving the political transformation just discussed by left/Socialist parties. The change is documented through the strong negative impact of manual workers and the positive impact of professional and high-tech workers on the rise of ecological organizations, urban growth control, percentages of women mayors and council members, and support for social issues like abortion and sex education. These studies chart specific dynamics of class and post-industrial politics, which change following many of the propositions formulated earlier in Clark and Lipset 1991 and Clark et al. 1993.

Cross-National Studies: Results

The issues in this exchange over the decline of class politics have been addressed in a few cross-national studies. Inglehart's (1990, 1997) continuing work, he suggests, documents a general decline of class cleavages and the rise of what he earlier termed "post-materialist" issues. Such results have been reported not only by Inglehart but also by others who have used the World Values Surveys (WVS), which he has coordinated (but see Van Deth and Scarborough 1995). It remains a rich data source that one-country analysts might consider using. Many Oxford- and Berkeley-based writers criticize Inglehart, but none to my knowledge has yet reanalyzed his data, now in the public domain (David Weakliem is currently analyzing this data). Hout did propose work in this direction: "Instead of speculating on the existence of 'two lefts' or trying to read the tea-leaves of the association model's parameters, for example, we might go out and measure how parties make materialist, postmaterialist, and immaterialist appeals to classes" (Hout 1999: 316).

Second is a major international project coordinated by Mark Franklin, Tom Mackie, Henry Valen, et al. (1992), extending a book on the decline of class politics in Britain (Franklin 1985). The international project pursued similar issues, involving leading national experts writing on their countries, using national citizen surveys and internationally comparable modeling methods. The authors in most countries found a decline in class (or cleavage) politics. A more general point was when and how cleavages declined, since it was not in the same years across countries. In general they show the decline of "cleavage politics" first in the United States and Canada, next in most Western European countries, and last in Italy and Norway. They interpret shifts as driven by the decline of industrial manufacturing, large working-class populations, strong unions, and militant left parties. New patterns emerged with higher education and income. In brief, the patterns broadly support a shift from industrial to post-industrial politics.

Third, Nieuwbeerta (1995; Nieuwbeerta and De Graaf 1999; and Nieuwbeerta in chap. 6 of this volume) and his associates study 16 countries, mostly in Western Europe, using the Goldthorpe occupational categories and logistic regression methods developed by the Oxford group. They report declines in class politics in countries that had the highest levels of class cleavages. Specific results vary with their several parallel analyses, but in general declines hold most consistently for Norway, Britain, and Germany. They also admirably seek to measure the impact of the size of the working class, as we have proposed, albeit using just a manual/nonmanual dichotomy. Even this crude measure explained as much as 52 percent of the class politics in Denmark and 41 percent in Italy, while in other countries like Germany, it was just 18 percent and in Britain 17 percent. Might not these results be usefully interpreted as how fully the left parties adapted to changes in their constituencies? That is, the German SPD and British Labour Party embraced the New Politics only after this empirical work, while the Danish and Italian left parties were among the earliest to change programs (cf. Mouritzen 1992; Ercole quoted in Clark and Hoffmann-Martinot 1998: 79–83).

I have conducted several cross-national studies with colleagues to test some 25 propositions about shifts from class toward post-industrial politics, reported in three books. Here are just a few findings related to the class politics exchange. I analyze national surveys of U.S. mayors (Clark:

1994) showing initially that large race cleavages in an urban electorate generate pro–welfare state/redistributive-spending preferences among mayors. But race is in turn explained away (Clark 1996) when four inequality indexes are introduced (for income, education, occupational, and national origin), computing inequality with the method of Atkinson (1975), economist at Nuffield College, Oxford (suggesting a Clark-Oxford filiation!). But conversely, cities low in inequality illustrate the New Political Culture: in high Sierra Club membership and growth-control movements, elected leaders favoring socially liberal policies, and adopting productivity-improvement and ecological policies.

Clark and Rempel (1997) analyze citizen surveys in up to 20 countries. Linkages are pursued between class and party, which clarify shifts since the 1960s: more independent voters, more education, more reliance on media news, weakened impact of social background characteristics on public policy preferences. In the same volume, Brint et al. show a rise in social liberalism and fiscal conservatism, especially among professionals in several countries. Mayer shows similar shifts in party campaign materials and candidates' speeches. Butts charts analogous rises in civic and women's associations.

Clark and Hoffmann-Martinot (1998: esp. chap. 4) document political transformation by political parties in 20 countries, especially left/Socialist parties. Many gradually shifted programs from class politics to post-industrial issues after the 1970s. The dynamics of class versus post-industrial politics are also documented through the strong negative impact of manual workers and positive impact of professional and high-tech workers, on-the-rise of ecological organizations, urban growth control, percentages of women mayors and council members, and support for social issues like abortion and sex education. Strong national parties weaken these dynamics in most countries outside the United States, however, pointing up the disparities between party leaders and citizens. Citizens in many European countries shifted toward post-industrial politics long before their party leaders. Many shifts in citizen policy preference consistently hold cross-nationally, but parties are nationally distinct, making them critical for implementing change.

Death, Decline, Dealignment, and Realignment

These four labels convey quite different meanings, but have been variously applied to the same results. The last is favored by some Oxford and Berke-

ley authors. Why? Realignment keeps class "alive." How? The first three *d*
words—*death, decline,* and *dealignment*—imply a weakened relation between class and voting. Realignment implies not a weakening but a new relationship or alignment between an occupational group and political party.
A major example is professionals, an occupational category not distinguished by Goldthorpe in his class schema: he lumped them with managers
as upper-class persons. But Hout et al. (1999) and Weakliem and Heath
(1999a,b) examined professionals separately, finding that unlike managers
they "realigned" their voting from the 1950s to the 1990s: from Republican to Democratic in the United States. Yet this did not occur in Britain
(Weakliem and Heath 1999a,b).

Realignment is preferred by some Berkeley and Oxford writers, since it can
be interpreted as an adaptation of "class politics." Realignment contrasts with
death, decline, and dealignment, since one can interpret some logistic regression results as showing "no decline." How? Simply put, in a logistic regression
model to explain party voting, the key variables considered by the Oxford and
Berkeley participants are usually the impact of *all* the occupational categories.
This reading of the printout comes from looking narrowly at a statistical measure (like the bic in the Hout et al. models) of the explanatory power of *all*
occupational categories combined, ignoring changes in strength or even direction of *individual* occupational categories. Consequently the original empirical analysis by Hout et al. (1995) could "find" the common first-generation "result": trendless fluctuation. Yet this was observed by considering the
overall bic measure, not coefficients of each occupational category. "Class voting," so the interpretation could go, was thus unchanged, even if there was
"realignment" by professionals and skilled workers.

These four labels, as the examples suggest, are quite narrowly descriptive, close to the data, and fail to join broader interpretations. Yet one of
the main arguments that Clark and Lipset have repeatedly made is the importance of transcending the inherently narrow and descriptive results
from any single country, short time period, and small number of variables.

Can we link such "realignments" with more general competing interpretations? Indeed. The rise in number and political independence of professionals is an archetypal shift posited by the New Political Culture. In the
United States, it is a shift by some of the younger, most politically informed and active persons in the electorate in the years when progressive
positions on social issues were increasingly stressed by Democrats. Republicans did the opposite after Goldwater's candidacy and especially after
Richard Nixon's 1968 "Southern Strategy" (of courting whites over blacks
in an effort to win southern "Dixiecrat" voters).

Manza and Brooks moved rapidly beyond their first-generation paper with Hout to show how and why professions "realigned" their votes. The crucial point here is that their later, deeper analysis asked how and why a single occupational category, professionals, changed. They both located the change dynamics conceptually as testing competing general theories and showed empirically specific factors explaining change, especially social liberalism attitude items. That is, professionals shifted parties primarily because of their own socially liberal views, not because of their incomes or education or other factors. Brooks and Manza (1997) read this as consistent with the New Political Culture (NPC) interpretation rather than three other general interpretations. Related work by Brint et al. (1997) extends this interpretation for the United States, as does work internationally by Inglehart (1990) and Kriesi (1989), which Nieuwbeerta and De Graaf (1999: 48) concur with, again stressing the importance of analyzing professionals separately from managers.

Such labels as "dealignment" and "realignment," then, gain conceptual significance if they are linked to more general interpretations.

Emerging Issues and Future Challenges

Serious discussion of class and related topics in this exchange has also unearthed issues that future work can hopefully extend.[4]

The Greening of Parties

In Germany the Green Party has redefined the rules of the game for politics, as partly documented by Müller (1999) and Gabriel et al. (1998). More generally the Scandinavian, Swiss, and many other parties have seriously added ecology and women's politics themes in ways that deserve much more precise analysis for their more general implications. The factors stressed by Inglehart to interpret such shifts hold reasonably well in Germany but far less well in France (Hoffmann-Martinot 1991). We should address why in a broader context.

Rise of the Nationalist Right

Did embracing new social issues by classic left parties contribute to the rise of highly nationalist right parties that now win some 15–20 percent of the vote in most Western European countries? This seems plausible but needs closer study. What proportion of traditional working-class voters switched from old Left to new Right, driven away by the new social issues and attracted by anti-immigrant and patriotic themes? In the non-PR (proportional representation) countries, how much have voluntary groups or occasional elected officials similarly moved to the new Right? The controversy and complexity of this question are illustrated by the European scandal over the Austrian Freedom Party joining a government coalition in 2000. Much of the Freedom Party program reads quite like Tocqueville, while attacking European-wide government. The Freedom Party's leader, Haider, even published a newspaper article, "Blair and Me", maintaining that he was seeking to fight conservative elements in his party, like Blair. How do new parties advance their appeals?

Emergence of New Democracies and Greater Democratization by Older Party Systems: Primary Elections, Direct Election of Mayors, Transparency, and More

The emergence of democratic practices in countries like those in Eastern and central Europe as well as areas like Taiwan or Mexico has led to new interest in democratic institutions and their impacts. Taiwan and Mexico in recent years joined the United States in adopting primary elections of voters inside the political parties to choose the parties' candidates for general elections. Primarylike practices have been discussed in Europe. Such concerns spread as the "nondemocratic" elements of parties and cleavage politics are confronted in a more egalitarian value climate.

Similarly, the two major parties in Italy from 1945 to 1989 virtually collapsed along with leadership of the entire Italian political system in the early 1990s. New democratic laws were adopted, seeking to enhance democratic responsiveness to citizens rather than to party leaders, to policy issues over clientelism, and to transparency of decisions to the public over "closed deals." Similar trends are actively debated or in progress in many countries of the world, potentially with drastic implications for political cleavages. These trends may both enhance class politics (as Mair et al. 1999 and Evans and Whitefield 1999 suggest) and suppress class cleavages if broader subpopulations feel more confidence and thus more legitimacy in the political system.

Voter Turnout

Hout et al. (1995) creatively added voter turnout in their analyses. Others should too: modeling nonvoting as a serious alternative to "transitioning" to another party has not been pursued by most party politics analysts. It grows more critical as nonvoting rises to over 50 percent of the electorate. It is particularly high among former left party, manual workers in countries like Britain and the United States, where no right parties exist (largely thanks to majority election or, as the British say, first past the post rules). The interrelations among party program shifts and confidence in parties and leaders (or conversely alienation from them) demand linking to turnout, as suggested in the broader interpretations of Clark and Hoffmann-Martinot (1998: 41–48, 198ff.) and Weakliem and Heath (1999b: 306). Note that some social sectors like women and African Americans in the United States have recently increased turnout (Manza and Brooks 1999), perhaps because of a shift in relevance to them of Democratic Party programs, which may simultaneously lower turnout by blue-collar workers who are white and male.

Values and Value Conflicts

Concepts like "confidence" and turnout are hard to explain without reference to underlying values of population subgroups, which may support or conflict with party programs and policies. Similarly, anger can generate protest activity and new party voting among ecologists as well as nationalist–anti-immigrant groups. Fields like class voting and community power emerged from neo-Marxist traditions that long omitted values as serious explanations. But as new issues arise (gender equality, human rights, the environment) and party-voting dynamics change, the analyst can go much further with clear attention to values. Lipset's work in the last decade has grown far more explicit about such values-voting linkages. This followed the Lipset and Rokkan (1967) work that showed how the period of enfranchisement marked the programmatic focus of parties in most of Europe for almost a century. The rise of new politics issues makes such concerns all the more important. The explosion of work on political culture, trust, and civic associations since Putnam (1993, 1995) is critical here.

Income and Inequality

There has been minimal mention in this exchange of growing income inequalities as a political issue. But clearly this issue can spark classlike conflicts, even though it seems to have done so minimally to date in the United States, where inequality is growing fastest. Still the same income trends are emerging globally, creating new class cleavages between the globally sophisticated who benefit from world markets and the more local and limited in bargaining who fall in income. Similarly, unions are rapidly falling in some countries like the United States and France as global markets rise, but less in others like Scandinavia. This interacts with values: if most citizens feel that "wealth is theft," then more income inequality is politically explosive. The lack of such reactions in the United States leads some to conclude that this indicates a more broadly shared legitimacy of the economic and social system than in other countries of the world (see Clark and Hoffmann-Martinot 1998: 140–145).

Age Groups and Retirement Benefits

As the elderly increase in number and voting strength, retirement systems may grow more fiscally strained and politicized. Elderly assistance programs have been partly decentralized to local government in countries like Germany, Korea, and Japan in ways that seem "unthinkable" in the United States, where the American Association of Retired Persons is the largest single membership group in the country and perhaps the most politically influential. How do such issues cross-cut class politics?

Deeper Analysis of Critical Subpopulations, like Professionals

We need to push analysis of professionals and their subtypes further (conservative versus socially critical, etc.) because they have been growing rapidly in numbers while blue-collar voters have dropped by over half in the last 20–30 years in most advanced post-industrial countries. Brooks and Manza (1997) and Brint et al. (1997) have pioneered in this area. We should extend such efforts. In-depth case studies with a variety of methods can usefully complement quantitative survey research, following the "deviant case" analysis of outliers that Paul Lazarsfeld stressed and Lipset pursued in works from *Union Democracy* (Lipset et al. 1956) to *American Exceptionalism* (Lipset 1996).

More Comprehensive Modeling of Political Systems and Their Transformation Rules

As one grows more conscious of the critical roles of processes considered in these last sections and how they shift traditional class voting, the importance of more complex and more comprehensive models joining them grows clearer. Cross-national comparisons highlight critical variables that

one may not notice in single-country studies. A first effort in this modeling direction is in chapter 12 of this volume, joining the core issues from
this exchange over class politics with those emerging from post-industrial
politics work. Successive volumes from the British General Election Surveys by Anthony Heath et al. (1985, 1991) have measured and analyzed
many related phenomena, some of which have been joined in mathemati-
cal-like models. Manza and Brooks 1999 and their subsequent papers similarly illustrate a synthesis of many of the best contributions from the exchange that has continued over the last decade on the changing dynamics
of class and politics. The next decade looks promising for related work.

Notes

1. As ever, Stinchcombe provoked reflection through humorous overstatement. The quote has
its own microhistory:

> I said it in a class that Eric Wright was in at Berkeley. I was being sarcastic about sociolo-
> gists' lack of imagination, that they couldn't think of politics except as stratification, of
> friendship except as stratified, of marriage as anything but a market, of childcare as placing
> kids in the class system, of ethnicity and race prejudice as a sense of group position, of pol-
> itics as an extension of the class structure. Eric knew I was being sarcastic, but when he re-
> peats it he is the sort of scholar of whom it might seem that he took it literally.
>
> A Trotskyist leader (of 9 people) once told me that you should never make jokes in
> politics, because your enemies will take you literally and pin it on you. So sociology is
> evidently a continuation of politics by other means. (from an email to Jeff Manza and
> Terry Clark, March 16, 2000)

Stinchcombe is not alone in stressing sociologists' great concern with nuances of stratification. See
for instance Grusky 1994; and Meyer 1994: 733, 737.

2. An earlier exchange has parallels and lessons for this one: studies of national power elites and
community power, debating political power and the role of business. The exchange was long and
conflictual, but it sharpened and substantially refined core concepts like power, influence, hierarchy, coalitions, and resources, which are used in several fields of social science today. Nelson Polsby,
a Berkeley colleague of Stinchcombe and Michael Hout, reviewed the literature and debates in his
Ph.D dissertation ([1963] 1980.) He maintained that sociologists were more sensitive to stratifi-
cation-based interpretations than were political scientists confronting the same evidence. There was
also considerable debate over methods: Floyd Hunter and his followers used the reputational
method, asking about the overall importance of different leaders, while Robert Dahl and associates
like Aaron Wildavsky and Raymond Wolfinger reconstructed some key concrete decisions in their
decisional method. (Polsby completed an M.A. in sociology at Chicago with Peter Rossi and a
Ph.D. in political science at Yale with Robert Dahl. He also links the 1990s class politics exchange
to the earlier debate on the back cover of Evans 1999, noting that the book is "an important gathering of studies illustrating the continuing vitality of social stratification as a theory.") A central issue was how much class and business drive political leadership processes, as neo-Marxist interpretations suggest. To document his claims, Polsby conducted an extensive review but clearly offered
a personal reading while citing a large number of works. Others conducted more careful, quantitative analyses of the same basic evidence (166 studies) and found quite conflicting results: zero dif-

ferences according to method or discipline. The differences in political leadership that did emerge across cities were explained by socioeconomic characteristics (size, income, economic diversification, etc.) (Clark et al. 1968; Gilbert 1968; Clark 1968).

The 1990s exchange over class politics illustrates remarkable similarity on three key points from that earlier debate. First, most work in both consists of "case studies," that is, studies of one nation. Second, researchers use different methods. Third, results differ. Fourth, some researchers are in sociology; others in political science. In the 1960s exchange, Polsby suggested that the causality ran:

Discipline → Method → Results

Similarly, many early 1990s criticisms of Clark and Lipset suggest that their results derived from their Alford Index, that is, the "wrong" method. Yet later work suggests that the method is insignificant in generating results. Concepts are being redefined and measured more precisely, the same data have now been reanalyzed with multiple methods to compare results, and as in the power debate, methods are not at all as important as the early critics held. Historical studies of longer time periods and comparative cross-national studies generate different results and sharpen more general interpretations, even refuting earlier case studies of short periods. Several are reviewed below that challenge the persistence of class view. The more general studies both permit testing and encourage more specific propositions about why and how class politics are or are not important.

3. This result was in the Clark paper prepared for the 1995 Oxford conference and was circulated in advance to all conference participants. (I fell ill and unfortunately did not present it in person but continued email correspondence with several participants and met with them at other conferences.) In the empirical papers at the Oxford conference, and in subsequent revisions for the Evans (1999) book, there was no shift of attention to incorporate these party concerns. By contrast, in the commentaries and interpretations of many papers for that conference, there is far more explicit attention to this "Achilles heel" of the first-generation papers, and party concerns, finally, loom large. They are the main focus of three of the four official commentators: Peter Mair, Seymour Martin Lipset, and Michael Hout. Hout even went so far as to outline a mathematical model that would systematically measure party effects. As he put it: "Our work in this volume is all about support and has tended to ignore appeals. The little conjecture I have presented with respect to the association model is one way, within our paradigm, of dealing with the issue of appeals" (in Mair et al. 1999: 317). Only the fourth discussant, Goldthorpe, resisted this recognition of party effects. Presumably his statement was from the time of the conference, two years before the Blair election, and he did not yet have available his results quoted above. This may explain his different conclusion: "I remain a strong supporter of the null hypothesis: not very much is happening" (in Mair et al. 1999: 321). While Evans similarly continues to support "the null hypothesis" in the introduction and conclusions to Evans 1999, he is visibly concerned to address and seeks to counter arguments of some of the more important studies stressing party change (Kitchelt 1994; Sartori 1969; Mair et al. 1999; and others). Perhaps these summaries respond to concerns of publishers and nonspecialist readers who prefer a livre-à-these to a subtly balanced discussion.

4. This account demands at least a tip of the hat to the sociology of knowledge. This subfield of sociology specifies social and institutional conditions that encourage knowledge in different directions. Its core in the last half century is the sociology of science, pioneered by Robert K. Merton (1973), who stressed the scientific community, cosmopolitans, peer review, global competition, and related factors that tend to internationalize science and keep it "honest." But for a decade or so, around the 1980s, some British contributors sought to develop a new approach, the sociology of scientific knowledge (SSK), building up from case studies of microsocial relations of individual laboratories and broadly concluding that hierarchy, domination, and power overwhelmed the Merton-like factors (e.g., Barnes 1977; Latour 1986). Rather, they held, bad ideas could live on for decades if a senior professor at a leading university backed them. They usually did not seek to define limits to this second view (such as only in the U.K.) but implied it generally held. This debate led Kim (1994) to build a synthesis in the form of a self-demonstrating interpretation. He

reinterpreted a famous case used by MacKenzie and Barnes (1979) to document the domina-tion/power view of science. Kim's innovation was detailing how domination was not the whole story and specifically how the scientific community shifted paradigms. The basic answer was third-party outsiders: a journal editor at Harvard was distant and open enough to review and publish pa-pers rejected by the leading English journals. Initially papers by "lesser minds" were dismissed by the brilliant Pearson, but as they accumulated over time, they convinced most researchers world-wide that even Pearson could be wrong on Mendelian genetics, despite his major works in other areas (like the Pearson r). He held to the old theory, in good part because of his general social and ethical support for the common man, countering the elitist Bateson.

Are there any parallels in our exchange on class politics? One might suggest that two distin-guished professors at two leading universities had a spark of insight in extending their methods from social mobility to politics. They each completed an empirical paper reporting parallel results in both fields: "trendless fluctuation." This absence of change was a shocking result to specialists and to others, since it implied that decades of well-intended policies (scholarships, the huge ex-pansion of higher education, government hiring and procurement programs including affirmative action, unions and political parties that sought to help the common person, and many high-minded elected officials) were insignificant in changing the core of class-based social relations. The rich were still rich and the poor still poor, while schools, universities, parties, voting, and government func-tioned without fundamental change. These shocking results were based on the insightful and so-phisticated tools of logistic regression, subtly applied and published in dry scientific papers. They were presented not in a muckraking expose but with high-tech statistics and graphics. But as nu-merous participants joined the discussion, they came from many different institutions and were more intellectually and institutionally independent. Conferences where multiple views could be aired and criticisms could be frank led at least some of the less rigid and younger to pursue new questions. "Rigid" is perhaps a strong label and too psychological for sociologists: we all have our blinders. Perhaps it is best to stress the institutional context of the large, decentralized, competitive American university system, where frequent horizontal mobility by especially younger faculty heightens the importance of fresh ideas and undercuts any local hierarchy. Small countries like Britain have few horizontal options, certainly from its Oxbridge pinnacle from which mobility is only downward.

These general institutional patterns would lead one to predict the slowest change in revising in-tellectual paradigms in the smallest university systems and by persons who participate least in the "cosmopolitanizing" institutions, like international conferences, that create more open intellectual markets. We thus find that younger scholars like Clem Brooks and Jeff Manza and the fairly young David Weakliem published very large numbers of papers that quickly advanced new results and in-terpretations, while the senior scholars Goldthorpe and Hout were mainly busy elsewhere. These general institutional reflections also suggest that Hout at Berkeley would be more open to change than his Oxford counterpart. Their commentaries on the field (in Mair et al. 1999) clearly fit these general tendencies: Goldthorpe concluded: "I remain a strong supporter of the null hypothesis that not very much is happening" (321), while Hout's commentary almost playfully advances a frankly revolutionary change from past models, stressing political parties, albeit defending it as "consistent with our paradigm" (317). This is noteworthy in that the paradigm he invokes seems to refer pri-marily to the methodology of logistic regression rather than past substantive results or their guid-ing ideas; indeed, his new formulation would refute them. Contrast this paradigmatic approach with Pakulski's chapter on the "class paradigm" (in this volume).

These institutional reflections may help interpret the introductory and concluding chapters of the Oxford conference book (by Evans in Evans 1999), which basically reflect the tone of Goldthorpe's comments. Perhaps the design of the book and some writing was completed ear-lier (the conference was in 1995, the book published in 1999). Over time, contributors kept adding new twists and finding new results, leading us to label a "second generation" of work by 1999.

References

Alford, Robert. 1963. *Party and Society,* Chicago: Rand McNally.

Atkinson, A. B. 1975. *The Economics of Inequality.* London: Oxford University Press.

Barnes, Barry. 1997. *Interests and the Growth of Knowledge.* London: Routledge and Kegan Paul.

Bell, Daniel. 1973. *The Coming of Post-Industrial Society.* New York: Basic Books.

Brint, Steven. 1994. *In an Age of Experts.* Princeton: Princeton University Press.

Brint, Steven, William L. Cunningham, and Rebecca S. K. Li. 1997. "The Politics of Professionals in Five Advanced Industrial Societies." In Terry Nichols Clark and Michael Rempel, eds., *The Politics of Post-Industrial Societies,* 113–143. Boulder, Colo.: Westview Press.

Brooks, Clem, and Jeff Manza. 1977. "Partisan Alignments of the 'Old' and 'New' Middle Classes in Post-Industrial America." In Terry Nichols Clark and Michael Rempel, eds., *The Politics of Post-Industrial Societies,* 143–160. Boulder, Colo.: Westview Press.

Butts, Paul. 1997. "The Social Origins of Feminism and Political Activism: Findings from 14 Countries." In Terry Nichols Clark and Michael Rempel, *The Politics of Post-Industrial Societies,* 209–244. Boulder, Colo.: Westview Press.

Clark, Terry Nichols. 1995. "Who Cares if Social Class Is Dying, or Not? Being an Effort to Articulate a Framework to Deepen the Meaning of Such Questions." Prepared as background for a conference on social class at Nuffield College, Oxford.

Clark, Terry Nichols. 1996. "Structural Realignments in American City Politics: Less Class, More Race, and a New Political Culture." *Urban Affairs Review* 31, no. 3 (January): 367–403.

Clark, Terry Nichols, ed. 1968. *Community Structure and Decision-Making.* San Francisco, New York: Chandler/Halstead/Wiley.

Clark, Terry Nichols, ed. 1994. *Urban Innovation: Creative Strategies in Turbulent Times.* London, Newbury Park, New Delhi: Sage Publications.

Clark, T. N., and L. C. Ferguson. 1983. *City Money.* New York: Columbia University Press.

Clark, Terry Nichols, and Vincent Hoffmann-Martinot, eds. 1998. *The New Political Culture.* Boulder: Westview Press.

Clark, Terry Nichols, and Ronald Inglehart. 1988. "The New Political Culture." Presented to the annual meeting of the American Political Science Association, Atlanta, Georgia.

Clark, Terry Nichols, and Seymour Martin Lipset. 1991. "Are Social Classes Dying?" *International Sociology* 6 (December): 397–410.

Clark, Terry Nichols, and Michael Rempel, eds. 1997. *Citizen Politics in Post-Industrial Societies.* Boulder: Westview Press.

Clark, Terry Nichols, Seymour Martin Lipset, and Michael Rempel. 1993. "The Declining Political Significance of Social Class." *International Sociology* 8, no. 3 (September): 293–316.

Clark, Terry Nichols, William Kornblum, Harold Bloom, and Susan Tobias. 1968. "Discipline, Method, Community Structure and Decision-Making: The Role and Limitations of the Sociology of Knowledge." *American Sociologist* 3, no. 3 (August): 214–217.

Dahrendorf, R. 1959. *Class and Class Conflict in Industrial Society.* Stanford: Stanford University Press.

Evans, Geoffrey. 1999. *The End of Class Politics?* Oxford: Oxford University Press.

Evans, Geoffrey, and Stephen Whitefield. 1999. "The Emergence of Class Politics and Class Voting in Post-Communist Russia." In Geoffrey Evans, ed., *The End of Class Politics?* 254–280. Oxford: Oxford University Press.

Franklin, Mark, 1985. *The Decline of Class Voting in Britain.* Oxford: Oxford University Press.

Franklin, Mark, Thomas T. Mackie, Henry Valen, et al. 1992. *Electoral Change: Responses to Evolving Social and Attitudinal Structures in Western Countries.* New York: Cambridge University Press.

Gabiel, Oscar, Katja Ahlstich, Frank Brettscheneider, and Volker Kunz. 1998. "Transformations in Policy Preferences of Local Officials." In Terry Nichols Clark and Vincent Hoffman-Martinot, eds., *The New Political Culture,* 219–234. Boulder, Colo.: Westview Press.

Giddens, Anthony. 1980. *The Class Structure of the Advanced Societies*. New York: Harper and Row.

Gilbert, Claire. 1968. "Community Power and Decision-Marking: A Quantitative Reexamination of Previous Research." In Terry Nichols Clark, ed., *Community Structure and Decision-Making*, 139–158. San Francisco, New York: Chander/Halstead/Wiley.

Goldthorpe, John. 1999. "Modelling the Pattern of Class Voting in British Elections, 1964–1992." In Geoffrey Evans, ed., *The End of Class Politics?* 59–82. Oxford: Oxford University Press.

Grusky, David B. 1994. *Social Stratification*. Boulder: Westview Press.

Heath, Anthony, Robert Jowell, and John Curtice. 1985. *How Britain Votes*. Oxford: Pergamon Press.

Heath, Anthony, et al. 1991. *Understanding Political Change: the British Voter 1964–1987*. Oxford: Pergamon Press.

Hoffmann-Martinot, Vincent. 1991. "Grüne and Verts: Two Faces of European Ecologism." *West European Politics* (October): 70–95.

Hout, M., C. Brooks, and J. Manza. 1993. "The Persistence of Classes in Post-Industrial Societies." *International Sociology* 8, no. 3 (September): 259–277.

Hout, Michael, Clem Brooks, and Jeff Manza. 1995. "The Democratic Class Struggle in the United States, 1948–1992." *American Sociological Review* 60, no. 6 (December): 805–828.

Inglehart, Ronald. 1990. *Culture Shift in Advanced Industrial Society*. Princeton: Princeton University Press.

Inglehart, Ronald. 1997. *Modernization and Postmodernization*. Princeton: Princeton University Press.

Kim, Kyung-Man. 1994. *Explaining Scientific Consensus*. New York: Guilford Press.

Kitchelt, Herbert. 1994. *The Transformation of European Social Democracy*. Cambridge: Cambridge University Press.

Kriesi, H. "New Social Movements and the New Class in the Netherlands." *American Journal of Sociology* 94, no. 5: 1078–1116.

Latour, Bruno. 1986. *Laboratory Life*. 2d ed. Princeton: Princeton University Press.

Lee, David J., and Brian S. Turner, eds. 1996. *Conflicts about Class*. London: Longman.

Lipset, Seymour Martin. 1981. *Political Man: The Social Bases of Politics*. Baltimore, Md.: Johns Hopkins University Press.

Lipset, Seymour Martin. 1996. *American Exceptionalism*. New York: W. W. Norton.

Lipset, Seymour Martin. 1998. "Paul F. Lazarsfeld of Columbia." In Jacques Lautman and Bernard-Pierre Lecuyer, eds., *Paul Lazarsfeld (1901–1976): La sociologie de Vienne a New York*, 255–270. Paris: Editions L' Harmattan.

Lipset S., and S. Rokkan, eds. 1967. *Party Systems and Voter Alignments: Cross-National Perspective*. New York: Free Press.

Lipset, Seymour Martin, Martin Trow, and James S. Colemen. 1956. *Union Democracy*. Glencoe, Ill.: Free Press.

MacKenzie, Donald, and Barry Barnes. 1979. "Scientific Judgement: The Biometry-Mendelism Controversy." In B. Barnes and S. Shapin, eds., *Natural Order*, 191–210. Beverly Hills: Sage.

Mair, Peter, Seymour Martin Lipset, Michael Hout, and John H. Goldthorpe. 1999. "Critical Commentary: Four Perspectives on the End of Class Politics?" In Geoffrey Evans, ed., *The End of Class Politics?* 308–322. Oxford: Oxford University Press.

Manza, Jeff, and Clem Brooks. 1999. *Social Cleavages and Political Change*. Oxford: Oxford University Press.

Mateju, Petr, Blanka Rehakova, and Geoffrey Evans. 1999 "The Politics of Interests and Class Realignment in the Czech Republic, 1992-1996." In Geoffrey Evans, ed., *The End of Class Politics?* 231–253. Oxford: Oxford University Press.

Mayer, G. Allen. 1997. "New Fiscal Populism: Innovations in Political Candidates and Campaigns in Illinois, 1956–1992." In Terry Nichols Clark and Michael Rempel, eds., *The Politics of Post-Industrial Societies*. Boulder, Colo.: Westview Press.

Merritt, Dennis. 1999. "The Rise of the New Political Culture in Britain." M. A. thesis, De Paul University.

Merton, Robert K. 1973. *The Sociology of Science*. Edited by Norman W. Storer. Chicago: University of Chicago Press.

Meyer, John. 1994. "The Evolution of Modern Stratification Systems." In David B. Grusky, ed., *Social Stratification*, 730–737. Boulder: Westview Press.

Mouritzen, Poul-Erik. 1992. *Managing Cities in Austerity*. London and Newbury Park: Sage Publications.

Munson, Ziad. 1995. "Modeling Class Effects." Presented to Social Science History Association, annual meeting, Chicago.

Nieuwbeerta, Paul. 1995. *The Democratic Class Struggle*. Amsterdam: Thesis Publishers.

Nieuwbeerta, Paul and Nan Dirk De Graaf. 1999. "Traditional Class Voting in Twenty Postwar Societies." In Geoffrey Evans, ed., *The End of Class Politics?* 23–58. Oxford: Oxford University Press.

Pakulski, Jan. 1993. "The Dying of Class or Marxist Class Theory." *International Sociology* 8, no. 3 (September): 279–292.

Polsby, Nelson. [1963] 1980. *Community Power and Political Theory*. Rev. ed. New Haven: Yale University Press.

Przeworski, Adam, and John Sprague. 1988. *Paper Stones*. Chicago: University of Chicago Press.

Przeworski, Adam, and Henry Teune. 1970. *The Logic of Comparative Social Inquiry*. New York: Wiley Interscience.

Putnam, Robert. 1993. *Making Democracy Work*. Princeton: Princeton University Press.

Putnam, Robert. 1995. "Bowling Alone." *Journal of Democracy* 6, no. 1 (January): 65–78.

Ringdal, K., and K. Hines. 1999. "Changes in Class Voting in Norway 1957–1989." In Geoffrey Evans, ed., *The End of Class Politics?* 181–202. Oxford: Oxford University Press.

Sartori, G. 1969. "From the Sociology of Politics to Political Sociology." In S. M. Lipset, ed., *Politics and the Social Sciences*, 65–100. Oxford: Oxford University Press.

Shavit, Yossi, and Hans-Peter Blossfeld, eds., 1993. *Persistent Inequality*. Boulder: Westview Press.

Van Deth, Jan W., and Elinor Scarborough, eds. 1995. *The Impact of Values, Beliefs in Government*. Vol. 4. New York: Oxford University Press.

Weakliem, David L., and Anthony F. Heath. 1999a. "The Secret Life of Class Voting: Britain, France, and the United States since the 1930s." In Geoffrey Evans, ed., *The End of Class Politics?* 97–136. Oxford: Oxford University Press.

Weakliem, David L., and Anthony F. Heath. 1999b. "Resolving Disputes about Class Voting in Britain and the United States: Definitions, Models, and Data." In Geoffrey Evans, ed., *The End of Class Politics?* 281–307. Oxford: Oxford University Press.

Wright, Erik O. 1985. *Classes*. London: Verso.

2

Are Social Classes Dying?[*]

TERRY NICHOLS CLARK AND SEYMOUR MARTIN LIPSET

Abstract New forms of social stratification are emerging. Much of our thinking about stratification—from Marx, Weber, and others—must be recast to capture these new developments. Social class was the key theme of past stratification work. Yet class is an increasingly outmoded concept. Class stratification implies that people can be differentiated hierarchically on one or more criteria into distinct layers, classes. Class analysis has grown increasingly inadequate in recent decades as traditional hierarchies have declined and new social differences have emerged. The cumulative impact of these changes is fundamentally altering the nature of social stratification—placing past theories in need of substantial modification.

This paper outlines first some general propositions about the sources of class stratification and its decline. The decline of hierarchy, and its spread across situses, is emphasized. The general propositions are applied to political parties and ideological cleavages, the economy, the family, and social mobility. These developments appear most clearly in North America and Western Europe, but our propositions also help interpret some of the tensions and factors driving change in Eastern Europe, the Soviet Union, and other societies.

Introduction

New forms of social stratification are emerging. Much of our thinking about stratification—from Marx, Weber, and others—must be recast to

[*]Originally published in *International Sociology* 6, no. 4 (December 1991): 397–410.

capture these new developments. Social class was the key theme of past stratification work. Yet class is an increasingly outmoded concept, although it is sometimes appropriate to earlier historical periods. Class stratification implies that people can be differentiated hierarchically on one or more criteria into distinct layers, classes. Class analysis has grown increasingly inadequate in recent decades as traditional hierarchies have declined and new social differences have emerged. The cumulative impact of these changes is fundamentally altering the nature of social stratification—placing past theories in need of substantial modification.

We begin with a brief review of class stratification from Marx and Weber, as their formulations remain influential. We next show how class-based analyses have declined in explanatory value for political behavior and suggest three propositions that explain why. Toward an alternative framework, we examine changes in two arenas of stratification: the economy and family. In each section we consider how hierarchy has declined and new patterns are emerging, illustrating the decline of social classes and the fragmentation of social stratification.

Classical Formulations: Marx and Weber

Marx and Weber developed an approach to class stratification that heavily influenced most later work.[1] We briefly summarize their contributions, then assess how they need revision.

Karl Marx

Karl Marx started from the premise that the primary function of social organization is the satisfaction of basic human needs—food, clothing, and shelter. Hence, the productive system (the economy) is the nucleus around which society is organized. From the assumption of the primacy of production flows the Marxist definition of class: any aggregate of persons who play the same part in the production mechanism. Marx, in *Capital,* outlined three main classes, differentiated according to their relations to the means of production: (1) capitalists, or owners of the means of production; (2) workers, or all those who are employed by others; (3) landowners, who are regarded as survivors of feudalism. Although Marx differentiated classes in objective terms, his primary interest was to understand and facilitate the emergence of class consciousness among the depressed strata. He wished to see them create a sense of shared class interests, as a basis for conflict with

the dominant class. The fact that a group held a number of objective characteristics in common, but lacked class consciousness, meant for Marx that
it could not play the role of a historically significant class. He analyzed many
conditions that facilitate working-class consciousness: consolidation of small
into larger workplaces, nationalization of communication, and so forth.

Marx was not very concerned with the specifics of the capitalist upper class.
Basically, he assumed that the powerful parts of such a class must be self-
conscious and that the state as a vehicle of power serves the interests of the
dominant class, in the long run. The dilemma of the Marxist theory of class
is also the dilemma of every other single-variable theory. We can locate a class
member objectively, but this may tell us little about the subjective correlates
(social outlook, attitudes, etc.) of class position. Marx never actually said that
there would necessarily have to be a relationship between class position and
the attitudes of class members. But if he recognized "exceptions" in his historical and journalistic writings, they did not change his main theory.

Max Weber

While Marx emphasized economic factors as determinants of social class,
Weber suggested that economic interests were only a special case of the
larger category of "values," which included many things that are neither
economic nor interests. For Weber, the Marxist model was a source of
fruitful hypotheses, yet it remained too simple to handle the complexity of
stratification. He therefore sought to develop an analytical alternative, one
which distinguished the various sources of hierarchical differentiation and
potential cleavage. Weber's key contributions to social stratification were
in showing how class, status, and bureaucracy can operate independently,
such as to influence political decisions.

Class

Weber reserved the concept of class for economically determined stratification. He defined a class as composed of people who have life chances in
common, as determined by their power to dispose of goods and skills for
the sake of income. Property is a class asset but not the only criterion of
class. For Weber, the crucial aspect of a class situation is, ultimately, the
market. His examination of past class struggles suggested that conflicts between creditors and debtors are perhaps the most visible economic cleavage. The conflict between employers and workers is highly visible under
capitalism but is just a special case of the more common struggle between

buyers and sellers. Weber, like Marx, was concerned to identify conditions encouraging class consciousness. Yet for him there was no single set of classes or form of class consciousness. Rather, which groups develop a consciousness of common interest opposing other groups is a specific empirical question; different groups join or conflict at different times and places. Variations depend heavily on the general culture of a society, including its religion and fundamental beliefs. These can foster or inhibit the emergence of class-conscious groups in ways that cannot be understood solely from a society's economic base.

Status

Writing about class, Weber broadened the concept but did not essentially break from Marx. His dramatic difference came in relativizing class by introducing his second major dimension of stratification, status, which Weber defined as the positive or negative estimation of honor, or prestige, received by individuals or positions. Thus it involves the felt perceptions of people. Since status involves the perception of how much one is valued by others, people value it more than economic gain. Status may flow from wealth, religion, race, physical attractiveness, or social skills.

Power, Status, and Bureaucracy

Power, which in the Marxist analysis derives from class position, is a much more complex phenomenon in the Weberian model. Weber defined power as the chance of a person or group to realize their will even against the opposition of others. Power may be a function of resources possessed in the economic, status, and political systems; both status and class are power resources. Since people want higher status, they tend to try to orient their behavior to that approved by those with the higher status that they value. Power resources can also be found in institutions that command the allegiance of people—religions, parties, trade unions, and the like. Anyone with followers or, like the military, with control of force may have access to power. In large measure, the relative weight of different power resources is determined by the rules of the political game, which vary in different societies. Such rules of the game are found in the structure of legal authority and its degree of legitimacy, which in turn influence how power is secured.

For Weber, the key source of power in modern society is not in the ownership of the means of production. Rather, the increased complexity of modern industrial society leads to the development of vast bureaucracies that grow increasingly interconnected and interdependent. The modern state, with its monopoly of arms and administration, becomes the dominant institution in bureaucratized society. Because of the increasing complexity of operating modern social institutions, even most economic institutions are brought into a close dependent relationship with the administrative and military bureaucracies of the state. Increasingly, therefore, the key power resources become rigidly hierarchical large-scale bureaucracies—"the iron cage." Weber's insightful analysis, especially of bureaucracy, stressed early twentieth-century changes. As we move into the twenty-first century, bureaucracies are being curtailed.

Reconceptualizing Class: Post Marx and Weber

If one looks closely at class theories in recent decades, it is striking how much class has changed. This is not immediately obvious, since most theorists claim direct descendance from Marx and Weber. But many have in fact fundamentally altered the concept of class toward what we term the fragmentation of stratification. Consider some examples of class theory and social stratification. Dahrendorf (1959: 157–206) stressed that many lines of social cleavage have not erupted into class conflict. For a Marxian revolution, the working class should suffer immiserization and grow more homogeneous; capitalists should join in combat against them. But Dahrendorf points instead to the "decomposition of labor": workers have become more differentiated by skill level—into skilled, semiskilled, and unskilled. Unions often separate more than join these groups. Perhaps even more important is the expansion of the "middle class" of white-collar nonmanual workers. Such a middle class was largely ignored by Marx; it was expected to join the capitalists or workers. Instead it has grown substantially and differentiated internally, especially between lower-level salaried employees and managers. Dahrendorf might have abandoned the concept of class but instead retained the term while redefining it to include all sorts of groups in political or social conflict: " 'class' signifies conflict groups that are generated by the differential distribution of authority in imperatively coordinated associations" (Dahrendorf 1959: 204).

Many writers have, like Dahrendorf, retained terms from Marx while substantially changing their meaning. Erik Wright (1985: 64–104) has sought to capture some of the same changes as Dahrendorf. He does so by developing a 12-category "typology of class location in capitalist society" that includes: (1) bourgeoisie, (2) small employers, (4) expert managers,

(5) expert supervisors, (8) semicredentialed supervisors, and continues up to (12) proletarians. It explicitly incorporates not just ownership but also skill level and managerial responsibility. It is striking that Wright, a self-defined Marxist, incorporates so much post-Weberian multidimensionality.

Giddens (1980: 108–112) similarly emphasizes the emergence of multiple cleavages within the workplace, the distinct importance of management, and the rise of an autonomous middle class, as undermining the classical Marxist approach.

These analyses stress changes in workplace relations. Yet social relations outside the workplace are increasingly important for social stratification. If "proletarians" are visibly distinct in dress, food, and lifestyle, they are more likely to think of themselves and act as a politically distinct class. In the nineteenth and early twentieth centuries, this was often the case, as novels and sociologists report. The decreasing distinctiveness of social classes is stressed by Parkin (1979: 69), who holds that this brings the "progressive erosion of the communal components of proletarian status." Specifically, "the absence of clearly visible and unambiguous marks of inferior status has made the enforcement of an all-pervasive deference system almost impossible to sustain outside the immediate work situation. It would take an unusually sharp eye to detect the social class of Saturday morning shoppers in the High Street, whereas to any earlier generation it would have been the most elementary task."

The same tendency toward fragmentation emerges from assessments of political leadership and power. The elitist and hierarchical assumptions that lie behind ruling class analysis as developed by Marx, Pareto, and Mosca have been increasingly weakened. When Hunter's *Community Power Structure* appeared in 1953, it confirmed the view of many social scientists that upper-class power elites ruled. But over the next three decades, this class domination view was supplanted by a pluralistic, multidimensional conceptualization. The paradigm change did not come easily: it cumulatively evolved from some 200 studies of national and community power, accompanied by considerable debates about power elites and class domination (see Dahl 1961; Clark 1975; Clark and Ferguson 1983). Stressing historical changes, Shils (1982: 31) suggests that by the late twentieth century "these reflections seem to lead to the conclusion that Mosca's conception of a political class is no longer applicable in our contemporary societies."

Should the social class concept be abandoned? In a 1959 exchange, Nisbet suggested that class "is nearly valueless for the clarification of the data of wealth, power and social status in the contemporary United States"

(1959: 11). Commenting on Nisbet in the same journal, Bernard Barber and O. D. Duncan both argued that his position had not been substantiated and that a sharper analysis and evidence were necessary. This was over 30 years ago. Yet today class remains salient in sociologists' theories and commentaries. We do not suggest it be altogether abandoned but complemented by other factors.

The Decline of Social Class, and the Multiplication of Status Dimensions

Theories lag behind social changes. Major social changes have occurred since Marx and Weber wrote and have accelerated since 1970. Their cumulative effects remain inadequately conceptualized. We extend the critique of Marx that Weber began and others continued. But we push further.

Many stratification analysts used class analysis longer and more extensively than empirically warranted because of their focus on Europe. Analysts of American society are often defensive, suggesting that America is somehow "behind" Europe. Marxists were among the most outspoken in this regard but not unique (e.g., Wilson 1978). However, things changed as new social movements emerged in the 1970s and 1980s. The United States then often seemed more a leader than a laggard. This seemed even more true in the dramatic changes of the late 1980s as the former Communist societies, led by Eastern Europe, sought to throw off their central hierarchical planning and move toward free economic markets and political democracy.

What do these changes imply for theories of stratification? A critical point is that traditional hierarchies are declining; economic and family hierarchies determine much less than just a generation or two ago. Three general propositions state this argument, developed below:

1. *Hierarchy generates and maintains rigid class relations.[2] The greater the hierarchical (vertical) differentiation among persons in a social unit, the deeper its class divisions tend to become.*

Since the degree of hierarchy may vary with a society, we add:

2. *The greater the hierarchical differentiation in each separate situs[3] (or separate vertical dimension, e.g., economic institutions, government organizations, and families), the more salient are class-defined patterns in in-*

formal social relations, cultural outlooks, and support for social change, such as support for social movements and political behavior.

But note the converse of 1 and 2:

  3. *The more the hierarchy declines, the more structured social class relations diminish in salience. And the larger the number of situses which evidence declining hierarchy, the less salient are class relations in the society.*

As class conflict declines, there may be less conflict, or conflict may be organized along different lines (for instance, gender).

Not all hierarchies generate counterreactions. There must be sufficient acceptance of democratic processes to permit opposition to surface. And the more that legal structures, the media, and other institutions permit or enhance the articulation of social conflict, the more antihierarchical themes can spread and win social support. That hierarchy generates efforts to dismantle it is a social proposition analogous to the psychological frustration-aggression hypothesis: frustrated persons act aggressively. But this social psychological resonance complements the social dynamics in our propositions 1, 2 and 3. While there may be rational individual choice, leaders and institutional arrangements have distinctive impacts.

We consider next separate situses of social stratification in terms of our three general propositions. In each situs we consider some of the specific dynamics by which social classes have declined or are declining. The cumulative effect, across situses, is the emergence of a new system of social stratification.

Politics: Less Class, More Fragmentation

Political behavior is an ideal area to assess changes in stratification. It was central to Marx and Weber; it is highly visible today; it has been studied in detail; it permits tests of competing hypotheses. Lipset's *Political Man* stressed class politics in its first edition (1960). But the second edition (1981, especially pp. 459ff.) focused on the declines in class voting. A striking illustration of this change is in the results from the 1940s to the 1980s on the Alford Index of class voting. This index is based on the percentage of persons by social class who vote for left or right parties. For instance, if 75 percent of the working class votes for the Left, and only 25 percent of the middle class does so, the Alford Index score is 50 (the difference between these two figures). Figure 2.1 shows that the Alford Index has declined in every country for which data are available.

Figure 2.1

Class voting has declined in all Western democracies from 1947 to 1986.

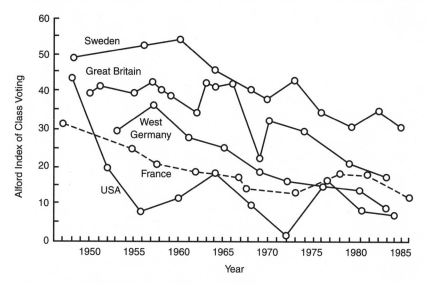

Source: Lipset 1981; updated in Clark and Inglehart 1991.

What is replacing class? The classical left-right dimension has been trans-formed. People still speak of the Left and the Right, but definitions are changing. There now are two Lefts, with distinct social bases. The tradi-tional Left is blue-collar based and stresses class-related issues. But a sec-ond Left is emerging in Western societies (sometimes termed New Poli-tics, New Left, Post-Bourgeois, or Post-Materialist), which increasingly stresses social issues rather than traditional class political issues. The most intensely disputed issues for them no longer deal with ownership and con-trol of the means of production. And in many Socialist and even Commu-nist parties (in the 1970s in Italy, in the 1990s in Eastern Europe) sup-porters of these new issues are supplanting the old:

1. *Political issues shift with more affluence: as wealth increases, people take the basics for granted: they grow more concerned with lifestyle and amenities. Younger, more educated and more affluent persons in more affluent and less hierarchical societies should move furthest from traditional class politics.*

Much evidence supports this proposition. Consider the strength of the correlation between fiscal issues (should government spend more or not?) and social issues (abortion, tolerance of minorities, etc.). Figure 2.2 shows

Figure 2.2

Only older French mayors report traditional ideology: correlations between fiscal and social liberalism for U.S. and French mayors, by age.

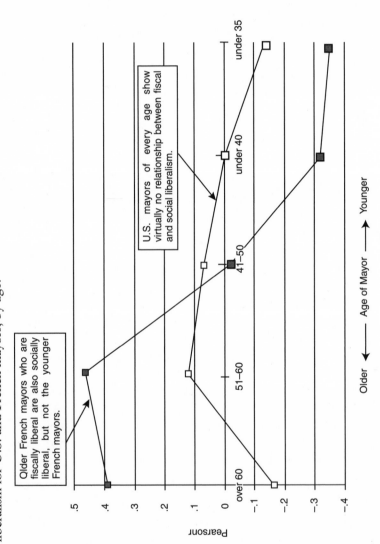

that older French mayors (those over 50) show the traditional class-political association between fiscal and social liberalism.

But for French mayors from 40 to 50, the relationship drops to zero, while for those under 40, it flips to negative. By contrast, for U.S. mayors of every age, fiscal and social liberalism are virtually unrelated. Pursuing this analysis in multiple regressions, using nine variables (party, wealth, etc.), we find similar results: adjusted R^2s for the French are high (.25 to .44); about six times higher than for U.S. mayors (.03 to .08)! This survey was carried out in 1983; in another survey just a decade earlier, the U.S. mayors were close to the French (Clark and Ferguson 1983: 189). Hierarchy and class effects, these results suggest, have declined dramatically in just a few years.[4]

These trends are congruent with the "post-industrial" trends identified by Daniel Bell and Alain Touraine, and the "post-materialist" (earlier termed "post-bourgeois") patterns identified by Ronald Inglehart (1990), stressing "self-actualization" via aesthetic intellectual and participatory concerns. Scott Flanagan (1980) suggests a shift from traditional consciousness to libertarian consciousness. But one should not overstate the changes: Alan Marsh, analyzing British data, finds that "materialists" and "post-materialists" do not differ in their concern for having enough money, which both share. The post-materialists, however, "are distinguished by their relative youth, wealth, education and by their concern for ideology" (Marsh 1975: 28).

Politics is normally analyzed as a consequence of class. We turn next to two situses—the economy and family—that generate class relations and suggest how they have changed in content.

Economic Organization Changes: Sources of a New Market Individualism

One simple, powerful change has affected the economy: growth. And economic growth undermines hierarchical class stratification.

2. *Affluence weakens hierarchies and collectivism, but it heightens individualism.*

With more income, the poor depend less on the rich. And all can indulge progressively more elaborate and varied tastes. But as such complexity increases, it grows harder to plan centrally; decentralized, demand-sensitive decision-making becomes necessary. These contrasts particularly affect centrally planned societies like the Soviet Union. But they operate too for firms like General Motors and U.S. Steel.

3. *Markets, ceteris paribus, grow in relevance as income rises.*

Many private goods come increasingly from more differentiated and sub-market-oriented small firms, especially in such service-intensive fields as "thoughtware," finance, and office activities. By contrast huge firms are in relative decline, especially for traditional manufacturing products like steel and automobiles. Some two-thirds of all new jobs are in firms with 20 or fewer employees, in many countries (Birch 1979). These small firms emerge because they outcompete larger firms. Why? Technology and management style are critical factors.

4. *The more advanced the technology and knowledge base, the harder it is to plan in advance and control administratively, both within a large firm and still more by central government planners.*

Technological changes illustrate how new economic patterns are no longer an issue of public versus private-sector control but bring inevitable frustrations for hierarchical control by anyone. As research and development grow increasingly important for new products and technologies, they are harder to direct or define in advance for distant administrators of that firm, and even harder for outside regulators or political officials seeking to plan centrally (as in a Soviet five-year plan, to use an extreme case). Certain plastics firms have as much as one-third of staff developing the chemistry for new products. Computers, biological engineering, and robotics illustrate the dozens of areas that are only vaguely amenable to forecast and hence central control.

A major implication for social stratification of these economic changes is the *decline in traditional authority, hierarchy, and class relations.* Current technologies require fewer unskilled workers performing routine tasks or a large middle management to coordinate them than did traditional manufacturing of steel, automobiles, etc. High tech means increasing automation of routine tasks. It also demands more professional autonomous decisions. More egalitarian, collegial decision-making is thus increasingly seen as a hallmark of modern society, by analysts from Habermas and Parsons to Daniel Bell and Zbigniew Brzczinski, and to consultants in business schools who teach the importance of a new "corporate culture"—as illustrated by *In Search of Excellence* (Peters and Waterman 1982), the number-one nonfiction bestseller in the United States for some time and widely read by business leaders in the United States and Europe. Even Soviet scholars as early as 1969 noted "a sweeping qualitative transformation of productive forces as a result of science being made the principal factor in the development of social production" (Richta et al. 1969: 39).

The occupations that are expanding are white-collar, technical, professional, and service-oriented. The class structure increasingly resembles a diamond bulging at the middle rather than a pyramid. Higher levels of education are needed in such occupations; the number of students pursuing more advanced studies has rapidly increased in the past few decades.

5. *The larger the extent of the market, the less likely are particularistic decisions (preference for family members, city residents, or nationals) to prevail. Local stratification hierarchies are correspondingly undermined as markets grow—regionally, nationally, and internationally.*

The force of this proposition has grown in the 1970s and 1980s with the globalization of markets for manpower, capital, and sales. Big and small firms have experienced major consolidations, enhanced by the growth of multinationals, the 1970s' oil boom and subsequent bust, leveraged buyouts, the rise of the Eurodollar market, and worldwide trade expansion. The growth of the U.S. economy has been fueled by massive in-migration, especially from Mexico, Latin America, and Asia. More immigrants came into the United States in the 1980s than in any decade since before World War 1. These factors combine to undermine the familistic–quasi-monopolistic tradition of business hierarchy and class stratification patterns.

A Slimmer Family

Major trends here parallel those in the economy.

6. *The family and intimate personal relations have increasingly become characterized by more egalitarian relations, more flexible roles, and more tolerance for a wider range of behavior. Hierarchical stratification has weakened.*

The traditional family has been slimmed. The authoritarian paternalistic family is decreasingly the model for stratification in the rest of society. Fewer young people marry; they wed later, have fewer children; far more women work outside the home; divorce rates have risen; parents and grandparents live less often with children (e.g., Cherlin 1981; Forse

1986). Paralleling these sociodemographic changes are changes in attitudes and roles concerning the family. Children and wives have grown substantially more egalitarian in a very short period of time. Indeed, attitudes toward the family have changed more than almost any other social or political factor in the past 20–30 years, especially questions like, Should women work outside the home?

Social Mobility

Besides these internal family dynamics, the slimmer family determines less the education and jobs of individual family members. Increased wealth and government support programs have expanded choices to individuals and cumulatively transferred more functions than ever away from the family. The magnitude of these changes rose in the 1970s and 1980s.

7. *The family has grown less important as a basis of stratification in relation to education and jobs.*

Families are decreasingly responsible for raising children and placing them in jobs. Fewer children work in family firms (farms, shops, etc.). Social mobility studies show decreasing effects of parents' education and income in explaining childrens' occupational success; simultaneously the effects of education have increased.[5] The proportions of wives and mothers working in jobs outside the home have grown dramatically, first and especially in the United States but in many European countries too.

Conclusion

New patterns of social stratification are emerging. The key trend could be described as one of "fragmentation of stratification":
–the weakening of class stratification, especially as shown in distinct class-differentiated life-styles
–the decline of economic determinism and the increased importance of social and cultural factors
–politics organized less by class and more by other loyalties
–the slimming of the family
–social mobility less family-determined, more ability- and education-determined

Notes

1. A further discussion of Marx, Weber, and functionalist contributions to stratification can be found in Lipset 1985, chap. 2.

2. We broadly follow Marx and Weber in understanding social class as social differentiation emerging from structured socioeconomic life chances of distinct social categories of persons. Social classes can emerge from differential access to the means of production (as Marx stressed), or to trade or consumption (as Weber added). Class consciousness may be said to emerge if these social categories develop distinct subjective outlooks, culture, and behavior patterns. Social class membership may be important for a wide range of social and political behavior in so far as social class membership is a criterion for social and political decisions (such as who is admitted to college or a political caucus). Empirical analysis must assess the importance of class compared with other potential explanatory variables.

By hierarchy we understand the vertical differentiation of individuals and subunits in terms of specific criteria, such as income, status, and power. Hierarchies may be continuous, ranking persons from high to low, but need not include any distinct classes. We consider both objective and subjective assessments of hierarchy. While the subjective may be more important in generating social protest and political ideology, it is also harder to measure systematically. Hierarchy is similar to but distinct from social class. Two examples illustrate the differences. A society could have a sharply hierarchical but smoothly continuous income distribution and have no distinct social classes. A second society could include persons relatively similar in income level but be sharply divided into two opposing classes, for example, blue- and white-collar workers.

3. We adapt the concept of situs from Benoit-Smullyan (1944) and Bell (1973: 377), to refer to parallel but distinct sectors of social organization, each with its partly distinct rules of the game (or culture).

4. The mayor results are from the Fiscal Austerity and Urban Innovation Project, discussed in Baldersheim et al. 1989; Clark 1985–1988; and Clarke 1989. See Inglehart 1990 for similar findings about citizens.

5. U.S. mobility studies from the late nineteenth century onward report few changes until the 1960s (Lipset and Bendix 1991; Grusky 1986) but major changes since: Hout's (1988) replication of Featherman and Hauser (1978) showed that the effect of origin status on destination status declined by 28 percent from 1962 to 1973 and by one-third from 1972 to 1985. Hauser and Grusky (1984, 1987) analyzed 16 and 22 countries, finding more mobility in countries with socialist and social democratic political leadership. This reflects the dramatic changes in the occupational and ownership structure across many societies in recent years.

References

Baldersheim, H., et al., eds. 1989. *New Leaders, Parties, and Groups.* Bordeaux, France: CERVEL-IEP.

Barber, B., and Duncan, O. D. 1959. "Discussion of Papers by Professor Nisbet and Professor Heberle." *Pacific Sociological Review* (spring): 25–28.

Bell, D. 1973. *The Coming of Post-Industrial Society.* New York: Basic.

Benoit-Smullyan, E. 1944. "Status, Status Types and Status Interrelationships." *American Sociological Review* 9: 151–161.

Birch, D. L. 1979. *The Job Generation Process.* Cambridge, Mass.: MIT Program on Neighborhood and Regional Change.

Cherlin, A. J. 1981. *Marriage, Divorce, Remarriage.* Cambridge, Mass. Harvard University Press.

Clark, T. N. 1975. "Community Power." In Inkeles, A., Coleman, J. and Smelser, N.J. (eds). *Annual Review of Sociology* 1: 217–296. Palo Alto: Annual Reviews.

Clark, T. N. 1985, 1986, 1987, 1988. *Research in Urban Policy,* vols. 1, 2A, 2B, 3. Greenwich, Conn.: JAI Press.

Clark, T. N., and Ferguson, L. C. 1983. *City Money.* New York: Columbia University Press.

Clark, T. N., and Inglehart, R. 1991. "The New Political Culture: An Introduction." Prepared for Clark, T. N., and Hoffmann-Martinot, V. (eds.), *The New Political Culture.* Boulder, CO: Westview, 1998.

Clarke, S., ed. 1989. *Urban Innovation and Autonomy.* Newbury Park: Sage.

Dahl, R. A. 1961. *Who Governs?* New Haven: Yale University Press.

Dahrendorf, R. 1959. *Class and Class Conflict in Industrial Society.* Stanford: Stanford University Press.

Featherman, D. L., and Hauser, R. M. 1978. *Opportunity and Change.* New York: Academic Press.

Flanagan, S. C. 1980. "Value Cleavages, Economic Cleavages, and the Japanese Voter." *American Journal of Political Science* 24.

Forse, M. 1986. "La diversification de la société française vue à travers le mariage et l'idéologie." *The Tocqueville Review* 7: 223–233.

Giddens, A. 1980. *The Class Structure of the Advanced Societies.* New York: Harper and Row.

Grusky, D. B. 1986. "American Social Mobility in the Nineteenth and Twentieth Century." Ph.D. diss., Department of Sociology, University of Wisconsin–Madison.

Hauser, R. M. 1972. *Socioeconomic Background and Educational Performance.* Washington, D.C.: Rose Monograph Series, American Sociological Association.

Hauser, R. M, and Grusky, D. B. 1984. "Comparative Social Mobility Revisited." *American Sociological Review* 49: 19–38.

Hauser, R. M., and Grusky, D. B. 1987. "Cross-National Variation in Occupational Distributions, Relative Mobility Chances and Intergenerational Shifts in Occupational Distributions." Draft paper.

Hout, M. 1988. "More Universalism, Less Structural Mobility." *American Journal of Sociology* 93: 1358–1400.

Inglehart, R. *Cultural Shift in Advanced Industrial Society.* Princeton: Princeton University Press.

Lipset, S. M. 1981 [1960]. *Political Man: The Social Bases of Politics.* Baltimore: Johns Hopkins University Press.

Lipset, S. M. 1985. *Consensus and Conflict.* New Brunswick, N. J.: Transaction Books.

Lipset, S. M., and Bendix, R. 1991 [1959]. *Social Mobility in Industrial Society.* New Brunswick, N.J.: Transaction Books.

Lipset, S. M., and Schneider, W. 1983. *The Confidence Gap.* New York: Free Press.

Marsh, A. 1975. "The Silent Revolution, Value Priorities, and the Quality of Life in Britain." *American Political Science Review* 69.

Nisbet, R. A. 1959. "The Decline and Fall of Social Class." *Pacific Sociological Review* 11–17.

Parkin, F. 1979. *Marxism and Class Theory: A Bourgeois Critique.* New York: Columbia University Press.

Peters, T. J., and Waterman, R. H. 1982. *In Search of Excellence.* New York: Warner Books.

Richta, R., et al. 1969. *Civilization at the Crossroads.* White Plains, N. Y.: International Arts and Sciences Press.

Sihls, E. 1982. "The Political Class in the Age of the Mass Society." In Czudnowski, M. M., ed., *Does Who Governs Matter?* DeKalb, Ill.: Northern Illinois University Press.

Wilson, W. J. 1978. *The Declining Significance of Race.* Chicago: University of Chicago Press.

Wright, E. O. 1985. *Classes.* London: Verso.

3

The Persistence of Classes in Post-Industrial Societies[*]

MIKE HOUT, CLEM BROOKS, AND JEFF MANZA

Abstract Class structures have undergone important changes in recent decades with the rise of post-industrial societies. Clark and Lipset have recently interpreted these changes as evidence that class is fragmenting and losing its importance. We reject their analysis. The birth of new sources of inequality does not imply the death of the old ones. We review empirical evidence that shows how class-based stratification continues to be a central factor in social stratification. Clark and Lipset also argue that class affects politics, the economy and the family less than it used to. Their conclusion is based on a selective reading of the empirical literature. We discuss the countervailing evidence and conclude that class effects persist.

> *Rumors of my death are greatly exaggerated.*
> (Mark Twain on hearing that his obituary had been published)

At the 1958 meetings of the American Sociological Association, Robert Nisbet announced the "decline and fall of social class" (Nisbet 1959). While the concept of social class was still "useful in historical sociology

[*]Originally published in *International Sociology* 8, no. 3 (September 1993): 259–277.

We have received useful comments on an earlier draft of this paper from Michael Burawoy, Glenn Carroll, Iona Mara Drita, Theodore P. Gerber, David Knoke, Maurizo Pisati, Yossi Shavit, Paul Sniderman, Arthur L. Stinchcombe, Donald Treiman, Loic Wacquant, David Weakliem, Aaron Wildavsky, Erik Wright, and Maurice Zeitlin. Our correspondents are, of course, not responsible for the use we have made of their comments. The Survey Research Center, UC Berkeley, provided financial and other support.

[and] comparative or folk sociology," according to Nisbet, it is "nearly useless for the clarification of data of wealth, power, and social status in contemporary United States and much of Western society in general" (11). Nisbet argued that class was no longer significant in the political sphere because "political power is spread in an unstratified way among voters," and in the economic sphere because of a "massive change from an economy based preponderantly upon primary and secondary sectors to one based increasingly upon tertiary occupations" in which "it is too obvious that the majority of jobs falling within the tertiary sector in modern times are not easily subsumed under any class system" (15). Finally, Nisbet argued that "the general elevation of level of consumption and the disappearance of clear and distinct strata of consumption" make it "unlikely that self-conscious and mutually antagonistic groups will arise" (16). As a result of such trends, he concluded that "class lines are exceedingly difficult to discover in modern economic society except in backwater areas" (ibid.). A key piece of empirical evidence in support of these theses offered by Nisbet was an apparent decline in the use of class themes in popular novels (11, 16).

The suggestion that class is declining in importance has been an oft-repeated theme in social science literature in the years since Nisbet's essay. Many scholars have claimed to discover, yet again, the disappearance (or impending disappearance) of classes in the years since Nisbet's essay (Goldthorpe and Marshall 1992). Theorists of post-industrial society emphasized the decline of class in the emerging social structures of modern societies in their writings (Bell 1973; Lipset 1981; Touraine 1971; see also the "post materialist" analysis of Inglehart 1990). Functionalist theories of social stratification deny the relevance of inequality in the ownership of property for the division of society into groups (Davis and Moore 1945; Parsons 1968, 1970; Sørensen 1991). Theorists of the "new social movements" have also rejected the use of class in understanding the social and political dynamics of contemporary societies (Cohen 1982; Laclau and Mouffe 1985; Hall and Jacques 1989).

The recent paper by Terry Nichols Clark and Seymour Martin Lipset (1991) in the journal *International Sociology* brings together a number of these arguments to offer an updated version of the declining significance of class argument. They give an unequivocal "yes" to the question in the title of their essay, "Are Social Classes Dying?"[1] They echo Nisbet's claim that class analysis is strictly for historians in asserting that class "is an increasingly outmoded concept" (Clark and Lipset 1991: 397) and that new forms of stratification are replacing class. They support these large claims with data selected to indicate that class has less of an effect on political, economic, and family outcomes than it used to, and go beyond routine reports that some of the parameters of social stratification are changing to announce the decline of classes and the fragmentation of social stratification. They lament that, 30 years after Nisbet's essay, "class remains salient in sociologists' theories and commentaries" (401), and they seek to bring this state of affairs to an end.

Clark and Lipset have joined with other writers past and present who leap from data on trends to conjectures about the future. The death and dying metaphors suggest more finality than the data will support. For, while we would be contradicting our own results if we were to deny that there have been trends toward a diminished effect of class on important social indicators, for example, the openness in mobility (Hout 1988), we see those trends as the outcome of a class-political process that is neither immutable nor irreversible. The past 25 years of class research reveal a mix of upward and downward trends in the effects of class. The mix is confusing for those who view them through the lenses of Marxist and functionalist theories that specify the economy as cause and politics as consequence in the political economy of class. The empirical record is becoming clearer and clearer, however, that the causal arrow needs to be reversed. The mix of increasing, unchanging, and decreasing class effects reflects the important role of politics in determining such mainstays of class analysis as the class structure itself, the mobility regime, and class voting in a society (Esping-Anderson 1990; Heath et al. 1991; Erikson and Goldthorpe 1992).

Coming from Seymour Martin Lipset, whose earlier work taught us much about the link between class and political life, this latest challenge to class analysis should not be ignored. Unlike Nisbet, who explicitly dismissed empirical research, arguing that "statistical techniques have had to become ever more ingenious to keep the vision of class from fading away altogether" (1959: 12), Clark and Lipset summarize a wealth of empirical data to make their case. On closer examination, however, we find that much of the evidence they cite is highly selective and cannot withstand critical scrutiny. We are especially troubled by their complete neglect of other evidence that shows the continuing, and even rising, importance of class. Altogether, we believe it is impossible to sustain their conclusion, and in the discussion that follows we seek to show that, while class may be defined and used by social scientists in a number of different ways, the concept remains indispensable. Whether they treat it as an independent or a dependent variable, sociologists will turn away from class at their own peril.

The Persistence of Classes

Sociologists did not invent the concept of class. But we have made more out of it than others have, mainly by emphasizing the point that it is how one makes a living that determines life chances and material interests. We differ from economists' nearly exclusive focus on the quantity of income or wealth and commonsense conceptions that blend lifestyle and morality with economic and sociological considerations (Jencks 1991).[2] The part-time school teacher, the semiskilled factory worker, and the struggling shopkeeper may all report the same income on their tax returns, but we recognize that as salaried, hourly, and self-employed workers, they have different sources of income and, consequently, different life chances.

At various points in their paper, Clark and Lipset (1991: 397, 401–402, 405) seem to equate class and hierarchy, but they are separate dimensions. *Hierarchy,* in sociological usage, could refer to any rankable distinctions. *Class* refers to a person's relationship to the means of production and/or labor markets, and it is an important determinant of an individual's income, wealth, and social standing.[3] Hierarchy or related concepts might be used as an explanation of stratification processes, as in Erikson and Goldthorpe 1992 or Hout and Hauser 1992, but to use the concepts as explanandum and explanans they must be defined independently and the relationship must be spelled out.

Class is an indispensable concept for sociology because (1) class is a key determinate of material interests; (2) structurally defined classes give rise to, or influence the formation of, collective actors seeking to bring about social change; and (3) class membership affects the life chances and behavior of individuals. The first concern refers to the intrinsic importance of class. The other two are relevant for "class analysis"—the investigation of how class affects other aspects of social life. Clark and Lipset state their case—which refers to all three of these concerns—without acknowledging that each concern raises different sets of issues. As a result of these confusions, Clark and Lipset's argument collapses analytically distinct processes.

Clark and Lipset also confuse trends in society with trends in writing about society. To be sure, our conceptions of class have grown more complex over the years. Marx's initial codification of the importance of whether one works for a living or expropriates a profit from the sale of goods produced by others has been supplemented over the years by additional distinctions, most of which are ignored by Clark and Lipset. In addition to workers and capitalists, contemporary Marxist accounts of class structure recognize professionals and crafts persons, who extract rents on their expertise, and managers and supervisors, who extract rents on their organizational assets (Wright 1985) These are not mere status distinctions, as Clark and Lipset would have it.[4] They are class distinctions because they specify economic roles with respect to labor markets and material interests. Contemporary Weberian theories of class also admit to complexity without negating the existence of classes. Weberians focus on the closure strategies that professionals and skilled workers use to influence labor markets to their collective advantage (Parkin 1979; Goldthorpe 1980: 39–46; Erikson and Goldthorpe 1992: 42–43; Manza 1992) and the internal labor markets that select managers and supervisors (Parkin 1979; Kalleberg and Berg 1987). While sociologists' models of class are a lot more complicated than they used to be, complexity alone does not imply that class is dead or dying.

Clark and Lipset's conclusions about the decline of class in post-industrial societies hinge on the claim that "traditional hierarchies are declining; economic and family hierarchies determine much less than just a generation or two ago" (1991: 401). However, hierarchy is never defined, and the assumed link between *hierarchy* and *class* in their formulation is at best vague. In moving back and forth between a materialist analysis of class to the vaguer concept of hierarchy, Clark and Lipset are tacitly shifting the terrain of debate away from class per se. This conceptual slippage makes it easier for them to conclude that classes are dying. Their emphasis on hierarchy is also potentially misleading in that forms of hierarchy could decline without any change in class structure or the general importance of class for systems of stratification or political behavior.[5] They persistently conflate class-based inequalities with nonclass forms of stratification. Perhaps as a consequence, Clark and Lipset conveniently ignore some of the most salient aspects of class inequalities in contemporary capitalist societies. First, they completely ignore the remarkable persistence in the high levels of wealth controlled by the bourgeoisie in these societies.[6] Further, they ignore the capacity of wealth-holders to influence political processes, either directly through financial contributions, intraclass organizational and political networks, and government agencies, or indirectly through control over investment decisions (Clawson et al. 1992; Domhoff 1990; Useem 1984; and Bottomore and Brym 1989 on direct control; and Block 1987, 1992; Lindblom 1977 on indirect control).[7]

Private fortunes are still predicated on ownership of the means of production. During the 1980s when inequality of wealth and earnings was growing in the United States and elsewhere, the private fortunes at the forefront of resurgent inequality were in almost all cases built through ownership. High-tech champions like Gates, merchandisers like Walton, and developers like Trump got rich because they owned the means of production. Arbitragers collected high fees and executives were "overcompensated," but they gained more from ownership of shares of stock than from their wages and salaries (Crystal 1991).

One important test for class analysis is the demonstration that some classes have material advantages over others. If classes are dying, then we would expect incumbents of different classes to earn similar amounts; that is, all of the income or earnings inequality should be within classes. Table 3.1 shows previously unpublished evidence regarding the relationship between class and earnings in the United States in late 1991.[8] The two leading class schemes in the current literature—Wright 1985 and Erikson and Goldthorpe 1992—are used. We are confident that other carefully crafted class schemes would also show significant variation in earnings levels.[9]

The class differences in earnings are statistically and substantively significant. Wright's capitalist class is at the top of the earnings distribution and his bottom class—workers—is at the bottom. The ratio of earnings from top to bottom is 4.2:1 for men and 2.5:1 for women. Wright's class scheme explains 20 percent of the variance in earnings. Adjusting for sex, education, age, and hours worked mediates some of the class differences, but the adjusted means show significant variation. The Erikson-Goldthorpe scheme also shows a pattern of significant variation. The ratio of the top class's earnings to the earnings of the lowest class is 4.9:1 among men and 3.6:1 among women.[10] The ratio of class variance to total variance in the Erikson-Goldthorpe scheme is 0.17. From both class schemes it is clear that changes in the class structure have not eroded the important effects of class on earnings.

The growth of the proportion of the population that is middle-class and the proliferation of middle classes has also not negated the persistence of income inequality (Smeeding 1991) and the growing proportions of the populations of industrial societies that are living in extreme poverty. The broad outlines of this "new poverty" (Markland 1990) are becoming increasingly clear (Wacquant 1993).[11] The existence of long-term joblessness or occupational marginality among sectors of the populations of these societies and the growth of low-income areas characterized by multiple sources of deprivation for residents (Massey 1990; Massey and Eggers 1990) do not fit very well with Clark and Lipset's claims about the decline of "traditional hierarchies."

In general, the persistence of wealth and power at the top and growing poverty and degradation at the bottom of contemporary class are struc-

Table 3.1

Earnings by Class: United States, 1991 (N = 1,557)

Class	Annual Earnings[a]		Annual Earnings (Adjusted)[b]	
	Men	Women	Men	Women
Wright Schema				
Employers				
10 or more employees	$71,300	$27,800	$52,200	$22,300
1–9 employees	$34,400	$23,000	$29,900	$19,100
No employees (petty bourgeoisie)	$20,800	$9,200	$21,200	$11,200
Employees				
Expert managers	$46,500	$30,600	$32,100	$22,000
Expert supervisors	$44,900	$26,600	$37,500	$23,700
Expert nonmanagers	$32,500	$24,900	$27,200	$20,800
Semicredentialed managers	$32,300	$22,100	$31,500	$20,800
Semicredentialed supervisors	$20,800	$19,700	$23,100	$21,600
Semicredentialed nonmanagers	$25,800	$17,700	$26,700	$17,000
Uncredentialed managers	$22,200	$14,400	$26,000	$16,800
Uncredentialed supervisors	$23,100	$16,300	$23,600	$17,500
Workers	$16,800	$11,400	$20,900	$14,600
Erikson-Goldthorpe Schema				
Upper professional (Ia)	$39,200	$28,400	$32,300	$21,700
Upper manager (Ib)	$56,200	$27,200	$40,300	$22,400
Lower professional (IIa)	$24,400	$18,700	$23,400	$17,400
Lower manager (IIb)	$33,400	$18,100	$30,300	$18,000
Clerk or sales worker (IIIb)	$22,800	$13,300	$23,300	$15,900
Service worker (IIIb)	$14,500	$7,800	$20,300	$12,000
Employer (IVa)	$41,800	$21,600	$35,300	$19,000
Petty bourgeosie (IVb)	$20,000	$9,000	$22,000	$11,100
Technician or supervisor (V)	$24,700	$17,000	$26,300	$18,700
Skilled worker (VI)	$22,600	$15,100	$26,000	$15,100
Semiskilled worker (VIIss)	$19,100	$13,500	$21,500	$14,500
Unskilled worker (VIIus)	$11,500	$10,000	$16,800	$12,500
Farmer w/employees (IVc)	$27,400	—[c]	$24,400	—[c]
Farmer, no employees (IVd)	$26,600	$4,500	$18,100	$3,300
Farm laborer (VIIf)	$16,700	—[c]	$17,600	—[c]

[a] We calculated the geometric mean instead of the usual arithmetic mean because of the well-known positive skew of the earnings distribution.

[b] We adjusted the geometric mean for the effects of education, age (including a term for age-squared), hours worked, and class (dummy variables) by regressing the log of earnings on these variables for men and women separately. The adjusted means are the antilog of the value expected for a 40-year-old person with a high school diploma who worked 40 hours per week for a full year.

[c] Fewer than five cases.

tures suggest that Clark and Lipset's conclusions about the impending death of classes are premature. In the United States, the country which we know best, it is becoming increasingly common in urban communities for privileged professionals and managers to live in secluded enclaves and suburbs (often behind locked gates) or in secured high-rise condominiums, while marginalized sectors of the population are crowded into increasingly dangerous inner-city areas (a trend discussed at length by the former secretary of labor in the United States, Robert Reich, in his 1991 book; see also Davis 1991). As long as such conditions prevail, we are skeptical that sociologists would be wise to abandon the concept of class, whatever other evidence might be adduced to show that the importance of class is declining.

Are Social Classes Dying? No

The evidence presented above should be enough to sustain our thesis that class divisions persist in post-industrial societies. But Clark and Lipset base their critique less on the existence of class divisions than on the supposed decline in the effects of class in three "situses" (politics, the economy, and the family) in these societies. We shall show that, even on their own terms, Clark and Lipset's empirical evidence cannot support their conclusions about the declining significance of class.

Politics

To demonstrate the declining significance of class in the political arena, Clark and Lipset attempt to show that class voting has declined. Their evidence is based on the claim that "the Alford Index [of class voting] has declined in every country for which data are available" (1991: 403).[12] Four observations about their data undermine these assertions, however.

First, their reliance on the Alford Index as the proper measure of class voting in highly dubious. That index is based on a two-class model of society. It is computed by simply subtracting the percentage of nonmanual occupations voting for left parties from the percentage of persons in manual occupations voting for left parties (Alford 1963: 79–80). By lumping together all persons employed in nonmanual occupations into one "class" and all persons working in manual occupations into the other "class," the Alford Index creates artificially high levels of cross-class voting among both groups. For example, secretaries, low-level clerks, and service-sector employees, who may have very similar class interests to manual workers, are counted as deviant if they vote for left parties. It has been apparent for some time that the two-class model used in the Alford Index is overly simplistic and does not capture the full complexity of class voting (Korpi 1972; Robertson 1984). The two classes invoked by Alford have no relation to Marxist class categories and are far too crude for Weberian or functionalist approaches (Blau and Duncan 1967: 432–433), so it is useless for testing hypotheses.

It will come as no surprise, then, to learn that the crude two-class model significantly underestimates the extent of class voting. By constructing a much more careful conception of the class structure than that employed by Clark and Lipset, Przeworski and Sprague (1986) derived very different estimates of both the cross-sectional differences and the trends in class voting. They found that class voting between 1990 and 1975 was relatively stable in three countries (Germany, Norway, and Finland), declined in one country (Denmark), and *increased* in the other three countries (Sweden, Belgium, and France) (Przeworski and Sprague 1986: chap. 5).[13] Przeworski and Sprague's evidence is not above criticism, but it leads us to reject Clark and Lipset's generalization about a monotonic decline in class voting in advanced capitalist societies.

Second, there are important technical limitations of the Alford Index that have substantive implications for our ability to understand trends in class voting (Heath et al. 1987). The Alford Index is subject to sampling error, yet Clark and Lipset use it uncritically without testing for significance. As Heath and his colleagues have pointed out, "It is a straightforward matter to test whether changes in that index are statistically significant," and therefore "scholars who use it should surely be expected to carry out such tests" (1987: 265). More serious than this lapse of scientific practice is the fact that the range of values that the Alford Index can take on is constrained by the marginal totals. This means that whenever the marginals change, for example, when new parties or candidates enter the electoral arena or the electoral balance among parties shifts significantly, the index can fluctuate wildly, even if the overall logic of class voting remains unchanged. Simple models for assessing association controlling for changes in the marginal distributions have been available to social scientists for 20 years (Goodman 1972) and are part of all widely disseminated computer packages,[14] so there is no need to rely on the potentially misleading Alford Index.

Third, the cross-national differences among the five countries they consider raise serious doubts about their proposition that "hierarchy generates and maintains rigid class relations" (Clark and Lipset 1991: 402). Problems with the Alford Index notwithstanding, reasonable estimates of class voting are likely to show Sweden as the nation with the strongest association between class and voting (among the five countries considered by Clark and Lipset) and the United States as the weakest. And yet, with respect to income inequality, Sweden is the most egalitarian country among the five by most indicators, and the United States the least among the five (Esping-Anderson 1990). Parkin (1971), Korpi (1983), and Esping-Anderson (1990), among others, have advanced the converse proposition that Sweden's class politics has produced the social policies responsible for Sweden's low levels of inequality. Not only are the data inconsistent, but the causal order between egalitarianism and class voting is reversed.

Fourth, Clark and Lipset seem to assume an unmediated connection between class and voting, ignoring completely the decisive role of unions, social movement organizations, and political parties in shaping the conditions under which voters make choices. When parties and other political organizations are organized around class, high levels of class voting can be expected. Przeworski and Sprague's (1986) analysis of the dynamics of social democratic parties based originally on working-class votes suggests that the strategic decision of these parties to weaken their class-based appeals to seek middle-class votes—a trend celebrated in Lipset 1990—has had a profound effect on the social bases of their political support. If workers' parties abandon or compromise their specific interests, does it mean those interests no longer exist? We say no. Class interests may remain latent in the political arena, but this does not mean they do not exist.

Clark and Lipset flesh out their case for the declining significance of class for politics by arguing that the traditional left-right cleavages characteristic of democratic capitalist societies have increasingly given way to more complex, multidimensional political ideologies. Such a claim shifts the focus from class as a determinant of political views to class or class inequalities as an *object* of public opinion. Clark and Lipset repeat the assertion that there are now "two Lefts," one based on the economic demands of subordinate classes, the other stressing "social issues" (1991: 403; Lipset 1981: 510–511). From this disjuncture of economy and society, they wish to infer that the class content of political struggles and public debate is declining. However, this contention is not supported either by the data they cite or by the existing research literature. For example, Weakliem's (1991) research on the dimensionality of class and voting casts doubt on the empirical adequacy of Clark and Lipset's interpretation of political trends. Weakliem finds that, while a second (plausibly post-materialist) dimension of politics *is* necessary to explain the relationship between class and party identification, it applies equally well to older and younger cohorts. The similarity of cohorts contradicts the claim that complexity is new, and Weakliem's crucial finding that "all classes have been moving toward the postmaterialist left" in his analysis of voting trends in Italy, the Netherlands, and France (1991: 1350) leads us to reject Clark and Lipset's assertions about the two Lefts.[15]

The complexities of political strategies and tactics make the distinction between class as a causal agent and class or inequality as an object of discussion absolutely critical. Merely because an issue is not directly couched in terms of class or traditional left-right politics does not mean that class is irrelevant to understanding it. Luker's (1984) research on the worldviews of pro-choice and pro-life activists exemplifies an issue that, while not ostensibly about class, turns in part on the contrasting class interests and experiences of the activists. What if some "new" social issues have become the object of political struggles and public debate in part because they resonate with people's traditional left-right political heuristics (Sniderman et al. 1991)? Could it be that controversies over affirmative action or the extension of rights to new categories of citizens (such as the disabled) gain their ideological strength from being about "old" (class) issues, such as equality or social democracy?

Finally, we note that Clark and Lipset supplement their arguments about the declining significance of class in politics with an analysis of the political attitudes of French and American mayors. They argue that the "traditional class-political association between fiscal and social liberalism" (1991: 403) is true for older French mayors but not for younger French mayors or for American mayors of any age. We are not sure what to make of this evidence. It is not immediately clear what relationship "social liberalism" (defined by the authors as issues such as "abortion" and "tolerance toward minorities") has ever had to class politics. The pattern they predict seems to hold for the French mayors (youngers generations being significantly less "traditional" in the terms defined by Clark and Lipset) but not for the American mayors (where the data show that there is not association between age and traditional liberalism).

Even if these data somehow did tell us something useful about the ideologies of mayors, we are unconvinced that it is relevant for their thesis that "younger, more educated and more affluent persons in more affluent and less hierarchical societies should move furthest from traditional class politics" (Clark and Lipset 1991: 403). First, it is not self-evident that younger mayors are more affluent (than older mayors are? than younger mayors used to be?). More important, generalizing from elites to the mass public is extremely risky. Elites have consistently been found to have more coherent, stable, comprehensive political belief systems than nonelite actors (Campbell et al. 1960; Converse 1964). In this particular case, mayors' views are likely to have been forged under more pressure than the average citizen experiences, because mayors are caught between the rock of fiscal constraint and the hard place of public opinion (Clark and Ferguson 1983). While elites' attitudes might be interesting in their own right, they cannot be generalized to the views of the publics they represent (McClosky and Brill 1983: 418–419).

In short, Clark and Lipset's evidence on class politics is incomplete and unconvincing. They have failed to make the case that class is declining in importance for politics. Class never was the all-powerful explanatory variable that some intellectual traditions assumed in earlier periods; class was always only one source of political identity and action alongside race, religion, nationality, gender, and others. To say that class matters less now than it used to requires that one exaggerate its importance in the past and understate its importance at present.[16] Class is important for politics to the extent that political organizations actively organize around class themes. Hence, in some periods the political consequences of class may appear latent, even if the underlying logic of class is unchanged.[17] We believe that on balance, however, the evidence shows that class remains important and that Clark and Lipset fail to demonstrate that class voting and traditional political values have declined.

Post-Industrial Economic Trends

Clark and Lipset argue that "economic growth undermines hierarchical class stratification" (1991: 405). They argue markets are growing in relevance as a consequence of rising incomes and that "decentralised, demand-sensitive decision-making" is growing to meet ever more complex consumer demand (ibid.). While huge firms are in relative decline and smaller niche-oriented ventures are increasing in at least some countries (Sabel 1982; Piore and Sabel 1984), we question whether any of the other claims they make in this section can stand up to critical scrutiny.

We first note that Clark and Lipset's claims about the growing "marketness" of capitalist societies in comparison to earlier periods is very difficult to sustain empirically (Block 1990: 56–66), and no substantial evidence is provided by these authors. Further, it ignores completely the steady and spectacular growth of the state throughout the course of the twentieth century in all industrial societies (Esping-Anderson 1990).

Even if Clark and Lipset's claims about growing marketness were true, there is good reason to question their analysis of how this affects class-based stratification. For example, they note that most job growth in recent years has taken place in small firms (1991: 405, citing Birch 1979). But they fail to point out that smaller firms are rarely able to offer their employees all of the income benefits, and job security of larger firms and that most unstable, low-paying jobs are located in small firms (Gordon et al. 1982; Edwards 1988; O'Connor 1973; Stolzenberg 1978).

Clark and Lipset then argue that more advanced technologies make it "harder . . . to plan in advance and control administratively" and that these economic changes are leading to a "*decline in traditional authority, hierarchy* and class relations" (1991: 406; emphasis in the original). Their discussion of technology takes the most optimistic conceivable scenarios as reality, ignoring the more complex institutional patterns actually emerging in post-industrial societies. The use of new management styles in response to the appearance of high technology is heavily dependent on the context in which it is embedded (Zuboff 1988; Shaiken 1984). In many firms, managers resist any transfer of authority to lower-level employees, even if the new "smart machines" make possible a democratization of decision-making within firms (Zuboff 1988). Far from eliminating class struggle, the introduction of new technology and management styles often creates new forms of class conflict. The jury is still out on the fate of hierarchy in post-industrial firms.

Finally, Clark and Lipset argue that economic growth is undermining "local stratification hierarchies as markets grow—regionally, nationally, internationally" (1991: 406). Mills (1946) effectively countered such observations nearly half a century ago by arguing that the gulf between decision centers in metropolitan skyscrapers and the dispersed loci of production and consumption was yet another layer of statification, not a pattern that "combine[s] to undermine the familistic-quasi-monopolistic tradition of business hierarchy and class stratification patterns" (1991: 407), as Clark and Lipset would have it.[18]

Family

Clark and Lipset argue that the "slimmed" family in post-industrial society has "increasingly become characterised by more egalitarian relations . . . [as] hierarchical stratification has weakened" (Clark and Lipset 1991: 407). While the patterns they refer to in support of these arguments (greater freedom of marriage and divorce, greater opportunities for women to work in the paid labor force and the decline of extended family arrangements) are clearly important, they provide no evidence that the slimmed family is a more egalitarian one. The modern family is a good deal more complex than Clark and Lipset imply (Connell 1987: 120–125). Research on contemporary family life suggests that while egalitarian *beliefs* are more widespread than in earlier periods, a clear gender division of labor remains in place in most families (Hochschild 1989). In the United States, for example, the evidence overwhelmingly suggests that the rise in female-headed slimmed families with the liberalization of divorce law has led to *rising* rates of poverty in female-headed families (Thistle 1992: chap. 4; Weizman 1985). For the urban poor, the slimmed family celebrated by Clark and Lipset is a major source of poverty and inequality (Wilson 1987). This is attributable in part to the positive association between husbands' and wives' occupations that *increases* differences among families even as differences within families decrease (Bianchi 1981; Hout 1982).

Under "family," Clark and Lipset also address recent changes in social mobility, arguing that "the slimmer family determines less the education and jobs of individual family members" and that "social mobility studies show decreasing effects of parents' education and income in explaining children's occupational success" (citing Featherman and Hauser 1978 and Hout 1988). However, Clark and Lipset fail to take due note of the sources of those changes. It is true that class origin affects students' progress through the educational systems of most industrial societies less than it used to, but the cause of diminished educational stratification is *not* less class-based selection but less selection of any kind at the early transitions, where class matters most (Mare 1980, 1981). Replications of Mare's results for the United States in 15 industrial societies show that only Sweden, Hungary, and the former Czechoslovakia had real declines in class-based selection (Shavit and Blossfeld 1992; Raftery and Hout 1993). In Hungary and Czechoslovakia political party tests replaced class selection; only Sweden saw a real growth in the openness of the educational stratification process.

Likewise, falling class barriers to social mobility cannot be attributed to "affluence" or other indirect forces. The expansion of higher education in the United States—a class-conscious policy designed to benefit youth of lower-middle and working-class origins—has brought down class barriers to achievement (Hout 1988). It works because throughout this century a college diploma served to cancel the effect of social origins on occupational success. By making college accessible to working-class youth, the expansion of higher education in the United States removed class barriers for those who took advantage. Elsewhere, different mechanisms affected mobility. In Sweden, the social democratic welfare state assured more equal access not only to universities but also to jobs in desirable occupations (Esping-Anderson 1990: 144–161). In Hungary, political tests for professions and managerial positions guaranteed a dramatic weakening of class barriers during the first generation of Communist rule; it slacked after the first generation (Wong and Hauser 1992). Where class-conscious action does not organize opportunity, as in Ireland (Hout 1989, chap. 11), class barriers are unshaken, even by industrialization on a scale that might be said to lead to an increase in "affluence."[19]

Conclusion: Classes Are Not Dying

Class structures have undergone important changes in recent decades, with the rise of post-industrial societies. The birth of new sources of inequality does not imply the death of the old ones. In arguing that Clark and Lipset have failed to show that social classes are dying, we do not wish to imply that there have been no changes in the class structures of advanced capitalist societies, or in the association between class and other social phenomena. The manual working class *has* declined in size in recent decades in most countries, while the proportion of the labor force working in the service sector has increased. Such changes are important; they tell us that nineteenth-century models of class are no longer adequate. Yet moving to more complex, multidimensional models of class does not imply that classes are dying. The persistence of classbased inequalities in capitalist societies suggests that in the foreseeable future the concept of class will—and should—play an important role in sociological research.

While the research evidence on the persistence of class as a factor in life chances and politics is abundant and convincing, explanations for that persistence are not. As a profession we have documented the parameters of class relations to a high degree of precision, while simultaneously demolishing the older theories that framed our work. We have discovered that class structures are more complex than Marxist and other theories that assign class structure a causal role in the evolution of societies *and* less subject to the calming effects of affluence than modernization theories posit. The theoretical question for the next decade is, Why is class so complex and why is it dependent on politics instead of determinative of politics? As citizens and sociologists we would very much like to live in a world in which class inequalities have disappeared. But, to paraphrase Gramsci, class society is not yet dying, and truly classless societies have not yet been born.

Notes

1. Clark and Lipset do say at one point in their paper that their goal is not to "suggest that it [i.e., class] be abandoned altogether, but complemented by other factors" (1991: 401). The general thrust of their argument, however, is to throw out class altogether. For example, they never indicate in what concrete ways they believe the concept of class remains relevant. It is this general thrust to which we respond.

2. We note, however, that Clark and Lipset (1991: 4000) put great stock in lifestyle when they cite Parkin's contention that "the absence of clearly visible and unambiguous marks of inferior *status* has made the enforcement of an all-pervasive deference system almost impossible to sustain outside the immediate work situation. It would take an unusually sharp eye to detect the social class of Saturday morning shoppers in the High Street, whereas to any earlier generation it would have been the most elementary task" (Parkin 1979: 69; our emphasis). To our minds, this is evidence of waning status distinctions, not waning class distinctions. Thus it *counters* Clark and Lipset's general point that status distinctions are on the rise as class is on the wane. See Manza 1992 for a discussion of the class themes latent in Parkin's "closure theory."

3. In this chapter we adopt a generic definition of class that we hope is compatible with the contemporary versions of both neo-Marxist and neo-Weberian concepts. We wish to avoid distracting from our main point that class continues to affect social stratification and politics by discussing the ongoing debates among class theorists over how best to understand both the concept of class and the ways in which classes have importance in contemporary societies. Scholars who infer that class has become irrelevant just because class analysts disagree on the best way to codify their structure or measure their effects fall into the same logical error as the creationists who infer that evolution does not describe natural history because biologists disagree about sequences and causes.

4. We must note the misreading of Wright's work by Clark and Lipset. They argue that even a "self-described Marxist" such as Wright is forced to "incorporat[e] so much post-Weberian multidimensionality" in his models of class structure (1991: 400). They imply that Wright and other contemporary class analysts are implicitly abandoning the concept of class in their work, ignoring the underlying class logic of Wright's analysis of the mechanisms of exploitation.

5. For example, one could imagine a class society in which traditional hierarchies based on gender or race had completely disappeared, if one's life chances were completely uninfluenced by one's gender or race. Wright (1990) compares the logic of classless versus genderless societies.

6. The pattern of the amount of wealth controlled by the richest 1 percent of the populations of different capitalist societies seems to be remarkably consistent and seems to hold across different societies. Wolff's (1991) careful reconstruction of trends in the distribution of household wealth in Sweden, Britain, and the United States shows a common decline from the early 1920s to the early 1970s and no change or actual *increases* in bourgeois wealth over the last two decades (see also Levy 1987 and Phillips 1991 on the United States; Sharrocks 1987 on Britain; and Spånt 1987 on Sweden). Including an augmented measure of household wealth which includes retirement benefits. Wolff concludes that the top 1 percent in all three societies controls more than 20 percent of all household wealth. The essays contained in Bottomore and Brym 1989 provide useful overviews of the persistence of the economic power controlled by the capitalist class in seven countries. Maurice Zeitlin's (1989) provocative essays have influenced our thinking on these issues.

7. We would further note that elite educational institutions play an important role in transmitting privilege from one generation to another. For a discussion of these issues, see Baltzell 1958 and Domhoff 1970 on the general mechanisms of transmission of privilege, and Useem and Kara-

bel 1986 on the way such privileges operate in pathways to corporate hierarchies in the United States: see Marceau 1977 on France: and the essays in Bottomore and Brym 1989 on capital class privileges in seven leading countries. Finally, Marceau (1989) discusses the making of an international capitalist elite.

8. The data are from a national telephone survey of American adults over 18 years old conducted by the UC Berkeley Survey Research Center under the direction of Michael Hout, Erik Olin Wright, and Martín Sánchez-Jankowski (1992).

9. The well-known positive skew of earnings data is controlled by taking the geometric mean instead of the usual arithmetic mean, i.e., by logging earnings, taking the means of the logs, and then reporting the antilog of the mean of the logs. Class differences in earnings are shown in gross and adjusted form. The gross earnings are the observed data. The adjusted means are the earnings expected for a 40-year-old person who has 12 years of schooling and worked 40 hours per week for the full year based on a regression of logged earnings on education, age, age squared, and hours worked for men and women separately.

10. The classes on the top and bottom differ by gender. For men the top class is upper-level managers and the bottom is unskilled workers; among women the top and bottom classes are upper-level professionals and service workers, respectively.

11. For discussions of the new poverty in the United States, England, Italy, and the Netherlands, respectively, see Jencks and Petersen 1991; Townsend et al. 1987; Mingione 1991; Engbersen 1989. See also Wacquant 1993 for an excellent analysis of some of the similarities and differences of the new poverty in France and the United States.

12. The amateurish presentation of this data in their paper makes it difficult to assess because of the lack of technical details, but we will suspend disbelief and take them at face value here. We would note, however, that the title of the graph reporting these data misleadingly claims class voting has declined in *all* Western democracies, when the authors in fact have data for only five countries.

13. We would point out that the magnitude of the increase in France, Belgium, and Sweden is substantial: from 0 and 9 in 1900 and 1914 in Belgium to 27 in 1975, from 32 in 1914 to 69 in 1975 in Sweden, and from *negative* levels of class voting in the period before the 1930s in France to 34 in 1975.

14. The much greater analytical power of such techniques and their importance in estimating class voting is demonstrated in the lively debates over class voting in Britain. The use of the Alford Index and related measures by Sarlvik and Crewe (1983) to show a purported decline in class voting has been decisively refuted by the more nuanced analysis of Heath and his colleagues (1985, 1987, 1991), who find "trendless fluctuation" but no concrete evidence of declining class voting in Britain (see also Marshall et al. 1988: chap. 9; Weakliem 1989). Halle and Romo (1991) apply some of these techniques in an effective analysis of class voting in the United States.

15. To be sure, there may be new political issues, or at least older issues which have once again become the object of increased ideological conflict, such as gender or the environment in the post-1960s period. But this does not mean that the reemergence or politicization of these issues is sufficient either to displace or reconstitute fundamental dimensions such as the left-right continuum in politics. This point is indirectly supported by a recent strand of theorizing in public opinion research (Sniderman et al. 1991), which demonstrates the centrality of heuristics for understanding the political reasoning of the average citizen. In the context of class analysis, we want to propose that insofar as class and left-right identification operate as heuristics, they provide people with a source of readily comprehensible likes and dislikes, as well as attitudes and values. This means that, in contrast to Clark and Lipset's argument, there is reason to expect left-right worldviews to be quite robust, providing a framework for *incorporating* new issues of conflicts. It is also reasonable to infer that class issues and left-right political identification are ideological resources that political parties or social movements have at their strategic disposal. This point is relevant when considering how the class-voting relationship is mediated by parties and other organizations. Strategic actors may, on the one hand, attempt to mitigate the effect of class differences by making cross-class ap-

peals. But they may also choose to make active use of class-based appeals as well. Both these strategies underscore the latent power of class.

16. We echo Duncan (1959:28) here: "It is therefore entirely possible that the confidence with which one sets forth an account of class structure in 18th or 19th century England is partly a function of a paucity of the data on occupational differentiation, income levels, budget patterns, public attitudes, styles of life, and the like that the investigator of contemporary society demands."

17. We would suggest that the same is true of other sources of social inequality and differentiation. Race and gender, for example, have always been important to the social fabric of American society, but they have not always been central loci of political organization and struggle.

18. Evidence from diverse sources support Mills (Featherman and Hauser 1978: 482–494; Hodson 1983; Harrison and Bluestone 1988).

19. The policies that expanded equality of educational opportunity have been eroded by "taxpayers' revolts" and diminished economic growth. If the argument in Hout 1988 is correct, such developments should eventually lead to a reemergence of class barriers to mobility. An updating of the analysis through to 1992 shows no change in mobility patterns since 1982, but it is likely that not enough time has passed for the effects of reduction in spending for education to be felt.

References

Alford, R. 1963. *Party and Society*. Chicago: Rand McNally.

Baltzell, E. D. 1958. *Philadelphia Gentlemen : The Making of a National Upper Class*. New York: Free Press.

Bell, D. 1973. *The Coming of Post-Industrial Society*. New York: Basic.

Bianchi, S. 1981. *Household Composition and Racial Inequality*. New Brunswick, NJ: Rutgers University Press.

Birch, D. L. 1979. *The Job Generation Process*. Cambridge, MA: MIT Program on Neighborhood and Regional Change.

Blau, P. and Duncan, O. D. 1967. *The American Occupational Structure*. New York: Wiley.

Block, F. 1987. *Revising State Theory*. Philadelphia: Temple University Press.

Block, F. 1990. *Postindustrial Possibilities*. Berkeley: University of California Press.

Block, F. 1992. "Capitalism without Class Power." *Politics and Society* 20: 277–302.

Bottomore, T. and Brym, R., eds. 1989. *The Capitalist Class*. New York: Harvester Wheatsheaf.

Campbell, A. et al. 1960. *The American Voter*. Chicago: University of Chicago Press.

Clark, T. N. and Ferguson, L. C. 1983. *City Money*. New York: Columbia University Press.

Clark, T. N. and Lipset, S. M. 1991. "Are Social Classes Dying?" *International Sociology* 6(4): 397–410.

Clawson, D., Neustadt, A., and Scott, D. 1992. *Money Talks: Corporate PACs and Political Influence*. New York: Basic.

Cohen, J. 1982. *Class and Civil Society*. Amherst: University of Massachusetts Press.

Connell, R. 1987. *Gender and Power*. Stanford: Stanford University Press.

Converse, P. E. 1964. "The Nature of Belief Systems in Mass Publics." In Apter. D. (ed), *Ideology and Discontent*, 206–261. New York: Free Press.

Crewe, I. 1986. "On the Death and Resurrection of Class Voting: Some Comments on *How Britain Votes*." *Political Studies* 34: 620–634.

Crystal, G. 1991. *In Search of Excess: Executive Compensation in the 1980s*. New York: Norton.

Davis, K. 1991. *City of Quartz*. London: Verso.

Davis, K. and Moore, W. 1945. "Some Principles of Stratification." *American Sociological Review* 50: 242–249.

Domhoff, G. W. 1970. *The Higher Circles: The Governing Class in America*. New York: Vintage.

Domhoff, G. W. 1990. *The Power Elite and the State*. New York: Aldine de Gruyter.

Duncan, O. D. 1959. "Discussion." *Pacific Sociological Review* 2: 27–28.

Edwards, R. 1988. "Segmented Labor Markets." In Hearn, F. (ed), *The Transformation of Industrial Organization*, 85–98. Belmont, CA: Wadsworth.

Engbersen, G. 1989. "Cultures of Long-Term Unemployment in the West." *The Netherlands Journal of Social Sciences* 25: 75–96.

Esping-Anderson, G. 1990. *The Three Worlds of Welfare Capitalism*. Princeton, NJ: Prinecton University Press.

Erikson, R. and Goldthorpe, J. H. 1992. *The Constant Flux: Class Mobility in Industrial Societies*. Oxford University Press.

Featherman, D. L. and Hauser, R. M. 1978. *Opportunity and Change*. New York: Academic.

Goldthorpe, J. H. 1980. *Social Mobility and Class Structure in Modern Britain*. Oxford: Clarendon Press.

Goldthorpe, J. H. and Marshall, G. 1992. "The Promising Future of Class Analysis: A Response to Recent Critiques." *Sociology* 26: 381–400.

Goodman, L. A. 1972. "A General Model for the Analysis of Surveys." *American Journal of Sociology* 77: 1035–1086.

Gordon, D., Edwards, R. and Reich, M. 1982. *Segmented Work, Divided Workers*. New York: Cambridge University Press.

Hall, S. and Jacques, M. eds. 1989. *New Times: The Changing Face of Politics in the 1990s*. London: Lawrence and Wishart.

Halle, D. and Romo, F. 1991. "The Blue-Collar Working Class: Continuity and Change." In Wolfe, A. (ed.), *America at Century's End*, 152–184. Berkeley: University of California Press.

Harrison, B. and Bluestone, B. 1988. *The Great U-Turn: Corporate Restructuring and the Polarizing of America*. New York: Basic.

Heath, A., Jowell, R. and Curtice, J. 1985. *How Britain Votes*. Oxford: Pergamon.

Heath, A., Jowell, R. and Curtice, J. 1987. "Trendless Fluctuation: A Reply to Crewe." *Political Studies* 35: 256–277.

Heath, A. et al. 1991. *Understanding Political Change: The British Voter, 1964–1987*. Oxford: Pergamon.

Hochschild, A. 1989. *The Second Shift: Working Parents and the Revolution at Home*. New York: Viking.

Hodson, R. 1983. *Workers' Earnings and Corporate Economic Structure*. New York: Academic.

Hout, M. 1982. "The Association between Husbands' and Wives' Occupations in Two-Earner Families." *American Journal of Sociology* 88: 397–409.

Hout, M. 1988. "More Universalism, Less Structural Mobility." *American Journal of Sociology* 93 (March): 1358–1400.

Hout, M. 1989. *Following in Father's Footsteps: Social Mobility in Ireland*. Cambridge, MA: Harvard University Press.

Hout, M. and Hauser, R. M. 1992. "Hierarchy and Symmetry in Social Mobility." *European Sociological Review* 8: 239–266.

Hout, M., Wright, E. O. and Sánchez-Jankowski, M. 1992. "1991–1992 Class Structure and Consciousness Survey" [Machine Readable Data File and Documentation]. Berkeley: UC Berkeley Survey Research Center.

Inglehart, R. 1990. *Culture Shift in Advanced Industrial Society*. Princeton, NJ: Princeton University Press.

Jencks, C. 1991. "Is the American Underclass Growing?" In C. Jencks and P. Petersen, eds., *The Urban Underclass*, 28–100. Washington, D.C.: Brookings Institution Press.

Jencks, C. and Petersen, P. eds. 1991. *The Urban Underclass*. Washington, DC: Brookings Institution Press.

Kalleberg, A. L. and Berg, I. 1987. *Work and Industry: Structures, Markets, and Processes*. New York: Plenum Press.

Korpi, W. 1972. "Some Problems in the Measurement of Class Voting." *American Journal of Sociology* 78: 627–642.

Korpi, W. 1983. *The Democratic Class Struggle*. London: Routledge and Kegan Paul.

Laclau, E. and Mouffe, C. 1985. *Hegemony and Socialist Strategy*. London: Verso.

Levy, F. 1987. *Dollars and Dreams: The Changing American Income Distribution*. New York: Russell Sage Foundation.

Lindblom, C. 1977. *Politics and Markets*. New York: Basic.

Lipset, S. M. 1981. *Political Man: The Social Bases of Politics*. Baltimore, MD: Johns Hopkins University Press.

Lipset, S. M. 1990. "The Death of the Third Way: Everywhere but Here, That is." *The National Interest* 20: 25–37.

Luker, K. 1984. *Abortion and the Politics of Motherhood*. Berkeley: University of California Press.

McClosky, H. and Brill, A. 1983. *Dimensions of Tolerance: What Americans Believe about Civil Liberties*. New York: Russell Sage Foundation.

Manza, J. 1992. "Classes, Status Groups, and Social Closure: A Critique of Neo-Weberian Social Theory." *Current Perspectives on Social Theory* 12: 275–302.

Mare, R. D. 1980. "Social Background and Educational Continuation Decisions." *Journal of the American Statistical Association* 75: 295–305.

Mare, R. D. 1981. "Change and Stability in Educational Stratification." *American Sociological Review* 46: 72–87.

Marceau, J. 1977. *Class and Status in France: Economic Change and Social Immobility*. New York: Oxford University Press.

Marceau, J. 1989. *A Family Business? The Making of an International Business Elite*. New York: Cambridge University Press.

Markland, S. 1990. "Structures of Modern Poverty." *Acta Sociologica* 33: 125–140.

Marshall, G. et al. 1988. *Social Class in Modern Britain*. London: Hutchinson.

Massey, D. S. 1990. "American Apartheid: Segregation and the Making of the Underclass." *American Journal of Sociology* 96: 329–357.

Massey, D. S. and Eggers, M. L. 1990. "The Ecology of Inequality Minorities and the Concentration of Poverty, 1970–1980." *American Journal of Sociology* 95: 1153–1188.

Mills, C. W. 1946. "The Middle Class of Middle-Sized Cities." *American Sociological Review* 11: 520–529.

Mingione, E. 1991. "The New Urban Poor and the Crisis of Citizenship/Welfare Systems in Italy." Paper presented at the Working Conference on "Pauverté, immigrations et marginalités urbaines dans les sociétés avancées." Paris, Maison Suger, May.

Nisbet, R. 1959. "The Decline and Fall of Social Class." *Pacific Sociological Review* 2: 11–17.

O'Connor, J. 1973. *The Fiscal Crisis of the State*. New York: St. Martin's.

Parkin, F. 1971. *Class Inequality and Political Order*. New York: Praeger.

Parkin, F. 1979. *Marxism and Class Analysis: A Bourgeois Critique*. New York: Columbia University Press.

Parsons, T. 1968. "Professions." In Sills, D. (ed)., *The International Encyclopedia of the Social Sciences*. vol. 12, 536–547. New York: Free Press.

Parsons, T. 1970. "Equality and Inequality in Modern Society, or Social Stratification Revisited." *Sociological Inquiry* 40: 13–72.

Phillips, K. 1991. *The Politics of Rich and Poor: Wealth and the American Electorate in the Reagan Aftermath*. New York: Harper.

Piore, M. and Sabel, C. 1984. *The Second Industrial Divide: Possibilities for Prosperity*. New York: Basic.

Przeworski, A. and Sprague, J. 1986. *Paper Stones: A History of Electoral Socialism*. Chicago: University of Chicago Press.

Raftery, A. E. and Hout, M. 1993. "Maximally Maintained Inequality: Expansion, Reform and Opportunity in Irish Education, 1921–1975." *Sociology of Education* 66: 41–62.

Reich, R. 1991. *The Work of Nations.* New York: Knopf.
Robertson, D. 1984. *Class and the British Electorate.* Oxford: Basil Blackwell.
Sabel, C. 1982. *Work and Politics.* New York: Cambridge University Press.
Sarlvik, B. and Crewe, I. 1983. *Decade of Dealignment.* New York: Cambridge University Press
Shaiken, H. 1984. *Work Transformed: Automation and Labor in the Computer Age.* New York: Holt, Rinehart and Winston.
Sharrocks, A. F. 1987. "U.K. Wealth Distribution: Current Evidence and Future Prospects." In Wolff, E. (ed.). *International Comparisons of the Distribution of Household Wealth,* 29–50. New York: Oxford University Press.
Shavit, Y. and Blossfeld, H.-P. 1992. *Persistent Inequality: Changing Educational Stratification in Thirteen Countries.* Boulder, CO: Westview.
Smeeding, T. M. 1991. "Cross-National Comparisons of Inequality and Poverty Position." In Osberg. L. (ed.). *Economic Inequality and Poverty: International Perspectives,* 39–59. Armonk, NY: Sharpe.
Sniderman, P., Brody, R. A. and Tetlock, P. 1991. *Reasoning and Choice: Explorations in Political Psychology.* New York: Cambridge University Press.
Sørensen, A. B. 1991. "On the Usefulness of Class Analysis in Research on Social Mobility and Socioeconomic Inequality." *Acta Sociologica* 34: 71–87.
Spånt, R. 1987. "Wealth Distribution in Sweden: 1920–1983." In Wolff, E. (ed.). *International Comparisons of the Distribution of Household Wealth,* 51–71. New York: Oxford University Press.
Stolzenberg, R. M. 1978. "Bringing the Boss Back In: Employer Size, Employee Schooling, and Socioeconomic Achievement." *American Sociological Review* 43: 813–828.
Thistle, S. 1992. "Between Two Worlds." Unpublished Ph.D. dissertation. Department of Sociology, University of California, Berkeley.
Touraine, A. 1971. *The Post-Industrial Society.* New York: Random House.
Townsend, P., Corrigan, P. and Kowarzick, U. 1987. *Poverty and Labour in London.* London: Low Pay Unit.
Useem, M. 1984. *The Inner Circle.* New York: Oxford University Press.
Useem, M. and Karabel, J. 1986. "Paths to Corporate Management." *American Sociological Review* 51: 184–200.
Wacquant, L. 1993. "Urban Outcasts: Stigma and Division in the Black American Ghetto and the French Urban Periphery." *International Journal of Urban and Regional Research* 17 (Sept): 366–383.
Weakliem, D. 1989. "Class and Party in Britain, 1964–83." *Sociology* 23: 285–297.
Weakliem, D. 1991. "The Two Lefts? Occupation and Party Choice in France, Italy, and the Netherlands." *American Journal of Sociology* 96 (May): 1327–1361.
Weizman, L. 1985. *The Divorce Revolution.* Stanford, CA: Stanford University Press.
Wilson, W. J. 1987. *The Truly Disadvantaged: The Inner City, the Underclass, and Public Policy.* Chicago: University of Chicago Press.
Wolff, E. 1991. "The Distribution of Household Wealth: Methodological Issues, Time Trends, and Cross-Sectional Comparisons." In Osberg. L. (ed.). *Economic Inequality and Poverty: International Perspectives,* 92–133. Armonk, NY: Sharpe.
Wong, R. S.-K. and Hauser, R. M. 1992. "Trends in Occupational Mobility in Hungary under Socialism." *Social Science Research* 21: 419–444.
Wright, E. O. 1985. *Classes.* London: Verso.
Wright, E. O. 1990. "Explanation and Utopia in Marxism and Feminism." Paper presented at the annual meeting of the American Sociological Association, Washington, DC, August 11–15.
Zeitlin, M. 1989. *The Large Corporation and Contemporary Classes.* Cambridge: Polity.
Zuboff, S. 1988. *In the Age of the Smart Machine: The Future of Work and Power.* New York: Basic.

4

The Declining Political Significance of Social Class[*]

TERRY NICHOLS CLARK, SEYMOUR MARTIN LIPSET, AND
MICHAEL REMPEL

Abstract Social classes have not died, but their political significance has declined substantially; this justifies a shift from class-centered analysis toward multicausal explanations of political behavior and related social phenomena. This contribution extends key propositions from Clark and Lipset and adds new empirical evidence to the commentaries by Hout et al. and Pakulski.

Four general propositions are stated concerning where and why class is weaker or stronger. The propositions are then applied to several areas, considering how class has weakened in its impact, especially on politics. We cite several writers of Marxist background to show how they have converged with others in interpreting central developments. The paper notes the impact of organizations like parties and unions, independent of classes, in affecting political processes. It points to the rise of the welfare state as generally weakening class conflict by providing a safety-net and benefits. The diversification of the occupational structure toward small firms, high tech, and services weakens class organizational potentials. So does more affluence. Political parties have correspondingly shifted from class conflict to noneconomic issues like the environment. The Socialist and Communist parties have drastically altered their programs in dozens of countries, away from traditional class politics toward new social issues and often even toward con-

[*]Originally published in *International Sociology* 8, no. 3 (September 1993): 293–316.

straining government. New nationalist parties have arisen stressing national identify and limiting immigration. These developments cumulatively weaken class politics.

Social classes may not have died, but their political significance has declined substantially; this justifies a shift from class-centered analysis toward multicausal explanations of political behavior and related social phenomena. These were the central claims of Clark and Lipset's "Are Social Classes Dying?" (1991). It encouraged commentaries by Jan Pakulski, "The Dying of Class or of Marxist Class Theory?" (1993), and Michael Hout, Clem Brooks, and Jeff Manza, "The Persistence of Classes in Post-Industrial Societies" (1993). We certainly agree with Hout et al. that "funeral arrangements are premature" but warn the hurried reader that Clark and Lipset never claimed the need for a funeral. The funeral image invokes a strawman—and a dead one at that. *Our point is that social class has* declined *in its ability to explain social and especially political processes. But it still lives.*

This contribution (1) extends and clarifies certain key propositions from Clark and Lipset, (2) adds new empirical evidence to respond to the commentaries by Hout et al. and Pakulski, and (3) considers recent Marxist theorizing about these developments. The reason for point 3 is that it frequently affects a clear assessment of points 1 and 2. For many sociologists, reworking Marxist theory sometimes seems more important than recognizing or interpreting profound social changes. We thus consider both some major social changes of our time associated with the decline of social class and how shifts in theorizing, especially by writers of neo-Marxist background, have addressed these changes. Pakulski rightly stresses the profound implications for Marxist theory brought on by the self-destruction of Communism in the short past decade. While his Polish background makes him acutely aware of such intellectual cataclysms, Western observers may be less sensitive to such changes. His commentary can thus be insightful for those of us who have not lived through the intellectual, political, and economic revolutions he has seen first hand.

Definitions of "Social Class" and "Hierarchy"

Pakulski's review of alternative conceptions of class helpfully contrasts that of Clark and Lipset with Hout et al. and appropriately cautions that because of its many definitions, social class engenders debates that often become enmeshed more in semantics than in substance. He makes clear that because they introduce a quite different conception of class, Hout et al., in much of their reply, "can hardly serve in engaging the Clark and Lipset arguments about the fragmentation of stratification and dealignment." Much of the Hout et al., commentary seems to imply disagreement over issues about which we in fact hardly differ. To help join the issues, in several sections below we operate with definitions of class and hierarchy proposed by Hout et al.: "Hierarchy, in sociological usage, could refer to any rankable distinctions. Class refers to a person's relationship to the means of production and/or labor markets...." This provides an "objectivist" definition of classes as subgroups discernible to the theorist through an objective empirical study of labor markets. As compared with a society's "class structure," which consists only of its social classes, a "hierarchy" consists of either classes, Weberian "status groups," races, ethnic groups, or any other vertically ranked social groupings.

By using these objectivist conceptions, we can distinguish (1) the existence, and (2) the political significance of social classes or other hierarchical groupings. The existence of social classes can be ascertained by studying solely labor market stratification patterns. However, their political significance depends on the *strength* of the *relationship* between those stratification patterns and political outcomes. Thus when Hout et al. offer evidence that social classes exist, as exemplified by distinctions between small- and large-firm employees or managers and supervisees, or by statistical relationships such as between imputed class membership and income, this does not refute the Clark and Lipset position that classes have declining politically relevant effects.

Theoretical Propositions

The Impact of Hierarchy

Clark and Lipset provide a summary of much work in progress, which is perhaps occasionally too brief. Nevertheless, it is surely a mistake by Hout et al. to write of Clark and Lipset, "They give an unequivocal 'yes' to the question in the title of their essay," or that, "they *lament* that 'class remains salient in sociologists' theories and commentaries'" (our emphasis). Our concern was and is not to assert that classes have declined everywhere, or that class analysis is no longer of any contemporary value, but to identify where and why classes persist in some social locations yet decline in others. Our intent becomes explicit in the conceptual core of the paper, where several propositions of "the greater the X, the greater the Y"–type format were stated to specify conditions supporting or weakening social classes. This contextual/relativist approach informs work in progress where we are comparing developments in Eastern and Western Europe, Japan, Australia, Canada, and the United States. To clarify interactions between class and hierarchy, we state the following propositions:

1. *The more polarized are hierarchical divisions in a situs (or vertical dimension, such as in economic institutions, political institutions, or families), the more prevalent are hierarchically defined political and cultural patterns which stem from those divisions.*
1a. *The more polarized is the class structure (i.e., divisions in the labor market situs), the more prevalent are class-defined political and cultural patterns.*
2. *The more polarized and pervasive are hierarchical divisions throughout a society, the more prevalent are hierarchically defined political and cultural patterns which stem from the divisions in each individual situs.*
2a. *The more polarized and pervasive are hierarchical divisions throughout a society, the more prevalent are class-defined political and cultural patterns.*

Propositions 1a and 2a specifically concern social conditions promoting class politics. Proposition 1a suggests that as class divisions become more objectively polarized (i.e, more rigidly differentiating experiences, opportunities, and life outcomes), they grow more subjectively salient and thus more politically influential. Conversely, class divisions that are less polarized and more flexible and open have fewer effects on political opinions and behavior.

Proposition 2a states that as the combination of class-related and other hierarchical divisions grows more polarized and inescapably permeates social experiences, class divisions are more salient and politically significant. Conversely, where hierarchy is less omnipresent, political preferences and conflict patterns stem more from cultural values or "tastes," some of which are not class derived.

Propositions 2 and 2a assert a positive relation between the general pervasiveness of hierarchy and the political significance of particular hierarchies. We now contextualize them with the following caveat, expressed in both general and class-specific formulations:

3. *The more the different hierarchies create overlapping rather than cross-cutting divisions, the more prevalent are hierarchically defined political and cultural patterns.*

3a. *The more the class structure creates divisions that overlap rather than cross-cut divisions created by non-class-based hierarchies, the more prevalent are class defined political and cultural patterns.*

Proposition 3 incorporates "cross-cutting cleavages," which as Lipset (1981a) showed often discourage political action. Correlatively, strongly overlapping cleavages *encourage* forceful political action. For instance, consider class and race in American politics. In Clark and Ferguson 1983 and subsequent work, we find that African Americans are the most likely subgroup in the United States to initiate antihierarchical political activity. Proposition 3 suggests that this is encouraged by their overlapping subjugation in both "race" and "class" hierarchies. Many African Americans have improved their *class* status since the 1950s, and African-American led protest has concurrently subsided (Wilson 1987)—consistent with proposition 3 above and propositions about the economy in Clark and Lipset. The flip side of the African-American case is, of course, the relative political weakness of the American "working class" for most of the United States' history. Proposition 3 indicates this by pointing to workers ambiguous, cross-cutting memberships concerning class, race, and national background (see Lipset 1985; Roedigger 1991).

The Impact of Organization

Many theorists agree that collective action is advanced by a strong internal organization or mobilization capacity (McCarthy and Zald 1977; Smelser 1962; Olson 1965; Tilly 1978). This holds especially for the "working class," which lacks the economic resources of its "capitalist" adversaries. Instead, to influence policy, the working class relies more on the power of numbers generated by channeling members' political activities through strong worker organizations (Offe 1981; Panitch 1980). Hout et al. recognize this in writing, "Class is important for politics to the extent that political organisations actively organise around class themes."

We generalize from this observation to stress that organization is often a distinct, influential factor, complementing the macrostructural factors of earlier propositions. So we add:

4. *The greater the internal organization of those at the bottom of a hierarchy, the more likely they are to initiate and succeed at antihierarchical politics.*

4a. *The greater the internal organization of those at the bottom of a soci-*

ety's class structure, the more likely they are to initiate and succeed at class politics.

These propositions frame selected empirical results, which we review below. These are drawn from several projects of Lipset, Clark, Rempel, and others which analyze with more elaborate propositions and multiple-data sources where and how social class cleavages persist in certain societies, cities and time periods—but decline in others. We seek to continue the tradition of Marx and Weber in specifying contexts defining where and why simpler relationships hold.

The Declining Political Significance of Social Class in the West

Social class was clearly influential in the late nineteenth and early twentieth centuries. In the United States and Western Europe, this was the classic period of industrial society and its conflicts, which Marx and Weber so stressed. Later, neo-Marxists characterize the period by its large, sometimes monopolistic firms, which employed great numbers of low-wage, "blue-collar" workers in "Fordist" production systems to perform simple, menial manufacturing tasks. While employed in unsatisfying work when they did have jobs, many workers also faced highly unstable employment prospects because of severe swings of Western economies from "boom" to "bust." These conditions produced high levels of worker militancy, which encouraged some political interpreters to anticipate revolution. Yet as the twentieth century progressed, the militancy subsided. Why? Two important reasons were the rise of the welfare state and diversification of the occupational structure.

The Rise of the Welfare State

The "welfare state" brought state-administered social welfare programs and economic regulatory policies. Together they stabilized the "boom-bust" tendencies of Western economies, and as several critical theorists have stressed (e.g., Bowles and Gintis 1987; Habermas 1975; Offe 1987; Pollock 1982), they diffused class conflict in two ways. First, the state emerged as a powerful economic actor. Bargaining changed as state actors joined capitalists, managers, and workers. Second, the welfare state improved social and economic conditions faced by workers and other low-income persons. By stabilizing formerly severe economic fluctuations, the

welfare state increased workers' employment stability; by establishing a social welfare net for the economically disadvantaged, the welfare state directly alleviated the suffering of society's potentially most antagonistic social strata.

Many Western countries that established welfare states did so by adding
benefits like health insurance and unemployment compensation for workers. In some cases these came from "corporatist" bargains among the state,
managers, and workers. These bargains improved workers' benefits and
thereby diffused previous radicalism; but in the process of recognizing
workers as important political actors, the bargains paradoxically reinforced
class-based political organization and voting patterns. Conversely, as these
arrangements began to break down under the economic strains of the
1970s and 1980s, the prior importance of these arrangements in reinforc-
ing class consciousness grew more appreciated. Nevertheless, perceiving
the success which state intervention brought to an organized working
class, other disadvantaged subgroups—the elderly, handicapped, and
women, for instance—followed and at times succeeded in the same path.
In each case it was the lure of potential benefits from the state that provided value added beyond that which came from the relation to the means
of production for workers (and other benefiting social categories). The
state thus became a new means to create and reinforce "group consciousness" and political behavior, but an increasingly important one in the
1980s and 1990s. Farmers, in countries like France, have been particularly
visible in protesting against cuts in state subsidies.

Diversification of the Occupational Structure

Occupational diversification involves the much discussed shift from
"Fordist" manufacturing techniques toward more flexible task structures
and more service and information-intensive industries (Bell 1973; Gouldner 1979; Lipset 1981a; Piore and Sabel 1984). As Clark and Lipset note,
these changes created more middle management and high skill positions
and less hierarchical authority relations. With more "mental laborers"
came a diverse array of new knowledge domains, like computers, automation, and high finance. The consequent proliferation of jobs and
forms of knowledge caused workers less and less to share comparable labor
market experiences, making their objective class locations increasingly ambiguous.

Some theorists have sought to adapt Marxist analysis to these changes
by developing schemas specifying several intermediate classes between the

traditional "proletariat" and "bourgeoisie" (e.g., Giddens 1980; Wright 1985). But as Clark and Lipset point out, if this flexible redefinition of class helps these theorists to adapt "class-analysis" to late twentieth-century society, it is achieved by redefining "class structure" away from the classic proletariat into a more fragmented and less "polarized" entity. In some sections below, we follow these writers and Hout et al. in using *class* in this broader sense. Class membership, thus redefined, becomes more subtle and less socially grating, as well as less politically salient.

While high tech and a more abstract knowledge base may have created more satisfying work opportunities for professionally trained persons in the new service sector, this same "service sector" includes many menial and low-paying jobs, like janitor, fast food employee, or household laborer (e.g., Gorz 1989; Wilson 1987). This fosters a new, potentially antagonistic class (or "underclass") of menial laborers which might initiate a new form of class-based protest. However, members of this class tend to work apart from each other or in relatively small operations and are seldom unionized. This lowers their organizational capacity below that of the former manufacturing plant-based working class, which could share and collectively react to daily experiences of subordination. Thus, while occupational changes may not have objectively improved for all types of workers, the changes have nonetheless consistently fostered a decline of organized class politics.

The following sections discuss several subsequent and more specific trends that often further the decline of class politics.

Rising Affluence

As the welfare state stabilized, Western economies and occupational diversification created more high-skilled jobs, and Western societies became more affluent. Clark and Lipset posit that rising affluence fosters new non-class-based forms of political behavior, especially on social value issues like environmentalism, peace, or civil liberties.

The concept of affluence can be conceived on either of two levels. On the macrolevel, *affluence* commonly refers to economic development, measured, for example, by the gross national product (GNP). Growth in the GNP in the past several decades has made possible declining concern for production and for jobs as an economic driving force; it has moved us toward an advanced consumer economy, oriented toward providing a diverse, exciting, and ever-changing array of consumable goods and services. Some critical theorists have sought to address these developments in suggesting that by making available and creating demand for a wider range of consumer opportunities, consumer economies constitute the "leisure domain" as a newly vital locus of the differentiation of political and personal identities (Gorz 1989; Harvey 1989). With leisure experiences more subjectively salient, political solidarity based on "class," or in other words on common workplace experiences, becomes increasingly problematic.

On the microlevel, *affluence* can refer to the wealth of individual persons, as captured in census or survey data. Coming from a micro/social psychological tradition of Michigan voting studies, Inglehart (1990) reasons that when money is "in short supply" for individuals, they tend to emphasize obtaining more of it. This may cause them to become politically active on class-based economic issues like wage levels, working hours, or social welfare policies. By contrast, for more affluent individuals, financial concerns seem less pressing; such persons consequently emphasize more "nonmaterialist" issues like promoting a clean environment, possessing plentiful and diverse consumption opportunities, or having more democratic input in the decisions that affect them (see also Bowles and Gintis 1976; Lipset 1981a).

Both macro- and micro-affluence generate a shift from class-relevant "materialist" issues to more symbolic "post-materialist" issues. Analyzing changes in responses by several thousand citizens to surveys over the past 20 years, Inglehart and Abramson (1993) confirm this linkage. They find that per capita GNP is strongly correlated with a country's mean score on Inglehart's post-materialism indexes. Those countries that grew more affluent in the 1980s saw declines in materialist attitudes; those whose economies languished experienced less change. Their finding is important. Even if, as Hout et al. claim, "post-materialist issues" are not "new," consistent with Clark and Lipset's affluence propositions (especially propositions 1 and 2), Inglehart's past work and Inglehart and Abramson show that these issues have become *relatively more politically salient* as affluence has risen.

Has affluence in fact risen? In a short term for one country, results will vary somewhat depending on which specific indicators are used; if shifts are small the specific indicators selected and measurement errors will affect results. Also, independent of the results obtained from aggregate mean indicators, there also may be a redistribution of income among different socioeconomic groups. Blue-collar, unionized workers in traditional manufacturing seem to have lost income relative to more entrepreneurial, self-employed persons in recent decades, for instance. Still, in the longer term and in considering more countries, these measurement issues recede in importance, and major increases in affluence become clear. Since World War II, all Western societies have experienced substantial economic growth, and income structures have concurrently evolved from a pyramidal shape to one with a larger bulge in the middle. Yet, as Hout et al. observe, the 1970s and 1980s have seen both economic ups and downs, making shorter-term interpretations more complex.

Changing Political Party Dynamics

Hout et al. criticize Clark and Lipset for ignoring the mediating impact of political parties. While Clark and Lipset did not elaborate on parties, this was only for reasons of space. They have frequently stressed parties elsewhere and certainly concur on their importance (e.g., Lipset 1991, 1993).

Our main point about parties in Clark and Lipset 1991 was the decline of the left-right continuum. This has led traditional leftist parties to become more moderate while also generating the rise of new parties stressing new issues. For instance, in Denmark, Sweden, the Netherlands, and Germany, both Green parties and "left-libertarian" parties oriented around issues like environmentalism and peace have attained a moderate degree of electoral success (Franklin et al. 1992; Kitschelt 1990; Kuechler and Dalton 1990). These parties have appealed to the young, the highly educated, and cosmopolitan voters, especially in Germany and Scandinavia.

We may be on the threshold of even more profound changes in parties in many countries. France, Italy, Japan, and Taiwan are all in the middle of scandals, lawsuits, and fundamental attacks not just on individual leaders or parties but on the basic rules of the game that many parties have followed. We elaborate on this below.

Many of the issues that mobilize the Greens (peace, world environmental degradation) imply a denial of traditional, primordial attachments—to nation, religion, and ethnic group. Religious belief and church attendance dropped by about half in many Western European countries in the 1970s and 1980s (Flora 1986). Thus religion now anchors fewer individuals. The creation of the European Community potentially disrupts national attachments of the past; for many Western Europeans nationhood itself seems threatened. More specifically, workers and unions in some industries (like farmers, steel workers) may find that efforts to lower tariffs and create broader international exchanges jeopardize the subsidies and special arrangements that they won in the past. Yet the "market" for many citizens remains a cold, scary, international symbol, long attacked by left, religious, and peasant parties.

If the Greens were a major party innovation of the 1970s, the 1980s saw the rise of nationalist. anti-immigrant and neofascist parties in Germany, France, Spain, and other Western European countries. This was due in part to the decline of the Communist and Socialist cadre parties and of unions of the past in these countries, which had (usually) prevented workers from articulating nationalist and anti-immigrant concerns. At least this was the apparent consequence of the official humanitarian program of Socialist and Communist parties in general. However, more was simmering under the surface. In France, the Communist Party even took the lead in the 1980s in seeking to impose national limits on immigration. Many years earlier it had sought to deny full citizenship rights to immigrants for local services, including schools, health, and public housing. This was part of an effort to drive immigrants away to other localities, in order not to weaken the political power base Communists had established in certain low-income suburbs of Paris and other industrial communes. Communist officials pursued these local anti-immigrant policies in the 1970s and 1980s, following narrow considerations of electoral strategy, at the same time that the national Communist Party program and policy statements continued to stress internationalist, humanitarian concerns, especially toward Third World countries. (These findings come from many years of close fieldwork on the French Communist Party by Martin Schain [1988].) Thus, when the traditional Communist and Socialist parties weakened, anti-immigrant sentiment translated into the rise of support among workers for nationalist and anti-immigrant national-level parties, like the National Front in France.

A related major force driving the decline of class voting for parties is the rise of regional and ethnic-based parties. As traditional class issues decline, locally based identities rise in salience: Basques in France and Spain, the many regions of Italy, and so on. These trends have been documented in such countries as Belgium, Switzerland, Canada, and the United Kingdom (Franklin et al. 1992). Of course, these are but pale imitations of the profound and politically aggressive ethnic cleavages that surfaced with the demise of Communism in the former Soviet Union and Yugoslavia.

Finally, parties of all ideologies have declined in political influence. The reasons are many. A few are: increased voter education and consequent ideological independence from party-defined programs, mass media replacing parties as sources of voting cues, voters' greater willingness to support issue-specific groups and hence the rising proportional influence of special interest groups over parties. Even among elected party officials, one notes declining dependence on party endorsements and campaign activities for their election and on party programs for their opinions (e.g., see Berger 1981; Dalton 1988). Since the working class has traditionally been heavily dependent on parties and unions, the declining influence of parties is especially deleterious to the articulation of a distinct working-class position. Result: less class politics.

The Rise of Dual Labor Markets

Clark and Lipset stress the rise of small firms as contributing to the "fragmentation of stratification." Hout et al. respond that small firms create a new, distinct layer of class stratification, writing: "But they fail to point out that smaller firms are rarely able to offer their employees all of the income, benefits and job security of larger firms and that most unstable, low-paying jobs are located in small firms." This adds a new consideration but does not question the general Clark and Lipset interpretation. While workers in some small firms may face inferior wage and working conditions, this does not imply that these conditions generate class politics as Marx, Weber, and Clark and Lipset defined it.

Consider the implications for class politics of the "dual labor market" argument. The separation of labor markets into a large firm–dominated "core" and small firm–dominated "periphery" stifles class-based political activity for several reasons. First, since smaller peripheral firms are more flexible, expanding or contracting with short-term economic fluctuations, their staffs are more vulnerable to layoffs. Bigger firms in the core are relatively less economically vulnerable, in the short term at least, because of larger capitalization. This allows them to provide their employees greater wages, benefits, and employment stability and to invest more in their training. Consequently, workers in the core may be more satisfied and less militant. Second, peripheral workforces tend not to be unionized. Despite their relatively poor working conditions and employment stability, they are thus organizationally unprepared to initiate effective political protest. Third, the existence of a large, unstably employed "stand-by" peripheral workforce gives employers in the core the upper hand in negotiating with workers there who become militant. If need be, employers in the core can simply draw on the large and growing peripheral workforce to replace militant employees. In the 1980s, major employers like General Motors thus demanded "give backs," reducing worker salaries and benefits. These sorts of policies have led some theorists, neo-Marxists and others, to posit that the creation of dual labor markets constituted an intentional capitalist tactic to combat growing worker militancy of the late 1960s and early 1970s (e.g., Brown 1990; Hardiman 1990; Offe 1985). Whether or not this is so, these considerations suggest that the ironic *effect* of dual labor markets is simultaneously to create a new form of class stratification and to diffuse class conflict.

Nevertheless, more generally one might ask if positing a "dual" labor market is not in part a defensive theoretical strategy which seeks "structure" where there is little. The assumption that the "core" remains dominant, economically and politically, is not so clearly valid. The General Motors example reminds us of the vulnerability if even the largest multinational "core" firms, which in the 1980s suffered from international competition, leveraged buyouts, and market losses to more innovative and agile smaller firms. In the 1980s, the pages of *Fortune* magazine, oriented toward the leadership of the largest 500 U.S. corporations, were filled with fears and rumors of *possible,* and descriptions of dozens of *actual,* takeovers and dismantlements of the largest corporations by hostile outside investors. The outlook that Galbraith and others described just a short decade or so earlier as corporate hubris thus seems far gone. The examples of the former Communist countries, which are dismantling the largest state-operated industries, show similar aggressive efforts to impose "market discipline" on big firms. In sum, the "dual labor market" theory starts from a key assumption: that large firms are more buffered from market forces than small firms. From this assumption, the theory then derives most of the corollaries that we discussed above. However, the assumption may be less true now than in years past. This area demands more precise research to update the theory.

The Rise of Other Institution-Based Class Divisions

Clark and Lipset point out that while in earlier decades class background exerted strong effects on future class location, it has become progressively less important since the 1960s. Hout et al. do not disagree but point out with respect to educational outcomes that not only selection based on class background but also differential selection based on other structural criteria has declined simultaneously. Just the same, the net outcome is that, instead of ascriptive factors, class location has become based more on institution-specific processes. These include the following examples:

1. Credentialism: Increasingly, access to high-skill, professional jobs requires as a prerequisite advanced educational credentials, like college or other degrees (Collins 1979; Parkin 1979). This holds even though the credentials do not always actually bear on the ability to perform the tasks.

2. New labor market distinctions: As the dual labor market example illustrates, new forms of class stratification can arise within occupational institutions. Other occupational institution-specific factors, which have been documented by sociologists as affecting future class location, include industry of employment and access to specific training (e.g., Baron 1984; Beck et al. 1978; Spillerman 1977).

3. Neighborhood and local social structure: Different cities and neighborhoods vary in employment opportunities and types of industrial specialization. This in turn affects labor market opportunities for residents. Areas with heavy manufacturing concentration and unionization in the past suffered the highest unemployment and social distress in the 1980s and 1990s, like Chicago and Pittsburgh in the United States; Birmingham and Liverpool, England; areas in northern France near Rennes; and the Ruhr in Germany. All showed similar problems. Different cities and neighborhoods not only offer differential employment opportunities but also provide residents with a differential quality of educational, recreational, and social-support institutions. For instance, Wilson (1987) stresses the unique conditions of social isolation and institutional abandonment faced by residents of America's inner-city ghettos. Structural deprivations there are especially severe, since middle-class minority residents moved away from many underclass neighborhoods by the 1980s. While birth in an inner-city ghetto immediately places one at a disadvantage, the source is not just family class but also the socially isolating institutional and structural conditions of the ghetto neighborhood. Persons of similar class and racial background born in other neighborhoods can avoid these deprivations. For these and related reasons, specialists on American minorities in the 1980s and 1990s, like William Julius Wilson and his associates, have recently stressed the increasing salience of race over class, which a decade or so earlier they felt was supplanting racial cleavages.

Political Outcomes: The Decline of Class Politics

The Decline of Class Voting

Clark and Lipset present Alford Index scores from 1947 to 1986, which show a decline in "class voting" in five countries. Hout et al. question these results on methodological grounds. We concur with the methodological weaknesses of the Alford Index. We used it to illustrate a simple trend and because it is a widely replicated index. Since our paper was written, we have learned of two substantially more sophisticated and detailed studies of related issues. Both reach generally similar conclusions. The first is a major new work that provides a much more sensitive and rigorous analysis of class and the social bases of voting among citizens than does the Alford Index. Franklin et al. 1992 is a collective effort of voting experts across the world who assembled national samples of citizen data over several decades. They use a standard regression model to explain voting for left parties, including in most countries these core socioeconomic variables: low income, working-class occupation, trade-union membership, minimal education, under 45 years old, rural residence, sex, and major region of the country. They add subjective working-class identification and church attendance as further independent variables. Their regressions show general declines in the impact of class-related variables. Their regressions show general declines in the impact of class-related variables on left voting in most countries, often by half, from the 1960s to the 1980s. But not in all countries; declines are minimal in Italy and Germany, for instance. The authors introduce a number of variables to help interpret these patterns: age cohort effects, economic growth, and more.

Second is a set of 10 or so papers presented at the Limerick 1992 annual conference of the European Consortium for Political Research by participants in a panel on the decline of class voting. These papers generally report results similar to those of Franklin et al., again using regression-type methodologies that controlled many other factors.

Still, to consider briefly the Hout et al. critique of the Alford Index in Clark and Lipset, we note that they do not call into question the basic Clark and Lipset conclusion. A simple visual inspection reveals significant and *sustained* declines in class voting of 15 or more index points for every country represented. Although the index is not ideal for measuring class divisions, we would at least expect that those classified as "working class" were in the same category in the past; thus the index results imply rising cross-over voting from that group. The increase in working-class "right" voting is epitomized by the 1972 U.S. presidential election, when the Democrat George McGovern ran on an extremely social value–oriented platform. This caused him to lose the votes of many "blue-collar" workers, who reacted against his social liberalism. Reflecting this, the Alford Index dropped to near zero in the United States in 1972.

Hout et al. also point to Sweden: "—the most egalitarian country among the five by most indicators (Esping-Anderson 1990)—exhibits the highest degree of class voting." However, the suggestion that class voting trends in Sweden refute our hierarchy proposition is overstated. This was not Clark and Lipset's only proposition but one of three general and seven more specific ones, which combined to generate a decidedly multicausal theory. Without considering variables implied by several propositions, the validity of just the first cannot be tested by citing a single counterexample. Furthermore, class voting *within* Sweden, as in every other country shown, declined since 1948. In Sweden, left voting also fell still further in the latest national election (subsequent to the chart), in which Social Democratic votes dropped in the 30 percent area. Other countries have seen similar transformations in socialist voting (see below).

The Rise of Social Value Issues

Clark and Lipset posit that "social issues have risen in salience relative to fiscal/economic issues." Recent evidence supporting this position comes from Inglehart and Abramson (1993), who find that from 1970 to 1992 (years of mixed results on the Alford Index), scores on Inglehart's postmaterialism index rose significantly for national samples of citizens in seven of eight Western countries. Similarly, it is generally recognized that since the 1960s, "new social movements" concerned with issues like environmentalism, peace, feminism, or gay rights have grown increasingly influential (e.g., Lipset 1981 b; Dalton, 1988; Dalton and Kuechler 1990; Inglehart 1990; Offe 1987). Dalton (1988) cautions that because relatively affluent persons tend to support these movements, their rise may have the indirect effect of displacing from the political landscape working-class-based movements.

The growing salience of social value issues led Clark and Lipset to posit that they now constitute a distinct political dimension from more traditional economic or fiscal issues. By contrast, Hout et al. suggest, "What if some "new social issues" have become the objective of political struggles and public debate in part because they resonate with peoples' traditional Left-Right heuristics?"

While it may be reasonable for intellectuals to invoke social class as an "ideological resource," we are surprised that Hout et al. impute such thinking to "the average citizen." This flies in the face of decades of public opinion research indicating that only an extremely small proportion of citizens use broad ideological dimensions to evaluate political issues. Converse's classic paper (1964) reported that only 12 percent of voters mentioned an "overarching" dimension such as the "Left-Right," and that fewer than 4 percent actually relied on such a dimension to order their views on specific issues. More recently, Neumann (1986) reports that only one-fifth of American citizens can define *liberalism* and *conservatism* in enough breadth to subsume multiple issues and that only one-tenth offer definitions that are tolerably acceptable. Neumann concludes that excepting a highly active and sophisticated 5 percent or so of the population, most citizens base their political thought on the most publicized issues and "pseudo-issues" of the day. So when Hout et al. ask, "Could it be that controversies about affirmative action or the extension of rights to new categories of citizens (such as the disabled) gain their ideological strength from being over 'old' (class) issues such as equality or social democracy?" it is hard to be persuaded of this argument for most citizens.

To support the two-dimensional model, Clark and Lipset present results from a survey of French and United States mayors indicating low correlations between their fiscal and social liberalism. The point of this evidence was to indicate that a mayor ostensibly elected as a "leftist" candidate may not anymore have the commitment to leftist *economic* policies, which could have been expected in the past. Instead, the figure indicates that such a mayor may be economically or fiscally *conservative* but may have been elected as leftist purely on the basis of positions taken on new social value issues. In disputing this evidence, Hout et al. write, " . . . generalizing from elites to the mass public is extremely risky. Elites have consistently been found to have more coherent, stable, comprehensive political belief systems than non-elite actors." This response is perplexing, for if elites do have more stable, comprehensive belief systems than citizens, that might imply that if we had observed significant correlations for mayors, to ascribe the same to citizens would be inappropriate. However, the main point of the table was to show that the correlations for mayors were *insignificant* in the United States and declined with age for French mayors. If anything, one should only expect weaker correlations for citizens.

We offer two pieces of evidence further supporting these patterns. Table 4.1 reports correlations between fiscal and social issues for citizens in Europe and the United States. Most relations are near zero, suggesting minimal "constraint" or "ideological clustering"—consistent with Converse (1964) and others. Figure 4.1 replicates the same analysis reported earlier for mayors. It reveals low correlations of social and fiscal liberalism in Canada, Japan, and Australia (in addition to those for the United States and France reported in Clark and Lipset). The correlations also seem to decline with age in several countries, suggesting a declining impact of traditional left-right cleavages in the political socialization of the young that takes place in these several countries.

Table 4.1

Citizens in the U.S. and Europe Show Low Ideological Clustering: Correlations between Fiscal and Social Liberalism Items Are Low or Insignificant

For European Citizens

Age		V148 Less Govt. in Economy
60–80	V57 Less different sex roles	.01
	V150 Protect the environment	-.01
45–59	V57 Less different sex roles	-.06
	V150 Protect the environment	-.03
33–44	V57 Less different sex roles	.01
	V150 Protect the environment	-.05
15–29	V57 Less different sex roles	-.03
	V150 Protect the environment	-.02

For U.S. Citizens

	Federal Taxes Are Too High	Federal Taxes Should Be Cut by 1/3	Support Proposition 13 (tax cut)
Civil liberties/crime	.01	.08	-.09
Race—govt. should play an active role	.05	.06	-.11
School integration	.02	.01	-.07
Women's rights—govt. should play an active role	-.03	.02	-.04
Abortion	-.03	-.02	-.07
ERA	.01	-.02	.01

Source: Euro Barometer 19, April 1983. Survey of 9,790 citizens in France, Belgium, Netherlands, Germany, Italy, Luxembourg, Denmark, Ireland, Great Britain, Northern Ireland, Greece

Note: The data shown for the four European age groups in the panel above are correlations between attitudes concerning less government and attitudes concerning sex roles and the environment. These age-specific results for Europeans could not be replicated for the United States because the numbers were too low. The main point is that the correlations were similarly low in all instances.
V57=Q. 136. "Do you agree or disagree with women who claim that there should be fewer differences between the respective roles of men and women in society? 1. Agree 2. Disagree"
V150 = Q. 236 "< Do you agree or disagree that > Stronger measures should be taken to protect the environment against pollution? 1. Agree strongly 2. Agree 3. Disagree 4. Disagree Strongly"
V148 = Q. 234. "<Do you agree or disagree that > Government should play a smaller role in the management of the economy? 1. Agree strongly 2. Agree 3. Disagree 4. Disagree strongly"

Source: Data are for 2,000 U.S. citizens surveyed in the 1978 National Election Study, University of Michigan.

Statistics are Pearson r's, with values exceeding about .05 significant at the .01 level. See also Clark and Ferguson 1983: 372.

Figure 4.1
Correlations between fiscal and social liberalism decline among younger
mayors, in several countries.

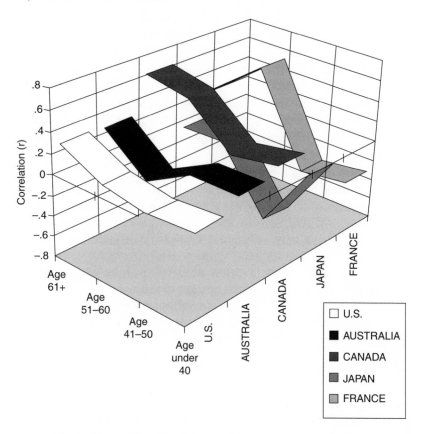

Note: These are Pearson r's between fiscal liberalism (mayor's responses to "would
you prefer more, same, or less spending" in several policy areas) and social liberalism (support for abortion).
Source: Fiscal Austerity and Urban Innovation Project.

Hout et al. discuss Weakliem's (1991) study, which reports unusual results, contradicting most past work on the same issue. Weakliem used a
new methodology from Leo Goodman, dichotomizing variables rather
than using all available continuous data. Further work should examine
whether his essentially weak findings are due to his methodology or remain
robust across methodologies.

The Political Rise of the "Middle Class" and Transformation of Left Party Programs

Despite the new salience of social issues, fiscal and economic issues persist. The change is clearest and most dramatic on the left. The policy positions of Socialist parties, which Lipset (1991) reviewed on five continents, showed a consistent abandonment of social welfare state and distribution issues and a general acceptance of market economics and of curtailing government growth. The self-destruction of the Soviet Communist regimes and dramatic shifts by most other Communist parties of the world illustrate the generality of this same trend. Many have abandoned their names as well as their Leninist programs; in Italy the PCI has become the Democratic Party of the Left.

In February 1993, a month before the national elections where the Socialists lost their majority in France, Michel Rocard called for Socialist Party regulars to join in a Big Bang Revolution and submerge the party into a larger "gathering" of ecologists, human rights activists, reform communists, and others. Radical change was needed, he said, since

> we have become a market society where inequalities translate into multiple forms, but where the sentiment of belonging to a class, to a collective movement, is no longer perceived as a reality.... The perception of the general interest has been so diluted as to disappear.... This explains, across Europe, the fundamental questioning of parties and traditional organizations. And that explains the success in France of the ecologists.... (*Le Monde* 1993)

As President Mitterand's main rival within the Socialist Party, Rocard lamented the party's decline and advocated the Big Bang transformation to effect a fundamental realignment to bring it in touch with the voters. Soon after the election, Rocard was named to lead the Socialist Party.

How should we interpret these drastic changes? A new literature is starting to emerge here, but we suggest that the worldwide trends are illuminated by looking closely at the origins of the "taxpayer revolt" in the United States, arguably the first and best-documented manifestation of the general pattern. Indeed, when Western Europeans learned of these U.S. developments in the 1970s, they found them inconceivable in the left-right ideological framework then still dominant (see Balme et al. 1986–1987). What changed and why? Clark and Ferguson (1983) pursued this question and found that the new pattern began not with Ronald

Reagan's election in 1980, nor with California's Proposition 13 tax revolt in 1978, but in local elections and fiscal policies implemented starting in the early 1970s. New types of leaders emerged then, which Clark and Ferguson labled New Fiscal Populists (NFPs): socially liberal, fiscally conservative, populist in appealing to citizens rather than parties, unions, or organized groups, and supporting more productive government. The large number of U.S. municipalities (N = 1,030 over 25,000) permitted multicausal analysis of leaders and their implemented policies in ways impossible to do for national states. While several factors entered, a key social characteristics was the size of the middle income sector in a city; it drove the emergence of NFPs in many multiple regression models. These NFPs served as political advocates of a new "middle-class" income sector. These are persons who do not depend much on government for welfare state–type services, yet are not affluent enough to ignore the tax bite in their incomes due to government growth. The rise in political salience of this broad middle class heightened fiscally conservative demands to reduce taxes and government deficits in the United States and other countries (Clark and Ferguson 1983; Flora 1986; Franklin et al. 1992; Wilensky 1981).

It might be argued that the fiscally conservative "middle class" is a politically active social class, but this would be inconsistent with Marxist class theory. First, the "middle class" takes its designation from an income category, not from a distinct shared labor market experience as posited by class analysis. Second, there is little evidence that "middle-class" voters possess a "class consciousness," causing them to act collectively for a "class interest." Rather, their main impact has been via electoral politics, not via collective actors. Evidence on this point is in figure 4.2, from surveys of mayors in seven Western countries, which rank the importance of major organized groups. It shows that "taxpayer groups," which quintessentially represent this middle-class fiscally conservative position, are the least active of all 11 types of organized groups. Third, while Marxist theories of class conflict posit a struggle for cultural and political *power*, the new fiscal conservatives do not seek power but enhanced freedom for individuals to pursue their economic wants less constrained by government taxation. Finally, the impact of "middle-class" political action is the removal from Western political agendas of issues that most concern persons who are the least economically secure, especially the "underclass," which depends most on welfare state support. Thus a class politics that society's lowest strata might support declines with "middle-class" activism.

Figure 4.2
City governments respond very weakly to taxpayers' groups, in seven countries.

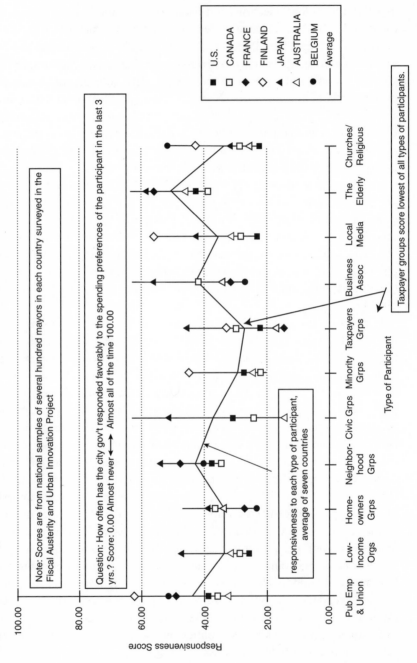

Note: Scores are from national samples of several hundred mayors in each country surveyed in the Fiscal Austerity and Urban Innovation Project

Question: How often has the city gov't responded favorably to the spending preferences of the participant in the last 3 yrs.? Score: 0.00 Almost never ←→ Almost all of the time 100.00

responsiveness to each type of participant, average of seven countries

Taxpayer groups score lowest of all types of participants.

Legend:
U.S.
CANADA
FRANCE
FINLAND
JAPAN
AUSTRALIA
BELGIUM
Average

Responsiveness Score

Type of Participant

Pub Emp & Union
Low-Income Orgs
Home-owners Grps
Neighbor-hood Grps
Civic Grps
Minority Grps
Taxpayers Grps
Business Assoc
Local Media
The Elderly
Churches/Religious

The Rise of a "New Class"?

Many characteristics of our New Fiscal Populists resemble the "new class," which some theorists posit in an effort to retain a class-centered analysis. This "new class" consists of college-educated, technically trained professionals (e.g., Berger 1981; Kristol 1978; Gouldner 1979). Although Pakulski (1993) points out that "orthodox" Marxist class theory normally applies only to the traditional manufacturing-based proletariat, some suggest that the new class constitutes a Marxist class in that it is defined by a distinct labor market experience. Gouldner (1979) argues that this experience is in applying technical, humanistic, or social knowledge through critical analysis. He argues that "new class" members thus develop a unique "culture of critical discourse."

Gouldner holds that the "new class" advances two political agendas. The first is to increase its economic and political power vis-à-vis the "old class" of property-owning capitalists. The second is to promote the socially liberal causes of new social movements. Some theorists argue that support for new social movements applies only to new class members working with forms of "social and cultural knowledge" (e.g., Brint and Kelley 1993; Kriesi 1989). Such knowledge has a more humanistic, value-laden content, which should make its users more sensitive to the legitimacy of diverse values and generally to noneconomic concerns. Kriesi (1989) confirms that social and cultural professionals are more likely than persons from other occupational groupings to support new social movements. Brint (1993) extends this analysis to multiple countries and finds that new class theory explains variation in social liberalism in selected northern European countries noted for the large scope of their welfare states, but not elsewhere.

Although these new class results show support for social liberalism within a distinct class, the theory also supports our point that the class *content* of Western politics has declined. By advancing a universalistic social agenda on issues such as peace and the environment, the new class helps displace specifically economic, class-relevant issues that are traditionally part of "class politics."

Also, even in rallying to a socially liberal agenda, new class members do not act as a self-conscious, united class but usually as voters and members of "single-issue" groups. Pakulski (1993) points out that these can be minimally organized but depend on the media, which help create "imagined communities," like smokers. In sum, the new class both contributes to and helps explain the decline of old class politics.

Figure 4.3
Alford Index of class voting shows decline over time.

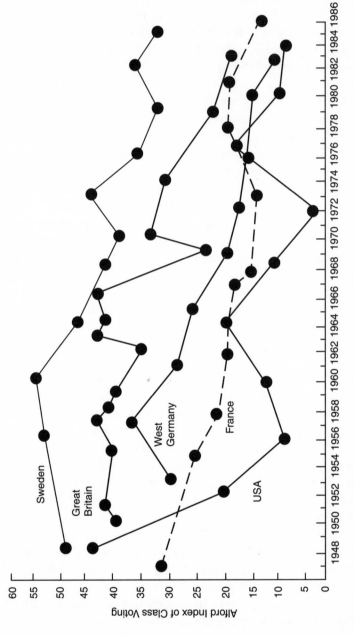

Adapted from Lipset 1981a: 505; updated in 1993 with results from more recent elections.

Conclusion: The Future of Class Analysis in Political Explanations

We agree that class analysis can still be useful and have considered many examples above, like "new class" theory, which illuminate the structural sources of social liberalism. Combined with our propositions, several modern class and stratification theories that we have considered confirm our conclusion that the political significance of social classes has declined. These theories specify the multiple layers implicated in current class structures and their more institution-centered, less family-based origins. They imply that classes have become more fluid and complex and consequently less inescapably polarizing. This makes class membership less subjectively salient and less politically influential. It is thus an ironic contribution of modern class theories to clarify why the class structures that they uncover exert a declining influence over political events.

Still, while class theories can illuminate many patterns, they must increasingly be supplemented by considerations of non-class-based hierarchies. This follows because, while class distinctions have become less rigid, other hierarchies, especially ascriptive ones like those based on sex, race, or ethnicity, continue to polarize many countries of the world, differentiating them, for example, by residential location, by educational opportunities, or of course by future class location. Consider some of the most salient political issues of the late 1980s and 1990s: the feminist movement, race, and vicious ethnic and national conflicts in many areas of Europe. These all involve nonclass hierarchies that have come to play prominent roles in Western politics. Their growing salience suggests that "hierarchy" rather than "class" has become the more comprehensive and pivotal theoretical tool to explain the widest range of structurally determined political behavior.

While hierarchy transcends class, all structural explanations are sometimes insufficient. This is because many currently prominent issues do not directly concern structurally defined subgroup interests, but more qualitative, culturally based concerns. Even though structural explanations *can* explain the propensities of members of certain subgroups to support these general *types* of issues, such explanations cannot specifically account for activism on problems such as environmental devastation, war, heightened threats to civil liberties posed by modern state power, or, under the former Communist regimes, demands for democracy. To account for these trends, it is likely to be a more promising strategy not to stretch class analysis further but to recognize that structural-cleavage-based explanations must be supplemented by others: that the new many indeed be quite new. Social science theory might then begin to catch up with the profound changes that we observe across the world.

References

Balme, R. et al. 1986–1987. "New Mayors: France and the United States." *Tocqueville Review* 8: 263–278.

Baron, J. N. 1984. "Organizational Perspectives on Stratification." *Annual Review of Sociology* 10: 37–69.

Beck, E. M., Horan, P. M. and Tolbert II, C. M. 1978. "Stratification in a Dual Economy: A Sectoral Model of Earnings Differentiation." *American Sociological Review* 43: 704–720.

Bell, D. 1973. *The Coming of Post-Industrial Society*. New York: Basic.

Berger, S. 1981. "Introduction," in Berger, S. (ed.), *Organizing Interests in Western Europe: Pluralism, Corporatism, and the Transformation of Politics*. New York: Cambridge University Press.

Bowles, S. and Gintis, H. 1976. *Schooling in Capitalist America: Educational Reform and the Contradictions of Economic Life*. New York: Basic.

Bowles, S. and Gintis, H. 1987. *Democracy and Capitalism*. New York: Basic.

Brint, S. 1993. "The Social Bases of Liberalism and Dissent." Draft manuscript prepared for volume edited by Terry Clark and Mike Rempel.

Brint, S. and Kelley, S. 1993. "The Social Bases of Political Beliefs in the United States." *Research in Political Sociology* 6: 277–317.

Brown, W. 1990. "Class and Industrial Relations: Sociological Bricks without Institutional Straw." In Clark, J. et al. (eds.), *John Goldthorpe: Consensus and Controversy*. New York: Falmer.

Clark, T. N. and Ferguson, L. C. 1983. *City Money*. New York: Columbia University Press.

Clark, T. N. and Lipset, S. M. 1991. "Are Social Classes Dying?" *International Sociology* 6(4): 397–410.

Collins, R. 1979. *The Credential Society*. New York: Academic Press.

Converse, P. E. 1964. "The Nature of Belief Systems in Mass Politics." In Apter, D.E. (ed.), *Ideology and Discontent*. New York: Free Press.

Dalton, R. J. 1988. *Citizen Politics in Western Democracies: Public Opinion and Political Parties in the United States, Great Britain, West Germany and France*. Chatham, NJ: Chatham House.

Dalton, R. J. and Kuechler, M. eds 1990. *Challenging the Political Order: New Social and Political Movements in Western Democracies*. New York: Oxford University Press.

Esping-Anderson, G. 1990. *The Three Worlds of Welfare Capitalism*. Princeton, NJ: Princeton University Press.

Flora, P. 1986. *Growth to Limits: The Western European Welfare State since World War II*. New York: Walter de Gruyter.

Franklin, M. et al. 1992. *Electoral Change: Responses to Evolving Social and Attitudinal Structures in Western Countries*. New York: Cambridge University Press.

Giddens, A. 1980. *The Class Structure of the Advanced Societies*. New York: Harper and Row.

Gorz, A. 1989. *Critique of Economic Reason*. Translated by G. Handyside and C. Turner. New York: Verso.

Gouldner, A. W. 1979. *The Future of Intellectuals and the Rise of the New Class*. New York: Seabury.

Habermas, J. 1975. *Legitimation Crisis*. Boston, MA: Beacon Press.

Hardiman, N. 1990. "Capitalism and Corporatism: The Political Economy of Advanced Capitalist Societies." In Clark, J. et al. (eds.), *John Goldthorpe: Consensus and Controversy*. New York: Falmer.

Harvey, D. 1989. *The Condition of Postmodernity*. Cambridge, MA: Basil Blackwell.

Hout, M., Brooks, C., and Manza, J. 1993. "The Persistence of Classes in Post-Industrial Societies." *International Sociology* 8, no. 3: 259–277.

Inglehart, R. 1990. *Culture Shift in Advanced Industrial Society*. Princeton, NJ: Princeton University Press.

Inglehart, R. and Abramson, P. R. 1993. "Economic Security and Value Change." Unpublished draft manuscript.

Kitschelt, H. 1990. "New Social Movements and the Decline of Party Organization." In Dalton, R. J. and Kucheer, M. (eds.), *Challenging the Political Order: New Social and Political Movements in Western Democracies*. New York: Oxford University Press.

Kriesi, H. 1989. "New Social Movements and the New Class in the Netherlands." *American Journal of Sociology* 94(5): 1078–1116.

Kristsol, I. 1978. *Two Cheers for Capitalism*. New York: Basic.

Kuechler, M. and Dalton, R. J. 1990. "New Social Movements and the Political Order: Inducing Change for Long-Term Stability?" In *Challenging the Political Order: New Social and Political Movements in Western Democracies*. New York: Oxford University Press.

Lipset, S. M. 1981a. *Political Man: The Social Bases of Politics*. Baltimore, MD: Johns Hopkins University Press.

Lipset, S. M. 1981b. "What Ever Happened to the Proletariat?" *Encounter* 56 (June): 18–34.

Lipset, S. M. 1985. *Consensus and Conflict*. New Brunswick, NJ: Transaction Books.

Lipset, S. M. 1991. "No Third Way: A Comparative Perspective on the Left." In Chirot, D. (ed.), *The Crisis of Leninism and the Decline of the Left*, 183–232. Seattle/London: University of Washington Press.

Lipset, S. M. 1993. "Reflections on Capitalism, Commerce, Socialism, and Democracy." *Journal of Democracy* 4(2): 43–55.

McCarthy, J. D. and Zald, M. N. 1977. "Resource Mobilization and Social Movements: A Partial Theory." *American Journal of Sociology* 82(6): 1212–1241.

Neuman, R. W. 1986. *The Paradox of Mass Politics: Knowledge and Opinion in the American Electorate*. Cambridge, MA: Harvard University Press.

Offe, C. 1981. "The Attribution of Public Status to Interest Groups: Observations of the West German Case." In Berger, S.(ed.), *Organizing Interests in Western Europe: Pluralism, Corporatism, and the Transformation of Politics*. New York: Cambridge University Press.

Offe, C. 1985. *Disorganized Capitalism: Contemporary Transformations of Work and Politics*. Cambridge, MA: MIT Press.

Offe, C. 1987. "Challenging the Boundaries of Institutional Politics: Social Movements since the 1960s." In Maier, C.S. (ed.), *The Changing Boundaries of the Political*. New York: Cambridge University Press.

Olson, M. 1965. *The Logic of Collective Action: Public Goods and the Theory of Groups*. Cambridge, MA: Harvard University Press.

Pakulski, J. 1993. "The Dying of Class or of Marxist Class Theory?" *International Sociology* 8, no. 3: 279–292.

Panitch, L. 1980. "Recent Theorizations of Corporatism: Reflections on a Growth Industry." *British Journal of Sociology* 31(2): 159–187.

Parkin, F. 1979. *Marxism and Class Theory: A Bourgeois Critique*. New York: Columbia University Press.

Piore, M.J. and Sabel, C. F. 1984. *The Second Industrial Divide: Possibilities for Prosperity*. New York: Basic.

Pollock, F. 1982. "State Capitalism." In Arato, A. and Gebhardt, E. (eds.), *The Essential Frankfurt School Reader*. New York: Continuum.

Roediger, D. 1991. *The Wages of Whiteness: Race and the Making of the American Working Class*. New York: Verso.

Shain, Martin. 1988. "On Changes in French Communism." Paper Presented to annual meeting of the American Political Science Association.

Smelser, N. 1962. *A Theory of Collective Behavior.* New York: Free Press.

Spillerman, S. 1977. "Careers, Labor Market Structure, and Socioeconomic Achievement." *American Journal of Sociology* 83: 551–593.

Tilly, C. 1978. *From Mobilization to Revolution.* Reading, MA: Addison-Wesley.

Weakliem, D. 1991. "The Two Lefts? Occupation and Party Choice in France, Italy and the Netherlands." *American Journal of Sociology* 96 (May): 1327–1361.

Wilensky, H. L. 1981. "Leftism, Catholicism, and Democratic Corporatism: The Role of Political Parties in Recent Welfare State Development." In Flora, P. and Heidenheimer, A.J. (eds.), *The Development of Welfare States in Europe and America.* New Brunswick, NJ: Transaction.

Wilson, W. J. 1987. *The Truly Disadvantaged: The Inner City, the Underclass, and Public Policy,* Chicago, IL: University of Chicago Press.

Wright, E. O. 1985. *Classes.* London: Verso.

5

Class and Politics in Advanced Industrial Societies[*]

JOHN H. GOLDTHORPE

The significance of social class in the politics of modern nations is an issue of long-standing controversy. A hundred years ago, it held a central place in the "debate with Marx," in which many of the great founders of sociology and of political science were engaged. And, today, the issue of class and politics is still one that provokes vigorous and complex argument. However, in order fully to appreciate this latest phase in the controversy, it is important to recognize that for several decades following World War II a period of relative consensus intervened. In this period, a broadly similar understanding of the relationship between class and politics could in fact be shared by analysts of widely differing ideological persuasions.

The essentials of this consensus, formed chiefly under the influence of the work of Lipset and Rokkan, were the following (see esp. Lipset and Rokkan 1967). On the one hand, it was accepted that, as the Western world had industrialized, fundamental changes had occurred in lines of social cleavage. Divisions deriving from processes of "nation-building" and state formation—for example, ones grounded in religion or region—had

[*]Formerly adapted and revised for *Conflicts about Class,* edited by David J. Lee and Brian S. Turner [London: Longman, 1996), this chapter was orginally a lecture given to the Hellenic Political Science Association in February 1994, a version of which was subsequently published (in translation) in the *Greek Political Science Review.* I am indebted for helpful conversations to Geoffrey Evans and Paul Nieuwbeerta.

105

tended to decline in political importance, while the importance of divisions based on class had steadily grown. In "mature" industrial societies, political organization and political partisanship were in fact largely class-based. On the other hand, it was also accepted that although class conflict had often played a part in the creation of liberal democratic polities, such conflict did not necessarily—or even typically—lead in turn to the revolutionary overthrow of such polities. Rather, liberal democracy provided an institutional context within which class-based political action might be contained, yet at the same time allowed an effective expression. Thus, Lipset (1960) could write, from an American liberal standpoint, that the participation of citizens in the electoral politics of Western nations represented "the democratic translation of the class struggle"; and more than 20 years later Korpi (1983) could entitle *The Democratic Class Struggle* a work examining the possibilities, as seen from the left wing of the Swedish Social Democratic Party, for a nonrevolutionary transition to socialism.

It is the breakdown of this postwar consensus that is now at hand. While the consensus prevailed, most of the objections that were raised against it came from unreconciled Marxists, who remained firm in the belief that "bourgeois democracy" was a sham which working-class revolution would, sooner or later, sweep away. But, from the 1980s, a challenge of a quite different character has gained in strength. What is now maintained is that, at least in the more advanced societies of the late twentieth century, the political importance of class is on a decisively downward curve. The contention is not simply that class cleavages and conflict can no longer be seen as "the engine of history"—as the source of collective action that creates epochal change. What is further held is that even at the level of the everyday, and especially of the electoral, politics of liberal democracies, the influence of class on individuals' attitudes and allegiances is steadily waning.

However, while arguments to this effect have been advanced with growing frequency in recent years, it must be noted at the outset that, in their more detailed content, these arguments vary a good deal. Although the "decline of class" is an increasingly common theme, quite diverse explanations of this decline are in fact proposed. At least four different positions can be identified.

First, it has been claimed that, at the present time, the main lines of social cleavage are, once more, being redrawn. Just as religious and regional divisions earlier gave way to those of class in determining the broad pattern of political alignments, so class is now giving way to new forms of cleavage that are characteristic of advanced industrial or "post-industrial" society. For example, it is held that important divisions—with evident political implications—are emerging along *sectoral* lines and in regard both to production and consumption. Conflicts, actual or potential, arise, on the one hand, between those who are employed in the public as opposed to the private sectors of the economy, and, on the other hand, between those who rely on public as opposed to private provision in such respects as health, housing, education, and transport (e.g., Kitschelt 1994; for Britain see Dunleavy 1980; Dunleavy and Husbands 1985; and Saunders 1984, 1990).

Second, one has the argument that in the more advanced societies of today, individuals' social structural locations, *however* defined, are becoming of less importance in shaping their political outlook than are their general belief and value systems. Previously, a close connection might be supposed between, say, class position and ideological position. But now such connections are weakening, among younger generations especially, as material interests become less compelling and as belief and value systems become more autonomous. In turn, then, the old bread-and-butter issues of politics give way to the "new agendas" of "post-materialism," which center on such issues as personal liberty, women's and minority rights, the environment, and so forth. In this regard, the most influential work has been that of Inglehart (Inglehart 1977, 1984, 1990; Ingelhart and Rabier 1986; see also Eder 1993).

Then, third, there are those who maintain that the impact of class on politics is declining primarily because of a process of change in the nature of political action itself. The citizens of advanced societies are increasingly making political decisions on the basis of a rational assessment of particular issues and policies, rather than responding more or less automatically in ways that might be predicted either from the social positions they hold or from some overarching ideology to which they are committed. For example, it is claimed that in elections voters are now beginning in a genuine sense to *choose* which party they will support, in the light of the prevailing circumstances, instead of voting more or less unthinkingly for the "natural" party of their class or political creed. And, thus, far greater variation—or "volatility"—can be seen, from election to election, both in the strength of party support and in its social composition (see especially Rose and McAllister 1986; also various contributions in Franklin et al. 1992).

Fourth, and finally, the emphasis may be placed simply on the decline of class per se. In modern societies, it is argued, class is ceasing to be a major determinant of life chances, lifestyles, and collective identities, and its influence on politics is therefore weakening *along with* its influence in virtually all other aspects of social life. Advancing industrialism or emerging post-industrialism not only creates greater wealth overall and a more equal distribution of material resources but, in addition, more equal opportunities for economic and social advancement. Old ascriptive hierarchies break down and social selection becomes increasingly based on individual merit, while at the same time the decline of former solidarities of community and workplace encourage men and women to pursue their own individual projects. In turn, then, the very rationale for thinking and acting politically in terms of class membership is progressively undermined. Of particular interest is the change in Lipset's position (in Clark and Lipset 1991) from that described earlier (see also Pahl 1989).

In these differing accounts there are, of course, various complementary elements—but a number of contradictory ones also. In various respects, their exponents are in disagreement with each other. It is, for instance, difficult to reconcile arguments that new structural cleavages have superseded those of class with arguments that claim the end of "cleavage politics" of any kind. However, the aim here is not to proceed with further exegesis, critical or otherwise. It is, rather, to challenge the *initial* thesis that each of the arguments presented above is intended to uphold—that is, the thesis that in the economically advanced societies of the late twentieth century there is a comprehensive and secular tendency for the class basis of politics to be eroded. In raising this challenge no attempt will be made to rehabilitate the postwar consensus previously referred to—which could be thought, if anything, to have *exaggerated* the importance of class in the politics of the *mid*-twentieth century. Nor will it be maintained that the relationship between class and politics in modern societies reveals no changes of any kind. The attempt will rather be to show that these changes are too complex, and also far too variable cross-nationally, to be captured by *any* single thesis that is couched in quite general and "developmental" terms.

Flogging a Very Dead Horse

To begin with, one may observe that many of those who now take up the theme of the decline of class politics seem set on conducting "the debate with Marx" all over again—and that this is not at all helpful to their case. The main empirical claim would appear to be that in modern democracies there is little sign of class-based political action that is of a revolutionary or even of a determinedly radical character. Labor and Social Democratic parties now form an integral part of the established political system and no longer view themselves as the organizational spearheads of transformatory social movements, while Communist parties have become largely ineffectual and, since the collapse of the Soviet bloc, have often just disappeared from the political scene.

Now with all of this, one may readily agree. The Marxist theory of class and of the class determination of politics has undoubtedly been undermined, and by events still more than by social research. However, very little then follows for the matter in hand. Marx's theory of class is not, and never has been, the *only* one on offer. It is here worth remembering that many of the great figures who, as mentioned at the start, engaged with Marx at the time when to debate with him had real relevance, did not reject the concept of class as such—nor its significance for political analysis. Think only of Max Weber, Vilfredo Pareto, or Josef Schumpeter. It should not then be too difficult to recognize that many, probably most, of those who today believe that class remains a key factor in the politics of advanced societies are themselves *not* Marxists. They operate with different—and, they would maintain, more sophisticated—understandings of how class inequalities are formed, of how these inequalities are subjectively experienced, and of how this experience is in turn reflected in politics.

It ought, then, to be obvious that the case for the decline of class politics cannot be made simply by pointing to the failure either of Marxist theory or of Marxist practice. Nor, moreover, is there much merit—or even logic—in another argument that has been advanced by those who are preoccupied with the critique of Marx. That is the argument that if, today, a more refined form of class analysis is indeed required than that provided by Marx, then this in itself *implies* that the political impact of class is less than it once was. Thus, for example, Clark, Lipset, and Rempel (1993) in a response to Hout, Brooks, and Manza (1993) acknowledge that analyses of the class structures of modern societies are now available that go far beyond such crude dichotomies as "bourgeoisie" and "proletariat." But, they contend, to abandon such Marxist categories, in favor of ones that recognize a more differentiated, less polarized, class structure is in itself to concede that class membership has became "less politically salient" (see also Holton 1996).

However, what could be more convincingly argued is more or less the opposite of this position. That is, only when one has an understanding of class that is appropriate to the complexities of modern societies will it be possible fully to comprehend the kinds of relationship that now prevail between class and politics. And, one could go on, it is largely *because* commentators such as those cited have difficulty in appreciating class analysis other than in its Marxist versions that they fail to see the extent to which class politics persists. In other words, a rather strange paradox may be suggested. Those who maintain the thesis of declining class politics are led to do so because they cannot themselves escape from ways of thinking about class, and about politics, that are too much influenced by the Marxism that they so obsessively attack.

Since this is perhaps a rather difficult point to accept, it may be helpful to develop it in more specific terms. One of the principal claims advanced by those who argue for a decline in class politics (Clark, Lipset, and Rempel included) is that over recent decades the association between class and vote in Western democracies has steadily weakened. To support this claim, a resort is typically made to the "Alford Index" of class voting (Alford 1962, 1963). This index is one easily calculated from social survey data, that is, by taking the percentage of the working class who vote for left-wing parties and then subtracting from this the percentage of those not in working class who vote for such parties. The larger the index, the stronger, it is supposed, is the class-vote link.

The Alford Index has for long been known to have serious statistical deficiencies (see Hout et al. 1995a). However, what, for present purposes, is of greater significance is that the index directly reflects, and is indeed entirely dependent upon, the idea of a simple class dichotomy—working class *versus* a residual nonworking class—taken together with a corresponding party dichotomy—left *versus* a residual nonleft. If such a *marxisant* approach is rejected, and more than two classes or more than two kinds of party are recognized, then the Alford Index simply cannot be used.

It is, furthermore, of interest to observe that essentially the same limitation applies with the alternative index of class voting devised by Rose and McAllister (1986), to sustain their argument that voters are now "beginning to choose," and, again, that a dependence upon the same dichotomies of class and of party underlies the seemingly more sophisticated methods followed by Franklin and his associates (1992) in their comparative study of electoral change in Western democracies, in which a weakening in almost all forms of cleavage politics is alleged. The analyses presented in these latter studies, it should be said, are no less open to technical objections than those that rely upon the Alford Index.[1] But the point of main relevance here remains the crude conceptual treatment of both class and party that is entailed, which may itself very easily lead analysts into drawing quite mistaken substantive conclusions.

For example, where no more than a dichotomy of working class/nonworking class is recognized, major problems necessarily arise over the class allocation of various "intermediate" groupings—such as self-employed artisans, foremen and supervisors, technicians, or routine workers in services—whose members together make up a quite substantial component of modern electorates. With more refined forms of class analysis, it is possible for these groupings to be treated in a theoretically differentiated way; and, it turns out, the distinctions that are made often do matter a good deal for the issue of class and party support. Thus, it has been found in several nations that self-employed artisans, along with other "own account" workers, have a particularly high level of *right-wing* voting—often in fact higher than that which prevails among white-collar employees (for Britain, see Heath et al. 1991: chap. 5). Consequently, if such self-employed individuals are included along with manual wage-earners in the working class, as usually happens with dichotomous schemes, then a quite misleading impression will be gained of the political heterogeneity of this class, and, in turn, the strength of the class-vote link is likely to be underestimated.

Likewise, where attention is concentrated simply on support for left, as opposed to nonleft, parties, it becomes difficult to assess the influence on class voting patterns of relatively complex party structures—and of changes therein. If, for instance, in a multiparty system, a new right-wing party were to arise with quite homogeneous class support—say, a "tax revolt" party backed chiefly by higher-level salaried employees and the petty bourgeoisie—then this development could easily be overlooked, and even if it led to class voting being intensified. That is, merely because it occurred within the residual, nonleft range of the political spectrum, in contradiction with the underlying supposition that class voting is of interest only as a phenomenon of the Left.

Finally in this connection it is relevant to note that what also lies beyond the scope of all merely "two-valued" treatments of the class-party link is the question of *non*voting and of *its* relationship to class. In several cases, however, most notably, perhaps, that of the United States (on which see further below), this question is one that any serious analysis of the social bases of electoral politics must take fully into account.

This, then, is the burden of the more negative part of the critique that may be made of the thesis of class politics in decline: that those who seek to uphold this thesis do so largely on the basis of simple, and indeed conceptually inadequate, dichotomies of class and of party, and by then focusing their attention primarily on the working class and on left voting. It is found preferable, it would seem, to continue with an implicit, if not explicit, attack on Marxist class theory—which is surely flogging a very dead horse—rather than to attend to the analytical developments that are required if the relationships that actually do prevail between classes and parties within modern democracies are to be more profitably examined.[2]

Against Class Dealignment—Some Recent Findings

In the remainder of this chapter the aim is to pursue the critical argument in a more positive fashion. A number of illustrations will be given of findings from recent research that does actively seek to raise conceptual and technical standards in electoral sociology; and, as will be seen, these findings in fact provide ample empirical grounds for questioning the idea that a progressive weakening of the class-vote link represents a *generic* feature of the politics of advanced societies. The studies to which reference will be made have several features in common. First, they abandon class dichotomies in favor of more differentiated categories. Second, they take into account voting for all parties and also, where relevant, nonvoting. And third, instead of relying on indexes of an essentially ad hoc kind, they seek to test different hypotheses about class voting by embodying these in formal statistical models. Of course, by concentrating on the relationship between class and *vote,* the question of class and *politics* is being considerably narrowed down. However, the proponents of the thesis of "class politics in decline" have themselves largely based their arguments on the supposed weakening of the class-vote link—insofar as these arguments have been given any clear empirical reference at all.

The first illustration comes from the British case, where the issue of class and party has perhaps been for longest disputed. A process of "class dealignment" in British politics was initially claimed after the general election of 1959, when Labour lost for the third time running. The working class, it was held, no longer provided Labour with the same solid support as previously. Then, when Labour defeated the Conservatives at elections in the 1960s and 1970s, a different twist was given to the argument: the emergence of a new kind of middle-class "leftism" was now suggested. But, finally, with Labour's four successive defeats at the polls from 1979 onward, the idea of "the end of working-class politics" was again taken up. In attempted explanations of these differing phases and forms of class dealignment, it may be added, versions of all of the theories previously reviewed have at some point or other been invoked (see, e. g., Abrams et al. 1960; Sarlvik and Crewe 1983; Robertson 1984; Franklin 1985; Rose and McAllister 1986; Butler and Kavanagh 1992). However, in more recent years, the entire debate on class voting in Britain has been transformed as a result of a major program of research undertaken by Heath and his associates. This has involved the systematic reanalysis of data from the full series of British General Election Surveys that have been carried out after each election from that of 1964 to that of 1992—nine elections in all (see especially Health et al. 1985; Heath et al. 1991; Heath et al. 1994; Heath et al. 1995). The two findings of key significance to have emerged from this research are the following.

First, when appropriate statistical techniques are applied to the data, it is apparent that there has been *no* steady tendency for the net association between class and vote to weaken over the period in question. A rather sharp decline in class voting does show up between the elections of 1964 and 1970, but this decline was not maintained and, after 1970, only trendless fluctuation in the level of class voting can be discerned.[3]

Second, then, Labour's failure in recent elections cannot be attributed to any *specific* weakening in the political solidarity of the working class. It is true that, since 1979 especially, workers have been clearly less likely to vote for Labour than before. However, such a tendency to desert Labour has in no way been confined to the working class but is apparent throughout the electorate. What is indicated is that Labour has just been a rather unattractive party "across the board" and also that "third" parties, that is, the Liberals and others, have tended to increase their appeal. Furthermore, Labour has suffered from the fact that the working class, in the sense of the body of manual wage-earners, has been declining in size in Britain, as in all other advanced societies. Thus, even though there has been no particular defection of the working class from Labour, there are simply fewer manual workers in the electorate to vote for Labour as their "natural" party.

In addition, one other finding of present interest may be obtained from the data set that Heath and his colleagues have assembled. That is, that class voting in Britain, at least since the 1970s, is more or less as strong on the right as it is on the left (Goldthorpe 1999; see also Evans 1993a). For example, the propensity for Conservative visiting among the service class or "salariat" of professionals, administrators, and managers or again among the petty bourgeoisie is almost as marked as is the propensity for Labour voting among the working class. It can, it is true, also be shown that from the 1970s through to the election of 1992, the Conservatives enjoyed, *in addition to* the support of those classes for whom they represent the "natural" party, a clearly higher level of "nonclass" appeal than Labour within the electorate at large (Goldthorpe 1999). Nevertheless, the idea that Labour can be set in contrast with the Conservatives as being a distinctively "class" party must be thrown into serious doubt.

The second set of findings to be noted derives from research being currently undertaken by Hout and his associates of voting in United States presidential election from 1956 to 1992 (Hout et al. 1995b). There are good grounds for believing that in the United States the influence of class on vote has been, historically, at a lower level than in European nations (Nieuwbeerta and De Graff 1999) and especially relative to the influence of such other factors as region, race, and ethnicity. Nonetheless, the thesis of class dealignment in voting has also been applied to the United States, and the research project in question is specifically aimed at testing its validity in this case.

The main conclusion reached thus far is that, just as in British electoral politics, no steady tendency is apparent for the net class-vote association to weaken; again, there is merely trendless fluctuation over the three-and-a-half decades that the analyses cover. Two supplementary findings of obvious importance are, however, also reported.

First, while there is little evidence of class *de*alignment in voting, processes of class *re*alignment would appear to be in train: that is, processes which, while leaving the overall *level* of class voting unchanged, nonetheless imply some shift in the *pattern* of association between class membership and party support. In particular, a tendency is revealed on the part of routine nonmanual employees—that is, workers in lower technical, clerical, and service occupations—to give increasing support to Democratic candidates while, however, skilled manual workers show some movement, albeit of an erratic kind, toward greater Republican voting.

Second, it is confirmed that, in the American case, nonvoting, just as much as voting, is class-linked and rather stably so. Members of the working class, in the sense of manual wage-earners, are clearly less likely to vote in presidential elections than are members of all other classes. Furthermore, differences in nonvoting as between skilled and nonskilled manual workers would appear if anything to be diminishing; that is, skilled workers have in recent elections become almost as likely not to vote as nonskilled workers. This findings helps bring out a general point that has been often overlooked in the debate on class voting: that the extent of such voting depends not only on features of the class structure but on features of the *party* structure also. Thus, class voting, as opposed to nonvoting, might well be higher in the United States if there were actually a working-class party for workers to vote for. As two other American investigators,

Vanneman and Cannon (1987), have observed, nonvoters in the United States are in their class composition very similar to Labour voters in Britain, but, they conclude, the United States has no leftist party so workers "sit out."

A third instructive illustration of recent research findings is provided by a comparative study carried out by Weakliem (1991) of electoral politics in three European nations: France, Italy, and the Netherlands. Weakliem analyzes data on class and vote for these nations, taken from repeated surveys over the years 1973 to 1985. His concern is again that of examining the thesis of declining class politics, but with special reference to one of the more detailed underlying arguments that were earlier noted: the argument that class is a declining force in modern politics because, among younger generations especially, "new agendas" are emerging that are not primarily related to class interests. In this case, as Weakliem observes, the class-vote link is seen as being loosened through the tendency of left-wing parties to take up "post-materialist" rather than old-style "class" issues. In this way they gain in appeal for affluent white-collar voters who are the main bearers of post-materialist beliefs and values—but at the cost of alienating some of their more traditional supporters in the working class, who may then move to the right, attracted, say, by populist rhetoric.

In the outcome, Weakliem's findings in regard to class voting are much in line with those previously considered. In France, Italy, and the Netherlands, just as Britain and the United States, there is little evidence of class voting being in progressive decline. Rather, class cleavages in party support appear to fluctuate around a fairly level trend. Moreover, while there is evidence of a post-materialist "dimension" in the electoral politics of all three nations, this remains generally weaker than the materialist "dimension" that reflects class interests—and even among voters in younger age-groups (see on the related issue of "gender politics," Evans 1993b). In other words, the importance of "new agendas" is easily exaggerated.

Furthermore, Weakliem's analysis allows him to put forward an explanation of why post-materialism has failed to reduce the level of class voting in the manner anticipated. This is because, insofar as post-materialist ideology has strengthened, it has done so *across all classes alike*. Thus, left-wing parties' pursuit of post-materialist issues has not, in itself, led to a significant loss of working-class, relative to nonworking-class, support. Rather, left party support may have helped post-materialist beliefs and values to develop within the working class.

The fourth, and final, instance of research to be discussed concerns what may appear to be a rather special case, that of the Irish Republic. Irish electoral politics have indeed been regarded as quite exceptional, in that it has proved difficult to find any clear social bases for party support (see especially Whyte 1974). The two main parties in the republic, Fianna Fáil and Fine Gael, have their origins in the Civil War of 1922–1923, and subsequent support for them has appeared to be largely a matter of family tradition that, over time, has come to have an essentially symbolic significance. However, recent research by a number of Irish sociologists and political scientists has led to some revision of this view.

To begin with, more refined forms of class analysis have revealed a greater degree of class-linked voting than was previously supposed, even if still well below the general European level. Further, though, and more interesting, there are indications that in recent Irish elections the influence of class on party support has been growing. In particular, Fine Gael is beginning to look more like a center-right party with distinctive appeal for the expanding salariat, while the previously insignificant Labour Party is coming into greater electoral prominence on the basis of chiefly working-class support (see, e.g., Mair 1979, 1992; Laver et al. 1987; Breen and Whelan 1994). What, in other words, would seem to be happening is that at last, after some 70 years, symbolic politics are on the wane and class interests are beginning to pattern party support somewhat more strongly.

Ireland can then count as another national case where the thesis of the decline of class politics scarcely applies. However, its significance might perhaps prove be a good deal wider than this. The Irish case, taken as one of *the decline of symbolic politics,* may prove to be of particular relevance to our understanding of the development of the new, postcommunist democracies of Central and Eastern Europe. Here, too, the electoral politics that have followed immediately on the creation of new democratic systems have contained a largely symbolic element, reflecting divisions in the predemocratic period and in the struggle to throw off foreign domination. And the Irish example does indeed suggest that such symbolic politics may have great durability. But it further suggests that, sooner or later, the influences of material, and especially class, interests are likely to be felt. During the decades ahead, then, at least the ethnically less fragmented nations of Central and Eastern Europe—assuming, of course, that they keep their democracies intact—may provide instances of just the opposite of class dealignment, that is, of nothing less than a reassertion of electoral politics as primarily the democratic translation of the pursuit of class interests and of the conflicts thus engendered.

Conclusions

Three points may thus be emphasized. First, if Marxist approaches are to be abandoned, the concept of class should be alternatively understood—and rendered operational. (One approach which has influenced several of the empirical studies referred to above is Goldthorpe 1987: chap. 2; see also Erikson and Goldthorpe 1992: chap. 2; Evans 1992, 1993c, 1994). The thesis of declining class politics can then be directly challenged on the basis of current research of greater conceptual and technical refinement than that on which the thesis itself has been maintained.

It is not, it must be stressed, an implication of the research and analysis that have been considered that sustained class dealignment in electoral politics *never* occurs. To the contrary, there appears to be good evidence now emerging that something of this kind did indeed take place over the postwar period in both Norway (Ringdal and Hines 1999) and Sweden (Holmberg 1984). Further cases may well be documented. However, what the illustrations provided do indicate is that the decline of class politics cannot be seen as a quite general tendency that is in some way "built into" the developmental logic of modern democracies. The far more typical finding is that, in the short term, the class-vote link shows a good deal of fluctuation in its strength and, on a longer-term view, displays either stability or a trend of only a very uncertain kind.

Second, although class dealignment is not an integral feature of the politics of modern societies, class realignment may be reckoned as a far more probable occurrence. That is to say, without the level of class voting necessarily weakening overall, the pattern of class-party linkages is susceptible to change. The actual forms that are taken by such realignment may be expected to display considerable cross-national variation, since realignment is likely to result more from changes in party structure—and party strategies—than from changes in the class structure directly. The arguments reviewed at the start of this chapter would all appear to underestimate not just the persisting force of class as a factor in democratic politics but, further, the readiness and capacity of political parties to respond purposively to the development of class structures in order to maintain and increase their electoral support.

Third, research of the kind illustrated should be seen as that which points the way for the future. It is not research undertaken in the interests of Marxism, nor yet of anti-Marxism. It aims to go beyond this now quite sterile confrontation. What those who engage in such research have chiefly in common is a commitment not to some political worldview but rather to a particular conception of social science (see Goldthorpe 1990). Central to this is the insistence that, whatever may be the motivations, political or otherwise, that underlie a research enterprise, the attempt must be made to conduct it according to the best available methodological standards— *and* that such standards *can* be specified. In its current phase at least, the debate on class and politics is perhaps as much about whether or not such a conception of social science is to prevail as it is about sociopolitical realities.

Notes

1. Rose and McAllister's index shares with the Alford Index the basic flaw that it is not "margin insensitive." This means that when these indices are used to assess trends in class voting, measurement of the class-vote association itself is confounded with the effects of changing marginal distributions in successive class-by-party tables. In the case of Franklin and his associates, the fact that they persist in working with a merely dichotomous dependent variable—i.e., left/nonleft voting— should then have led them to the use of logistic, rather than ordinary least squares, regression.

2. Exception should here be made of certain authors who have later attempted to offer a defense of the thesis, or at least a reasoned responses to its critics, by taking seriously the conceptual and technical issues that they have raised. For example, Nieuwbeerta and De Graaf (1999) examine the effect on estimates of trends in class voting of moving from dichotomous to more elaborate class categories but are forced by their comparative strategy to retain the simple left-nonleft party division.

3. Weakliem and Heath (1999), using Gallup data that extend back to 1935, find that class voting in Britain actually peaked between 1945 and 1950; between 1935 and 1945 it appears to have been at a rather lower level than after 1970. Unfortunately, the degree of reliability of the Gallup data seems to be difficult to determine.

References

Abrams, M., R. Rose, and R. Hinden. 1960. *Must Labour Lose?* Harmondsworth: Penguin.
Alford, R. 1962. "A Suggested Index of the Association of Social Class and Voting." *Public Opinion Quarterly* 26: 417–425.
Alford, R. 1963. *Party and Society: Anglo-American Democracies.* Chicago: Rand McNally.
Breen, R., and C. Whelan. 1994. "Social Class, Social Origins and Political Partisanship in the Republic of Ireland." *European Journal of Political Research* 26: 117–134.
Butler, D. E., and D. Kavanagh. 1992. *The British General Election of 1992.* London: Macmillan.
Clark, T. N., and S. M. Lipset. 1991. "Are Social Classes Dying?" *International Sociology* 6 (December): 397–410.
Clark, T., S. Lipset, and M. Rempel. 1993. "The Declining Political Significance of Social Class." *International Sociology* 8, no. 3: 293–316.
Dunleavy, P. 1980. "The Political Implications of Sectoral Cleavages and the Growth of State Employment." *Political Studies* 28: 364–383 and 527–549.
Dunleavy, P., and C. Husbands, 1985. *British Democracy at the Crossroads.* London: Allen and Unwin.

Eder, K. 1993. *The New Politics of Class*. London: Sage.

Erikson, R., and J. Goldthorpe. 1992. *The Constant Flux: A Study of Class Mobility in Industrial Societies*. Oxford: Clarendon.

Evans, G. 1992. "Testing the Validity of the Goldthorpe Class Schema." *European Sociological Review* 8: 211–232.

Evans, G. 1993a. "The Decline of Class Divisions in Britain? Class and Ideological Preferences in Britain in the 1960s and 1980s." *British Journal of Sociology* 44: 449–471.

Evans G. 1993b. "Is Gender on the New Agenda?" *European Journal of Political Research* 24: 135–158.

Evans G. 1993c. "Class, Prospects and the Life-Cycle: Explaining the Association between Class Position and Political Preferences." *Acta Sociologica* 36: 263–276.

Evans, G. 1994. "An Assessment of the Validity of the Goldthorpe Class Schema for Men and Women." In R. M. Blackburn, ed., *Social Inequality in a Changing World*. Cambridge: Cambridge Social Research Group.

Franklin, M. 1985. *The Decline of Class Voting in Britain*. Oxford: Clarendon Press.

Franklin, M., et al. 1992. *Electoral Change: Responses to Evolving Social and Attitudinal Structures in Western Countries*. New York: Cambridge University Press.

Goldthorpe, J. (With C. Llewellyn and C. Payne). 1987. *Social Mobility and Class Structure in Modern Britain*. 2d ed. Oxford: Clarendon Press (1st ed., 1980).

Goldthorpe, J. 1990. "A Response." In J. Clark, C. Modgil, and S. Modgil, eds. *John H. Goldthorpe: Consensus and Controversy*. London: Falmer.

Goldthorpe, J. 1999. "Modelling the Pattern of Class Voting in British Elections, 1964 to 1992." In G. Evans, ed., *The End of Class Politics?* 59–82. Oxford: Oxford University Press.

Heath, A., G. Evans, and C. Payne. 1995. "Modelling the Class/Party Relationship in Britain, 1964–92." *Journal of the Royal Statistical Society* (ser. A) 158: 563–574.

Heath, A., R. Jowell, and J. Curtice. 1985. *How Britain Votes*. Oxford: Pergamon Press.

Heath, A., R. Jowell, and J. Curtice, eds. 1994. *Labour's Last Chance? The 1992 Election and Beyond*. Aldershot: Dartmouth.

Heath, A., et al. 1991. *Understanding Political Change: The British Voter, 1964–1987*. Oxford: Pergamon.

Holmberg, S. 1984. *Väljare: Förandring*. Stockholm: Liber.

Holton, R. 1996. "Has Class Analysis a Future?" In D. Lee and B. Turner, eds., *Conflicts about Class: Debating Inequality in Late Industrialism*, 23–26. New York: Longman.

Hout, M., C. Brooks, and J. Manza. 1993. "The Persistence of Classes in Post-Industrial Societies." *International Sociology* 8, no. 3: 259–277.

Hout, M., C. Brooks, and J. Manza. 1995a. "Class Voting in Capitalist Democracies since World War II: Dealignment, Realignment or Trendless Fluctuation." *Annual Review of Sociology* 21: 137–163.

Hout, M., C. Brooks, and J. Manza. 1995b. "The Democratic Class Struggle in the United States, 1948–1992." *American Sociological Review* 60, no. 6 (December): 805–828.

Inglehart, R. 1977. *The Silent Revolution: Changing Values and Political Styles among Western Publics*. Princeton: Princeton University Press.

Inglehart, R. 1984. "The Changing Structure of Political Cleavages in Western Society." In R. J. Dalton, S.C. Flanagan, and P. A. Beck, eds., *Electoral Change in Advanced Industrial Democracies*. Princeton: Princeton University Press.

Inglehart, R. 1990. *Culture Shift in Advanced Industrial Society*. Princeton: Princeton University Press.

Inglehart, R., and J.-R. Rabier. 1986. "Political Realignment in Advanced Industrial Society: From Class-based Politics to Quality-of-life Politics." *Government and Opposition* 21: 456–479.

Kitschelt, H. 1994. *The Transformation of European Social Democracy*. Cambridge: Cambridge University Press.

Korpi, W. 1983. *The Democratic Class Struggle*. London: Routledge and Kegan Paul.

Laver, M., M. Marsh, and R. Sinnot. 1987. "Patterns of Party Support." In M. Laver, P. Mair, and R. Sinnot, eds., *How Ireland Voted: The Irish General Election of 1987*. Dublin: Poolbeg Press.

Lipset, S. 1960. *Political Man. The Social Bases of Politics*. New York: Doubleday; 2d ed., Baltimore: Johns Hopkins University Press, 1981.

Lipset, S., and S. Rokkan, eds. 1967. *Party Systems and Voter Alignments: Cross-National Perspective*. New York: Free Press.

Mair, P. 1979. "The Autonomy of the Political: The Development of the Irish Party System." *Comparative Politics* 11: 445–465.

Mair, P. 1992. "Explaining the Absence of Class Politics in Ireland." In J. Goldthorpe and C. Whelan, eds., *The Development of Industrial Society in Ireland*. London: British Academy.

Nieuwbeerta, P., and N. D. De Graaf. 1999. "Traditional Class Voting in Twenty Postwar Societies." In G. Evans, ed., *The End of Class Politics?* 23–58. Oxford: Oxford University Press.

Pahl, R. 1989. "Is the Emperor Naked?" *International Journal of Urban and Regional Research* 13; no. 4: 709–720.

Ringdal, K. and K. Hines. 1999. Changes in Class Voting in Norway, 1957–1989. In G. Evans, ed., *The End of Class Politics?* 181–202. Oxford: Oxford University Press.

Robertson, D. 1984. *Class and the British Electorate*. Oxford: Blackwell.

Rose, R., and I. McAllister. 1986. *Voters Begin to Choose: From Closed Class to Open Elections in Britain*. London: Sage.

Sarlvik, B., and I. Crewe. 1983. *A Decade of Dealignment*. Cambridge: Cambridge University Press.

Saunders, P. 1984. "Beyond Housing Classes: The Sociological Significance of Private Property Rights in Means of Consumption." *International Journal of Urban and Regional Research* 8: 202–207.

Saunders, P. 1990. *A Nation of Home Owners*. London: Unwin.

Vanneman, R., and L. W. Cannon. 1987. *The American Perception of Class*. Philadelphia: Temple University Press.

Weakliem, D. 1991. "The Two Lefts? Occupation and Party Choice in France, Italy, and the Netherland." *American Journal of Sociology* 96 (May): 1327–1361.

Weakliem, D., and A. F. Heath. 1999. "Resolving Disputes about Class Voting in Britain and the United States." In G. Evans, ed., *The End of Class Politics?* 281–307. Oxford: Oxford University Press.

Whyte, J. H. 1974. "Ireland: Politics without Social Bases." In R. Rose, ed., *Electoral Behavior: A Comparative Handbook*. New York: Free Press.

6

The Democratic Class Struggle in Postwar Societies
Traditional Class Voting in Twenty Countries, 1945–1990*

PAUL NIEUWBEERTA

Introduction

A common feature of elections in Western societies, which are commonly regarded as the platform of "the democratic class struggle" (Anderson and Davidson 1943; Lipset 1960; Korpi 1983; Przeworski and Spraque 1986), is that people from the lower classes are more likely to vote for left-wing parties than people from other classes are. The purpose of this chapter is to describe the strength of the relationship between class and voting behavior in Western industrialized countries in the postwar period of 1945–1990.

From the start of research on stratification and politics, studies have been concerned with the relationship between social class and voting behavior. (For an extensive review of the history of research on the relationship between class and voting behavior, see Nieuwbeerta 1995,

---

*This chapter is based on a presentation that I gave in the "Special Session on Class and Voting Behavior," organized by Terry Nichols Clark and Seymour M. Lipset, at the annual meeting of the American Sociological Association, Washington D.C., August 21–23, 1995.

1996.) The first studies on this topic were characterized by the use of a dichotomous manual/nonmanual class scheme. In addition, the focus was on the absolute levels of class voting, measured by the so-called Alford Index. These studies showed that in all Western democratic countries, members of the manual classes were more likely to vote for left-wing political parties than members of nonmanual classes were. They also revealed that the strength of the link between class and voting behavior was different from country to country and that declines in class voting occurred in most countries in the postwar period (Kemp 1978; Andeweg 1982; Korpi 1983: 35; Lipset 1983; Lane and Ersson 1991: 94; Franklin 1985; Dalton 1988; Inglehart 1990; Clark et al. 1993: 312).

Nevertheless, scholars from later generations argue that, although differences and trends in class voting were found in earlier studies, it is not clear whether these differences and trends would be found when examining levels of class voting in a more appropriate way (Korpi 1983; Heath et al. 1985; Hout et al. 1993; Goldthorpe 1994). First, they claim that the traditionally used measure of class voting (i.e., the Alford Index) is sensitive to variation in the general popularity of political parties. Therefore, they argue, one should focus on levels of relative class voting instead of absolute class voting and measure this by means of odds-ratios, or log-odds-ratios instead of Alford Index scores. Second, they argue that earlier studies used class schemes too crude to take into account relevant developments in the class structure in these countries.

The critique on the approach of traditional class voting studies has led to strong debates in the literature between scholars advocating one standpoint or the other (see, e.g., Clark and Lipset 1991; Crewe 1986; Heath et al. 1985, 1991; Hout et al. 1993). In these debates, however, these scholars could refer to only a very limited number of studies using measures of relative class voting and detailed class schemes and examining levels of class voting in many countries simultaneously and over a long period. In fact, the only studies done (Heath et al. 1995; Hout et al. 1995, Ringdal and Hines 1995) focused on trends in single countries: Britain, France, Norway, and the United States.

It is against this background that in this chapter I raise the following descriptive research questions: To what extent did levels of relative class voting differ across democratic industrialized countries in the postwar period? And to what extent was there a decline in levels of relative class voting in these countries over that period? In order to answer these questions, I follow a long line of studies that have examined this relationship, but I endeavor to improve on these studies, first, by analyzing data from 20 countries over the period 1945–1990, second, by employing both the traditionally used manual/nonmanual class scheme and a detailed class scheme (the EGP class scheme), and, third, by using measures of both absolute and relative class voting. A comparison of the results for (absolute) manual/nonmanual class voting and relative EGP class voting will indicate to what extent conclusions from traditional studies were flawed.

Data

To address the research questions of this study, data from 20 countries over the period 1945–1990 were analyzed. These countries can be considered as having been basically democratic over a substantial period of time (Lijphart 1984: 37). My set of 20 countries included all countries in Western Europe (except Iceland), two countries from the continent of North America (Canada and the United States), and Australia.

In the analyses two kinds of data were employed for the 20 countries under investigation in the postwar period. The first kind of data, the aggregated country data, includes information about the levels of class voting for each of the 20 Western industrialized countries in each year since the end of World War II. These data were obtained from two groups of sources: tables published in various articles and books, and tables calculated using data from several national representative surveys available on tapes (i.e., my individual data set). In total for all 20 countries, 324 tables cross-classifying class (manual/nonmanual) by party voted for (left-wing/right-wing) were found. The sources of these class voting tables are listed in Nieuwbeerta 1995 and 1996.

Data of second kind, the individual-level data, were used from national representative surveys of these countries. These data pertain to 75,783 male respondents aged 18 years or older from 113 national surveys held in 16 out of the 20 countries and covering the period 1956–1990. For Greece, Luxembourg, Portugal, and Spain, no useful individual-level data files were found. These data sets have been extracted, made comparable, and collected in one large combined file, the "International Stratification, Mobility and Politics File." For detailed information on this file, I refer to the accompanying codebook (Nieuwbeerta and Ganzeboom 1996).

Manual/Nonmanual Class Voting

Class Voting Indexes

Traditionally, to measure the level of class voting in a country at a certain point in time, the Alford Index has been used (Alford 1962, 1963). For a two-by-two table cross-classifying class (manual/nonmanual) and voting behavior (left-wing/right-wing),[1] the index score is obtained by taking the difference between the percentage of manual workers that voted for left-wing political parties and the percentage of nonmanual workers that voted for these parties.

Recently, scholars have proposed the log-odds-ratio as a measure of the strength of the class-vote relationship (Heath et al. 1985; Thomsen 1987; Hout et al. 1995; Manza et al. 1995). The log-odds-ratio is the natural logarithm of the odds-ratio, where the odds-ratio is the odds for manual workers voting left-wing rather than right-wing divided by the odds for nonmanual workers doing the same.[2] This log-odds-ratio can also be re-garded as the log-odds for manual workers voting for a left-wing political party rather than a right-wing party minus the log-odds for nonmanual workers voting in this way. If voting behavior is not dependent on class, the log-odds-ratio has the value of zero. As a tribute to the scholar who was one of the first to apply the log-odds-ratio in research on stratification and politics, we call this log-odds-ratio the Thomsen Index (Thomsen 1987). The Thomsen Index has advantages over the Alford Index in its in-sensitivy to changes in the general popularity of the political parties.

However, in practice, for two-by-two class voting tables the advantages of the Thomsen Index over the Alford Index should not be overstated. As the arguments given by Goodman (1975: 86) imply, it is only when the distribution of the general popularity of political parties or the distribution of social classes is more skewed than 25:75 or 75:25 that the Alford and Thomsen indexes might yield substantially different conclusions. In my data sets such distributions occur only in Canada and Ireland, where left-wing parties have fewer than 25 percent of the votes. Consequently, in the aggregated country data set the Pearson correlation between the Alford and the Thomsen indexes of the 324 country-year combinations in the 20 countries has the value .97 (p = .000). So, although we follow the theo-retical advantages of the Thomsen Index over the Alford Index (Heath et al. 1985; Hout et al. 1993), in practice descriptions of levels of class vot-ing using both indexes yield very much the same conclusions.

Differences between Countries

In order to answer my research questions, that is, to describe levels of class voting in postwar societies, I calculated the mean value of the Alford and Thomsen indexes of each country in four periods. These mean values are given in tables 6.1 and 6.2. My analyses confirm the findings of previous, more limited studies that use only the Alford Index. That is, there is a clear indication of substantial differences in levels of both absolute and relative manual/nonmanual class voting across democratic industrialized countries in the postwar period. The lowest levels of class voting are found in the United States and Canada. In these countries we find low positive Thomsen Index scores. This implies that manual workers do vote more left-wing than nonmanual workers, but the difference in voting behavior between these classes, especially in Canada, is small. The Thomsen Index scores of these countries rarely exceed 0.50. Furthermore, some countries have somewhat higher, but still relatively low, levels of class voting. These countries are France, Greece, Ireland, Italy, Netherlands, Portugal, Spain, and Switzerland. In these countries, the Thomsen Index scores are rarely higher than 1.0. Then follows a group of countries with intermediate levels of class voting. These countries are Australia, Austria, Belgium, Germany and Luxembourg. In these countries the Thomsen Index scores are predominantly between 1.0 and 1.5. Finally, in some countries we find relatively high levels of class voting, the Thomsen Index scores are higher than 1.5. These countries are the four Scandinavian countries and Britain. In the Scandinavian countries the Thomsen Index scores are occasionally even higher than 2.0.

Trends within Countries

My findings also show that a substantial decline in the levels of class voting occurred in most democratic countries in the postwar period. A first indication is provided by the higher index scores for earlier periods than for more recent years. A second, more precise indication of the decline in levels of class voting in most countries is provided by the trend parameters in tables 6.1 and 6.2. These trend parameters report the decline or rise in the level of class voting for each country measured by the Alford Index and the Thomsen Index. For every country, a linear regression analysis was performed on the indexes with the exact year of observation as an independent variable. A decline in the level of class voting should be indicated by

Table 6.1

Levels of Class Voting (Measured by Alford Index) in 20 Countries, 1945–1990 (Aggregated Country Dataset)

	Mean Levels of Class Voting per Period				Linear Trend (Change/10 Years)		N of Cases	Range of Years
	1945–1960	1961–1970	1971–1980	1981–1990	Parameter	s.e.		
Australia	32.9	29.3	27.8	19.4	-4.2*	0.7	17	1946–90
Austria	—	27.4	28.9	18.3	-6.1*	3.0	5	1968–89
Belgium	—	25.4	17.9	16.4	-4.3*	2.4	20	1968–90
Britain	37.3	38.3	24.3	23.4	-5.9*	1.2	30	1945–90
Canada	7.0	7.7	—	4.0	-0.7	1.4	13	1945–84
Denmark	39.8	52.0	28.1	20.9	-4.9*	0.8	29	1945–90
Finland	48.4	50.2	36.9	35.7	-6.1	4.6	5	1958–87
France	24.4	18.3	17.0	11.7	-3.7*	0.8	25	1947–90
Germany	36.0	24.8	14.9	13.4	-7.0*	1.0	25	1953–90
Greece	—	—	12.3	9.7	4.4	5.7	10	1980–89
Ireland	26.6	14.1	8.7	7.3	-2.3	1.3	18	1969–90
Italy	—	14.5	17.8	13.1	-4.3*	1.2	20	1953–90
Luxembourg	—	—	24.8	18.8	-3.8	4.1	17	1973–90
Netherlands	14.0	14.7	21.8	15.5	-0.2	1.0	25	1950–90
Norway	52.5	32.0	33.8	20.5	-9.1*	1.5	11	1949–90
Portugal	—	—	—	14.9	5.9	6.0	5	1985–89
Spain	—	—	18.4	15.5	-4.1	7.1	6	1979–89
Sweden	51.0	40.7	37.3	32.7	-5.5*	0.9	12	1946–88
Switzerland	—	—	17.6	12.8	-3.8	4.4	4	1972–87
United States	16.2	7.7	10.9	8.1	-2.8*	1.0	27	1948–90
Mean	32.2	26.5	22.2	16.6				
s.d.	14.9	14.2	8.6	7.8				

Note: The variable year is centered around 1980.

* p < .05

a negative trend-parameter. I should point out that I do not argue that a negative linear trend-parameter for a country implies a strict linear declining trend in the level of class voting in that country. The parameters are regarded as only a summary measure of the overall increase or decrease in class voting in a country, and not as the best representation of the developments in class voting over time.

In tables 6.1 and 6.2, negative trend-parameters are reported for 18 out of the 20 countries for both indexes. The only two countries with a positive (nonsignificant) trend-parameter are Greece and Portugal. However, for these two countries data are available only over the periods 1980–1990 and 1985–1990, respectively. Of the 18 slope-parameters that are negative in both tables, 11 are statistically significant at the .05 level. The pertinent countries are: Australia, Austria, Belgium, Britain, Denmark, France, Germany, Italy, Norway, Sweden, and the United States. Furthermore, the finding of statistically insignificant slope-parameters for Finland, Spain, and Switzerland might be caused by the limited number of years that we have data for these countries. Thus, in general, our data lend support to the statement that levels of class voting in Western industrialized societies have declined over the postwar period. The only countries for which we do not find significant declines in their levels of class voting, but where we have data for a sufficient number of years to detect significant trends, are Canada, Ireland, Luxembourg, and the Netherlands.[3]

EGP Class Voting

The next question that can be raised—and has been raised frequently by scholars of the third generation of research on social stratification (Heath et al. 1985; Hout et al. 1993)—is, To what extent would the above results on cross-national and over-time patterns of class voting be different if a more detailed class scheme were used? Heath et al. (1985), Hout et al. (1993), and Goldthorpe (1994), for instance, posit that in industrialized countries declines in the levels of class voting, when measured by a manual/nonmanual class distinction, can be explained, at least to some extent, by changes in the composition of these two classes. In recent years many countries have seen the service class grow substantially relative to the other nonmanual subclasses. In addition, the percentage of skilled workers within the manual class has grown, and the percentage of unskilled workers has diminished. Under the conditions that members of the service class tend to be more left-wing than the other nonmanual subclasses and the

Table 6.2

Levels of Class Voting (Measured by Thomsen Index) in 20 Countries, 1945–1990 (Aggregated Country Dataset)

	Mean Levels of Class Voting per Period				Linear Trend (Change /10 Years)		N of Cases	Range of Years
	1945–1960	1961–1970	1971–1980	1981–1990	Parameter	s.e.		
Australia	1.38	1.22	1.16	0.80	-0.18*	0.03	17	1946–90
Austria	—	1.12	1.28	0.76	-0.27*	0.13	5	1968–89
Belgium	—	1.21	0.87	0.80	-0.20*	0.11	20	1968–90
Britain	1.64	1.67	1.07	0.90	-0.22*	0.03	30	1945–90
Canada	0.30	0.31	—	0.27	-0.01	0.06	13	1945–84
Denmark	1.82	2.33	1.18	0.97	-0.30*	0.05	29	1945–90
Finland	2.17	2.24	1.60	1.52	-0.30	0.21	5	1958–87
France	1.01	0.76	0.72	0.48	-0.15*	0.00	25	1947–90
Germany	1.55	1.06	0.61	0.55	-0.31*	0.04	25	1953–90
Greece	—	—	0.53	0.47	0.15	0.34	10	1980–89
Ireland	—	0.88	0.77	0.70	-0.15	0.13	18	1969–90
Italy	1.13	0.66	0.73	0.53	-0.19*	0.05	20	1953–90
Luxembourg	—	—	1.10	0.86	-0.14	0.19	17	1973–90
Netherlands	0.61	0.65	0.94	0.68	-0.01	0.05	25	1950–90
Norway	2.39	1.38	1.43	0.84	-0.44*	0.06	11	1949–90
Portugal	—	—	—	0.62	0.27	0.72	5	1985–89
Spain	—	—	0.75	0.63	-0.16	0.30	6	1979–89
Sweden	2.26	1.73	1.57	1.36	-0.27*	0.04	12	1946–88
Switzerland	—	—	0.82	0.80	-0.07	0.25	4	1972–87
United States	0.67	0.36	0.46	0.34	-0.12*	0.05	27	1948–90
Mean	1.41	1.17	0.98	0.74				
s.d.	0.66	0.59	0.33	0.30				

Note: The variable year is centered around 1980.
* p < .05

skilled workers are less left-wing than the other manual subclasses, these developments in a country will lead toward a more left-wing nonmanual class, a less left-wing manual class, and a lower level of manual/nonmanual class voting. Analysis of levels of class voting using a more detailed class scheme—and thus controlling for changes in the composition of the manual and nonmanual classes—therefore might show less pronounced declines in class voting.

In line with the arguments of these third-generation scholars, I therefore also use a more detailed class scheme, that is, the seven-class version of a class scheme originally introduced by Goldthorpe for the Oxford Mobility Inquiry and later elaborated by Erikson and Goldthorpe (1992: 38–39). The seven-class version of this class schemes called the EGP class scheme for brevity's sake, distinguishes four classes within the nonmanual class (the service class, routine nonmanual class, petty bourgeoisie, and farmers) and three within the manual class (skilled workers, nonskilled workers, and agricultural laborers). I have chosen this EGP class scheme, since it has been useful in comparative studies of intergenerational class mobility (Ganzeboom et al. 1989; Erikson and Goldthorpe 1992) and in studies examining the relationship between social class and voting behavior (Heath et al.1985; Evans et al. 1991), as well in studies of the effects of class mobility on voting behavior (De Graaf et al. 1995; Nieuwbeerta 1995; Nieuwbeerta and Ultee 2000).

To measure levels of class voting using the EGP class scheme, also log-odds-ratios can be applied. Here the advantages of the log-odds-ratio over the Alford Index are more relevant, since in this case the distribution of the classes and the voting behavior are regularly more skewed than 25:75 (Heath et al. 1985; Hout et al. 1995). Use of the seven-class EGP scheme takes six log-odds-ratios to measure all the differences in voting behavior (left/right) between these classes. However, as proposed by Hout et al. (1995), the standard deviation of these log-odds-ratios can be used as an overall measure of the level of EGP class voting. They named this overall measure the kappa index.

In table 6.3 I present the kappa index scores as measures of EGP class. These measures reveal that very much the same picture comes up as when describing levels of class voting using a manual/nonmanual class distinction. Again, the differences in voting behavior between the classes vary substantially from country to country. Furthermore, the ranking of the countries with respect to levels of class voting is similar to the ranking for manual/nonmanual class voting.[4] For example, in Norway during the period 1971–1980 the difference between the most left-wing class and the

Table 6.3
Levels of Class Voting (Measured by the Kappa Index) in 16 Countries, 1961–1990 (Individual Dataset)

	Mean Levels of Class Voting per Period			Linear Trend (Change/10 Years)		N of Cases	Range of Years
	1961–1970	1971–1980	1981–1990	Parameter	s.e.		
Australia	0.81	1.00	0.78	-0.04	0.07	9	1965–90
Austria	—	1.14	1.18	0.24	0.22	4	1974–89
Belgium	—	0.83	—	—	—	1	1975
Britain	0.99	1.12	0.74	-0.15*	0.06	12	1964–90
Canada	—	—	0.50	—	—	1	1984
Denmark	—	1.62	1.71	-0.34	0.38	6	1971–81
Finland	—	1.23	—	-0.77	—	2	1972–75
France	—	0.76	—	—	—	1	1978
Germany	1.37	1.05	0.73	-0.41*	0.08	13	1969–90
Ireland	—	—	1.08	-0.62	—	2	1989–90
Italy	0.55	0.61	0.42	-0.08	0.08	3	1968–85
Netherlands	0.90	0.98	0.68	-0.11	0.07	14	1970–90
Norway	0.96	1.01	0.52	-0.25*	0.07	7	1965–90
Sweden	—	1.33	0.89	-0.24	—	2	1972–90
Switzerland	—	1.00	—	-0.15	—	2	1972–76
United States	0.20	0.35	0.32	-0.04	0.04	24	1956–90
Mean	0.83	1.00	0.80				
s.d.	0.34	0.30	0.37				

Note: The variable year is centered around 1980.
* p < .05

most right-wing class, that is, between the unskilled manual workers and the farmers, is 2.75, while in the United States for the same period the difference between these classes is only 0.97. Besides, in each of the distinguished periods the countries from the continent of North America (Canada and the United States) have the lowest kappa index scores, while Britain and the Scandinavian countries have the highest.

To investigate whether the level of EGP class voting has declined over the postwar period, like the levels of manual/nonmanual class voting in these countries, I examine the linear trend parameters for the kappa index scores, which are also given in table 6.3. These figures show negative trend-parameters for all countries under investigation, except Austria. Thus, we can carefully conclude that, similar to the developments in levels of manual/nonmanual class voting, declines in the levels of EGP class voting in most countries have occurred. The trend-parameters differ significantly from zero only in Germany, Britain, and Norway. The absence of any statistically significant difference from zero, again, might be due to the availability of only a limited number of data sets for the pertinent countries. It is only for the United States and the Netherlands (i.e., countries where we have data from more than 10 years) that we can be reasonably sure no systematic decline in EGP class voting has occurred.

Conclusions

From the very beginning of research on class and voting behavior, studies have shown that the strength of the relationship between class and voting behavior differed between countries. In addition, these studies have shown that the strength of that relationship declined over the postwar period in most of these countries. These conclusions were especially drawn in studies of the first generation of social stratification and politics. In these studies levels of class voting were measured on the basis of the Alford Index, which distinguishes only between manual and nonmanual classes and measures absolute differences in voting behavior. However, in studies of later generations, doubts were raised about the conclusions of these first-generation studies. It was claimed that differences detected, when using measures of absolute class voting like the Alford Index, might not be due solely to differences in the strength of the relationship between class and voting behavior, but might also be due to differences in the general popularity of the political parties. Furthermore, it was argued that differences between countries or periods detected when using the manual/nonmanual class scheme might to some extent be due to differences in the composition of the manual and nonmanual classes between countries or periods, and not (only) to differences in the strength of the relationship between class and voting behavior. Consequently, in third-generation studies it was argued that when using a measure of relative class voting and distinguishing between more detailed classes, descriptions of levels of class voting might lead to different conclusions about between-country and over-time differences in class voting.

In the present study I tested the tenability of these arguments. The main finding is that the various measures of class voting yielded the same conclusions with respect to the ranking of the countries according to their levels of class voting and according to the speed of declines of class voting. The results indicated that substantial differences in levels of relative class voting existed between democratic industrialized countries in the postwar period. Of all countries under investigation, the Scandinavian countries and Britain had the highest levels of class voting, and the United States and Canada had the lowest. The differences were largest at the beginning of the period under investigation. In addition, substantial declines in levels of class voting occurred in many of the countries in the postwar period. The fluctuations in class voting within these countries, in our view, can be regarded in most of these countries—except the United States and Switzerland—as part of an overall declining trend, and not as trendless fluctuations (see Heath et al. 1985). The declines in the various countries were such that the countries slowly converged in a situation where class was relatively unimportant to voting behavior. Referring to the debate between Clark et al. (Clark and Lipset 1991; Clark et al. 1993) and Hout et al. (1993), we can therefore argue that with respect to politics, social classes are certainly not dead yet, but the rumors of their imminent death are not all that exaggerated.

These results, however, do not imply that the claims of the scholars of the third generation were wrong. Our findings showed that some of the between-country and over-time variations in manual/nonmanual class voting were due to variations in the composition of the manual and nonmanual classes, and not only to variations in the strength of the relationship between class and voting behavior. Furthermore, we did not fully use the possibilities offered by our data set and detailed class scheme. To begin with we dealt with a question that pertains only to the overall levels of class voting in countries. We thus did not examine the voting behavior of these detailed classes separately, nor did we investigate the specific trends in the voting behavior of these different classes. Such class-specific trends are of interest, since, for example, some classes might have started to vote less according to their class interest, as Heath et al. (1991) supposed for Britain, while others might have kept the same voting pattern or even started to vote more according to their class interests. These separate class-specific trends cannot always fully be detected when investigating the overall levels of class voting. Therefore, in future studies the focus should not be restricted to overall levels of class voting but should also include class-specific voting behavior.

In addition, with the discovery of substantial differences in overall levels of relative class voting between Western industrial countries in the postwar period and, during the same period, significant declines in class voting levels within these countries, future studies should focus on explaining these differences and trends. Various studies of stratification and politics from the first generation through the third have suggested how social and political characteristics affect levels of class voting in countries (Lipset 1983; Manza et al. 1995; Nieuwbeerta 1995; for more recent studies see also Nieuwbeerta and Ultee 1999; and Nieuwbeerta et al. 2000). The social characteristics raised by such studies range from variations in religious and ethnic diversity, via rises in the general standard of living and levels of intergenerational mobility, to post-materialistic value orientations. The political characteristics concern, among other things, the prominence of class issues in politics and the differences in policy preferences between political parties. The links between these social and political characteristics of countries and their levels of class voting need attention in future studies.

When testing political explanations for variation in levels of class voting in future studies, it would be worthwhile to distinguish between all the separate political parties that run in a country's elections. This would enable us to find out whether substantial changes in the voting patterns of social classes have occurred within left-wing or right-wing political blocs. For example, it might be that in the Netherlands, a country where we did not find a systematic decline in class voting, the manual workers are just as likely to vote for left-wing parties as before but are less apt to vote for extreme left-wing parties, choosing instead more moderate left-wing parties. Evans et al. (1991) and Heath et al. (1985, 1995) have already applied more detailed party classifications when investigating trends in Britain. Hout et al. (1995) have done likewise for the United States, and Ringdal and Hines (1995) for Norway. For trend analyses in other countries and for cross-nationally comparable studies on class voting, these examples deserve to be followed (for recent analyses see Evans 1999; Manza and Brooks 1999).

Notes

1. In Nieuwbeerta 1996 I present a list of the political parties that were classified as left-wing. Following Bartolini and Mair 1990: 42–43, all parties that were members of the Socialist International or the Communist Third International were included as left-wing. In the United States an exception to that criterion was made: the Democratic Party was defined as a left-wing party.

2. I prefer to use the log-odds-ratio over the odds-ratio, since the latter message does not adjust for floor effects. That is, if there is hardly a relationship between class and vote, a small change in the strength of that relationship results in a small alteration in the odds ratio, whereas if this relationship is strong, a small change results in a large alteration in this measure.

3. One could argue that our detailed class scheme also enables us to distinguish between class-specific processes of dealignment or realignment. For example, it is possible that the distances between the service class and skilled manual class become smaller, and at the same time the distances between the service class and the farmers grow. In this study, however, we focus on the overall change in levels of class voting and leave class-specific dealignment and realignment processes for future research (see also the "Conclusions" section).

4. Inspection of the index values for each year within these countries shows that, indeed, hardly any decline in class voting occurred in these countries.

5. I also compared all EGP class voting outcomes with the Alford and Thomsen indexes solely on the basis of our individual level dataset. This results in the same conclusions.

References

Alford, R. 1962. "A Suggested Index of the Association of Social Class and Voting." *Public Opinion Quarterly* 26: 417–425.

Alford, R. 1963. *Party and Society: The Anglo-American Democracies.* Westport: Greenwood Press.

Anderson, D., and P. Davidson. 1943. *Ballots and the Democratic Class Struggle.* Stanford: Stanford University Press.

Andeweg, R. B. 1982. "Dutch Voter Adrift: On Explanations of Electoral Change 1963–1977." Ph.D. dissertation, University of Leyden.

Bartolini, S. and P. Mair. 1990. *Identify, Competition and Electoral Availability: The Stabilisation of European Electorates, 1885–1985. Cambridge: Cambridge University Press.*

Clark, T. N., and S. M. Lipset. 1991. "Are Social Classes Dying?" *International Sociology* 6: 397–410.

Clark, T. N., S. M. Lipset, and M. Rempel. 1993. "The Declining Political Significance of Social Class." *International Sociology* 8: 293–316.

Crewe, I. 1986. "On the Death and Resurrection of Class Voting: Some Comments on How Britain Votes." *Political Studies* 34: 620–638.

Dalton, R. J. 1988. *Citizens Politics in Western Democracies: Public Opinion and Political Parties in the United States, Great Britain, West Germany and France.* Chatham: Chatham House Publishers.

De Graaf, N. D., P. Nieuwbeerta, and A. Heath. 1995: "Class Mobility and Political Preference: Individual and Contextual Effects." *American Journal of Sociology* 100: 997–1027.

Erikson, R., and J. H. Goldthorpe. 1992. *The Constant Flux: A Study of Class Mobility in Industrial Societies.* Oxford: Clarendon Press.

Evans, G., ed. 1999. *The End of Class Politics? Class Voting in Comparative Context.* Oxford: Oxford University Press.

Evans, G., A. Heath, and C. Payne. 1991. "Modelling Trends in the Class/Party Relationship, 1964–1987." *Electoral Studies* 10: 99–117.

Franklin, M. 1985. "How the Decline in Class Voting Opened the Way to Radical Change to British Politics." *British Journal of Political Science* 14: 483–508.

Ganzeboom, H. B. G., R. Luijkx, and D. J. Treiman. 1989. "Intergenerational Class Mobility in Comparative Perspective." *Research in Social Stratification and Mobility* 8: 3–84.

Goldthorpe, J. H. 1994. "Class and Politics in Advanced Industrial Societies." Paper presented at the XVII World Congress of Sociology, Bielefeld, Germany.

Goodman, L. A. 1975. "The Relationship between Modified and Usual Multiple-Regression Approaches to the Analysis of Dichotomous Variables." In D. R. Reise, ed., *Sociological Methodology 1976*, 83–110. San Francisco: Jossey-Bass.

Heath, A., G. Evans, and C. Payne. 1995. "Modelling the Class/Party Relationship in Britain, 1964–1992." *Journal of the Royal Statistics* (ser. A) 158: 563–574.

Heath, A., R. Jowell, and J. Curtice. 1985. *How Britain Votes*. Oxford: Pergamon Press.

Heath, A., J. Curtice, R. Jowell, G. Evans, J. Field, and S. Witherspoon. 1991. *Understanding Political Change: The British Voter, 1964–1987*. Oxford: Pergamon Press.

Holmberg, S. 1991. "Voters on the Loose: Trends in Swedish Voting Behavior." Unpublished paper Göteburg.

Hout, M., C. Brooks, and J. Manza. 1993. "The Persistence of Classes in Post-Industrial Societies." *International Sociology* 8: 259–277.

Hout, M., C. Brooks, and J. Manza. 1995. "The Democratic Class Struggle in the United States, 1948–1992." *American Sociological Review* 60: 805–828.

Inglehart, R. 1990. *Culture Shift in Advanced Industrial Society*. Princeton: Princeton University Press.

Kemp, D. A. 1978. *Society and Electoral Behaviour in Australia: A Study of Three Decades*. Brisbane: University of Queensland Press.

Korpi, W. 1983. *The Democratic Class Struggle*. London: Routledge & Kegan Paul.

Lane, J.-E., and S. O. Ersson. 1991. *Politics and Society in Western Europe*. 2d ed. London: Sage.

Lijphart, A. 1984. *Democracies: Patterns of Majoritarian and Consensus Government in Twenty-one Countries*. New Haven: Yale University Press.

Lipset, S. M. 1960. *Political Man: The Social Bases of Politics*. London: Heinemann.

Lipset, S. M. 1983. *Political Man: The Social Bases of Politics*. Expanded and updated ed. London: Heinemann.

Manza, J., and C. Brooks. 1999. *Social Cleavages and Political Change: Voter Alignments and U.S. Party Coalitions*. Oxford: Oxford University Press.

Manza, J., M. Hout, and C. Brooks. 1995. "Class Voting in Capitalist Democracies since WWII." *Annual Review of Sociology* 21: 137–163.

Nieuwbeerta, P. 1995. *The Democratic Class Struggle in Twenty Countries, 1945–1990*. Amsterdam: Thesis Publishers.

Nieuwbeerta, P. 1996. "The Democratic Class Struggle in Postwar Societies: Class Voting in Twenty Countries, 1945–1990." *Acta Sociologica* 39: 345–383.

Nieuwbeerta, P., and H. B. G. Ganzeboom. 1996. *International Social Mobility and Politics File: Documentation of a Dataset of National Surveys Held in Sixteen Countries, 1956–1990*. Amsterdam: Steinmetz Archive.

Nieuwbeerta, P., and W. C. Ultee. 1999. "Explaining Differences in the Level of Class Voting in 20 Western Industrial Nations, 1945–1990." *European Journal of Political Science* 35: 123–160.

Nieuwbeerta, P., N. D. De Graaf, and W. Ultee. 2000. "Effects of Class Mobility on Class Voting in Post-War Western Industrialized Countries." *European Sociological Review* 16, no. 14.

Przeworski, A., and J. Spraque. 1986. *Paper Stones: A History of Electoral Socialism*. Chicago: University of Chicago Press.

Ringdal, K., and K. Hines. 1995. "Patterns in Class Voting in Norway 1957–1989: Decline or 'Trendless Fluctuations'?" *Acta Sociologica* 38: 33–51.

Thomsen, S. R. 1987. *Danish Elections 1920–79: A Logit Approach to Ecological Analysis and Inference*. Aarhus: Politica.

7

Class Paradigm and Politics*

JAN PAKULSKI

I would like to restate here an argument about the declining relevance of "class perspective" or "paradigm"[1] for analyses of politics in advanced societies. This is not the first time such an argument has been presented. Perhaps the best-known classical formulations by Ossowski ([1958]1963) and Nisbet (1959) focused on the case of the United States. The more recent versions, taking a broader focus and backed by more compelling evidence, have appeared in major social science journals and in at least five books.[2] The current revival of critical interest in class, especially among sociologists (who seem to be more faithful to class than political scientists are), seems to mark the beginning of a critical reevaluation of the general class perspective. This perspective seems to be facing a rapidly growing number of "anomalies," that is, "new and unexpected phenomena" that cannot be accommodated within the dominant paradigmatic view (Kuhn 1970: 54). In this context, three points made by Kuhn are of particular relevance.[3]

First, Kuhn points out that competing paradigms are incommensurable and therefore hard to adjudicate. Advocates of challenged paradigms can defend them through "adjustments" and "developments" that accommodate at least some of the anomalies. These accommodative tendencies, one

---

*Many arguments presented in this chapter were developed in discussions with my colleague and collaborator Malcolm Waters and presented in more detail in Pakulski and Waters 1996a, b. Therefore many occurrences of *I* in the text should be *we*. However, mindful of the contentious nature of the claims I am making, I prefer to use the singular, if only to signal that the responsibility for possible errors is solely mine.

may add, are particularly strong in the case of socially "implicated" paradigms that underlie popular Weltanschauungen, ideological creeds, and disciplinary commitments. The deeper the implication and the heavier the investments in the paradigmatic view, the stronger the tendency to adjust a paradigm rather than abandon it. Indeed, the adjustments and reformulations proposed by some contemporary defenders of class paradigm seem to confirm that. Work of Wright (1985, 1989, 1994, 1996) and his collaborators, especially Baxter et al. (1991), represents one of the most sophisticated adjustments and reformulations of neo-Marxist class theory and perspective.

Second, as stressed by Kuhn (1970), paradigms never die out of sheer cumulation of anomalies. Rather, they deteriorate and are gradually superseded by more parsimonious and/or general paradigms, which are more capable of accommodating the most glaring anomalies. (Indeed, anomalies cease to be so when reinterpreted within alternative paradigms.) While in the natural sciences changes of paradigms are typically "revolutionary," in the social sciences, one may argue after Mulkay (1979), paradigmatic transformations occur typically through gradual deterioration and loss of interest rather than through sudden revolutionary replacement.

The third and closely related point concerns the incommensurate nature of paradigms. Because they are metatheoretical constructs, empirical adjudication between rival paradigmatic views is extremely difficult, and communication across paradigms is seldom successful. One of the key problems encountered when confronting interparadigmatic arguments is diversity of meanings attributed to the key terms. Therefore I begin by outlining the class paradigm and its core components before moving on to discuss the "anomalies" and outlining an alternative interpretation of politics. Finally, I conclude with a comment on the prospects for interparadigmatic adjudication.

Class Paradigm

It is worth starting by dispelling some possible misreadings of my argument. First, it does not imply that class, understood here as a social formation, is impossible and that class paradigm, class theory, and class analysis have never been useful. Rather, I argue that their utility was much more defensible in the analyses of politics in the early twentieth century, when class divisions, identities, and solidarities in Europe and North America were strong. Second, the rejection of class interpretation implies neither the end of capitalism, nor the disappearance of social stratification, nor a reduction in social inequality, nor the abating of social conflicts, nor, finally, the "end of social" or declining relevance of political sociology. Social inequalities, divisions, and conflicts persist and may even increase in their intensity, despite the decomposition of class. In fact, I argue that the demise of class and the accompanying waning of class organizations are likely to contribute to the broadening of social inequalities and sharpening of conflicts. This is because the nearly century-long egalitarian trends in advanced societies (that came to an end in the 1980s) reflected the impact of class conflicts and the pressures exerted by working-class organizations and because the class-based organizations played a crucial role in the "settlement" of social conflicts in the post-World War II decades. Third, I confine my argument to the so-called advanced industrial societies.

Class (in adjective form) refers here to a specific form of stratification and conflict and (as a noun) to specific strata and social formations they engender. *Class paradigm* or *class perspective* refers to a way of looking at societies, a view that contains the following assumptions about the key processes, causalities, and directions of change:[4]

1. About principal causality. Class is fundamentally an economic phenomenon; it reflects the primary (though not necessarily exclusive) causal role of capital ownership and market capacities, especially labor-market capacities, in structuring the material interests and social relationships, as well as sociopolitical cleavages.[5]
2. About groupness. Although class formation may differ in its strength and clarity, typically classes are more than statistical aggregates or taxonomic categories. They become real social formations reflected in observable patterns of inequality, association/distance, and, ultimately, conflict.
3. About sociopolitical and sociocultural articulation. Class inequalities and cleavages form, if not the principal, then at least important and persisting, bases for collective consciousness, identity, and action outside the arena of economic production (for example, political allegiances and voting preferences, etc).[6]
4 About transforming capacity. The major patterns of conflict and contestation in advanced capitalism reflect primarily (though not exclusively) class interests and class divisions. Classes are potential collective actors in the economic and political fields. Insofar as they consciously struggle against other classes, they can transform the general set of social arrangements of which they are a part.

It must be stressed that not all these assumptions are embraced in every class approach or with equal vigor. More orthodox Marxists tend to embrace all four of them and seek to relate all significant social phenomena to class structures and processes (e.g., Miliband 1977, 1989). Some neo-Marxist scholars, however, distance themselves from the assumption of transformative capacity and concentrate on groupness and sociocultural articulation. Some seek to develop a "weak" class analysis that "has as its central concern the study of relationships among class structures, class mobility, class-based inequalities, and class-based action" (Goldthorpe and Marshall 1992: 382).[7] Furthermore, there are differences of view among class theorists as to the precise meanings of "fundamentally economic phenomenon," "primary causal role," "real formations," and "transforming capacity." For example, Wright and some of his followers would object to unduly deterministic interpretations of the above propositions and would stress the contingency of class formation and the relative autonomy of politics (see Wright 1985, 1996; Western 1991).[8] In some formulations, class analysis becomes synonymous with stratification studies, with merely the focus on class (rather than, say, status hierarchy) seen as "a conceptual choice that must be made *a priori*" (Goldthorpe and Marshall 1992: 382).

Thus there are variations in the interpretation of class perspective and a tendency for an increasing modesty in the expectations as to what the class analysis can deliver. However, both class theorists and more modest class analysts assume some form of "class primacy." It would make little sense to apply the adjective *class* to a theory arguing that, say, race, gender, or civic status constitutes the primary source of social divisions and conflicts. Similarly, a "class analysis" that finds no evidence of important class divisions is clearly misnamed.[9]

Class analysts of politics endorse the notion of class primacy even when they reject economic determinism (a term that has many meanings). They focus on as causal link and correspondence between class divisions and political divisions on the aggregate level and between class membership and political preferences and behavior on the individual level. These links and correspondence have typically been analyzed in terms of class interest representation, class (party and ideological) alignment, class voting, class issues and programs, class consciousness, class ideology, and class action. Therefore a good test of adherence to class primacy and to the class paradigm is the acceptance of alternative (nonclass) causalities and divisions as important or even predominant in shaping politics—something that characterizes, as I argue below, Weberian approaches.

The Anomalies

The centerpiece anomaly raised by the critics of class interpretation of politics is party-class dealignment. It refers to a number of interrelated and parallel processes: a decline of class-based organizations and of class-specific political appeals and a waning of class imagery in politics (see, e.g., Dunleavy 1980, 1987; Sarlvik and Crewe 1983; and Rose and McAllister 1985). Dealignment, it is argued, is combined with the weakening of class voting, class identification, class consciousness and action and with the rise of new politics propelled by "post-ideological" values. These processes, diagnosed already in the 1970s and 1980s, accompany a dissolution of the corporatist frameworks within which national classes thrived (Crook et al. 1992: 79–105). I will comment on these processes under five subheadings:

1. Class Voting and Class-based Allegiance

Traditionally the most popular measure of dealignment was the Alford Index of party-class voting (Alford 1963: 79–80). This was constructed by taking the percentage of voters in manual occupations who cast votes for left-of-center parties and subtracting from it the percentage of voters in nonmanual occupations voting for such parties. The index has been declining since the 1940s in almost all advanced societies for which longitudinal data on voting behavior are available (Clark and Lipset 1991; Clark et al. 1993; Hout et al. 1995; Nieuwbeerta 1997). Although the decline varies in its pace and intensity, it appears nevertheless to be universal (tables 7.1 and 7.2).[10]

Critics of the Alford Index focus on its alleged crudeness. Thus Heath et al. (1985) criticize the index for its sensitivity to the variation in the popularity of the major political parties. Western et al. (1991), Hout et al. (1993), and Manza and Brooks (1996: 720) point out that it assumes a simplistic two-class model of society and politics and "cannot distinguish between realignment (structural change in the class bases of party support) and dealignment (statistical independence between class and party support)." While these criticisms are not entirely convincing,[11] there has been broad agreement that the Alford Index may distort the voting trends because it focuses on absolute rather than relative rates of class defection in voting and because it utilizes a dichotomous, and therefore overly crude, class scheme (Heath et al. 1985: 154; Marshall et al. 1988: 230–236; Hout et al. 1995: 807; Manza and Brooks 1996: 721). In response to

Table 7.1

Class Voting in Advanced Societies, 1960s–1980s: The Alford Index and the Proportion of Variance in Left Voting Explained by the "Social Structure" Variables

	Alford Index		Variance Explained	
	1960s	1980s	1960s	1980s
Sweden	46	34	28	18
Great Britain	42	21	19	10
West Germany	26	10	15	16
France	20	14	19	6
Untied States	18	8	10	11

Sources: Based on Lipset 1981: 505; Franklin et al. 1992: 387; Clark et al. 1993: 312.

Table 7.2

Class Voting in Fifteen Advanced Societies as Measured by Thomsen (T) and Alford (A) Indexes, 1945–1990

	1945–1960		1961–1970		1971–1980		1981–1990	
	T	A	T	A	T	A	T	A
Australia	1.38	32.9	1.22	29.3	1.16	27.8	0.80	19.4
Austria	—	—	1.12	27.4	1.28	28.9	0.76	18.3
Belgium	—	—	1.21	25.4	0.87	17.9	0.80	16.4
Britain	1.64	37.3	1.67	38.3	1.07	24.3	0.90	23.4
Canada	0.30	7.0	0.31	7.7	—	—	0.27	4.0
Denmark	1.82	39.8	2.33	52.0	1.18	28.1	0.97	20.9
Finland	2.17	48.4	2.24	50.2	1.60	36.9	1.52	35.7
France	1.01	24.4	0.76	18.3	0.72	17.0	0.48	11.7
Germany	1.55	36.0	1.06	24.8	0.61	14.9	0.55	13.4
Ireland			0.88	14.1	0.77	8.7	0.70	7.3
Italy	1.13	26.6	0.66	14.5	0.73	17.8	0.53	13.1
Netherlands	0.61	14.0	0.65	14.7	0.94	21.8	0.68	15.5
Norway	2.39	52.5	1.38	32.0	1.43	33.8	0.84	20.5
Sweden	2.26	51.0	1.73	40.7	1.57	37.3	1.36	32.7
United States	0.67	16.2	0.36	7.7	0.46	10.9	0.34	8.1

Source: Based on Nieuwbeerta's (1997: 45–53) analysis of aggregated country data sets. Countries with data missing for more that one decade were excluded from this table.

these criticisms, two additional measures of class voting have been proposed, both independent of variation in popularity of political parties and
utilizing more complex class schemes, one based on regression technique,
another on the odds-ratio (Franklin et al. 1992; Heath et al. 1985; Thomsen 1987; Niewbeerta 1997).

Franklin et al.'s (1992) study of electoral behavior in 16 industrialized
societies between the 1960s and 1980s focuses on the impact of class position on party support and voting patterns. The importance of this study
rests not only on its impressive comparative scope but also on the sophisticated methodology that uses regression techniques to reveal electoral
trends. The study confirms what the Alford Index has already shown,
namely, that contemporary electoral choice, with the possible exception of
the more recent trends in the United States (on which more below), is decreasingly influenced by class cleavages.[12]

Some critics point to the conjectural factors in elections and the possibility of political realignments along new class lines (Hout et al. 1995;
Weakliem and Western 1999). However, the empirical support for this
suggestion is rather weak. If one follows the suggestions of Franklin et al.
(1992) and looks at the longer electoral trends, one finds a decline in class
voting in most advanced societies but occurring at different times (earlier
in the United States and later in Western Europe and Australia). The same
applies to political/voting apathy, the area where some of the alleged
"class effects" have been diagnosed. Such apathy has been much more suc-
cessfully explained within a long-term rather than a short-term time frame
and by a combination of unemployment and racial inequality rather than
by class (Manza et al. 1995; Clark et al. 1993).

The similar results are shown when an odds-ratio-based Thomsen Index
is used in measuring the level of class voting (table 7.2). Unlike the Alford
Index, the Thomsen Index is not sensitive to the changing popularity of
parties and therefore offers a better measure of the class-vote relationship.
In a simple two-class version the index shows the odds for manual workers
voting for left-of-center parties divided by the odds for nonmanual workers voting in the same way. The natural logarithm of that ratio constitutes
the log-odds-ratio. The higher the odds-ratio and the log-odds-ratio, the
higher the level of class voting (Nieuwbeerta 1997: 39–41). Table 7.2
shows the results for a more complex seven-class scheme (introduced by
Goldthorpe) and thus counters also the criticism of oversimplification of
class scheme that has been directed against the users of the Alford Index.
As the table shows, the levels of class voting in 15 advanced societies for

which comprehensive data are available (except in the Netherlands) have declined between 1945 and 1990. This decline is evident in the Alford and the Thomsen indexes.

The observers of European, North American, and Australian politics in the 1990s would not be surprised by these findings. Dealignment there was diagnosed long ago, and attributed to the collapse and/or reformation of the traditional class-oriented parties, the spread of the catch-all appeals, and the rise of the left-libertarian and right-populist political movements. In Australia, Britain, and Germany, the dealignment was accompanied by the success of the "new Labour" in attracting the white collars. In other countries (such as Italy and France), it has been marked by high electoral volatility and partisan reshuffles. Thus, "the breakdown of linkages between particular social groups and political parties which used to represent the interests of those groups electorally" (Franklin et al. 1992: 408) seems to have continued in the late 1990s.

The Netherlands, the United States, and Canada appear as slightly deviant cases: they show a fluctuation rather than a continuous decline in class voting. Franklin et al. (1992) suggest an explanation for the North American cases. They argue that because the class dealignment in North America occurred largely before World War II, it is less likely to be detected in the more recent data. Hout et al. (1993, 1995) offer an alternative account. They see fluctuating class politics of de- and realignments in the United States. However, the evidence they offer of "trendless fluctuation" in American class voting (especially in the last 30 years) can hardly convince a class agnostic that class voting is alive.

Thus neither the unreliable measures of class voting nor the simplistic conceptualizations of class can be blamed for masking the allegedly significant and persistent impact of class location on voting. A decline in class voting diagnosed regardless of whether one uses the Alford Index or more complex regression models and regardless of whether class is conceptualized in the di- or trichotomous occupational terms (manual/nonmanual/farm) or in a more complex fashion.

The final line of defense for advocates of class analysis, such as Hout et al. (1993), is the argument that classes still exist as important social entities and forces, even when they lose their sociopolitical articulators and "remain latent in the political arena"(Hout et al. 1993: 266). While that may be true, the latency argument poses a particularly tricky question: How do we know that these "latent classes" and "latent class interests" exist?

2. The Weakening of Class Organizations

The major "class organizers" and "class persuaders," especially parties of the Left, have been destabilized by the process of class dealignment. After electoral defeats in the 1980s, the leadership of the parties weakened or completely abandoned class appeals and moved to the middle ground. This proved a winning strategy. The recovery of "new Labour" and "diluted Socialists" in the "pink wave" of 1997 was achieved by effective appeals to mass audiences across class divisions. The New Labour Party in Britain, following on the Australian model, became a typical "catch-all, middle-of-the-road" party attracting votes from all strata and occupational categories. In Italy, after the Socialist Party (PSI) literally decomposed in the early 1990s along with the Communist Party (PCI) and the Christian Democrats, the successful "Olive Tree" alliance marked the decline in class rhetoric and appeals.

Clearly, decline and rise in support for the socialist Left is contingent and periodical. However, the electoral cycles also show a trend of declining support for those political forces that appeal to and ally themselves with class-specific idioms, issues, programs, and rhetoric. The winners are those who adjusted their appeals and embraced the nonclass issues of market efficiency, international competition, deregulation, citizen autonomy, privacy, women's rights, and the environment.[13] Another aspect of this decline is the rapid rise of various "third" and unaligned forces, including single-issue movements and parties, and the proliferation of "independents." Although these "third forces," which most clearly abandon class appeals, formed marginal residua in the postwar period, they have been moving since the 1970s toward the political mainstream. Their rise to prominence mirrors the decline of class-based parties.

The organizations that are perhaps the most affected by the decline of class are the archetypal "representatives of the working class," the trade unions. Their decline has been universal in the industrialized world and most rapid among the young and highly skilled workers in the competitive sectors of the economy (Western 1995; Golden and Pontusson 1992; Regini 1992). The proportion of the workforce belonging to trade union in the United States has declined from 33 percent in 1955 to 16 percent in 1995, while participation in such "single-issue" civic groups as the National Organization for Women, the ecological Sierra Club, and the American Association of Retired Persons has increased rapidly. The symptoms of deunionization include not only declining membership but also the multiple fragmentation of union organizations. Large union bodies seem unable to cater to the increasingly diverse demands and interests of their constituencies. Indeed, such an interpretation seems to be increasingly popular among students of unionism and industrial relations (Kern and Sabel 1992).[14]

The most rapidly declining large trade unions have been the main organizations promoting class identification, consciousness, solidarity, and political behavior among the increasingly diverse workers. Their decline in the core areas of employment has been weakening a major mechanism of the social reproduction of the working class, thus contributing to its social dissolution. This decline has compounded the declining impact union membership has on class identification and political behavior.

The crisis of class organizations affects not only the Left but also those right-of-center parties that cultivate the economic and social class–issue repertoires and coat their appeals in class rhetoric and imagery. While many right-of-center coalitions (e.g., in Germany) have initially benefited from the decline of the organized Left, the more established right-of-center parties have also experienced the effects of dealignment. In the early 1970s, a whole family of right-of-center "progress," "populist," "protest," and "tax-revolt" parties appeared, first in northern Europe and then across the Continent (Betz 1994). Seen initially as typical "flash parties," they soon proved a consolidated political force and a permanent feature of the political landscape. Moreover, their allegedly "petty bourgeois" character proved to be a misnomer. The popularity of populist parties grows among both the manual working and new white-collar categories. Their programs bear little relation to the model of class issues and concerns (antiliberalism, antiindustrialism). They turn not so much against the welfare state—a quintessential class issue in the post–World War II period—as against what are called excesses and disfunctions of welfarism, uncontrolled immigration, and, more recently in Western Europe, the foreign *diktat* of the European Union, the World Bank, and the International Monetary Fund. These issues, it is suggested, represent the perception of threat to one's status, lifestyle, and values rather than the mobilizations of a class type.[15]

3. Class Identification, Consciousness, and Action

Popular images of social structure are still expressed predominantly in class terms, but the concept has taken on a variety of meanings that are often contradictory. However, empirical research on class imagery reveals "complex, diverse, fragmentary, ambiguous and even contradictory class conceptions" (Graetz and McAllister 1994: 238). Within this complexity, the "gradational model," typically interpreted in pecuniary fashion, is by far the most popular. In this model, "class" is identified with level of income and wealth (Lockwood 1966; Blackburn and Mann 1975; Graetz 1986; Emmison 1991). Moreover, there is little correspondence between class imagery and actual class location and little correspondence between class identification and political behavior (e.g., voting). Equally, there is only a weak relationship between imagery and what Graetz (1983: 80) calls "class sentiments" and little evidence of a relation to what Mann (1973: 13) identified as "class consciousness."[16] Indeed, the concept of class consciousness seems to lose its popularity rapidly, and it seldom figures in the repertoires of contemporary empirical research on social conflict.

Research fragmentation, differences in conceptualization of class and class consciousness, and methodological differences make it difficult to draw any clear conclusions as to the trends in class imagery, identification, and consciousness. However, if one follows the suggestion of Wright (1985) that class consciousness should be analyzed through both sentiments and *action*, there can be little doubt of a decline over the last decades. The waves of class conflicts that washed across Western societies in the 1950s and 1960s have since diminished to a ripple. In the mid-1990s industrial conflict in the Organization for Economic Cooperation and Development countries fell to its lowest level for over 50 years. In the 1990–1995 period an annual average of working days lost to labor disputes per 1,000 employees in 22 OECD countries was 100 compared with 145 in 1985–1990 and over 200 in the 1970s (*Financial Times*, September 4, 1996).

There are also indications that class has very little cultural and political significance. The participants in the Comparative Project on Class Structure and Class Consciousness in Australia, Emmison and Western (1991; see also Emmison 1991: 274) argue that class has little consequence for lived experience and little cultural significance. Their research findings confirm that the salience of class identification in Australia is extremely low, well below a whole range of such identity sources as gender, religion, ethnicity, age, and even support for a sport team. From this they have concluded that "the discursive salience of class for identity is almost minimal" (Emmison and Western 1990: 241). Other studies have confirmed the weak nexus among economic position, identification, political attitudes, and political activism.[17] While class identities seem to be dwindling, new political identities are being formed around such highly publicized and politically prominent issues as ethnicity, gender, and lifestyle. These identities, to which we now turn, seem to be displacing the old class identities as generators of political preference and action, at least among the young and among educated urbanites.

4. The Rise of New Politics

While diagnoses of detachment of politics from class divisions seem to proliferate (Rose and McAllister 1985; Crewe 1992; Franklin et al. 1992; Clark et al. 1993; Kitschelt 1994; Inglehart 1996), there is less agreement as to the nature and shape of new political divisions. In their pioneering analysis of political change in Germany, Baker et al. (1981) coined the term *new politics* to typify these new political configurations. Conceptualizations of new politics vary widely and include: new value preferences (Inglehart 1991, 1996), new issues and concerns (Dalton 1988), new political culture, especially the norms of direct involvement (Gibbins 1989; Clark 1995), new institutional forms, including the new social movements (Scott 1990), and new social bases and new political paradigms (Offe 1985). However, the new politics is invariably contrasted with "old," party-controlled, organized, bureaucratized, and class-based politics.

For Baker et al. (1981) a key feature of new politics is its generational base.[18] By contrast, the importance of class allegiances, identities, and behavior has been declining. In a passage that has been elaborated in Franklin et al.'s (1992) subsequent study, Baker et al. (1981: 192) declare that "the declining importance of class appears to be the major factor in accounting for the decline in the explanatory power of social characteristics as a whole." A similar diagnosis is offered by Inglehart (1991, 1996). He argues that new political configurations reflect new value preferences brought about by postwar generations. Inglehart defines the new value priorities as "postmaterialist," that is, as reflecting concerns that transcend the old concerns with material well-being and security. Post-materialist value hierarchies prioritize quality of life, self-actualization, and civil liberties and are carried by post–World War II generations sharing the formative experience of the "long boom." Their ascendancy in advanced West accompanies a "postmodern shift" and comes hand in hand with the declining importance of class.

This seems to confirm Kitschelt's (1994) account of the detachment of contemporary party politics from class divisions and ideologies and the emergence of new political divisions that cut across the left-right ideological spectrum. This class-related master-cleavage, according to Kitschelt, is ceasing to be an adequate conceptual guide to contemporary political divisions in advanced societies. Increasingly, voter preferences and party choices are based on such factors as organizational location, production sector, generation and life cycle, gender, and consumption style. New politics reflects the growing salience of these divisions and the corresponding decomposition of the old class ideological-political cleavages. Young and skilled blue-collar workers, for example, working in internationally competitive economic sectors turn against the traditional "working-class" packages of protection and welfare. Their older and less-skilled colleagues working in domestic services and manufacturing, together with low-skilled white-collar workers, support authoritarian and right-populist appeals. Highly educated "symbol-processors" working in the public sector and human services, especially women, show strong preferences for libertarian policies with a socialist bent.[19]

This diversification (diagnosed already in the 1950s and 1960s as "class decomposition" [Dahrendorf 1959]) seems to be gaining pace. Politics, as contemporary critics observe, ceases to be a distributive game monopolized by corporate class actors. Political agendas expand, and their social bases diversify. Like post-Fordist production, politics becomes specialized and issue-centered. It responds to specific sensitivities of increasingly diverse segments of population differentiated by education level, skills, gender, generation, family, religion, type of work, sector of the economy, exposure to international markets, and sexual preferences. This is a politics of fickle formations, where lasting party loyalties are as rare as brand loyalties in contemporary consumption.

5. Post-Ideological Values

Liberalism, conservatism, and socialism crystallized in the nineteenth century in the context of growing class divisions and conflicts. Socialism, in particular, was an ideological child of industrial class conflict, but liberalism and conservatism were also reformulated in response to the socialist challenge. The "imagined communities" of class grew increasingly reliant on such ideological constructs because of their increasing internal heterogeneity. The appropriation of the major political ideologies by national classes occurred via the class-oriented organizations, mainly working-class-oriented parties and trade unions. The ideological packages were products of activists and ideologists in these organizations striving for mass support. Party leaders and intellectuals defined class issues and formulated general strategies that were then used in political appeals. The supporters could now constitute social classes not so much on the basis of commonalities of fate—these commonalties have been declining with the growing industrial complexity—as on the basis of shared organizational loyalties and ideological commitments. This also resulted in the articulation of popular class discourses, class identities, and the strengthening of a left/right polarity in political attitudes.[20]

This ideological articulation of classes is now crumbling. A survey of the Socialist parties conducted by Lipset (1991) shows a "consistent abandonment of social welfare state/distributive issues" and of traditional socialist strategies. Throughout the early 1990s the egalitarian-etatist principles and the etatist strategies that formed the backbone of socialism were abandoned by most parties of the Left. The most ideologically committed organizations, such as the British and Australian Labour parties and the Communist parties in Italy and France, could be revived only by shedding their traditional ideological commitments. Similar developments are described by surveys of Social Democratic parties in Europe (Kitschelt and Hellmans 1990; Kitschelt 1994).

However, it is not merely socialism that is decomposing. Rather, the fundamental and underlying ideological polarity of left and right seems to be undermined by the emergence of new dimensions of politics, unaligned issues, and the mobilization of ideological melanges, such as those of North American "New Fiscal Populists," the Western European left-libertarians and right-populists, and the northern European right-progressionists. The emergence of civil rights concerns, "lifestyle politics," consumer choice, ecological prudence, and feminist concerns has exceeded the inclusive capacities of the old ideologies. Despite such desperate attempts at accommodation as the "green Left" and the "new Right," these new concerns are splitting and overshadowing the old ideological packages. Inglehart (1991, 1996), Dalton and Kuechler (1990), Poguntke (1993), and Giddens (1996) each argue that the class-related left/right division loses its polar character and is now cross-cut by an old-new dimension. In fact, Kitschelt (1994: 27) charts the new political-ideological orientations along three axes: socialist-capitalist, libertarian-authoritarian, and left-right, resulting in six major ideological clusters. These clusters, one should stress again, are detached from class positions and class interests.

Paradigmatic Shifts

All these "anomalies" prompt critical revisions of class theories and the paradigmatic shift to a more inclusive Weberian approach. This shift is in many ways analogous to the nineteenth-century shift that gave birth to the class paradigm. Even in late nineteenth-century Europe, social divisions and conflicts were comprehensible to most observers in terms of "status (estate) politics." What Marx and Engels saw as new entities—the bourgeoisie and the working class—appeared either as parts of the "third estate" (analogous to today's all-inclusive middle class) or as an altogether new "fourth estate" (an analogue of a "new class"). Indeed, the estate vision offered as useful a way of comprehending social conflicts in nineteenth-century Europe as class does: estates were the popular label, estate consciousness and identity predominated over class, and social conflicts were coated in the language of "rights" and "privileges" typical of the estate politics. For a nineteenth-century observer, one may even say for the budding social scientific community, there was no obvious need for a switch in imagery. The "death of estate" claims made by Marx and Engels were greeted with incredulity. To their contemporaries, estates were alive and strong. Perhaps there were just new "intra-estate divisions" or, possibly, the symptoms of a rising "new estate." This incompatibility of visions was reflected in a somewhat exasperated tone of a footnote Engels added to the 1885 German edition of Marx's *Poverty of Philosophy:* "The revolution of the bourgeoisie abolished the estates and their privileges. Bourgeois society knows only *classes*. It was, therefore, in contradiction with history to describe the proletariat as the "fourth estate," (quoted after Lopreato and Lewis 1974: 31; emphasis in original).

One may well argue that the estate vision of society was not so much incorrect as exhausted in nineteenth-century Europe. Its metanarrative was losing plausibility, and it faced cumulation of anomalies in the form of social divisions and conflicts that required constant "adjustments" (the defenders of estates would say "developments") of the scheme. As Engels' footnote testifies, such adjustments were made, and they doubtless satisfied the defenders of the estate vision. However, the class paradigm improved a capacity to engage the main social problems of the time, in particular, to make sense of what became known as the social question.

What we observe today is a similar deterioration of the class paradigm and a shift toward more diverse and inclusive interpretive schemes. As the class paradigm deteriorates, class explanations of politics lose consistency and parsimony. Advocates of class vision face a growing number of anomalies, especially when they try to identify the key political actors and account for conflict and change. Class accounts fail to make sense of the partisan shifts, libertarian and populist movements, gender politics, and neonationalism. The most damning evidence of their declining explanatory power comes from the most recent historical events: the ascendancy and decline of the Asian "tigers," the Eastern European "velvet revolutions," and the European unification. None of these crucial historical developments has involved what may plausibly be called class interests, class actors, class identities, class conflicts, or class ideologies. This is a most serious failure, because class paradigm proves impotent in the very task for which it was originally constructed: identifying the "rules of motion" of modern society.

In retrospect, we can see the period of "organized capitalism"(Lash and Urry 1987), especially the European "liberal corporatism,"[21] as the highest point in the historical life cycle of class formation and the zenith of class-paradigmatic domination. In the first half of the twentieth century, class cleavages in Western Europe were well articulated, and class-oriented milieu parties and trade unions acquired a central role in the political process defined and legitimized as a "democratic class struggle" (Lipset 1960; Korpi 1983) or "institutionalized class conflicts" (Dahrendorf 1959). The interests of large and heterogeneous social categories were defined by these organizations in a way that laid the foundations for broad class appeals and that generated recognizable sets of class issues. These issues of wages, working conditions, and welfare entitlements dominated the political agenda. Stimulated by appeals to class interests and solidarities, class identifications became popular even outside the working-class milieu as the concept of the middle class entered the popular vocabulary. With it, class discourses became the legitimate language of politics. The political organizers of class—trade unions, milieu parties, and their leaders—took over the dominant class-reproducing role. Within the political programs and platforms of these self-declared class bodies, class issues and interests were elaborated and disseminated. So were the class ideologies. Socialism, liberalism, and conservatism become associated with broad class interests because of their deployment as political formulas of the major class-organizing parties. Popular identifications and outlooks were increasingly shaped by political activism and ideological appeals of these class organizations. Working classes were closely identified with Labor and Social Democratic Party support and with allegiance to the socialist-left position (itself defined through Social Democratic Party platforms). Middle classes were defined in terms of the political programs of centrist and liberal-conservative parties and in terms of liberal-conservative outlooks and ideologies.[22]

Over the last decades we have been experiencing the reversal of these trends. Explanations of these reversals and "class-anomalous" developments vary widely. Dunleavy (1980) attributes ideological and political dealignment to detraditionalization. Baker et al. (1981) and Dalton (1988) argue that new cleavages represent new political-ideological dimensions reflecting educational upgrading and progressive individualism. Franklin (1985) attributes them to changing party appeals and breakdowns in class-party socialization. McAllister (1992) points to the growing importance of nonclass and marginal electorates. Inglehart (1991, 1996) links the decline of old (materialist and class-oriented) politics with increasing education, generational change, and the rise of post-materialist values. Franklin et al. (1992) identify the process of particularization that undermines the class-specific repertoires of concerns. Clark et al. (1993) link the new trends with increasing affluence, privatism, and mobility. Giddens (1996) points to increasing reflexivity, and Crook et al. (1992) suggest the combined impact of intensified differentiation, rationalization, and commodification. Whatever combination of factors are responsible, all these authors seem to agree that the combination of social change and new political formatting undermine the old social, ideological, and political-organization divisions and polarities of the class type and, with them, the relevance of the class paradigm.

Conclusion

While empirically incommensurate, paradigmatic interpretations can be assessed in terms of relative parsimony, plausibility—the capacity to generate anomalies—and overall relevance. The class paradigm, I would argue, has deteriorated beyond repair. Its capacity to "make sense" of the contemporary political configurations and processes in advanced societies and to deal with "anomalies" has declined. In spite of this decline and in spite of the rapidly shrinking intellectual return its offers, it is likely to persist. As Kuhn (1970) points out, paradigms can live with anomalies. Their resilience is proportional to the intellectual investments made by their advocates and to their ideological implications. The class paradigm was widely used and heavily implicated in the main ideological confrontations of the twentieth century. The advocates of class paradigm are less willing to abandon it than to "adjust" it through semantic stretch, "shrinking" and "morphing." The semantic stretch (Sartori 1970) involves extension of the meaning of the key concepts, such as class, so it applies to increasingly heterogeneous social entities and processes. Thus one may extend class maps and multiply classes to cover the skill and organizational assets (Wright 1985), educational credentials (Bell, 1973) and "cultural capital" (Bourdieu 1987), or even suggest that class is synonymous with occupation (Grusky and Sorensen 1997). The "shrinking" involves reduction in explanatory and/or research aspirations, increasing modesty regarding the scope of explained and researched phenomena. Thus many class analysts acknowledge the paradigm's inability to account adequately for "overdetermined," "complex," and/or "autonomous" processes of group formation, political activism and conflict, but still continue to embrace the class view of politics. The "morphing" strategy, described well by Waters (1994), consist of a gradual abandonment of the key assumptions of the class approach and a convergence with rival interpretive schemes. Thus many class schemes gradually converge with neo-Weberian and occupational-status ones, though they seldom abandon the original terminology.

Such adjustments face class analysts with several dilemmas. First, there is a dilemma of identity. The more successful the adjustments introduced to the class paradigm, the less distinguishable the adjusted "class models" and "class schemes" from their main competitors, especially neo-Weberian, status attainment, and human capital models. Class paradigm can maintain credibility only by sacrificing its identity. Second, there is a dilemma of theoretical relevance. As the class paradigm is adjusted by restricting its explanatory aspirations (through shrinking), the less relevant it becomes. The resulting increasingly modest versions tell us less and less about contemporary conflict and change. This is particularly apparent when they are compared with the original Marxist promise and the potential of its current competitors. Third, there is a dilemma of political and ideological salience. The more thorough and successful the adjustments proposed by contemporary class analysts, the less ideologically exciting the theoretical outcomes in terms of alignment with historical forces and emancipatory potential. The question these dilemmas pose is not so much, Can we save the class paradigm? but rather, Is it worth saving?

Notes

1. *Class paradigm, interpretation, vision* and *perspective* are used here as synonyms.
2. The recent debates are in the *American Sociological Review* 58, no. 1; *British Journal of Sociology* 44, nos. 2, 3; *International Journal of Urban and Regional Research* 15, no. 1; *International Sociology* 8, no. 3; 9, nos. 2–3; *Sociology* 24, no. 2; 26, nos. 2–3; 28, nos. 2, 2–4; and *Theory and Society* 25, no. 5. See also Marshall et al. 1988; Baxter et al. 1991; Lee and Turner 1996; Pakulski and Waters 1996a; Wright 1985, 1994, 1996; Holton and Turner 1989, 1994; Franklin et al. 1992; Clark et al. 1993; Clark 1995; Marshall 1997; and Hall 1997. The most comprehensive analysis of class voting can be found in Nieuwbeerta 1997.

3. These Kuhnian suggestions, however, are taken here not in the spirit of faithful exegesis but in an instrumental way, in order to highlight the point on the difficulties one encounters in challenging class interpretation. Some points I am making, in fact, depart from Kuhn's views. For example, my observations on the deterioration of paradigmatic models in the social sciences follow the ideas of Lakatos (1970) and Mulkay (1979).

4. Class theory specifies empirically testable causalities among socioeconomic, sociocultural, and sociopolitical aspects of class formation. The term *class analysis* is more contentious and less clear; it typically refers to a research program founded on some, but not all, core elements of class theory. While accepting the centrality of class, class analysts are more agnostic about the sociocultural articulation and transforming capacity of class (encapsulated in propositions 3 and 4 below).

5. "Ownership of the means of production and ownership of one's own labor power are explanatory of social action because these property rights shape the strategic alternatives people face in pursuing their material well being" (Wright 1996: 695).

6. This causal connection is the principal legitimizing claim for the continuing salience of class analysis.

7. See, in particular, Lee and Turner 1996; also Hout et al. 1993, 1995; and Manza and Brooks 1996.

8. Wright has also adjusted the class paradigm by multiplying the productive assets (to three) and therefore the ownership-exploitative class relations (thus increasing the number of classes to 12), and by further toning down the economic determination. Western et al. (1991) and Hout et al. (1995) propose significant adjustments in the fourth proposition and suggest a new way of measuring class effects in voting.

9. Wright (1996: 694) and Goldthorpe and Marshall (1992: 381) reject the claim that class analysis assumes "class primacy." However, they acknowledge that they believe in the "enduring importance of class divisions" (Wright 1996; 694), and/or they do not offer any alternative (to class) analytical and theoretical scheme, thus implicitly embracing class as the major analytical contender and class theory as the principal explanatory scheme.

10. This decline has been particularly steep in Australia. Cohort analysis indicates that class voting declines with age and that it was highest among the cohorts who voted for the first time in the 1930s (McAllister 1992: 161). Weakliem and Western (1999), however, suggest that much of the decline in the "general" class voting involves "realignment" of some middle-class groups.

11. For a start, while simple in its construction, the index is extremely useful in international and historical comparisons because of the clarity and universality of the manual/nonmanual division on which it relies. Moreover, the division discerned by the index corresponds very closely to the *major* industrial class division as defined by class theory, a fact that is recognized even by the harshest critics of the index. After all, dealignment is significant only if it affects the major classes and their political representatives and only if it can be confirmed in many societies. The critics also argue that the Alford Index allegedly assumes an "unmediated" connection between class and voting (Marshall et al. 1988; Hout et al. 1993). Again, this not a serious shortcoming. If sociopolitical "mediation" is the main means for class reproduction, a relaxation of the links between political organizations and their class constituencies will cause a failure in class patterning.

12. The analogous analyses of the 1987–1996 Australian Election Study data demonstrate a similar trend, thus confirming the diagnoses of a gradual decline in the importance of class voting since the 1960s by Kemp (1978: 348), Aitkin (1982: 315), and McAllister (1992: 158). "While social structure does appear to have been an important determinant of partisanship in most countries in the 1960s (explaining more than sixteen per cent of variance in left voting in eleven countries), by the 1980s there were only five countries left where this was still true. Even more telling, while in the 1960s there were eight countries in which more than twenty per cent of variance was explained by social structure (Norway, Belgium, Denmark, Netherlands, Sweden, Italy, France and Britain), by the 1980s only Norway and Italy were left in this position" (Franklin et al. 1992: 388).

13. Some left-of-center parties under strong reformist leadership have refashioned their appeals. For example, the Danish and German Social Democrats and the Labour parties in Australia, New

Zealand, and Britain remodeled themselves in that way and emerged in the late 1980s as champions of market reforms, the environment, civil rights, and affirmative action for women.

14. As Golden and Pontusson (1992) suggest, this is a crisis of *large* unions that attempt to represent large sections of employees in a general and indiscriminate idiom of sectional (class) interests.

15. The chauvinism of social entitlements, combined with a strong vision of us versus them, fits well the new dimension of "postindustrial materialism" (Andersen and Bjorklund 1990; Minkenberg and Inglehart 1989; Harmel and Gibson 1995; Betz 1994).

16. This has been confirmed by a comprehensive study of class consciousness and identity in Australia by Emmison and Western (1990, 1991). Mann identified four elements of class consciousness: identity, opposition, totality, and alternative (1993: 27–35). For the broader "class consciousness and action" debate, see Graetz 1983, 1986; Hindess 1987; Gorz 1982; Franklin 1985; Marshall et al. 1988; and Evans 1992.

17. Graetz's (1983, 1986, 1992) studies of the relationship among inequality, images, attitudes, and political activism show that popular beliefs are seldom dissensual in the way the class models would suggest; that beliefs about inequality and political opinions depend primarily on political orientations (rather than socioeconomic attributes); that such beliefs cut across class and status divisions; and that beliefs and opinions "exert no more than a marginal impact upon the propensity for political action" (1992: 172–173).

18. "A new generation has developed in the postwar years in Germany that is more involved in the democratic political system. In part, this has resulted from the accumulation of experience in the role of a participatory citizen, but it may also involve the inculcation of democratic norms of participation. Thus one source of increasing political involvement must be the growing size of the young participatory segment of the electorate, and the acceptance of their example by older generations." (Baker et al. 1981: 57).

19. As Kitschelt (1994: 33) points out, "Socialist appeals to class politics thus do not unite the working class, but divide it in different ways than a moderate pro-capitalist program [of corporatist welfarism]. On the socialist-capitalist axis then, social democrats chose . . . between mobilizing different segments of the working class. As a consequence, class politics is no longer a foundation of a broadly successful social democratic electoral coalition."

20. The best-known versions of this class-party ideology alignment can be found in Lipset 1960 and Parkin 1979. The latter placed the issue of inequality and state redistribution at the center of "class politics." Lipset added that smaller and less consistent packages were developed for "agrarian classes," as well as for sections of the population mobilized in nonclass terms (religious, regional, ethnic, etc.). He also interpreted mass social movements (fascist, communist, Peronist, etc.) in terms of their dominant class bases.

21. American politics, to repeat, has never approximated closely such highly articulated class politics. Racial and ethnic (status) patterning has always been dominant in American society, and the major political organizations have seldom appealed to class interests and categories. Class issues typically took the back seat, especially in election campaigns of the major political parties. Nevertheless, as pointed out by Lipset (1960, 1981), there was a rough correspondence between the general pattern of stratification and the "democratic class struggle" in the United States in the early 1950s.

22. This political articulation of classes involved not only the formation of class organizations and elites—the real "class actors" (Hindess 1987)—but also the development of uniform class symbolism, iconography, and the dissemination of national class identities and discourses. Organizational reconstitution coincided with a glorification of class parties, especially on the left of the political spectrum. Parties took over the heroic mantle of class in a way analogous to the appropriation of national sentiments by the states. In extreme cases, this identification was enforced through authoritarian means. For socialist revolutionaries, like Vladimir Lenin, and intellectuals, like Georg Lukács, the party was the only true expression of class. Class interest was identified with the party line.

References

Aitkin, D. A. 1982. *Stability and Change in Australian Politics.* Canberra: Australian National University Press.

Alford, R. 1963. *Party and Society: The Anglo-American Democracies.* Chicago: Rand McNally.

Andersen, J. G., and T. Bjorklund. 1990. "Structural Change and New Cleavages: The Progress Parties in Denmark and Norway." *Acta Sociologica* 33, no. 3: 195–217.

Baker K., R. Dalton, and K. Hildebrandt. 1981. *Germany Transformed: Political Culture and the New Politics.* Cambridge: Harvard University Press.

Baxter J., M. Emmison, J. Western, and M. Western, eds. 1991. *Class Analysis in Contemporary Australia.* Melbourne: Macmillan.

Bell, D. 1973. *The Coming of Post-Industrial Society.* New York: Basic Books.

Betz, H. G. 1994. *Radical Right-Wing Populism in Western Europe.* London: Macmillan.

Blackburn, R., and M. Mann. 1975. "Ideology in the Non-Skilled Working Class." In M. Bulmer, ed., *Working Class Images of Society,* 131–160. London: Routledge.

Bourdieu, P. 1987. "What Makes a Social Clan?" *Berkeley Journal of Sociology* 32: 1–17.

Clark, T. N. 1995. "Who Cares if Social Class Is Dying or Not?" Draft of the conference paper prepared as background for conference on social class at Nuffield College, Oxford, February.

Clark, T. N., and S. M. Lipset. 1991. "Are Social Classes Dying?" *International Sociology* 6, no. 4: 397–410.

Clark, T. N., S. M. Lipset, and M. Rempel. 1993. "The Declining Political Significance of Social Class." *International Sociology* 8, no. 3: 293–316.

Crewe, I. 1992 . "Labour Force Changes, Working Class Decline and the Labour Vote." In F. Piven, ed., *Labour Parties in Postindustrial Capitalism.* Oxford and New York: Oxford University Press.

Crook, S., J. Pakulski, and M. Waters. 1992. *Postmodernization: Change in Advanced Society.* London: Sage.

Dahrendorf, R. 1959. *Class and Class Conflict in Industrial Society.* London: Routledge.

Dalton, R. 1988. *Citizen Politics in Western Democracies.* Chatham: Chatham Publishers.

Dalton, R., and M. Kuechler. 1990. *Challenging the Political Order.* Cambridge: Polity.

Dunleavy, P. 1980. "The Urban Basis of Political Alignment." *British Journal of Political Science* 9: 409–444.

Dunleavy, P. 1987. "Class Dealignment Revisited." *Western European Politics* 10: 400–419.

Emmison, M. 1991. "Conceptualising Class Consciousness." In J. Baxter, M. Emmison, J. Western, and M. Western, eds., *Class Analysis and Contemporary Australia,* 246–278. Melbourne: Macmillan.

Emmison, M., and M. Western. 1990. "Social Class and Social Identify: A Comment on Marshall *et al.*" *Sociology* 24, no. 2: 241–253.

Emmison, M., and M. Western. 1991. "The Structure of Social Identities." In J. Baxter, M. Emmison, J. Western, and M. Western, eds., *Class Analysis and Contemporary Australia,* 279–306. Melbourne: Macmillan.

Etzioni-Halevi, E. 1992. *The Elite Connection.* London: Polity.

Etzioni-Halevi, E. 1997. "The Relationship between Elites and the Working Class: On Coupling, Uncoupling, Democracy and (In-)equality." In J. Higley, J. Pakulski, and W. Wesolowski, eds., *Postcommunist Elites and Democratization in Eastern Europe,* 251–279. London: Macmillan.

Evans, G. 1992. "Is Britain a Class Divided Society?" *Sociology* 26, no. 2: 233–258.

Field, L., and J. Higley. 1980. *Elitism.* London: Routledge and Kegan Paul.

Franklin, M. N. 1985. *The Decline of Class Voting in Britain.* Oxford: Clarendon Press.

Franklin, M. N., T. Macke, and H. Velen. 1992. *Electoral Change: Response to Evolving Social and Attitudinal Structures in Western Countries.* Cambridge: Cambridge University Press.

Gibbins, J. 1989. "Contemporary Political Culture." In J. Gibbins, ed., *Contemporary Political Culture,* 1–30. London: Sage.

Giddens, A. 1973. *The Class Structure of Advanced Societies*. London: Hutchinson.

Giddens, A. 1996. *Beyond Left and Right*. Cambridge: Polity.

Golden, M., and J. Pontusson, eds. 1992. *Bargaining for Change: Union Politics in North America and Europe*. Ithaca: Cornell University Press.

Goldthorpe, J., and G. Marshall. 1992. "The Promising Future of Class Analysis: A Response to Recent Critiques." *Sociology* 26 no. 3: 381–400.

Gorz, A. 1982. *Farewell to the Working Class*. London: Pluto.

Graetz, B. 1983. "Images of Class in Modern Society." *Sociology* 17, no. 1: 79–96.

Graetz, B. 1986. "Social Structure and Class Consciousness." *Australian and New Zealand Journal of Sociology* 22, no.1: 46–64.

Graetz, B. 1992. "Inequality and Political Activism in Australia." *Research in Inequality and Social Conflict* 2: 157–177.

Graetz, B., and I. McAllister. 1994. *Dimensions of Australian Society*. 2d ed. Melbourne: Macmillan.

Grusky, D. B., and J. B. Sorensen. 1997. "Can Class Analysis be Salvaged?" A redraft of a paper presented at the conference "Class and Politics," Washington, D.C. April 1995.

Hall, J. R., ed. 1997. *Reworking Class*. Ithaca and London: Cornell University Press.

Harmel, R., and R. K. Gibson. 1995. "Right-Libertarian Parties and the 'New Values': A Re-examination." *Scandinavian Political Studies* 18, no. 2: 97–118.

Heath, A., R. Jowell, and J. Curtice. 1985. *How Britain Votes*. Oxford: Pergamon.

Higley, J., and M. J. Burton. 1989. "The Elite Variable in Democratic Transitions and Breakdowns." *American Sociological Review* 54: 17–32.

Hindess, B. 1987. *Political and Class Analysis*. Oxford: Blackwell.

Holmwood, J., and S. Stewart. 1991. *Explanation and Social Theory*. Basingstoke: Macmillan.

Holton, R., and B. S. Turner. 1989. *Max Weber on Economy and Society*. London: Routledge.

Holton, R., and B. S. Turner. 1994. "Debate and Pseudo-Debate in Class Analysis: Some Unpromising Aspects of Goldthorpe and Marshall's defence." *Sociology* 28, no. 3: 799–804.

Hout, M., C. Brooks, and J. Manza. 1993. "The Persistence of Classes in Post-Industrial Societies." *International Sociology* 8, no. 3: 259–278.

Hout, M., C. Brooks, and J. Manza. 1995. "The Democratic Class Struggle in the United States, 1948–92." *American Sociological Review* 60: 805–828.

Inglehart, R. 1991. *Culture Shift in Advanced Industrial Society*. Princeton: Princeton University Press.

Inglehart R. 1996. *Postmodernization*. Princeton: Princeton University Press.

Kemp, D. 1978. *Society and Electoral Behavior in Australia*. Brisbane: University of Queensland Press.

Kern, S. and C. Sabel. 1992. "Trade Unions and Decentralised Production." In M. Regini, ed., *The Future of Labour Movements*, 217–249. London: Sage.

Kitschelt, H. 1994. *The Transformation of European Social Democracy*. Cambridge: Cambridge University Press.

Kitschelt, H., and S. Hellmans. 1990. *Beyond the European Left: Political Action in Left-Libertarian Parties*. Durham: Duke University Press.

Korpi, W. 1983. *The Democratic Class Struggle*. London: Routledge.

Kuhn, T. S. 1970. *The Structure of Scientific Revolutions*. 2d ed. Chicago: University of Chicago Press.

Lakatos, I. 1970. "Falsification and the Methodology of Scientific Research Programmes." In I. Lakatos and A. Musgrave, eds., *Criticism and Growth of Scientific Knowledge*, 91–97. Cambridge: Cambridge University Press.

Lash, S., and J. Urry. 1987. *The End of Organized Capitalism*. Cambridge: Polity.

Lee, D., and B. S. Turner, eds. 1996. *Conflict about Class*. London: Longman.

Lipset, S. M. 1960. *Political Man: The Social Bases of Politics*. New York: Doubleday.

Lipset, S. M. 1981. *Political Man*. 2d ed. Baltimore: Johns Hopkins University Press.

Lipset, S. M. 1991. "No Third Way: A Comparative Perspective on the Left." In D. Chirot, ed., *The Crisis of Leninism and the Decline of the Left.* Seattle: University of Washington Press.

Lipset, S. M., and S. Rokkan. 1967. "Cleavage Structures, Party Systems, and Voter Alignments: An Introduction." In S. M. Lipset and S. Rokkan, eds., *Party Systems and Voter Alignments: Cross-national Perspective,* 1–64. New York: Free Press.

Lockwood, D. 1966. "Sources of Variation in Working Class Images of Society." *Sociological Review* 14, no. 3: 244–267.

Lopreato, J., and L. Lewis, eds. 1974. *Social Stratification: A Reader.* London: Harper and Row.

McAllister, I. 1992. *Political Behaviour: Citizens, Parties and Elites in Australia.* Melbourne: Longman Cheshire.

Mann, M. 1973. *Consciousness and Action among the Western Working Class.* London: Macmillan.

Mann, M. 1993. *The Source of Social Power.* Vol. 2. Cambridge: Cambridge University Press.

Manza, J., and C. Brooks. 1996. "Does Class Analysis Have Anything to Contribute to the Study of Politics?" *Theory and Society* 25: 717–724.

Manza, J., M. Hout, and C. Brooks. 1995. "Class Voting in Capitalist Democracies since WWI." *Annual Review of Sociology* 21: 137–163.

Marshall, G. 1997. *Repositioning Class: Social Inequality in Industrial Societies.* London: Sage.

Marshall, G., H. Newby, D. Rose, and C. Vogler. 1988. *Social Class in Modern Britain.* London: Hutchinson.

Miliband, R. 1977. *Marxism and Politics.* Oxford: Oxford University Press.

Miliband, R. 1989. *Divided Societies.* Oxford: Clarendon.

Minkenberg, M., and R. Inglehart. 1989. "Neoconservatism and Value Change in the United States." In J. Gibbins, ed., *Contemporary Political Culture,* 81–109. London: Sage.

Mulkay, M. 1979. *Science and the Sociology of Knowledge.* London: Allen and Unwin.

Nieuwbeerta, P. 1997. *The Democratic Class Struggle in Twenty Countries, 1945–1990.* CIP-DATA Koninklijke Bibliotheek, Den Haag.

Nisbet, R. 1959. "The Decline and Fall of Social Class." *Pacific Sociological Review* 2, no. 1: 11–28.

Offe, C. 1985. "New Social Movements: Challenging the Boundaries of Conventional Politics." *Social Research* 52, no. 4: 817–868.

Ossowski, S. [1958] 1963. *Class Structure in the Social Consciousness.* London: Routledge.

Pahl, R. 1989. "Is the Emperor Naked?" *International Journal of Urban and Regional Research* 13: 709–720.

Pakulski, J., and M. Waters. 1996a. *Death of Class.* London: Sage.

Pakulski, J., and M. Waters. 1996b. "The Reshaping and Dissolution of Social Class in Advanced Society." *Theory and Society* 25, no. 5: 667–691.

Pakulski, J., and M. Waters. 1996c. "Misreading Status as Class: A Reply to Our Critics." *Theory and Society* 25, no. 5: 731–736.

Parkin, F. 1979. *Marxism and Class Theory.* London: Tavistock.

Poguntke, T. 1993. *Alternative Politics: The German Green Party.* Edinburgh: University of Edinburgh Press.

Regini, M., ed. 1992. *The Future of Labour Movements.* London: Sage.

Rose, R., and I. McAllister. 1985. *From Closed Class to Open Elections: Britain in Flux.* London: Sage.

Sarlvik, B., and I. Crewe. 1983. *Decade of Dealignment.* New York: Cambridge University Press.

Sartori, G. 1969. "From the Sociology of Politics to Political Sociology." In S. M. Lipset, ed., *Politics and the Social Sciences.* New York: Oxford University Press.

Sartori, G. 1970. "Concept Misformation in Comparative Politics." *American Political Science Review* 64, no. 4: 1033–1053.

Scott, A. 1990. *Ideology and New Social Movements.* London: Unwin Hyman.

Thomsen, S. R. 1987. *Danish Elections 1920–79.* Aarhus: Politica.

Waters, M. 1994. "Succession in the Stratification Order: A Contribution to the 'Death of Class' Debate." *International Sociology* 9, no. 3: 295–312.

Weakliem, D. L., and M. Western. 1999. "Class Voting, Social Change, and the Left in Australia, 1943–96." *British Journal of Sociology* 50, no. 43: 607–628.

Weber, M. 1978 [1922]. *Economy and Society*. Berkeley: University of California Press.

Western, M. 1991. "Class Structure and Demographic Class Formation in Australia." In J. Baxter, M. Emmison, J. Western, and M. Western, eds., *Class Analysis and Contemporary Australia*, 166–201. Melbourne: Macmillan.

Western, B. 1995. "A Comparative Study of Working Class Disorganization." *American Sociological Review* 60, no. 2: 179–201.

Western, M. 1998. "Class Biography and Class Consciousness in Australia." *Research in Social Stratification and Mobility* 16: 117–143.

Western, J., M. Western, M. Emmison, and J. Baxter. 1991. "Class Analysis and Politics." In J. Baxter, M. Emmison, J. Western, and M. Western, eds., *Class Analysis and Contemporary Australia*, 306–339. Melbourne: Macmillan.

Wright, E. O. 1985. *Classes*. London: Verso.

Wright, E. O. 1989. "A General Framework for the Analysis of Class Structure." In E. O. Wright, ed., *The Debate on Classes*, 3–43. London: Verso.

Wright, E. O. 1994. *Interrogating Inequality*. London: Verso.

Wright, E. O. 1996. "The Continuing Relevance of Class Analysis." *Theory and Society* 25, no. 5: 693–716.

8

Class, Culture, and Conservatism

*Reassessing Education as a Variable in Political Sociology**

DICK HOUTMAN

1. Introduction

A weakening relationship between social class and voting behavior ("class voting") is generally considered the litmus test for a declining political significance of social class, as several chapters in this volume reveal. This chapter argues that it is necessary to reconsider this conventional approach to the problem of class and politics. To demonstrate that it is less valid than generally assumed, we need to address the relationship between social class and political values first. Therefore, taking Lipset's classic article on working class authoritarianism (1959, 1981) as my point of departure, I review

---

*A first draft of this chapter was written during my stay at the University of Maryland at College Park, enabled by a TALENT-Fellowship granted by the Netherlands Organization for Scientific Research (NWO). Subsequent versions were presented at the Annual Research Institute of the District of Columbia Sociological Society, University of Maryland at College Park, April 29, 1995, the Comparative Institutions Seminar, University of California at Santa Barbara, May 9, 1995, the American Sociological Association Annual Meeting, Washington, D.C., August 20, 1995, and the conference on Social Class and Politics, Woodrow Wilson Center, Washington, D.C., April 20, 1996.

the most relevant research findings. Next, some new hypotheses, tailored to shed light onto an ongoing theoretical controversy over this relationship, are tested by means of data collected for this purpose in the Netherlands in 1997.

Next, I address the implications of my findings for the idea that the political significance of social class can be studied validly by focusing on the relationship between social class and voting behavior. I explain that this conventional approach is unsatisfactory because it tends systematically to underestimate the political significance of class and is likely to impede a theoretical understanding of why levels of class voting differ among countries and historical periods. Some important questions for future comparative research are suggested in this context.

2. Working-Class Authoritarianism

2.1. Introduction

Forty years after its publication as an article, Lipset's theory of working-class authoritarianism (1959, 1981) continues to stimulate empirical research and theoretical debate. Basically, it consists of two claims. First, Lipset argues, a distinction should be made between political values relating to (a rejection of) income redistribution and state regulation of the economic system on the one hand and values relating to (a rejection of) the primacy of individual liberty on the other. The former type of values is referred to as economic liberalism or conservatism, while the latter is called either noneconomic liberalism/conservatism or authoritarianism.

Lipset's second claim concerns the relationship between social class and both types of liberalism/conservatism. Compared with the middle class, members of the working class are held to be economically liberal but noneconomically conservative: "Economic liberalism refers to the conventional issues concerning redistribution of income, status, and power among the classes. The poorer everywhere are more liberal or leftist on such issues. . . . On the other hand, when liberalism is defined in non-economic terms—so as to support, for example, civil rights for political dissidents, civil rights for ethnic and racial minorities, internationalist foreign policies, and liberal immigration legislation—the correlation is reversed" (Lipset 1959: 485). Although I mean to refer to exactly the same type of political values, the last-mentioned type of liberalism will be called cultural rather than noneconomic in this chapter.[1]

2.2. Two Types of Liberalism/Conservatism

Now that 40 years have passed since the initial publication of Lipset's article, many studies have shed light onto the tenability of those two claims. What are the principal findings? As to the first claim, many studies have highlighted the importance of the distinction between both types of liberalism/conservatism. As it happens they are almost completely unrelated among the public at large. Accordingly, it cannot be predicted whether someone who favors redistribution of income will accept or reject, for instance, the maintenance of traditional general roles, the limitation of freedom of speech, homosexuality, capital punishment, et cetera (e.g., Felling and Peters 1986; Fleishman 1988; Middendorp 1991; Olson and Carroll 1992; Evans et al. 1996). Therefore, it does not make sense to speak of "liberalism" or "conservatism" in an unqualified way: being economically liberal, one might be culturally liberal or culturally conservative.

In Lipset's article noneconomic conservatism is alternatively referred to as authoritarianism, although the latter is often held to be a "personality characteristic" rather than a type of political value (Adorno et al. 1950). Nevertheless, research based on nationally representative data sets, collected among the Dutch population in 1975, 1980, 1985, and 1990, has demonstrated that the so-called F-scale for authoritarianism is strongly related to more conventional measures of cultural conservatism. Examples are intolerance regarding homosexuals, a preference for the maintenance of traditional gender roles, family traditionalism, harsh attitudes toward criminals, and a willingness to limit political freedom of expression (Middendorp 1991: 111). Those findings indicate that there is ample reason to reject too neat a distinction between authoritarianism and culturally conservative political values. Indeed, their strong correlation suggests that it makes more sense to consider them highly interchangeable concepts.

At face value, post-materialism, as conceptualized and operationalized by Ronald Inglehart, also seems to be tapping cultural liberalism, because "post-Materialist values emphasize individual self-expression and achieving a more participant, less hierarchical society" (1997: 179). Although postmaterialist values have most often been studied separately, Flanagan (1979, 1982, 1987) suggested, remarkably early, that post-materialism strongly overlaps with cultural liberalism, or "libertarianism" as he prefers to call it. Indeed, in his more recent work, Inglehart (1997: 41–42) acknowledges that post-materialism is merely a single element of a more en-compassing cluster of culturally liberal political values. Remarkably, how-ever, he still suggests that only "a poor empirical fit" exists between post-materialism and authoritarianism (Inglehart 1971: 997; Inglehart 1977: 68; Inglehart 1997: 47). Given the strong relationship between authori-tarianism and cultural conservatism, however, this is unlikely. Instead, Adorno et al.'s (1950) F-scale and Inglehart's index for post-materialism, two measures often kept strictly separate from more conventional mea-sures of cultural liberalism/conservatism in empirical research, seem to tap this general concept as well.

2.3. Social Class and Education: Theoretical Controversy

Many studies conducted since the 1960s have concluded that "the con-ceptualization and measurement of social class has a great deal of influence on whether . . . the theory of working-class authoritarianism (receives) sup-port or not" (Grabb 1980: 369; see also: Lipsitz 1965; Grabb 1979). More specifically, the more a class measure relies on education, the stronger the class effect found. In fact, those with little education, rather than the poor, are culturally conservative: "A consistent and continuing re-search literature has documented relationships between low levels of edu-cation and racial and religious prejudice, opposition to equal rights for women, and with support of, and involvement in, fundamentalist religious groups" (Lipset 1981: 478). This is revealed by research into tolerance for nonconformity (e.g., Stouffer 1955; Nunn et al. 1978; Grabb 1979, 1980; Bobo and Licari 1989), research into authoritarianism (e.g., Dekker and Ester 1987; Eisinga and Scheepers 1989), and research that shows level of education to be an important predictor of racial prejudice (e.g., Case et al. 1989; Eisinga and Scheepers 1989; Pedersen 1996) as well as cultural con-servatism in a more general sense (e.g., Zipp 1986; Woodrum 1988a, b; Davis and Robinson 1996). The decisive importance of level of education *in its own right* (i.e., independent of associated factors such as income or occupational conditions) has been underlined by studies of the cultural conservatism of (economically inactive) students with different levels of education (e.g., Feldman and Newcomb 1973, 1: 71–105; Schulz and Weiss 1993).

So, by and large, it is agreed nowadays that working-class authoritarian-ism (cultural conservatism) is basically authoritarianism (cultural conser-vatism) of the poorly educated. No agreement exists on the theoretical im-plications of this finding, however. On the one hand, there are those who consider education a key indicator for social class. As such, education's strong negative effect on cultural conservatism is held to support Lipset's theory of working, class authoritarianism (e.g., Kohn [1969] 1977; Middendorp and Meloen 1990). On the other hand, there are those who maintain that education is, of course, strongly related to social class but should nevertheless not be confused with it: "Education is not the same as social class and thus educational differences cannot be used as evidence for class distinctions" (Dekker and Ester 1987: 409; see also Grabb 1979, 1980). So, although there is hardly any disagreement about the finding that education is decisive for understanding authoritarianism or cultural conservatism, no agreement exists as to its implication for the tenability of Lipset's theory.[2]

Obviously, the issue is a theoretical one: What exactly does education indicate when we use it to explain cultural liberalism? Is it operating as an indicator of social class here? Actually, there are good reasons for doubt. After all, were education operating as an indicator for social class here, other class indicators should have basically similar effects. This is not the case, however. Especially the absence of a substantial income effect is telling (e.g., Kohn [1969] 1977; Kohn and Schooler 1983; Kohn and Slomczynski 1990; Zipp 1986), because income has traditionally been considered an important proxy for social class. Indeed, the ability to explain income differences is regarded as both a *conditio sine qua non* for the validity of class concepts (e.g., Marshall et al. 1988; Wright 1979, 1985; Middendorp and Meloen 1990) and an argument for the contemporary existence of social classes—in the Marxist sense of *Klassen an sich* rather than *Klassen für sich* (e.g., Hout et al., in this volume).

Research findings indicate that the low income of the working class accounts for a substantial part of its economic liberalism (e.g., Wright 1985: 259–278; Marshall et al. 1988: 179–183). This suggests that working-class economic liberalism results from its economic interests, thus confirming one of the core hypotheses of the class approach to politics, that is, the idea that a relationship between social class and political values may be expected precisely because different classes have different economic interests: "the lower-income groups will support [the leftist parties] in order to become better off, whereas the higher-income groups will oppose them in order to maintain their economic advantages" (Lipset et al. 1954: 1136; see also Svallfors 1991: 619; D'Anjou et al. 1995: 357–359).

Education's strong negative effect on cultural conservatism cannot be interpreted by means of this theoretical logic, however. After all, even when the absence of substantial income effects in studies into cultural con-

servatism is bypassed, it is quite unclear how and why the economic interests of the working class would lead to support for capital punishment, intolerance of homosexuality, or the maintenance of traditional gender roles.
Instead, education seems to be indicating something quite different here.
But what? Bourdieu's work on taste and cultural reproduction suggests a
plausible answer, because it considers education an indicator not for social
class but for cultural capital: the capacity to recognize cultural expressions
and to understand their meaning (e.g., Bourdieu 1973, 1984; Bourdieu
and Passeron 1977). Consequently, education is nowadays considered an
indicator not only for social class but for cultural capital as well (e.g.,
Kalmijn 1994).

It is not difficult to understand why cultural capital should affect cultural
conservatism negatively. After all, a capacity to recognize cultural expressions and to understand their meaning is unlikely to lead to an interpretation of unconventional lifestyles and patterns of culture as morally repre-
hensible deviations from an absolute, "extracultural" or "metasocial" moral
foundation. Instead, they are most likely to be recognized as *culture* (i.e.,
as humanly constructed and ultimately contingent and arbitrary), which is
expressed in their acceptance and in a more general emphasis on the value
of individual liberty (compare Gabennesch 1972; Bauman 1987: 81–95).

The foregoing suggests that education, like social class itself, is quite an
ambiguous variable in political sociology. Depending on the type of political values we are dealing with, education can operate as an indicator for either social class or cultural capital. Explaining *economic* liberalism, education
is likely to indicate social class, affecting it negatively; explaining *cultural* liberalism, however, it may instead be expected to affect it positively as an indicator for cultural capital. Because income has nothing to do with cultural
capital, it lacks education's ambiguity, tapping social class only. As a consequence, income effects are more readily interpretable. Along with education, income may be expected to affect economic liberalism negatively; unlike education, however, it should have no effect on cultural liberalism.

In short, education's negative effect on cultural conservatism cannot
simply be interpreted as support for Lipset's theory of working-class authoritarianism. Because the effects of ambiguous variables such as social
class and education are unlikely to provide theoretical clarity, the inclusion
of more explicit indicators for social class and cultural capital is necessary
to increase the interpretability of the findings. Moreover, it is important to
study economic liberalism and cultural conservatism simultaneously, to be
able to benefit theoretically from the probably divergent effects of (indicators for) social class and cultural capital.

2.4. Hypotheses

If we follow the logic of class analysis, as briefly outlined above, it is not too difficult to add two explicit class indicators to income. First, of course, wage dependence has traditionally been conceived as a key indicator for social class, because those who need to sell their labor power occupy a weaker position in economic life than those who own the means of production (Marx [1867] 1967; Marx and Engels [1848] 1948; Weber [1922] 1978, 1: 302–307; Wright 1979, 1985; Goldthorpe 1980). Job insecurity is a second indicator. After all, those with insecure jobs occupy weak economic positions as well. So, income, wage dependence, and job insecurity are three useful explicit indicators for social class.

Education is more ambiguous as an indicator for social class, for it also indicates cultural capital. As "institutionalized" cultural capital, however, it can be distinguished from "embodied" cultural capital: an interest in arts and culture (Bourdieu 1986; see also: Lamont and Lareau 1988; Böröcz and Southworth 1996).[3] Consequently, the amount of cultural capital is indicated not only by education but by cultural participation as well. Now, if education's culturally liberalizing effect should indeed be interpreted in terms of cultural capital rather than social class, cultural participation should have a similar result, whereas the three explicit indicators for social class should not affect cultural conservatism at all. Conversely, cultural participation should not affect economic liberalism, whereas education and the three explicit indicators for social class should.

A logical first step in the analysis would be to assess the relationship between social class and both types of liberalism/conservatism. What may be expected here is an economically liberal and culturally conservative working class. Next, in the second step, education and the explicit indicators for social class and cultural capital need to be entered to find out whether both types of liberalism/conservatism can, in fact, be explained from social class. It may be expected that this is true for economic liberalism. Therefore, the relationship between social class and economic liberalism is likely to stem from education, income, wage dependence, and job insecurity, while cultural participation may be expected to play no role at all. As to cultural conservatism, on the other hand, that of the working class may be expected to stem from its limited amount of cultural capital (low level of education and little cultural participation) rather than from its weak position in economic life (low income, wage dependence, and job insecurity).

So, only education is expected to affect economic as well as cultural liberalism/conservatism, albeit in opposite ways. As an indicator for a weak class position, like a low income, wage dependence, and job insecurity but unlike cultural participation, a low level of education is expected to lead to economic *liberalism*. On the other hand, like a low level of cultural participation but unlike a low income, it is expected to lead to cultural *conservatism*.

3. Data and Measurement

3.1. Data

Data were collected during the summer of 1997 by means of the panel of Centerdata (Catholic University Brabant, Tilburg, the Netherlands). This panel constitutes a representative sample from the Dutch population. Panel members had a home computer at their disposal, which enabled them to answer questions from Dutch researchers. The length of the questionnaire necessitated a two-part division, with the two parts answered at different times. The first part included questions for the economically active as well as the economically inactive (primarily questions about cultural participation and political values). The first part of the questionnaire involved 1,856 persons aged 18 years or older, who yielded a response rate of 90 percent. The second part included questions intended for the economically active panel members only (e.g., questions to measure social class, job insecurity, et cetera). Therefore, this second part of the questionnaire was answered only by those economically active for at least 20 hours a week. This yielded 792 respondents—again, a response rate of about 90 percent—with 711 of them having answered the first part of the questionnaire as well. Of course, the subsequent analysis is limited to those 711 respondents.

3.2. Measurement of Economic and Cultural Liberalism/Conservatism

Economic liberalism/conservatism was measured by means of six Likert-type items:(1) The government should raise the level of social security benefits. (2) Real poverty no longer exists in the Netherlands (item reversed for scale analysis). (3) Large income differences are unjust because people are equal in principle. (4) Nowadays the working class no longer needs to fight for an equal position in society (item reversed for scale analysis). (5) The government should take drastic measures to reduce income differences. (6) Companies should be forced to give their employees a fair share of their profits (Cronbach's α = 0.71). High scores indicate economic liberalism.

Cultural liberalism/conservatism was measured by means of a scale for authoritarianism, Inglehart's index for post-materialism, a scale for the rejection of traditional gender roles, and a scale measuring educational values. All of these tap values relating to individual liberty and maintenance of social order, so they are all expected to indicate cultural liberalism/conservatism.

Authoritarianism was measured by means of a short version of the F-scale, consisting of nine items: (1) Nowadays more and more people are prying into matters that should remain personal and private. (2) Familiarity breeds contempt. (3) Young people sometimes get rebellious ideas, but as they grow up they ought to get over them and settle down. (4) Our social problems would largely be solved if we could somehow remove criminal and antisocial people from society. (5) What we need are fewer laws and institutions and more courageous, tireless, and dedicated leaders whom the people can trust. (6) A person with bad manners, habits, and breeding can hardly be expected to get along well with decent people. (7) People can be divided into two distinct classes: the weak and the strong. (8) Sexual crimes, such as rape and assault of children, deserve more than just imprisonment; actually, such criminals should be corporally punished in public. (9) If people would talk less and work harder, everything would work out better. High scores indicate strong authoritarianism (Cronbach's α = 0.79).

Post-materialism was measured by means of the well-known short version of Inglehart's index, which is based on the ranking of four political goals. Two of these goals considered indicative of post-materialism ("giving the people more say in important government decisions" and "protecting free speech"), and two are indicative of materialism ("maintaining order in the nation" and "fighting rising prices"). To do justice to the ranking of the four individual goals, their relative priority has been factor analyzed. The first factor explains 44.2 percent of the variance, the lowest factor loading is 0.55, and the loadings of the materialist goals are the opposite of those of the post-materialist goals. Factor scores were used in the analysis, with higher scores indicating stronger postmaterialism.

Rejection of traditional gender roles was measured by means of five Likert-type items: (1) If a child gets ill, it is natural that the mother instead of the father stays at home. (2) As to the possession of leadership qualities, women are equal to men (item reversed for scale analysis). (3) Men are as fit as women to raise young children (item reversed for scale analysis). (4) It is best for young children if their mother does not work outside the home. (5) Failing to complete one's education is more problematic for women than for men. High scores indicate a rejection of traditional gender roles (Cronbach's α = 0.68).

Orientation toward education, the degree to which one believes that education should be directed at either economic-technological or cultural-intellectual goals ("instrumental," respectively "intrinsic" orientation toward education), was measured by means of seven Likert-type items: (1) If many students of an educational institution become unemployed after graduation, the government should restrict its number of first-year students. (2) It is a waste of public funds to have people receive a training that gives them only a slight chance of obtaining a job. (3) Education related to arts and culture is at least as important to society as technical training (item reversed for scale analysis). (4) The government should spend less money on branches of knowledge that fail to yield applicable knowledge. (5) Young people should be free to choose the education they are most interested in (item reversed for scale analysis). (6) Getting a well-paid job later is the principal motive for obtaining a degree. (7) The government should see that universities conduct research that is useful to the government and/or the business community. High scores indicate an "intrinsic" orientation toward education (Cronbach's α = 0.73).

Factor analyzing the five measures discussed above yields the two ex-

Table 8.1
Factor Analysis of Five Measures for Political Values (Varimax Rotation; N = 652)

	Factor 1	Factor 2
Authoritarianism	−0.84	0.11
Post-materialism	0.63	0.25
Rejection of traditional gender roles	0.69	0.05
Intrinsic orientation toward education	0.74	0.06
Economic liberalism	−0.05	0.98
Eigenvalue	2.15	1.00
R^2(%)	43.1	20.1

pected factors (table 8.1). Economic liberalism/conservatism proves unrelated to the four strongly interrelated others. This finding underscores the
necessity to distinguish systematically between cultural liberalism/conser-
vatism on the one hand and economic liberalism/conservatism on the
other. Therefore, the scale for economic liberalism/conservatism is used
separately in the subsequent analyses, whereas the four scales tapping cultural liberalism/conservatism are combined. Both resulting measures
range from 0 through 10, with high scores indicating economic liberalism
and cultural conservatism, respectively. The correlation between them is a
mere $-.13$ (two-sided test, $p < .01$).

3.3. Measurement of Social Class and Cultural Capital

Social class is measured by means of the class scheme developed by Erikson, Goldthorpe, and Portocarero (1979; Goldthorpe 1980: 39–42),
widely used in internationally comparative research nowadays (e.g.,
Nieuwbeerta 1995, 1996). The coding scheme for the Netherlands, published by Bakker et al. (1997), assigns EGP-class positions to those gain-
fully employed on the basis of (1) occupational title, (2) being self-employed or not, and (3) the number of people being supervised. This coding
procedure was restricted to the 711 respondents working at least 20 hours
a week.

   Class I (15.0 percent) consists of highly qualified professionals, administrators, and officials, as well as managers of large organizations and large
owners (including the liberal professions); class II (30.2 percent) consists
of less highly qualified professionals, administrators, and officials, as well as
managers of smaller organizations and supervisors of nonmanual workers.
Class III (21.2 percent) consists of routine nonmanual workers. In class IV
(5.3 percent) small self-employed businessmen are placed. Classes VI (5.8
percent) and VII (14.2 percent) together constitute the working class
("skilled" and "semi- and unskilled," respectively). Class V (7.5 percent)
is a sort of "upper layer" of the working class, or an "aristocracy of labor,"
consisting of highly skilled technicians and supervisors of manual workers,
distinguished from the working class proper.[4] This class scheme is not fully
hierarchical, for it is not possible to order all seven classes within a single
hierarchy ranging from class I (highest) to class VII (lowest). However,
classes I, II, and III do form a hierarchy, as do classes V, VI, and VII.

   Income was measured as net personal income as well as net family income. The former is used to assess the strength of the relationship between
EGP class and income, discussed in section 4.2 below, while the latter is

used to explain economic liberalism. Doing so, I follow Erikson's (1984) suggestion that with respect to the strength of the market position the household is the most significant unit of analysis. Mean net personal income is Fl 3,072 (s.d. = Fl 1,535); mean net family income, of course, is higher: Fl 4,468 (s.d. = Fl 1,119).

Wage dependence, a variable also used to construct the seven EGP classes, was established by asking whether one is self-employed (6.0 percent) or in paid employment (94.0 percent)

Job insecurity was operationalized by means of three questions. First, it was asked whether one is working on a temporary contract (5.3 percent were; 94.7 percent were not).[5] Second, the number of times one has been unemployed since the completion of one's education was ascertained. These answers were recoded into three categories: never (86.8 percent), once (7.2 percent), and twice or more (6.0 percent). Third, respondents were asked to estimate the likelihood of someone with a similar job and contract (either permanent or temporary) being forced to find another job within the next three years. Of the respondents, 20.4 percent answered "very unlikely"; 31.4 percent, "quite unlikely"; 36.6 percent "neither likely nor unlikely" or did not know; 8.3 percent "quite likely"; and 3.4 percent, "very likely." After standardization, the three indicators were added up and transformed into a scale ranging from 0 (lowest job insecurity) through 10 (highest job insecurity).

Education. Seven educational levels were distinguished: (1) no education or only primary education (6.1 percent); (2) lower vocational education (LBO) (15.5 percent); (3) lower general secondary education ((M)ULO/MAVO) (16.8 percent); (4) higher general secondary education (HAVO) or pre-university education (HBS/VWO/Gymnasium) (12.1 percent); (5) intermediate vocational education (MBO) (17.9 percent); (6) higher vocational education (HBO) (20.6 percent); (7) university education (5.9 percent).

Cultural participation was measured by means of seven questions: (1) number of books owned, (2) number of novels read during the three months preceding the interview, (3) frequency of attending concerts, (4) frequency of attending theater, cabaret, or ballet, (5) frequency of visiting art exhibitions (for instance, in a museum), (6) frequency of discussing arts and culture with others, and (7) degree to which one thinks of oneself as an "art lover." The seven scores were standardized and added up. Next, they were transformed into a scale ranging from 0 through 10, with higher scores indicating more cultural participation (Cronbach's $\alpha = 0.79$).

4. Results

4.1. Social Class, Economic Liberalism, and Cultural Conservatism

First, bypassing the distinction between social class and cultural capital for the moment, do we find an economically liberal and culturally conservative working class? If so, those belonging to EGP classes VI and VII, together constituting the working class, should display the highest scores on the measures for economic liberalism and cultural conservatism.

As to economic liberalism, four of the seven classes score above the grand mean of 4.89. Because this applies only marginally to classes III and (especially) V, it is evident that the two others, classes VI and VII (the working class), are most economically liberal. They deviate especially from class IV (small self-employed businessmen), which is the most conservative economically. Although those findings confirm the idea that the working class is more economically liberal than the other classes, it should be noted that the differences are quite small. Social class explains less than 7 percent of the differences with respect to economic liberalism.

With 12 percent of the variance explained, differences with regard to cultural conservatism are more substantial. Only classes I and II are less culturally conservative than the grand mean. The strongest cultural conservatism is found within the two classes constituting the working class: classes VI and VII. So, the idea that the working class is most culturally

Table 8.2
Economic Liberalism and Cultural Conservatism, by Social Class (Analyses of Variance: Deviations from Grand Means)

Social Class	Economic Liberalism	Cultural Conservatism
Class I	−0.27	−0.93
Class II	−0.30	−0.47
Class III	0.24	0.17
Class IV	−1.26	0.39
Class V	0.04	0.48
Class VI	0.67	1.05
Class VII	0.75	0.94
Grand mean	4.89	5.05
η	0.26*	0.34*
R^2(%)	6.5*	11.3*
N	697	695

* p <.001

conservative is also confirmed. Summing up, analyzing the relationship between social class and political values, we find exactly the pattern predicted by Lipset: an economically liberal and culturally conservative working class.

4.2. Opening up the Black Box

It has been argued that those relationships do not necessarily mean that both types of political values can be explained by social class. To find out whether they can, we need to introduce the distinction between social class and cultural capital, relying on the more explicit and less ambiguous indicators. The idea that the observed relationships stem from two different mechanisms—social class explaining economic liberalism, and cultural capital explaining cultural conservatism—assumes that measures of social class such as the one just used tap cultural capital as well as the strength of one's position in economic life. As a consequence, it is important to open up the black box of social class before testing hypotheses on the divergent effects of the more explicit indicators for social class and cultural capital.

I bypass differences regarding wage dependence among the seven classes in this analysis, because those are used in the coding procedure of the EGP-class scheme. For instance, all members of class IV are self-employed, whereas workers (classes VI and VII) cannot be by definition. As to the remaining indicators for social class and cultural capital, table 8.3 displays the contents of the black box—to the extent relevant to the current discussion, of course.

In regard to income, the seven classes differ substantially. Almost 30 percent of personal income differences can be explained by class membership. Because income is usually considered the preeminent standard when assessing the validity of class measures, this is not surprising, of course. The seven classes are likely to differ with respect to age, sex composition, and number of working hours—three variables known to have income consequences[6]—so table 8.3 also displays income differences after controlling for those. This hardly affects the size of the income differences among the seven classes, however (η decreases only slightly from 0.53 to 0.47).[7] On average, members of classes VI and VII, the working class, earn the lowest incomes.

As to job insecurity, the seven classes hardly differ: they tap only 5 percent of the differences, with classes III and VII characterized by most job insecurity. This is a remarkable finding, because the validity of a class mea-

Table 8.3

Net Personal Income, Job Insecurity, Education, and Cultural Participation, by Social Class (Analyses of Variance: Deviations from Grand Means)

Social Class	Income	Income (Corrected)[a]	Job Insecurity	Education	Cultural Participation
Class I	991	914	−0.11	1.3	0.98
Class II	224	261	−0.36	0.8	0.49
Class III	−621	−340	0.47	−0.5	−0.15
Class IV	556	−168	−0.53	−0.3	0.49
Class V	228	38	−0.11	−0.4	−0.76
Class VI	−512	−665	−0.12	−1.1	−1.48
Class VII	−692	−718	0.47	−1.7	−1.05
Grand mean	3,080	3,080	1.65	4.5	2.97
η	0.53*	0.47*	0.23*	0.59*	0.37*
R^2(%)	28.1*	48.0*	5.1*	34.2*	14.1*
N	678	678	706	689	705

[a]Corrected (by means of covariates) for age, sex, and number of weekly working hours.
* $p < 0.001$

sure that fails to capture differences with respect to economic security may be doubted:[8] Finally, differences regarding education and, to a somewhat lesser extent, cultural participation are substantial: 34 percent of the educational differences and 14 percent of those regarding cultural participation are captured by the distinction between the seven classes. The working class, classes VI and VII, is not only most poorly educated but least interested in arts and culture as well.

Summing up, the working class is characterized by both a relatively weak economic position and a limited amount of cultural capital. This confirms that EGP class taps the strength of not only one's position in economic life but one's cultural capital as well. Therefore, it is necessary to study which of these is responsible for the relationships between social class and both types of political values.

4.3. Social Class, Cultural Capital, and Economic Liberalism

How exactly does the economic liberalism of the working class come about? To answer this question, a regression analysis in two steps is performed. In the first step, education and the four explicit indicators for social class and cultural capital are entered. Next, in the second step, using

the "stepwise" option (SPSS), we assess whether or not the initial differences between the seven classes, as recorded in table 8.2, are attributable
to the variables already included in the analysis.[9] If neither of the class
dummies is able to improve significantly on the percentage of variance already explained, this means that the initial differences among the seven
classes were caused by the variables already entered in the first step. The
key question, then, is which of them are decisive?

What are the results of this analysis? First, the differences among the
seven classes recorded in table 8.2 above prove fully attributable to the
variables already included in the first step of the analysis (table 8.4). Second, a low family income, a low level of education, higher job insecurity,
and wage dependence—in short, a weak economic position—all lead to
stronger economic liberalism. Although none of these effects is very strong
(they range from 0.10 to 0.20), the variance explained is somewhat higher
than in the previous analysis, in which social class was used as the independent variable (10 percent and 7 percent, respectively). This difference
results mainly from the influence of job insecurity, which does affect economic liberalism, but is hardly captured by EGP class. Third, cultural participation, the only variable entered in the first step that does not indicate
social class, does not affect economic liberalism.

Table 8.4
*Economic Liberalism Explained by (Indicators for) Social Class and
Cultural Capital (β's; N = 661)*

Predictors	β
Step 1	
Cultural participation	0.08 (n.s.)
Education	−0.15**
Income	−0.12*
Job insecurity	0.18**
Wage dependence	0.15**
Step 2	
Class I	−0.00 (n.s.)[a]
Class II	−0.07 (n.s.)[a]
Class III	0.00 (n.s.)[a]
Class IV	0.04 (n.s.)[a]
Class V	−0.00 (n.s.)[a]
Class VI	0.05 (n.s.)[a]
Class VII	0.07 (n.s.)[a]
R2(%) 10.4**	

[a]Not included in regression equation
n.s. - not significant (p > .05); *p < .01; **p < .001

It can be concluded that the previously recorded economic liberalism of the working class is caused by its weak position in economic life. On a theoretical level this means not only that the working class does display economically liberal political values but also that this economic liberalism is, indeed, *caused* by its weak class position. As a consequence, Lipset's claim of an economically liberal working class is more than a descriptive one. It is also valid as an explanatory claim in a theoretical sense: the weak economic position of the working class causes its economic liberalism. This relationship results from the economic interests that are at stake: Because the working class in particular has an interest in state regulation of the economy and economic redistribution, it most strongly favors this.

4.4. Social Class, Cultural Capital, and Cultural Conservatism

Next, a similar type of analysis is performed for cultural conservatism (table 8.5). Education has a strong negative effect on cultural conservatism. So, as an indicator for social class, a high level of education leads to economic conservatism; however, it has a culturally liberalizing effect as well. Of course, this is not surprising; it has been demonstrated by many other studies (see section 2.3 above). We have seen that some consider this a class effect as well, whereas others claim that it is not. However, the effects of the other variables included in the analysis indicate that this educational effect has nothing to do with social class. There are three compelling reasons for this conclusion.

First, neither a low income, nor high job insecurity, nor wage dependence leads to cultural conservatism. This is not what we would expect to find if, like economic liberalism, cultural conservatism could be explained from a weak position in economic life as well. Indeed, education's indication of something else here is confirmed by a second finding: Cultural participation has an almost equally strong culturally liberalizing effect. So, the cultural conservatism of the working class is caused by its limited amount of cultural capital, unlike its economic liberalism, which is caused by its weak position in economic life. Third, indeed, the initial differences among the seven classes prove fully attributable to cultural capital. Moreover, in terms of variance explained, education and cultural participation provide quite a better explanation than social class. Working-class cultural conservatism, we can conclude, is caused not by its weak economic position but by its limited amount of cultural capital.

The implications of those findings for Lipset's hypothesis concerning working-class authoritarianism are obvious. Comparing classes with re-

Table 8.5

Cultural Conservatism Explained by (Indicators for) Social Class and Cultural Capital (β's; N = 659)

Predictors	β
Step 1	
Cultural participation	0.34[**]
Education	−0.24[**]
Income	−0.07 (n.s.)
Job insecurity	−0.07[*]
Wage dependence	−0.05 (n.s.)
Step 2	
Class I	−0.05 (n.s.)[a]
Class II	−0.02 (n.s.)[a]
Class III	0.01 (n.s.)[a]
Class IV	−0.04 (n.s.)[a]
Class V	0.03 (n.s.)[a]
Class VI	0.05 (n.s.)[a]
Class VII	0.02 (n.s.)[a]
R^2(%)	26.3[**]

[a]Not included in regression equation
n.s. = not significant ($p > .05$); [*]$p < .05$; [**]$p < .001$

spect to cultural conservatism, we find that, indeed, culturally conservative political values are most often found within the working class. On a theoretical level, however, Lipset's hypothesis is not confirmed. Unlike economic liberalism, cultural conservatism cannot be *explained* from the strength of one's economic position. Instead, it is caused by a limited amount of cultural capital.

4.5. Conclusion

Although many studies have demonstrated that working-class cultural conservatism is mainly a cultural conservatism of the poorly educated, no agreement exists on the question of whether this confirms Lipset's classical hypothesis of working-class authoritarianism. The analysis reported above sheds light onto this controversy.

Confirming Lipset's claim, economic liberalism and cultural conservatism—hardly related themselves—are remarkably differently related to social class. The working class is economically liberal and culturally conservative. This does not mean that both types of political values can be explained from social class, however. Economic liberalism can be: The eco-

nomic interests of the working class, related to its weak position in economic life, lead it to favor income redistribution and state regulation of the
economic system. Cultural conservatism cannot be explained from social
class: Values relating to the primacy of either individual liberty or maintaining social order cannot be explained from the strength of one's economic position. Instead, working-class cultural conservatism is caused by
its limited amount of cultural capital.

To conclude, it is necessary to complement Lipset's important distinction between economic and cultural liberal/conservatism with a
similar distinction, which has so far played no role within political sociology. Social class, affecting economic liberalism/conservatism, should be
systematically distinguished from cultural capital, affecting cultural lib-
eralism/conservatism. After all, measures of social class, such as the
EGP-class scheme used here, de facto tap both. Therefore, depending on
the type of political values with which we are dealing, their effects may or
may not be class effects. They are when we are dealing with economic lib-
eralism/conservatism, but they are not when social class is used to explain
cultural conservatism. Consequently, failing to open up the black box of
social class easily leads to misinterpretations of research findings and theoretical confusion.

5. Social Class, Political Values, and Class Voting

5.1. Class Voting Reconsidered

The study of class voting plays a key role in the debate about the political
significance of social class, as several chapters in this volume indicate. Recently, older studies of class voting have been criticized for methodological shortcomings, such as measuring absolute (Alford Index scores) instead
of relative class voting (log-odds-ratios) and the tendency to apply crude
manual/nonmanual class dichotomies instead of more detailed class
schemes such as the one used in this chapter (Hout et al., in this volume).
In his extensive study of class voting in 20 countries since 1945, however,
Nieuwbeerta has demonstrated that applying those methodological innovations does not yield substantially different conclusions: "The main finding is that the various measures of class voting [yield] the same conclusions
with respect to the ranking of the countries according to their levels of class
voting, and according to the speed of declines in class voting" (1996:
370).

Interestingly, notwithstanding methodological advances in subsequent generations of research (Nieuwbeerta 1995, 1996), the conceptualization of class voting itself has remained basically unchanged. The foregoing discussion of the relationships among social class, cultural capital, and political values, however, suggests that a new conceptualization is necessary to make theoretical advances as well.

Figure 8.1 displays the conceptualization of class voting shared by older and more recent studies of the topic, methodological advances notwithstanding. Applying this conventional conceptualization of class voting to the data for the Netherlands used in this chapter leads us to the conclusion that today no class voting exists in the Netherlands (table 8.6). Dichotomizing social class (working class versus nonworking class) does not affect this finding (Cramer's V = 0.05, p > .20). Furthermore, neither dichotomized social class (Cramer's V = 0.14, p > .05) nor the sevenfold class scheme used in table 8.6 (Cramer's V = 0.13; p > .20) is related to a nondichotomized version of the voting variable (see table 8.7 for the seven voting categories). Nevertheless, the foregoing analysis of the relationship between social class and political values suggests that we cannot simply conclude that social class is politically insignificant in the Netherlands today. As it happens, this conventional idea of class voting has two interrelated shortcomings, which necessitate a theoretical reformulation of the problem.

First, this conceptualization does not take into account *why* members of different classes are likely to vote differently. This question cannot simply be bypassed, however, for it does not make sense to consider as class voting the vote of an Italian worker for the Communist Party because he shares its commitment to garbage recycling, for instance (Clark, in this volume). Actually, the omission of voting motivations is remarkable, as Alford, discussing the problem of class voting 30 years ago, answers the question, Why expect class voting? with a logic similar to the one used above

Figure 8.1
Conventional conceptualization of class voting

Table 8.6
Voting Intention, by Social Class (% N = 537)

Social Class	Party on the Left[a]	No Party on the Left[b]	Total
Class I	44.0	56.0	15.6
Class II	37.6	62.4	33.7
Class III	45.0	55.0	20.3
Class IV	18.2	81.8	6.1
Class V	39.0	61.0	7.6
Class VI	42.3	57.7	4.8
Class VII	47.6	52.4	11.7
Total	40.4	59.6	100.0

[a]Social Democrats (PVDA), Greens (Groen Links), and Socialists (SP)
[b]Christian Democrats (CDA), Liberal Democrats (D66), Liberal Conservatives (VVD), and Christian Fundamentalists (SGP/GPV/RPF)
Cramer's V = 0.14 (p > .10)

to account for the relationship between social class and economic liberalism: "A relation between class position and voting behavior is a natural and expected association in the Western democracies, for a number of reasons: the existence of class interests, the representation of these interests by political parties, and the regular association of certain parties with certain interests. Given the character of the stratification order and the way political parties act as representatives of different class interests, it would be remarkable if such a relation were not found" (Alford 1967: 68–69). So, working-class support for parties on the left is assumed to stem from its desire for economic redistribution—that is, economic liberalism, which itself stems from its class-specific economic interests.

Table 8.7 demonstrates that this idea is as valid as it is one-sided: valid, because those voting for parties on the left—Labor Party (PVDA), Socialist Party (SP), and Greens (Groen Links)—are economically liberal, indeed; one-sided, because they are culturally liberal as well. Moreover, the relationships between party preference on the one hand and both types of political values on the other are equally strong. This means that cultural and economic liberalism/conservatism are equally important motivations for voting behavior. Indeed, a strong negative relationship exists between the average economic liberalism and the average cultural conservatism of the seven categories of party supporters (r = .62; N = 7; p = .07; one-sided test). So, whereas at the level of voters, economic and cultural liberalism/conservatism are almost unrelated, this is not so in regard to the level

Table 8.7

Economic Liberalism and Cultural Conservatism, by Voting Intention
(Analyses of Variance; Deviations from Grand Means [%]).

Voting Intention	Economic Liberalism		Cultural Conservatism	
Christian Democrats (CDA)	0.21	(12.1)	0.94	(12.3)
Liberal Democrats (D66)	−0.18	(16.0)	−0.31	(16.0)
Social Democrats (PVDA)	0.65	(27.9)	−0.71	(27.6)
Liberal Conservatives (VVD)	−1.19	(27.4)	0.84	(27.4)
Greens (Groen Links)	1.28	(7.8)	−1.80	(8.0)
Socialists (SP)	1.65	(4.3)	0.08	(4.3)
Christian Fundamentalists (SGP/GPV/RPF)	−0.49	(4.5)	0.92	(4.3)
Grand mean	4.82		4.96	
η	0.45[*]		0.44[*]	
R^2(%)	19.9[*]		19.8[*]	
N	537	(100.0)	536	(100.0)

[*] $p < .001$

of political parties: parties on the left are not only economically liberal but culturally liberal as well, while the opposite applies to parties on the right. The parties on the left (right), we can conclude, are chosen for reasons of economic liberalism (conservatism) as often as for reasons of cultural liberalism (conservatism).

With economic liberalism and cultural liberalism equally strongly contributing to a preference for parties on the left, a second shortcoming of the conventional conceptualization of class voting becomes apparent. In fact, there is no such thing as a "natural" relationship between the working class and parties on the left. There is an equally "natural" relationship between the middle class and parties on the left or, to formulate the same conversely, between the working class and parties on the right. As we have seen, as a consequence of its limited amount of cultural capital, the working class is the principal bearer of culturally conservative political values, represented by political parties on the right. In fact, of course, both of those conflicting ideas about the "natural" relationship between social class and political parties are one-sided simplifications of a complex reality.

We are dealing with a typical "cross-pressure mechanism" here, as it is discussed by Lazarsfeld et al. in The People's Choice ([1944] 1972: 53), their study of the American elections in 1940.[10] Confronted with the problem of selecting the party to vote for, members of the working class face a dilemma. Whereas their economic liberalism, stemming from their weak position in economic life, leads them to prefer parties on the left, their lack of cultural capital yields culturally conservative political values and a tendency to vote for parties on the right. Of course, the opposite applies to the middle class: It tends to vote for parties on the right as a consequence of its privileged economic position and for parties on the left as a consequence of its cultural liberalism, which stems from its cultural capital. In fact, what is conventionally called class voting constitutes the balance of those two opposite tendencies: economic voting (what class voting is intended to measure) and cultural voting (which has nothing to do with classes and economic interests).

Dealing satisfactorily with those two shortcomings of the conventional conceptualization of class voting requires (1) taking both types of voters' motivations into account rather than simply assuming one of them and (2) systematically distinguishing between social class and cultural capital. So, class voting should be conceptualized as *voting for a political party on the left (right), resulting from economically liberal (conservative) political values, which in turn stem from a weak (strong) class position.* Empirically, this means that class voting, properly conceived of as "economic voting," can be computed by multiplying path 1 and path 2 in figure 8.2. Likewise, the multiplication of path 3 and path 4 constitutes "cultural voting": *voting for a political party on the right (left), resulting from culturally conservative (liberal) political values, which in turn stem from a limited (large) amount of cultural capital.*

As we have seen, if the conventional idea of class voting is applied to the Netherlands today, no relationship between social class and party preference is found. We cannot conclude from this that social class is politically

Figure 8.2
Class voting reconceptualized as economic voting (path 1 × path 2) and distinguished from cultural voting (path 3 × path 4)

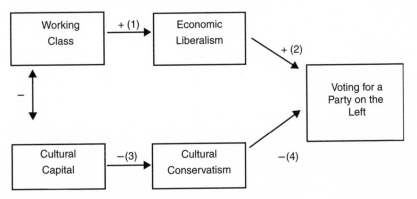

insignificant, however. This is demonstrated in figure 8.3, which displays the relationships among social class, both types of political values, and party preference. The distinction between the seven EGP classes has been labeled "working class" in this figure to make possible a substantially meaningful distinction between positive and negative effects (as we have seen, classes VI and VII—the working class—score highest on economic liberalism and cultural conservatism).[11] The seven categories of party preference have been quantified for this analysis by assigning to each of them the mean level of economic liberalism of those falling with it.[12]

Figure 8.3 demonstrates that we would be mistaken to conclude that social class is not politically significant in the Netherlands nowadays. After all, the working class is characterized by economically liberal political values, which lead it to prefer parties on the left. When the conventional conceptualization of class voting is applied, this is simply made invisible by the opposite tendency of the working class to vote for parties on the right as a consequence of its cultural conservatism. However, this is not an effect of social class: the limited amount of cultural capital of the working class is responsible for this countervailing tendency. In summation, the conventional conceptualization of class voting easily yields misleading conclusions. In this case, it would lead us to conclude wrongly that social class has no political significance in the Netherlands today. Nevertheless, the working class does vote for parties on the left as a consequence of its economic liberalism, stemming from its weak economic position.

Figure 8.3
Voting for a party on the left explained by social class, economic liberalism, and cultural conservatism (N = 527; R^2 voting: 26.5 percent)

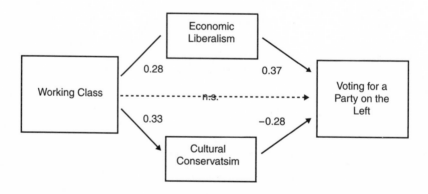

We are facing an interesting irony here. The very tendency of political sociologists to rely on a social class framework when studying voting behavior and political values proves to lead to a systematic *underestimation* of the political significance of social class. This framework gives rise to a blind spot for culture (Houtman 2000)—that is, a failure seriously to consider the possibility that education's culturally liberalizing effects might have nothing to do with social class and a failure to acknowledge the role of political values in the coming about of voting behavior. Precisely this failure to take culture seriously leads to an underestimation of the political significance of class.

5.2. Explaining Levels of Class Voting: Problems for Future Research

In the most extensive comparative study of class voting conducted so far, it has been demonstrated that class voting is strongest in Norway, Finland, Sweden, Denmark, and Great Britain and weakest in Canada and the United States. During the period 1945–1990 it has declined significantly in 11 of the 20 countries studied: in Australia, Austria, Belgium, Great Britain, Denmark, France, Germany, Italy, Norway, Sweden, and the United States. In most of the nine remaining countries, levels of class voting have declined as well, although this trend is not significant in those instances—in some cases, possibly as a consequence of the availability of data for only a limited number of years (Nieuwbeerta 1995, 1996).

The idea that political values and political life in general can be explained by economic factors is widely accepted within political sociology. Indeed, even Inglehart, who rejects the idea that the economic class struggle continues to structure political life, insists on the explanatory role of economic variables. Doing so, he focuses on processes of cultural and political change, which are held to be caused by the increase of affluence during the last few decades (e.g., Inglehart 1977, 1990, 1997). Given this general tendency in political sociology, it is hardly surprising that almost all hypotheses tested by Nieuwbeerta to account for the divergent levels of class voting relate to socioeconomic context variables. Typical examples are those about the consequences of the size of the income differences in a country, the general standard of living, the percentage of socially mobile persons, the union density, the degree to which social class is a political issue, and the proportion of manual workers in the population. It is striking to find that these hypotheses are rejected almost without exception (Nieuwbeerta 1995: 57–77).

Might the cultural context in which voting takes place be more important? Several studies suggest it might, indeed. As it happens, the level of cultural voting, which downwardly affects the level of class voting as traditionally conceptualized (figure 8.1), seems to be dependent on the cultural context in which voting takes place. So, macrocultural variables affecting the strength of paths 3 and 4 in figure 8.2 are quite likely to affect levels of class voting as they have been traditionally conceptualized.

The strength of path 3, education's effect on cultural liberalism/conservatism, proves to vary considerably among countries. It has been shown to be quite strong in the United States and Finland, substantially weaker in Costa Rica, and even absent in Mexico (Simpson 1972). Comparing its strength in the United States, West Germany, Austria, and France, Weil has concluded that "the impact of education on liberal values is weaker, nonexistent, or sometimes even reversed in nonliberal democracies or countries which did not have liberal-democratic regime forms in earlier decades, compared to countries which have been liberal democratic for a long time" (1985: 470). Indeed, this is confirmed by a recent comparative study based on an analysis of data from the World Values Survey, 1990–1993 (World Values Study Group 1994). If we control for religion, age, and sex, education proves to have negative effects on cultural conservatism in all of the 42 countries studied, except Belarus.[13] The strength of this effect varies considerably, however. It is dependent on the degree to which the values of individual liberty and acceptance of cultural diversity are institutionalized within a country. So, the more a country can be characterized as democratic, individualized or detraditionalized—culturally modern, in short[14]—the more strongly education negatively affects cultural conservatism (Houtman et al. 1999).

It is easy to understand why this should be so. After all, the educational system is the institution par excellence to transmit a country's culture to a new generation. As a consequence, precisely in those countries where individual liberty and acceptance of cultural diversity are most strongly institutionalized, we would expect the largest difference between the poorly and the highly educated in this respect. Conversely, in more traditional cultural settings, education and cultural liberalism/conservatism are only weakly related. So, the higher the level of cultural modernity of a country or historical period, the stronger the positive relationship between education and cultural liberalism (path 3 in figure 8.2).

Second, path 4—cultural liberalism/conservatism's effect on voting—may be expected to be weaker within more traditional cultural contexts as well. After all, the more culturally modern a social context, the less likely social action is to be determined by the force of habit. Indeed, to employ Max Weber's well-known ideal types ([1922] 1978, 1: 24–26), under conditions of cultural modernity social action is more likely to be value-rational than traditional.[15] By implication, the strongest relationships between values and lifestyles are to be expected under conditions of cultural modernity.[16] This idea is confirmed, for instance, by the finding that the well-known relationship between religion and cultural conservatism is strongest within the most culturally modern societies (Houtman et al. 1999; see also Kelley and De Graaf 1997). If Western societies have become more culturally modern during the last few decades,[17] research findings suggest that this logic applies to the relationship between political values and voting as well. Pooling data from Great Britain, France, Italy, West Germany, Belgium, and the Netherlands, Inglehart (1987: 1298) demonstrates that post-materialists tended to vote for parties on the left in 1985 more often than they did in 1970.

If, indeed, culturally modern social contexts give rise to higher levels of cultural voting, they necessarily lead to lower levels of class voting as conventionally conceptualized as well. Dealing with complex problems such as these, however, we cannot jump to conclusions just like that. Therefore, it is important to conduct systematic comparative research into this problem within the next few years. In doing so, it seems crucial to open up the black box of class voting, very much as this has been done in regard to the concept of social class itself in this chapter. Two research questions stand out as particularly relevant: First, to what extent do different levels of class voting in fact represent different levels of cultural voting? Second, to what extent are those affected by levels of cultural modernity rather than economic contextual variables? It is likely that answering those questions will lead us to conclude that cultural variables have been wrongly neglected not only at the individual level but at the societal level as well.

6. Conclusion and Debate

In his classical article on working-class authoritarianism, Lipset argues that there is no reason simply to consider the working class a liberating and progressive force in history. In fact, when it comes to the acceptance of individual liberty and cultural diversity, he explains, the working class is the most rather than the least conservative. Many studies, the current chapter included, have revealed that this is as true today as it was half a century ago. However, it has been demonstrated above that working-class cultural conservatism has nothing to do with its weak position in economic life. Instead, it is caused by its limited amount of cultural capital—that is, its low level of education and limited cultural participation. This finding has important implications for the debate about the declining political significance of class.

The widely accepted theoretical framework of social classes and economic interests has traditionally led political sociologists to conceive of political life as a struggle between social classes; to assume that cultural conservatism, like economic liberalism, can be explained from social class; to fail to consider seriously the possibility that education might be more than an indicator for social class; and to neglect the way political values, and especially cultural liberalism/conservatism, affect voting behavior. The rejection by Nieuwbeerta of most of the contextual hypotheses derived from this theoretical framework suggests that it cannot satisfactorily answer the questions it faces today: Why has the relationship between social class and voting behavior declined? Why do so many workers vote for parties on the right? And why do members of the middle class increasingly vote for parties on the left?

However, as Nieuwbeerta rightly points out, "full-blooming alternative approaches for explaining variations in class voting (are lacking)" (1955: 201). This lack of an alternative approach makes it all the more important to construct one.[18] When this is done, the conventional point of departure should be rejected as a one-sided simplification. So, it should be asked not (only) why the working class "naturally" or "normally" votes for parties on the left, but why it is equally "naturally" or "normally" attracted to parties on the right. Some building blocks for such a theoretical alternative have been suggested in this chapter. Its key concepts are cultural capital, cultural liberalism/conservatism, and cultural voting rather than social class, economic interest, and class voting.

It has been demonstrated that the working class is the most culturally conservative because it has substantially less cultural capital than the other classes. Although those political values have nothing to do with its weak position in economic life, they do lead to a preference for political parties on the right, which characteristically address issues of law and order. Conversely, the middle class is attracted to parties on the left, because the latter's defense of individual liberty and acceptance of cultural diversity resonates with middle-class cultural liberalism, which stems from its cultural capital rather than its privileged economic position. This relationship among cultural capital, cultural conservatism, and voting behavior, which leads the working class to vote for parties on the right and the middle class to vote for parties on the left, has been called cultural voting in this chapter.

Several research findings indicate that cultural voting is strongest within culturally modern social contexts (i.e., contexts characterized by a high level of institutionalization of the values of individual liberty and acceptance of cultural diversity) and weakest within more traditional ones. So, the more culturally modern the context in which voting takes place, the more strongly we underestimate the political significance of social class when we rely on the conventional idea of class voting. This is a less than valid measure for the political significance of class, because it is mixed up with a countervailing process of cultural voting. Therefore, in future research, it is necessary to open up the black box of class voting and study what is going on inside it within different cultural contexts. This is likely to reveal that the political significance of social class has declined less dramatically than we assume today but rather has simply been increasingly outstripped by an extension of levels of cultural voting.

Notes

1. This type of political value is usually referred to as social liberalism/conservatism in the American research literature (e.g., Zipp 1986; Phelan et al. 1995).

2. It has been argued, however, that the negative relationship between education and cultural conservatism is simply a methodological artifact caused by either the response set or the tendency among the highly educated to give socially desirable answers (e.g., Hamilton 1972: 455–456; Jackman 1973, 1978; Jackman and Muha 1984). Such attempts to explain away the cultural liberalism of the highly educated fail to convince. First, measures not susceptible to the problem of response set, such as Inglehart's (1977) index for post-materialism, yield basically the same relationship with education. Second, attempts to demonstrate the effects of social desirability yield specifications of the relationship between education and cultural conservatism rather than disprove its existence. As it happens, they boil down either (1) to demonstrating that the highly educated "know" the "right" (liberal) answers and subsequently raise the standards of cultural liberalism to a level at which education no longer makes a difference or (2) to interposing ideological or psychological variables between education and cultural conservatism to conclude that this (partly) explains the initial relationship (Weil 1985: 458–459).

3. Bourdieu also distinguishes objectified cultural capital, that is, the possession of cultural goods (books, painting, et cetera). In this chapter, objectified and embodied cultural capital have been combined into a single measure for cultural participation. Because it is hard to imagine that the possession of cultural goods in itself (i.e., independent of embodied cultural capital) affects cultural liberalism/conservatism, only a single indicator for objectified cultural capital has been used: number of books owned.

4. The information needed is lacking for 0.7 percent of the 711 cases.

5. Of course, this question was not asked of the self-employed. They were given the same score here as workers and employees with a permanent contract (0).

6. Given the type of work one does, one's income tends to be higher when one is older, male and, obviously, working more hours. As to the income differences between men and women, the reader is referred to Schippers 1995.

7. As expected, young people, women, and those working a limited number of hours earn lower incomes than the others do. The combined effect of those three variables is considerable, as the increase of variance explained from 28 percent to 48 percent indicates (the three separate effects are not displayed in table 8.3). Nevertheless, the initial income differences between the seven classes are hardly caused by disproportional numbers of young people, women, and part-time workers within the classes with the lowest average incomes. There is one exception to this, however, because the remarkably low mean income of class III (routine nonmanual) is caused by this phenomenon. The dramatic decline of the mean income of class IV after controlling for those three variables is, of course, especially caused by the relatively high number of working hours of the self-employed.

8. Steijn and Houtman (1998) have found this as well. There are two likely causes for this remarkable finding. First, as a consequence of recent socio-economic changes, analyzed by Beck (1992) as the rise of the risk society, it might be that job insecurity is no longer an exclusive characteristic of the working class. If this is the case, the usefulness of the EGP-class scheme has gradually declined as a consequence of changes in the real world. A second possibility, which is logically compatible with the one just mentioned, is that the EGP-class scheme has never tapped job insecurity adequately: it might have been a weak indicator for job insecurity in the past as well.

9. Using this stepwise option has the additional advantage that dummies for all seven classes can be offered for inclusion in the second step without creating problems of multicollinearity.

10. Thanks are due Jan Berting for drawing my attention to this study.

11. This path model has been constructed by means of ordinary least squares regression. The Combined effect of six EGP-class dummy variables on economic liberalism and cultural conservatism have been represented by means of the respective multiple determination coefficients (Rs). Their combined effect on party preference, controlling for both types of liberalism/conservatism, has been ascertained by means of a so-called sheaf variable. Such a sheaf variable for a nominal variable with n categories is simply computed as $(B_1^* D_1) + (B_2^* D_2) + B_{n-1}^* D_{n-1}$, with D referring to dummy variables for all except one of the n categories and B referring to the unstandardized regression coefficients those yield.

12. When this is done, of course, the effect of economic liberalism/conservatism is overestimated, while that of cultural liberalism/conservatism is underestimated. After all, the correlation between both possible quantifications of the seven party preferences is not -1.00 but -0.67. We have already seen that, in fact, both effects are about equally strong however (see table 8.7).

13. In the study referred to, cultural liberalism/conservatism has been operationalized as a linear combination of four composite measures: (1) Inglehart's index for post-materialism, (2) a scale tapping self-direction or conformity as parental values, (3) a scale measuring sexual permissiveness, and (4) a scale tapping the rejection of traditional gender roles (Houtman et al. 1999).

14. The level of cultural modernity has been measured as a linear combination of three indexes, which are strongly correlated among themselves: (1) an index for the level of democracy, based on the degree of acceptance of a considerable number of political rights and civil liberties (Inglehart 1997), (2) the length of the democratic tradition in number of years since 1920 (Inglehart 1997), and (3) women's position in society as measured by the gender empowerment measure (United Nations 1996), which is based on the percentage of female administrators and managers, the percentage of parliamentary seats occupied by women, the percentage of women with a technical or professional education, and the percentage of the national income earned by women.

15. Although both are culturally driven types of social action, only value-rational action involves a conscious selection of the value to guide social action. Precisely because of this reflexive process, value-rational action constitutes a type of *rational* action—like goal-rational action, but unlike traditional and affective action (Weber [1922] 1978: 24–26).

16. Indeed, under conditions of cultural modernity voting behavior may be more strongly affected by economic liberalism/conservatism as well. Although we have seen that it does not exist in the Netherlands today, a direct class effect on voting behavior may be expected within more traditional social contexts. It is likely to give way to indirect effects through both types of value-ratio-

nal voting as the level of cultural modernity increases (compare Middendorp's discussion of "the ideologization of the vote" in his excellent study *Ideology in Dutch Politics* [1991: 203–233]). So, when we study class voting in comparative perspective, it seems important to allow for a direct effect of social class ("traditional class voting"), in figure 8.2, and to study whether its decline goes along with stronger economic and cultural voting, as discussed in this chapter.

17. This assumption is hardly problematic, as Inglehart (1977, 1990, 1997) has demonstrated that among the younger age cohorts more postmaterialists are found than among the older ones, which is not a life-cycle effect, but indicates a process of cultural change.

18. Inglehart's theory of value change does not provide a fully satisfactory alternative. He is right in emphasizing the way post-materialist (culturally liberal) political values erode the relationship between social class and voting behavior. His claim that this value shift is caused by the circumstance that an increasing number of people have grown up under conditions of affluence is unjustified, however. Although I do not want to discuss this problem at length here, three things need to be pointed out shortly. First, Inglehart considers education an indicator of the affluence of the family one has grown up in ("formative affluence") (1977: 73–74). Although he does not include the latter variable in his analyses, those who have done so have unanimously concluded that it plays no role whatsoever, whereas education does (Lafferty 1976; De Graaf and De Graaf 1988; Elchardus 1991; Houtman 1998). Of course, counterarguing that in France a strong relationship exists between class background and education (Abramson and Inglehart 1994, 1995: 75–87) is not convincing in this context, because this does not demonstrate that parental affluence positively affects post-materialism (Duch and Taylor 1994: 819). Second, societal affluence during one's formative period proves not to affect post-materialism (Duch and Taylor 1993; De Graaf and Evans 1996). Third, although most post-materialists are found within the most affluent Western countries (Abramson and Inglehart 1995: 123–137), this cannot be interpreted as supporting Inglehart's theory. After all, if affluence fails to lead to post-materialism at the individual level, this theory cannot satisfactorily explain this relationship at the societal level: "One wonders how 'national affluence' could possibly reshape individuals' values, except by virtue of the fact that, at another level of analysis, it is reflected in the presence of affluent individuals," as Inglehart (1982: 471) himself remarks elsewhere. Indeed, it is quite likely that those affluent countries' cultural modernity is the decisive variable here. However, because the correlation between affluence and cultural modernity is no less than .88, while those two variables are equally strongly related to the percentage of post-materialists (minus the percentage of materialists) in a country (r = .70 and r = .71, respectively), it is impossible statistically to disentangle their effects (Houtman et al. 1999).

References

Abramson, Paul R., and Ronald Inglehart. 1994. "Education, Security, and Postmaterialism: A Comment on Duch and Taylor's 'Postmaterialism and the Economic Condition.'" *American Journal of Political Science* 38: 797–814.

Abramson, Paul R., and Ronald Inglehart. 1995. *Value Change in Global Perspective.* Ann Arbor: University of Michigan Press.

Adorno, Theodor W., Else Frenkel-Brunswik, Donald J. Levinson, and R. Nevitt Sanford. 1950. *The Authoritarian Personality.* New York: Harper and Row.

Alford, Robert R. 1967. "Class Voting in the Anglo-American Political Systems." In Seymour Martin Lipset and Stein Rokkan, eds., *Party Systems and Voter Alignments: Cross-National Perspectives,* 67–93. New York: Free Press.

Bakker, Bart, Inge Sieben, Paul Nieuwbeerta, and Harry Ganzeboom. 1997. "Maten voor prestige, sociaal-economische status en sociale klasse voor de standaard beroepen classificatie 1992" (Measures for prestige, socio-economic status, and social class for the standard occupational classification 1992). *Sociale Wetenschappen* 40: 1–22.

Bauman, Zygmunt. 1987. *Legislators and Interpreters: On Modernity, Post-Modernity, and Intellectuals.* Oxford: Polity Press.

Beck, Ulrich. 1992. *Risk Society: Towards a New Modernity.* London: Sage.

Bobo, Lawrence, and Frederick C. Licari. 1989. "Education and Political Tolerance: Testing the Effects of Cognitive Sophistication and Group Affect." *Public Opinion Quarterly* 53: 285–308.

Böröcz, Joszef, and Caleb Southworth. 1996. "Decomposing the Intellectuals' Class Power: Conversion of Cultural Capital to Income, Hungary, 1986." *Social Forces* 74: 797–821.

Bourdieu, Pierre. 1973. "Cultural Reproduction and Social Reproduction." In Richard K. Brown, ed., *Knowledge, Education and Cultural Change: Papers in the Sociology of Education*, 71–112. London: Tavistock.

Bourdieu, Pierre. 1984. *Distinction: A Social Critique of the Judgment of Taste.* London: Routledge and Kegan Paul.

Bourdieu, Pierre. 1986. "The Forms of Capital." In John G. Richardson, ed., *Handbook of Theory and Research for the Sociology of Education*, 241–258. New York: Greenwood Press.

Bourdieu, Pierre, and Jean-Claude Passeron. 1977. *Reproduction in Education, Society and Culture.* London/Beverly Hills: Sage.

Case, Charles E., Andrew Greeley, and Stephan Fuchs. 1989. "Social Determinants of Racial Prejudice." *Sociological Perspectives* 32: 469–483.

D'Anjou, Leo J. M., Abram Steijn, and Dries Van Aarsen. 1995. "Social Position, Ideology, and Distributive Justice." *Social Justice Research* 8: 351–384.

Davis, Nancy J., and Robert V. Robinson. 1996. "Are the Rumors of War Exaggerated? Religious Orthodoxy and Moral Progressivism in America." *American Journal of Sociology* 102: 756–787.

De Graaf, Nan Dirk, and Paul M. De Graaf. 1988. "Family Background, Postmaterialism and Life Style." *Netherlands Journal of Sociology* 24: 50–64.

De Graaf, Nan Dirk, and Geoff Evans. 1996. "Why Are the Young More Postmaterialist? A Cross-National Analysis of Individual and Contextual Influences on Postmaterial Values." *Comparative Political Studies* 28: 608–635.

Dekker, Paul, and Peter Ester. 1987. "Working Class Authoritarianism: A Re-Examination of the Lipset Thesis." *European Journal of Political Research* 15: 395–415.

Duch, Raymond M., and Michael A. Taylor. 1993. "Postmaterialism and the Economic Condition." *American Journal of Political Science* 38: 747–779.

Duch, Raymond M., and Michael A. Taylor. 1994. "A Reply to Abramson and Inglehart's 'Education, Security, and Postmaterialism.' " *American Journal of Political Science* 38: 815–824.

Eisinga, Rob, and Peer Scheepers. 1989. *Etnocentrisme in Nederland: Theoretische en empirische verkenningen* (Ethnocentrism in the Netherlands: Theoretical and empirical explorations). Nijmegen: ITS.

Elchardus, Mark. 1991. *Soepel, flexibel en ongebonden: Een vergelijking van twee laat-moderne generaties* (Pliable, flexible, and unattached: A comparison of two late-modern generations). Brussel: VUB Press.

Erikson, Robert. 1984. "Social Class of Men, Women and Families." *Sociology* 18: 500–514.

Erikson, Robert, John H. Goldthorpe, and Lucienne Portocarero. 1979. "Intergenerational Class Mobility in Three Western European Societies: England, France and Sweden." *British Journal of Sociology* 30: 415–441.

Evans, Geoffrey, Anthony Heath, and Mansur Lalljee. 1996. "Measuring Left-Right and Libertarian-Authoritarian Values in the British Electorate." *British Journal of Sociology* 47: 93–112.

Feldman, Kenneth A., and Theodor M. Newcomb. 1973. *The Impact of College on Students.* 2 vols. San Francisco: Jossey-Bass.

Felling, Albert J. A., and Jan Peters. 1986. "Conservatism: A Multidimensional Concept." *Netherlands Journal of Sociology* 22: 36–60.

Flanagan, Scott C. 1979. "Value Change and Partisan Change in Japan: The Silent Revolution Revisited." *Comparative Politics* 11: 253–278.

Flanagan, Scott C. 1982. "Changing Values in Advanced Industrial Societies: Inglehart's Silent Revolution from the Perspective of Japanese Findings." *Comparative Political Studies* 14: 403–444.

Flanagan, Scott C. 1987. "Value Change in Industrial Societies: Reply to Inglehart." *American Political Science Review* 81: 1303–1319.

Fleishman, John A. 1988. "Attitude Organization in the General Public: Evidence for a Bidimensional Structure." *Social Forces* 67: 159–184.

Gabennesch, Howard. 1972. "Authoritarianism as World View." *American Journal of Sociology* 77: 857–875.

Goldthorpe, John H. 1980. *Social Mobility and Class Structure in Modern Britain.* Oxford: Clarendon Press.

Grabb, Edward G. 1979. "Working-Class Authoritarianism and Tolerance of Outgroups: A Reassessment." *Public Opinion Quarterly* 43: 36–47.

Grabb, Edward G. 1980. "Marxist Categories and Theories of Class: The Case of Working Class Authoritarianism." *Pacific Sociological Review* 23: 359–376.

Hamilton, Richard F. 1972. *Class and Politics in the United States.* New York: Wiley.

Houtman, Dick. 1998. "Melvin Kohn, Ronald Inglehart en de verklaring van cultureel conservatisme: Een empirisch-theoretische kritiek" (Melvin Kohn, Ronald Inglehart, and the explanation of cultural conservatism: An empirical-theoretical critique). *Mens en Maatschappij* 73: 259–276.

Houtman, Dick. 2000. *Een blinde vlek voor cultuur: Sociologen over cultureel conservatisme, klassen en moderniteit* (A blind spot for culture: Sociologists on cultural conservatism, classes, and modernity). Assen: Van Gorcum.

Houtman, Dick, Jacques F. A. Braster, Manu Busschots, and Maria Del Mar Del Pozo-Andres. 1999. "Welvaart, moderniteit en cultureel conservatisme in internationaal vergelijkend perspectief" (Affluence, modernity, and cultural conservatism in internationally comparative perspective). *Sociologische Gids* 46: 24–50.

Inglehart, Ronald. 1971. "The Silent Revolution in Europe: Intergenerational Change in Post-Industrial Societies." *American Political Science Review* 65: 990–1017.

Inglehart, Ronald. 1977. *The Silent Revolution: Changing Values and Political Styles among Western Publics.* Princeton, N.J.: Princeton University Press.

Inglehart, Ronald. 1982. "Changing Values in Japan and the West." *Comparative Political Studies* 14: 445–479.

Inglehart, Ronald. 1987. "Value Change in Industrial Societies." *American Political Science Review* 81: 1289–1303.

Inglehart, Ronald. 1990. *Culture Shift in Advanced Industrial Society.* Princeton, N.J.: Princeton University Press.

Inglehart, Ronald. 1997. *Modernization and Postmodernization: Cultural, Economic, and Political Change in 43 Countries.* Princeton, N.J.: Princeton University Press.

Jackman, Mary R. 1973. "Education and Prejudice or Education and Response-Set?" *American Sociological Review* 38: 327–339.

Jackman, Mary R. 1978. "General and Applied Tolerance: Does Education Increase Commitment to Racial Integration?" *American Journal of Political Science* 22: 302–324.

Jackman, Mary R., and Michael J. Muha. 1984. "Education and Intergroup Attitudes: Moral Enlightenment, Superficial Democratic Commitment, or Ideological Refinement?" *American Sociological Review*, 49: 751–769.

Kalmijn, Matthijs. 1994. "Assortative Mating by Cultural and Economic Occupational Status." *American Journal of Sociology* 100: 422–452.

Kelley, Jonathan, and Nan Dirk De Graaf. 1997. "National Context, Parental Socialization, and Religious Belief: Results from 15 Nations." *American Sociological Review* 62: 639–659.

Kohn, Melvin L. [1969] 1977. *Class and Conformity: A Study in Values.* 2d ed. Chicago: University of Chicago Press.

Kohn, Melvin L., and Carmi Schooler. 1983. *Work and Personality: An Inquiry into the Impact of Social Stratification.* New York: Ablex.

Kohn, Melvin L., and Kazimierz M. Slomczynski. 1990. *Social Structure and Self-Direction: A Comparative Analysis of the United States and Poland.* Oxford: Basil Blackwell.

Lafferty, William M. 1976. "Basic Needs and Political Values: Some Perspectives from Norway on Europe's 'Silent Revolution.' " *Acta Sociologica* 19: 117–136.

Lamont, Michèle, and Annette Lareau. 1988. "Cultural Capital: Allusions, Gaps and Glissandos in Recent Theoretical Developments." *Sociological Theory* 6: 153–168.

Lazarsfeld, Paul F., Bernard Berelson, and Hazel Gaudet. [1944] 1972. *The People's Choice: How the Voter Makes up His Mind in a Presidential Campaign.* 3d ed. New York: Columbia University Press.

Lipset, Seymour Martin. 1959. "Democracy and Working-Class Authoritarianism." *American Sociological Review* 24: 482–502.

Lipset, Seymour Martin. 1981. *Political Man: The Social Bases of Politics.* Expanded ed. Baltimore, Md.: Johns Hopkins University Press.

Lipset, Seymour Martin, Paul F. Lazarsfeld, Allen H. Barton, and Juan Linz. 1954. "The Psychology of Voting: An Analysis of Political Behavior." In Gardner Lindzey, ed., *Handbook of Social Psychology,* 1124–1175. Cambridge, Mass.: Addison-Wesley.

Lipsitz, Lewis. 1965. "Working-Class Authoritarianism: A Re-Evaluation." *American Sociological Review* 30: 103–109.

Marshall, Gordon, Howard Newby, David Rose, and Carolyn Vogler. 1988. *Social Class in Modern Britain.* London: Hutchinson.

Marx, Karl. [1867] 1967. *Capital: A Critique of Political Economy.* Vol. 1. New York: International Publishers.

Marx, Karl, and Friedrich Engels. [1848] 1948. *Manifesto of the Communist Party.* New York: International Publishers.

Middendorp, Cees P. 1991. *Ideology in Dutch Politics: The Democratic System Reconsidered (1970–1985).* Assen: Van Gorcum.

Middendorp, Cees P., and Jos D. Meloen. 1990. "The Authoritarianism of the Working Class Revisited." *European Journal of Political Research* 18: 257–267.

Nieuwbeerta, Paul. 1995. *The Democratic Class Struggle in Twenty Countries, 1945–1990.* Amsterdam: Thesis Publishers.

Nieuwbeerta, Paul. 1996. "The Democratic Class Struggle in Postwar Societies: Class Voting in Twenty Countries, 1945–1990." *Acta Sociologica* 39: 345–384.

Nunn, Clyde Z., Harry J. Crockett, Jr., and J. Allen Williams, Jr. 1978. *Tolerance for Nonconformity: A National Survey of Americans' Changing Commitment to Civil Liberties.* San Francisco: Jossey-Bass.

Olson, Daniel V. A., and Jackson W. Carroll. 1992. "Religiously Based Politics: Religious Elites and the Public." *Social Forces* 70: 765–786.

Pedersen, Willy. 1996. "Working-Class Boys at the Margins: Ethnic Prejudice, Cultural Capital, and Gender." *Acta Sociologica* 39: 257–279.

Phelan, Jo, Bruce G. Link, Ann Stueve, and Robert E. Moore. 1995. "Education, Social Liberalism, and Economic Conservatism: Attitudes towards Homeless People." *American Sociological Review* 60: 126–140.

Schippers, Joop. 1995. "Pay differences between Men and Women in the European Labour Market." In Anneke Van Doorne Huiskes, Jacques Van Hoof, and Ellie Roelofs, eds., *Women and the European Labour Markets,* 31–52. London: Paul Chapman.

Schulz, Wolfgang, and Hilde Weiss. 1933. "Conservatism and the Political Views of Young Men in Austria." *European Sociological Review* 9: 79–90.

Simpson, Miles. 1972. "Authoritarianism and Education: A Comparative Approach." *Sociometry* 35: 223–234.

Steijn, Bram, and Dick Houtman. 1998. "Proletarianization of the Dutch Middle Class: Fact or

Fiction?" In Bram Steijn, Jan Berting, and Mart-Jan De Jong eds., *Economic Restructuring and the Growing Uncertainty of the Middle Class,* 73–91. Boston: Kluwer.

Stouffer, Samuel A. 1955. *Communism, Conformity, and Civil Liberties: A Cross-Section of the Nation Speaks its Mind.* New York: Wiley.

Svallfors, Stefan. 1991. "The Politics of Welfare Policy in Sweden: Structural Determinants and Attitudinal Cleavages." *British Journal of Sociology* 42: 609–634.

United Nations. 1996. *Human Development Report 1996.* New York: Oxford University Press.

Weber, Max. [1922] 1978. *Economy and Society.* 2 vols. Edited by Guenther Roth and Claus Wittich. Berkeley/Los Angeles: University of California Press.

Weil, Frederick D. 1985. "The Variable Effects of Education on Liberal Attitudes: A Comparative-Historical Analysis of Anti-Semitism Using Public Opinion Survey Data." *American Sociological Review* 50: 458–474.

Woodrum, Eric. 1988a. "Determinants of Moral Attitudes." *Journal for the Scientific Study of Religion* 27: 553–573.

Woodrum, Eric. 1988b. "Moral Conservatism and the 1984 Presidential Election." *Journal for the Scientific Study of Religion* 27: 192–210.

World Values Study Group. 1994. "World Values Survey, 1981–1984 and 1990–1993." Computer file. Ann Arbor, Mich.:. Institute for Social Research (producer), ICPSR (distributor).

Wright, Erik Olin. 1979. *Class Structure and Income Determination.* New York: Academic Press.

Wright, Erik Olin. 1985. *Classes.* London: Verso.

Zipp, John F. 1986. "Social Class and Social Liberalism." *Sociological Forum* 1: 301–329.

9

Social Class and Voting
The Case against Decline

DAVID L. WEAKLIEM

As mass representative democracy emerged in the nineteenth century, observers from all parts of the political spectrum believed that class was, or would soon become, an important influence on opinions and votes. Marx is remembered for his focus on class conflict, but liberals such as John Stuart Mill ([1861] 1962) and conservatives such as Sir Henry Maine (1886) were equally convinced of its importance; the difference is that the last two wanted to contain rather than encourage it. The development of representative national surveys in the 1930s and 1940s confirmed that class was important and made it possible to measure how large the differences among the classes were. In no case were the classes completely polarized: working-class conservatives and middle-class reformers or socialists were found in all countries. For example, in the 1940s and 1950s, about 25 percent of British manual workers voted for the Conservative Party, while about 20 percent of professionals and businessmen voted for Labour. Moreover, class was not the only systematic influence on vote, since significant ethnic, religious, and regional divisions were often present. At the same time, class was one of the leading influences in nearly all nations. Even in the United States, where class differences in party support were small by comparative standards, they were still about as large as racial and religious differences and far larger than differences by sex, age, or marital status (Campbell et al. 1954; Berelson et al. 1954). Taking Western democracies as a whole, class had more impact on party choice than any other "sociological" variable.[1]

Even as empirical research was establishing the importance of class, however, some observers were arguing that general social changes such as mass affluence, the expansion of schooling, and the growth of the mass media were working to reduce its influence. The evidence was inconclusive at first, but since the 1970s the hypothesis of a general decline of class has become widely accepted as a fact. Most contemporary observers believe that the impact of class has become considerably weaker over the last 50 years or so (Clark et al. 1993). Moreover, this decline is usually said to have occurred in all Western democracies, suggesting that it results from social trends common to industrial societies rather than factors specific to particular nations.

Beginning with Heath, Jowell, and Curtice's (1985) study of Britain, a number of critics have argued that the prevailing view is not supported by the evidence. Goldthorpe (1999), for Britain, and Hout, Brooks, and Manza (1995), for the United States, argue that there has been no systematic change in the influence of class on individual political behavior; at most, there has been some short-term fluctuation. Weakliem and Heath (1999; see also Weakliem and Western 1999) argue that class influences have declined in some nations, but not in all, and that there is no common pattern of change. Estimates of the strength of association between class and party in France, Britain, and the United States from Weakliem and Heath (1999) are displayed in figure 9.1.[2] Only the United States shows the steady decline that is supposed to be characteristic of all Western democracies. Britain shows some decline since the 1950s, but the association between class and party is almost exactly as strong in 1935 as in the 1980s and 1990s. France shows no trend in either direction. Despite their differences, critics of the prevailing view agree in rejecting the idea that a decline of class is a necessary feature of advanced industrial society.

This chapter will review this debate and offer some new evidence and suggestions for future research. It should be noted at the outset that class may affect many aspects of politics, including collective action, the behavior and opinions of elites, and structural constraints on government action. This chapter will consider only one of these, voting and general public opinion. Arguments for the decline of class, however, also focus on this aspect. More specifically, I focus on the strength of association between individuals' class position and voting choices, often referred to as class voting (Alford 1963).[3]

Figure 9.1
Estimated class voting in national elections, 1935–1993

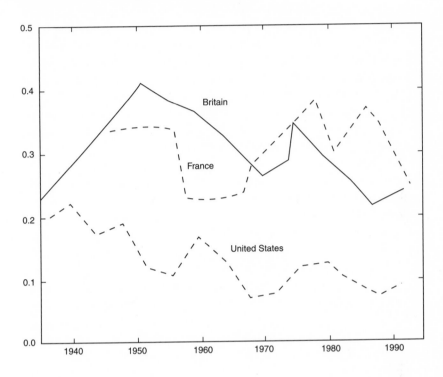

Direct Evidence on Changes in the Association of Class and Party

The best-known evidence of a decline of class is a table originally reported in Lipset 1981 and updated and extended several times, most recently by Clark, Lipset, and Rempel (1993). This table seems to show a fairly steady decline in class voting in a number of Western nations. In more comprehensive cross-national analyses, Franklin, Mackie, and Valen (1992) and Nieuwbeerta (1995) find evidence of a fairly general decline in class voting. All of this evidence, however, measures either class or party as dichotomies. Parties are grouped into the Left and the Right, while voters are grouped into working and middle classes, which are usually defined as manual and nonmanual occupations, with farmers excluded. At best, such definitions discard important information: at worst, they may produce illusory trends in estimates of class voting.

To collapse the parties into Left and Right essentially means that one is assuming that all parties in a group are equivalent for some purposes. For example, the British Liberals and Conservatives are usually counted as part of the Right, even though most observers perceive a significant ideological difference between them, and the Liberals receive a larger proportion of their votes from the working classes. Similarly, the French Socialist and Communists are usually combined into a single category despite large differences in the class composition of their voters. In principle, it is clear that being on the left or on the right is a matter of degree, and the custom of using a dichotomous classification seems to have arisen solely because of convenience. The practical consequence of using a dichotomous classification is that changes in the relative sizes of the parties are confounded with changes in class voting. For example, if the French Socialists grow relative to the Communists, as they have done since the 1960s, the class composition of the "Left" electorate will become more middle class, and class voting will necessarily appear to decline. The growth or decline of a party might reflect a change in class relations, a point that will be discussed below, but it might also result from general factors that are unrelated to class.[4]

The reliance on the manual/nonmanual distinction is also difficult to defend. Even observers who believe that people can be divided into two basic classes disagree about where to draw the line. Marx and Engels did not regard the distinction between manual and nonmanual employees as very important: in their theory, both were proletarians. Hamilton (1972), in an empirical analysis of the United States, argued that the major break was not between manual and nonmanual but between the upper and lower sections of the working class. Again, the use of the manual/nonmanual dichotomy seems to have arisen out of convenience; it was the only distinction that was consistently made in many of the surveys on which early researchers had to rely. Alford's (1963: 75–77) rationale for the use of the distinction is based on data availability and a small amount of empirical evidence and makes no claims of theoretical superiority.

Under other definitions of class, differences between manual and nonmanual workers can decline even when class differences are growing. That is, "realignment," or a change in the relative voting patterns of different groups, could be mistaken for "dealignment," a decline in class differences. As Harrop and Miller (1987: 187) point out, "Marx's apoca-

lyptic vision of a simple political dichotomy between workers and capitalists would show up as a decline in class divisions . . . between manual
and nonmanual employees." That is, many nonmanual workers will turn
to the left as they become aware of their interests as proletarians. Moreover, even if there is no realignment, changes in the sizes of groups within
manual and nonmanual categories will influence the size of the gap between manual and nonmanual workers. If lower-level nonmanual workers became more numerous relative to employers and top managers, support for the Left in the nonmanual category taken as a whole will
increase. Hence, the results of any analysis based on a dichotomy are necessarily ambiguous.

An adequate analysis of class voting must therefore use more complex
schemes of class and party. Ideally, it would be desirable to have a scheme
that encompasses all reasonable definitions of class as special cases. One
could determine whether conclusions about changes in class voting vary
depending on the definition of class. In practice, investigators dealing with
historical change are limited by the information available in the original
studies and have not been able to distinguish more than six or seven different groups. Nevertheless, investigators who use more complex class
schemes have found that a substantial part of the changes in class voting
involves realignment rather than a simple decline, a point that would have
remained invisible if they had used a dichotomy (Hout et al. 1995; Weakliem and Heath 1999; Weakliem and Western 1999).

Limitations of the Direct Evidence

The use of more complete information on class and party weakens the evidence for a decline of class but does not prove that no change has occurred. This point can be illustrated by considering an analysis of the
1964–1992 British General Election Survey (BGES) data using the five-
class scheme of Heath , Jowell, and Curtice (1985) and the "uniform difference" model proposed by Erikson and Goldthorpe (1992). This model
provides a good fit to these data and yields a convenient index of the
strength of class voting. If one makes the strength of class voting a linear
function of time, there is a modest but statistically significant downward
trend, amounting to about a 15 percent decline over the 30 year period.
However, if we take the 95 percent confidence intervals for the trend term,
the decline may be as small as 2 percent or as large as 38 percent. This uncertainty is simply the result of normal sampling variability. If we suppose

that some elections had unusually high or low levels of class voting because of circumstances specific to that time, even more variability is possible. Goldthrope (1999), for example, points out that class voting is estimated to be quite high in 1964, the first year of the BGES series. If we ignore 1964, the estimate of the linear trend is reduced by more than half and is no longer statistically significant. On the other hand, class voting is estimated to be quite low in 1970. If we ignore 1970, the estimate of the linear trend and its statistical significance increase. In other words, the results of fitting a uniform difference model to the BGES data can be interpreted in any of the following ways:

1. There has been a real downward trend in class voting over the last 30 years, but it may be as small as 2 percent or as large as 38 percent.
2. There has been no trend at all in class voting since 1966. All, or nearly all, of the change in class voting since that time is merely short-term fluctuation. Class voting was higher in 1964, but we don't know if this was characteristic of earlier elections or merely an aberration.
3. Class voting was unusually low in 1970. Perhaps this was associated with the cultural upheaval of the 1960s; class voting was also quite low in the United States at around the same time. If we omit the 1970 election as exceptional, there is definitely a downward trend. The estimated trend is –22 percent over the 30-year period, and the 95 percent confidence interval is from –7 percent to –48 percent.

The data simply do not permit a definite answer. This uncertainty does not result from a problem with data quality but from the laws of probability. Given the size of most election surveys, there is a substantial margin of error in estimates of class voting. It is possible to obtain additional data for some elections, but a deeper problem remains: there are few time points. Representative surveys are not available in any nation before the 1930s and were scarce until the 1960s. Given a little knowledge of political history, it is possible to argue that almost any election is a special case and should therefore be excluded from estimates of trends. As illustrated above, such decisions can have a large effect on conclusions.

Hence, analyses comparing class voting over time do not strongly support the idea of a general decline of class, but they do not rule it out either. This does not mean that nothing has been learned. It is fairly clear that the association between class and vote in Britain is stronger than that found in the United States at any time since the 1930s. Claims that class is now unimportant in Britain or that the United States and Britain have converged can thus be rejected. We cannot be sure, however, about whether class voting has declined or not. The data for Britain are more abundant than those for most other nations; hence, it is even more difficult to reach firm conclusions about industrial democracies in general.

Other Evidence

If the direct evidence is inconclusive, it is necessary to turn to circumstantial evidence. In fact, advocates of the conventional view generally do not devote much effort to analyzing or collecting direct evidence on class voting. Rather, they treat figures like that reported in Lipset 1981 as illustrations of a point that is already fairly clear and suggest that skeptics are putting their faith in exotic statistical techniques at the expense of common sense. For example, Clark, Lipset, and Rempel (1993) and Inglehart (1990) point to a variety of political changes that are said to be causes or reflections of a decline of class. Most of these changes can be divided into two basic categories: first, the rise of social movements that are not directly related to class interests, such as environmentalism, feminism, and various forms of religious fundamentalism; and second, the decline of parties and movements that appeal directly to class interests: Communist parties, socialism more generally, and the labor movement. Hence, the hypothesis of a general decline of class makes sense of a number of important developments; the decline of class voting is simply one more piece of evidence in its favor. Although the novelty of "new social movements" is sometimes exaggerated and socialism has gone through some difficult periods before, it seems clear that some important political changes have occurred. Opponents of the prevailing view argue that such changes are not necessarily related to class voting: rather, they may reflect general currents of opinion that affect all classes (Heath et al. 1985). For example, support for socialism may have declined among intellectuals and the middle classes as well as among the working classes. If one wants to describe this change, why call it a decline of class rather than a decline in support for socialism?

The opponents are certainly correct in a mathematical sense: the gap between classes is not the same as the average across classes, and a rise in class voting could go along with a decline in support for the Left.[5] Nevertheless, many observers still seem to have a sense that these developments must somehow be connected. This sense is not simply the result of confusion; rather, a particular model or theory that seems to be implicit in most accounts of class voting implies that they are connected. This model is found in the "Columbia school" of political sociology represented by

Lipset, Lazarsfeld, Barton, and Linz (1954) and Alford (1963), as well as in critics such as Sartori (1969) and Przeworski (1985). Ultimately, it can be traced back to the Marxist tradition, with its focus on the importance of working-class unity. The central idea is *competition among identities:* class competes with rival bases of political allegiance, such as religion, region, and gender.[6] Class will be a stronger influence when these rivals are weaker; conversely, if they become stronger, class must become weaker. In this case, the rise of new social movements will necessarily lead to the decline of class. The strength of class identity also is the key to the success of the traditional Left, which appealed primarily to class interests. If people come to think of themselves in terms of some other identity, such as religion, sexual orientation, or age, such appeals will become ineffective. Marxism, socialism, and even union activity will no longer hold much attraction. The decline of the Left will thus be another symptom of the decline of class. If the theory of competition of identities is correct, the decline of the Left, the rise of new political conflicts, and the decline of class voting are all part of the same general development. Conversely, the decline of the Left and the rise of new political conflicts are evidence that class voting either has declined or will decline. If the theory is wrong, however, they have no bearing on the question of class voting.

Testing this theory is difficult, because the primary focus is not on the individual but on larger social units such as nations, cities, or regions. There have been a few studies at the national level, such as Nieuwbeerta's (1995) effort to predict the level of class voting in different nations from characteristics such as ethnic heterogeneity. Analyses at the national level encounter the problems of limited data discussed above, especially when they consider historical change. An alternative approach to testing the theory is to consider its implications for the individual level, where data are more abundant. This is the approach taken in this chapter.

The Theory of Competition among Identities

Ethnicity, Religion, and Gender

The claim that ethnic and religious loyalties reduce the intensity of class conflict is a familiar one. Sombart ([1906] 1976) and many later authors argued that the ethnic diversity of the United States helped to explain the weakness of class consciousness among American workers. Sartori (1969: 76) holds that "class is the major determinant of voting behavior only if no other cleavage happens to be salient." Lijphart (1979: 453; see also Lipset and Rokkan 1967) holds that "primordial" loyalties interfere with the development of class identity, so that class "can become a factor of importance only in the absence of potent rivals such as religion and language." Many authors seem to take a rivalry as self-evident, but in fact it is based on an assumption that may or may not be true. As Parkin (1979: 34) observes, the assumption is "that the sense of identity with, or membership of, a class or ethnic [or other nonclass] group is essentially an either/or affair, such that a moral commitment to one precludes involvement in the other."

Traditionally, the main rivals of class were thought to be ethnic, religious, and sometimes regional identities. More recently, however, other identities have received attention as well. In addition to objective characteristics such as gender and age, identity may be based on lifestyle or ideology. Modern society is characterized by a multitude of identities, many of which are chosen rather than imposed from outside (Castells 1997). These "imagined communities" provide additional rivals to class (Pakulski 1993; the term was coined by Anderson [1983]). Few would deny that the political importance of some nonclass identities, such as sexual preference or commitment to environmentalism, has increased in recent years. The question at issue is whether class and other identities compete or merely coexist.

The alternative to thinking of competing identities is to think of a number of factors whose effects simply add together. For example, consider a married white woman employed in a working-class job. Being white and married are associated with a greater chance of voting Republican, whereas being a woman and having a working-class job are associated with a greater chance of voting Democratic. If the factors simply add together, they will offset each other and her chances of voting Democratic or Republican will be about equal. If there is a competition of identities, the factors will not simply offset; rather, the voter will choose one identity as primary and ignore or at least discount the others. The model of competition of identities is similar to the hypothesis that voters subject to "cross-pressures" will avoid political involvement, which is prominent in the work of the Columbia school (Berelson et al. 1954; Lipset 1981). Both are based on the idea that pressures in different directions do not simply cancel each other out but produce some kind of strain. The strain may be resolved either by focusing on one identity or by withdrawing from politics. This is plausible claim, but it is not a logical necessity.

The empirical implications of these different approaches can be understood by considering a remark of Rosenberg (1953: 25): "To the extent that people vote for or against a candidate because of his race, religion, nationality, geographical origin, etc., rather than on the basis of his economic principles or his position as a class symbol, to that extent do all classes in one group unite in opposition to all classes in another group." The model of competition of identities shows up in the claim that the nonclass groups "unite." Unity would occur only if the other factors completely eliminate the influence of class. In the additive model, people who are influenced by a given factor, say religion, would be more likely to vote for the party that is identified with their religion. They would not, however, "unite" in support of that party: just as the classes would be divided by religion, religious denominations would be divided by class; for example, working-class Catholics would be more heavily Democratic than middle-class Catholics.

The model of competition of identities might be evaluated by testing for interactions between class and other factors. General tests for interactions, however, usually require very large samples to yield conclusive results. More precise implications can be derived when the general model is combined with the idea that strong identities form in opposition to a dominant group, which is seen as neutral and unmarked (Young 1990: 168–173). For example, a white person may honestly say that he rarely thinks of race, while a black person will be constantly reminded of her racial identity. Consequently, if other identities prevent the development of class divisions, we can expect class voting to be lower in "marginal" or subordinate groups. According to Lipset (1968: 273; see also Alford 1963: 242–243; Hamilton 1972: 188–238), "as outgroup minorities, Catholics, Jews, and Negroes are much more likely to respond politically in terms of their ethnic-religious group identification. . . . Other bases of diversity, of which class is historically the most significant, should divide white Protestant reactions more than they do the others." Curiously, there seems to have been no empirical work on this question in the last two decades, despite the growth of interest in identity politics.

A full investigation of this issue would require international comparisons, but this preliminary study will be limited to the United States. Since whites have traditionally been dominant, class voting can be expected to be lower among blacks. Religion is more complicated. As Lipset (1968) suggests, Protestantism has traditionally been taken as the norm, and the Democratic Party came to be identified with the defense of religious minorities. Although anti-Catholic and anti-Jewish prejudice has weakened, the voting patterns established earlier in the twentieth century have been surprisingly resistant to change: the gap in Democratic support between

Jews, Catholics, and Protestants has narrowed little, if at all, since the
1940s (Manza and Brooks 1997). Hence, any tendency for Catholics and
Jews to unite across class lines could be expected to have endured as well.
While differences among Protestant denominations have traditionally been
less important, "fundamentalism" has emerged as a politically relevant
identity in recent years. Moreover, it is clearly marked as a distinctive identity: fundamentalists see themselves as an embattled minority in a predominantly secular culture. Fundamentalist Protestantism is therefore of
particular interest, since it is directly involved in current political debates.
To sum up, the influence of class on party choice is expected to be
strongest among mainline Protestants and weakest among the "minority"
religious groups: Catholics, Jews, and fundamentalist Protestants.

Gender was not considered a politically relevant identity until recently.
In the past 20 years, however, significant gender differences in voting and
attitudes have been observed, and it has become common to speak of
women's interests and sometimes of a distinctive women's view of politics.
Since males are the dominant and "unmarked" group, one would expect
lower class voting among women. That is, their common interests as
women should override class differences to some extent. Comparing class
voting among men and women is complicated, however, because married
women's votes are influenced by their husband's occupation as well as their
own.[7] Hence, a clearer picture can be obtained by comparing single men
and women. At the same time, marital status itself can be regarded as one
of the lifestyle groups that authors such as Pakulski (1993) point to as significant in contemporary politics. Remaining single after the usual age is
no longer regarded only as an individual peculiarity: now it is also regarded
as a lifestyle choice, especially with the rise of "traditional family values" as
a theme in political debate. Thus, marital status may become a politically
relevant identity or at least be linked to other politically relevant identities.
In fact, since the 1970s, single people have been significantly more likely
to vote democratic than married people have. Applying the general logic
of a conflict of identities, we can expect class voting to be lower among single people as a distinctive minority group. If the gender and marital differences are put together, class voting should be strongest among married
men, weaker among single men, and weakest among single women. The
expected ranking of married women is not clear because of the possible
confounding effects of husband's class.

Data for this and most subsequent analyses are taken from the
1972–1994 General Social Survey, or GSS. The cumulative GSS includes
a large number of cases and a wide range of questions on attitudes and de-

Table 9.1

Class Voting in Various Groups, United States, 1972–1992

	Percentage Voting Democratic	Class Effects (ϕ)	Std. Error of ϕ	Chi-square Test of Equality[a]
Whites	40.2	.342	.027	10.0[*] (1 d.f.)
Blacks	89.8	−.040	.120	
Fundamentalists	32.4	.443	.059	3.1 (3 d.f.)
Other Protestants	34.1	.364	.046	
Catholics		46.5	.315	.053
Jews		57.5	.503	.187
Married men	41.1	.530	.041	9.5 (3 d.f.)
Married women	46.3	.338	.048	
Single men		52.3	.524	.115
Single women	57.1	.499	.131	

[a] Each entry pertains to its entire category.
[*] p < .001

mographics. Since the GSS does not ask about congressional vote, all analyses will be restricted to presidential vote. Class is represented by six categories: professional, business (manager and proprietors), routine white collar, farmers, skilled manual, unskilled manual. Comparisons of class voting among various demographic groups are displayed in table 9.1. These comparisons are based on a logistic regression model of Democratic versus Republican voting in presidential elections:

$$\log(p_{ij}/(1 - p_{ij})) = \alpha_i + \phi_i s_j$$

where α_i represents the overall tendency of group i to vote Democratic, controlling for class, and s_j is a score representing the relative voting tendency of that class. The strength of class voting in a group is then given by the parameter ϕ.[8] The score could be assigned on prior grounds: for example, if one were to give all manual occupations a score of 1 and all nonmanual occupations a score of zero, α would be a logistic regression equivalent of the Alford Index (Alford 1963). For this investigation, however, I use scores that represent the actual class differences in voting patterns found in the United States in recent years: −1 for business, −0.5 for farmers, 0 for professionals and routine white collar, 0.5 for skilled manual, and 1.0 for unskilled manual.[9]

The first comparison involves blacks and whites. The ϕ parameter is essentially zero for blacks, indicating no class differences in Democratic support. Racial differences in the value of ϕ are statistically significant, as shown by the chi-square test for equality shown in the last column, supporting the conventional view that class voting is less in the out-group. The fact that class voting is essentially zero among blacks also suggests that all other comparisons should be restricted to whites.

The second comparison involves the four major religious groups, now restricting the sample to whites. The chi-square test in the final column shows that the group differences in ϕ are not statistically significant; that is, we cannot reject the hypothesis that class voting is the same in all religious groups. Moreover, the pattern of estimates is not consistent with expectations. Catholics show the least class voting, but fundamentalists show more than mainline Protestants. Jews are estimated to have the highest levels of class voting, although the estimate is very imprecise because of small numbers. Hence, there is no tendency for the out-groups to display less class voting. This is not to say that denomination has no impact on vote; as the figures in the first column show, Democratic support is considerably higher among Catholics and Jews than among Protestants. Although average Democratic support is about the same for fundamentalists and other Protestants, there have been substantial differences in particular elections. For example, in 1976, fundamentalists were more likely to support the Democratic candidate than other Protestants were; in 1992, they were substantially less likely. Thus, religious denomination is a significant influence on vote; its influence, however, does not appear to reduce the effect of class but simply seems to coexist with it, as suggested by the additive model.

The third comparison involves gender and marital status. Again, the sample is restricted to whites, and only single people of at least age 26 are included. The differences in ϕ are statistically significant, but only because class voting is substantially lower among married women. Although marital status has a substantial association with overall party support, there is no difference in the strength of class influences among single and married men. Moreover, class voting is virtually identical among single men and women. It is hardly credible to argue that gender overrides class divisions among married women but not single women. If anything, one would expect that gender would be more politically salient to single women. Thus, the lower level of class voting among married women probably reflects a tendency of their vote to be influenced by their husband's occupation rather than their own. Like denomination, gender and marital status are influences on vote, but there is no evidence that they replace class influences.

These results suggest that nonclass identities *may* override class divisions, as in the case of blacks, but they do not do so consistently. That is, other factors may be simply added to class, leaving class differences unaffected. Although regional differences were not analyzed here, previous research suggests that regional identity also does not consistently reduce class voting. I have found that class voting was once lower in the South than in the rest of the nation, but the difference has now disappeared (Weakliem 1997). In Great Britain, class voting appears to have once been somewhat stronger in the peripheral regions of Wales and Scotland than in England; although this difference has also largely disappeared (Weakliem and Heath 1995).

Why some identities override class differences is an important question, but for the purposes of this chapter, the important point is that not all identities do. If the idea that other identities necessarily conflict with class is abandoned, then the rise of political movements based on nonclass identities does not necessarily imply a loss of influence for class.

Ideological Groups

In recent years, more attention has been paid to communities based on ideology than those based on "primordial" attachments. The most elaborate account is that of Inglehart (1990), which focuses on groups defined by value priorities. The essential idea is, again, of competition: people must divide their attention among different priorities. Consequently, as nonmaterial issues become more important, material issues are becoming less important. A reasonable way to measure importance is by the association with party choice. Thus, Inglehart's account suggests that the association of party choice with opinions on nonmaterial questions will rise, while the association with opinions on nonmaterial issues will fall. Since few questions have been asked in identical form over a long period of time, the most effective way to test this hypothesis is by comparing cohorts—that is, people born in different periods—using the GSS data. Experimentation showed that the clearest contrast occurs when people born before 1935 are compared with those born in 1935 or later. Figure 9.2 presents estimates of the association of opinions on a variety of issues with Democratic versus Republican voting, using a logit model.[10] The opinion variables are standardized, so that the height of each bar indicates the relative strength of association for each issue. All are coded so that the response expected to be associated with Democratic voting is given a positive score. The first four items—spending on environmental protection, reaction to the statement that "women should take care of running their homes and leave running the country up to men," the morality of homosexual relations, and whether a communist should be allowed to teach in school—represent the type of nonmaterial or value issues that Inglehart (1990) suggests are becoming more important in politics. The next two—reactions to the statement that whites have a right to keep blacks out of their neighborhoods and spending to help blacks—concern race relations, an important issue in recent American politics. The last four—spending to help the poor, the desirability of government action to promote economic equality, and confidence in the leaders of both organized labor and large business—are the type of traditional economic issues that are supposed to be of declining importance.

Figure 9.2
Association of attitudes and vote, pre- and post-1935 cohorts, United States

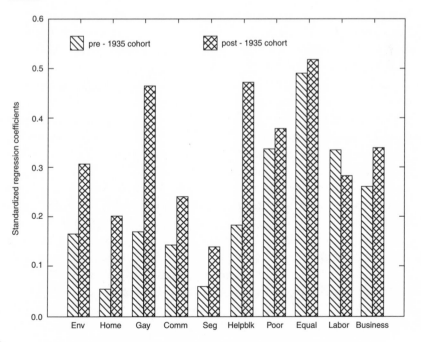

The association of party choice with opinions on nonmaterial and race relations issues has clearly increased. The association with traditional economic issues, however, has not declined but has remained essentially the same. The analysis suggested by Inglehart (1990) seems to be half right: nonmaterial issues have become more important, but material issues have not become less important. Again, the idea that class is in a competitive relationship with other social divisions is not supported.

The analysis reported in figure 9.2 does suggest a decline in class voting, at least according to some definitions. Education is associated with more liberal opinions on noneconomic issues, and the middle classes have more schooling than the working classes. Hence, if such issues become more important, some middle-class voters will tend to support the Democrats and working-class voters will tend to support the Republicans. Educational differences will increasingly work against occupational differences. In fact, most of the decline in class voting in the United States found by Weakliem and Heath (1999) seems to reflect a change in the effects of education; after controlling for education, any declines in the association of class with party choice are small. It is difficult to say whether this development is unique to the United States, but Weakliem and Western (1999) and Weakliem and Heath (1999) find some indirect evidence of it in Australia and Britain as well. A change in the effects of education, however, should be distinguished from a straightforward decline of class. Although it would partly offset the traditional differences between the working and middle classes, it would also produce a growing split between educated professionals and the "old middle classes" of small business.

The idea of a shift toward value conflict is based on the assumption that class conflict declines with economic satisfaction. This assumption deserves examination in its own right, since it is found in many accounts of modern politics (e.g., Clark et al. 1993). It seems obvious that a person who is dissatisfied with his material situation would tend to vote for the party that promises to look after his interests. In the middle class, this would generally mean conservative parties; in the working class, parties of the Left. In contrast, a person who is satisfied might let other concerns override material interests. This reasoning implies that class voting should be lower during times of prosperity and higher during times of economic hardship (Converse 1958). Moreover, if material satisfaction rises with economic growth, there will be a gradual decline in class voting over the long run.

The idea that material satisfaction reduces class voting may be tested directly using the GSS, which has regularly asked respondents about satisfaction with their financial situation. Another way to express the idea is to say that the effects of financial satisfaction on vote should differ by class: in the middle classes, greater satisfaction should increase support for the Democrats; in the working class, greater satisfaction should increase support for the Republicans. Results of an analysis based on a logit model are displayed in table 9.2. In all classes, financial satisfaction reduces the chance of voting for the Democrats; moreover, it is not possible to reject the hypothesis that the effect is the same in all classes. The same pattern is found when one compares income levels rather than occupations: financial dissatisfaction is still uniformly associated with greater support for the Democrats. The bottom panel compares class voting by level of financial satisfaction, using the class scores discussed above. The differences are marginally significant (p = .07) but are in the "wrong" direction: class voting is greater among more satisfied people. The reason for this difference can be seen by considering the estimates in the top panel. The estimated effects of financial satisfaction are smaller for manual workers than for the predominantly Republican classes of business, farmers, and white-collar workers; consequently, an increase in financial satisfaction increases the gap in party support between those classes.

On the individual level, if material satisfaction has any effect on class voting, it is to *increase* it. It is difficult to see why an increase would occur, and the statistical tests are inconclusive, so the most plausible conclusion is that material satisfaction has no effect on class voting. The results may be ex-

Table 9.2
Financial Satisfaction and Class Voting

	Parameter Estimate	Std. Error
Effects of Financial Satisfaction on Democratic Voting, by Class		
Professional	−.194	.057
Business	−.342	.058
White collar	−.247	.041
Farmer	−.263	.145
Skilled manual	−.196	.054
Unskilled manual	−.173	.058
Test of Equality	5.7 (5 d.f.)	
Class Voting, by Level of Financial Satisfaction		
Satisfied	.514	.065
Pretty satisfied	.330	.057
Not satisfied	.327	.084
Test of equality	5.3*(2 d.f.)	

*p < .05

plained by supposing that people are responding to the Democrats' traditional image as the party of the disadvantaged. In this case, whatever makes a person feel disadvantaged will increase his or her support for the Democrats. It is possible that the relationship between financial satisfaction and class voting is different at the societal level, but there is no obvious reason why this should be the case. Hence, we should not assume that there is any consistent relationship between general affluence and class voting, either in the short or the long term. This is not to say that economic growth has no effect on politics; Inglehart (1990) has presented strong evidence that societal affluence is associated with differences in public opinion. However, as seen above, a change in public opinion will not affect class voting in an additive model in which different influences coexist rather than compete.

The Effect of Parties

Many discussions of a general decline in class voting focus on changes in society, to which parties are assumed to respond more or less willingly. That is, social conditions make class interests more or less important to people, and this importance will be reflected in the strength of class voting. Where class is an important influence on people's experiences and opinions, it will be an important influence on vote. Authors such as Sartori (1969) and Przeworski (1985) have sharply criticized such accounts for neglecting the role of politics. Their criticisms, however, do not challenge the general idea of a competition among identities; in fact, they can be easily incorporated within it. The issue dividing "political" and "sociological" accounts is simply one of the weight of different influences.

The basic assumption of "political" accounts is that when parties do not offer distinctly different positions on questions involving class, people will be unable to use class as a guide to their vote (Converse 1958: 395–399). Social conditions might influence the *potential* for class voting, but the extent to which this potential is realized will depend on political parties. Some accounts go further and hold that even the potential is shaped by parties and other political organizations. Sartori (1969: 84), for example, states that "it is the class that receives its identity from the party. Hence class behavior presupposes a party that not only feeds, incessantly, the 'class image,' but also a party that provides the structural cement of 'class reality.' " In this view, classes, as political influences, are largely the creation of parties and other organizations such as labor unions. Przeworski and Sprague (1986: 9) hold that "the relative salience of class as a determinant of individual voting behavior is a cumulative consequence of the strategies pursued by political parties of the left." In particular, they argue that most parties of the Left have tried to appeal to nonclass interests, with the result that "class ideology becomes highly fragile and the efforts by left-wing parties to find electoral support profoundly undermine the salience of class as a cause of individual voting behavior" (Przeworski and Sprague 1986: 179).[11]

At first glance, the idea that party ideology and organization influence class voting seems to imply that there should be no uniform trends. Parties have their own traditions and internal politics, and it would be surprising if all made the same choices. Many observers of contemporary politics, however, believe that there has been a general ideological convergence in recent decades. As Lipset (1991; see also Clark et al. 1993) observes, nearly all major parties of the Left appear to have moved toward the center over the past few decades and have been particularly careful to avoid the language of class conflict. Party organizations have been declining for many years and have become increasingly dominated by middle-class people. Thus, in many nations, parties of the Left cannot be said to "organize" the working class in any real sense. These developments could be expected to cause the effect of class on party to decline almost everywhere.

However, despite many sweeping statements on the importance of parties, little is known about an actual relationship between parties and class voting. Is class voting greater among those who perceive large ideological differences? Do ordinary voters' perceptions of recent shifts in party ideologies match those of informed observers? Will the influence of class decay rapidly if parties do not cultivate it, as implied by Sartori (1969), or will there be considerable inertia? While there is not a great deal of information that can be brought to bear on these questions, it is nevertheless possible to make a start.

Since 1952, the American National Election Studies have regularly asked respondents if they think there are any important differences in what the parties stand for. Among those who thought there were no important differences and voted for one of the two major parties, 48.6 percent of the people in blue-collar jobs supported the Democrats, compared with 40.2 percent of those in white-collar jobs, a difference of 8.4. Among those who thought there were important differences, 56.0 percent of blue-collar workers and 41.8 percent of white-collar workers voted Democratic, and Alford Index score of 14.2. As expected, class voting is greater among those who perceive party differences. However, there has been no general decline in the percentage of respondents who perceive important differences. Between 1952 and 1976, it fluctuated in a relatively narrow range, from 49.1 in 1972 to 58.8 in 1964. Since 1980, it has regularly been above 60 percent. Thus, the public does not see an ideological convergence between the parties but rather a divergence.

Lipset (1991) holds that the United States is an exception in this respect. Britain, however, shows an even more striking case of perceived divergence. In 1979, 46 percent saw a "good deal" of difference between the parties; the figure rose to 82 percent in 1983 and 84 percent in 1987 before falling to 55 percent in 1992 (Heath and Jowell 1994: 196). Most expert observers would probably agree that the ideological gap between the parties increased sharply in 1983 as Labour moved toward the left but would see a substantial decrease in 1987 as Labour moved back toward the center. The public, however, apparently did not perceive much change until John Major replaced Margaret Thatcher as Conservative Party leader and prime minister. Even in 1992, the proportion seeing a large difference between the parties was considerably higher than it had been in the 1960s and 1970s, although Labour had moved away from its traditional commitment to nationalization and close ties with the trade unions.

Unfortunately, comparable information is not available for other nations. However, two important conclusions can be drawn from the American and British data: first, that popular perceptions of changes in party ideologies are not closely related to expert perceptions, and second, that it is necessary to pay attention to the Right as well as to the Left. Observers who see a decline of traditional class-centered ideology, such as Lipset (1991) and Inglehart (1990), focus almost exclusively on the Left. However, the difference between parties clearly depends on the position of the conservative parties as well. In the United States, the American National Election Studies have asked respondents to rate the Republicans and Democrats on a liberal-conservative scale since 1972. The perceived Democratic position has remained fairly constant, but the perceived Republican position became considerably more conservative after 1980. Whether or not the public is correct, to the extent that class voting is affected by the *perceived* differences between parties, one would expect it to have increased dramatically in Britain and the United States. The fact that it has not suggests that the link between perceived ideological differences and class voting is fairly weak.

A less sophisticated, but possibly more important, way in which parties can differ involves perceptions of their concern with different social groups. Campbell, Converse, Miller, and Stokes (1960: 234–240) observed that many people who had little grasp of conventional ideological terms nevertheless perceived differences between the group orientations of the parties. It seems possible that changes in the perceived orientations toward different classes could cause changes in class voting. Unfortunately, none of the major academic surveys has regularly asked questions on this subject, but the Gallup Poll has occasionally asked which party best serves the interests of farmers, business owners and professional people, white-collar workers, skilled workers, and "unskilled workers— such as manual workers." Figure 9.3 displays the difference between the percentages choosing the Democrats and Republicans for each group between 1947 and 1990. For example, in 1947, 50 percent of the sample thought the Republicans would be better for business and professional people, and 21 percent thought the Democrats would be better, with the remaining 29 percent seeing no difference or having no opinion. The number displayed for business and professionals in 1947 is consequently 21 – 50 = –29.

There have been some changes in the perception of the parties, but they have generally applied to all groups. For example, the Democrats were

Figure 9.3
Perceptions of which party serves groups best, United States, 1947–1990

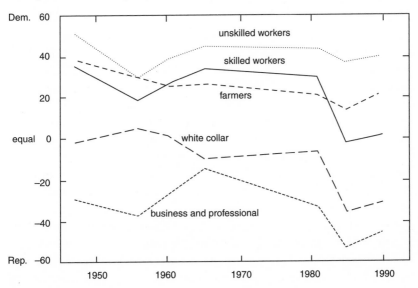

seen as better for all occupational groups in 1990 compared with 1985. These general shifts presumably reflect changes in perceptions of the parties in areas that apply to all classes, such as economic management or foreign policy. The *differences* between perceptions of service to different occupational groups are more relevant to class voting. Here, there is little systematic change. The Democrats are consistently seen as better for unskilled workers, skilled workers, and farmers; the Republicans, as better for white-collar and business and professional people. Moreover, the gaps between the perceptions of service to these groups show little change. In relative terms, it appears that white-collar workers and perhaps farmers are now somewhat more closely identified with the Republicans. The gap between the perceived service to business and professional and unskilled workers, however, did not decline over the period and may even have increased. Although there appears to be a substantial shift in the perceptions of service to skilled workers in the 1980s, this change may be artifact of a change in question wording.[12] Overall, there has been no major convergence in perceived party concern with different classes, although there may have been some small shifts.

The information in figure 9.3 suggests that party images, once established, are resistance to change. During the late 1940s, class and related issues such as labor relations were much more prominent in politics than they are today (Anderson 1988). Moreover, the Democratic Party had a much more impressive record of recent reforms intended to serve the working class than it did in the 1980s. Little or no sign of these historical differences can be discerned from the data in figure 9.3. While no comparable information is available for other nations, the United States is an extreme case with respect to the weakness of party organization and the absence of clear traditions of party ideology. Hence, if party images were to change anywhere, one would expect it to be in the United States. The evidence of these data counts against the "political" analysis of class voting in Sartori 1969 and Przeworski and Sprague 1986, an analysis that is based on the assumption that changes in party ideology and organization are soon reflected in changes in perceptions of the parties.

Hout, Brooks, and Manza's (1993: 272) idea of class as a psychological "heuristic" suggests an explanation for this stability. If people have become accustomed to seeing politics as a conflict over material equality, they will tend to think of one party as representing the rich and the other as representing the poor. To put it more strongly, people *expect* to see a party of the rich and a party of the poor; even if the parties try to go beyond the traditional categories of Left and Right, people will continue to put them into these roles. This is not to say that party images never change; this heuristic does not seem to have become firmly established in the United States until the twentieth century. But once established, it can continue even if the parties do not do much to encourage it.

Conclusions

The preceding investigation suggests that class sometimes competes with other social divisions but sometimes simply coexists with them. That is, we cannot assume that the rise of race, religion, or some other social division will drive out class. As discussed above, it seems fairly clear that the political importance of various nonclass identities has increased in recent decades. This is an important development in its own right but does not necessarily entail a decline of class. An important task for future research is to explain the circumstances under which class competes with other identities.

Another point that is implicit in the preceding discussion is that it is necessary to embed claims about class voting and class differences into general models of politics. Since there is an established research tradition on class voting, social scientists no longer ask *why* we should pay attention to class differences. Much sociological research is focused on differences among classes or other groups. For questions such as income or educational attainment, however, group differences are of interest in terms of equality: we want to know if they are justified and how they can be reduced if they are not. This rationale does not apply, however, to differences in voting tendencies or political opinions. On the face of it, the most important question seems to be, How many people hold a particular view? This question is the focus of most theoretical and general accounts of political change; they concentrate on general trends such as a move toward individualism or a decline of the Left. The great majority of research, however, has considered differences between groups. There certainly may be some connection between these questions; Marx, for example, argued that socialism would advance because of a rise of class consciousness in the working classes, not because of a growth of humanitarianism in the middle classes or a general spread of socialist sentiments in all classes. Since Marx's theories have had such a broad intellectual and historical influence, many observers have a sense that somehow the future of class voting is linked to the future of socialism, Marxism, or the welfare state. The connection, however, has not gone far beyond a vague sense; hence, it cannot be empirically confirmed or refuted. The preceding discussion suggests that to the extent that the model behind the "decline of class" thesis can be specified, it is not well supported by the evidence. On the other hand, opponents of the decline of class thesis have not made much progress in proposed clear alternatives of their own. Great progress in developing models of class voting was made in works such as Lipset et al. 1954, Campbell et al. 1960, and Alford 1963. In the last few decades, great progress has been made in collecting data and developing new techniques of analysis but very little has been made in specifying models. There are signs that this is now beginning to change, as Clark, Lipset, and Rempel (1993) and Manza, Hout, and Brooks (1995) have sought to situate class voting within broader theories of political and social change. This is a development that should be welcomed by all participants in the debate.

Notes

1. Some scholars have argued that religion, understood as including both denomination and religiosity, was of equal or greater importance (Sartori 1969: 86). Such claims, however, assume that religiosity can be treated as a cause of political preference. This assumption is almost certainly wrong; leftist political views can cause disenchantment with organized religion, or both political and religious views can reflect a more general attitude toward tradition. Denomination is often an important influence on vote but is usually smaller than class.

2. The measures of the strength of class voting are only roughly comparable across nations, although all reasonable measures show that the association is strongest in Britain and weakest in the United States.

3. One could also consider the class composition and voting patterns of certain aggregates, such as regions. However, most theorizing about class and electoral politics has focused on the individual level and has regarded aggregate data only as a means to make inferences about individual-level behavior (see Brustein 1988 for a recent exception).

4. There *is* a sense in which the growth or decline of a party might be said to represent a change in the importance of class. If class plays a major role in the ideology and public statements of a party, the decline of that party implies the decline of class as a theme in political discourse. This development might be important in its own right, but it is not the same as a decline in the influence of class on individual voting behaviour.

5. This is particularly true in the log-linear models favored by the skeptics but is also true when class voting is measured by correlations or differences in percentages. See Manza et al. 1995 for further discussion of measurement issues.

6. Clark, Lipset, and Rempel (1993), following a long tradition in sociological research, distinguish between "overlapping" and "crosscutting" hierarchies. They suggest that only crosscutting hierarchies discourage class-based political action. Unfortunately, neither they nor other authors in the tradition explain how to distinguish between them. In the United States, race and class are certainly overlapping in the obvious statistical sense—"lower" status on one tends to go with lower status on the other—but they are almost invariably treated as rivals.

7. For women, own occupation and husband's occupation have about equally strong influences on vote. For men, wife's occupation appears to have some influence, but it is much smaller than that of own occupation.

8. This model allows more or less class voting to occur in different groups but does not allow the relative positions of the classes to differ among groups. For example, professionals and routine white-collar workers are forced to be in the middle, in political terms, in all groups. The model nevertheless provides a good fit to the data, and the deviations from its predictions have no obvious interpretation.

9. Small changes in these scores produce only small changes in the estimates of ϕ. More radical changes, such as giving professionals a score of -1, might substantially change some of the comparisons. However, although the average socioeconomic status and income of professionals equal or exceed those of owners and managers, the fact is that the Democratic vote among professionals is much higher. Explaining the relative class positions is an important task in its own right; however, to compare the impact of class in different groups, it is best to take the relative class positions as given.

10. I refer to "association" rather than to "effects" because it is not clear that opinions should be regarded as an independent variable. To some extent, party loyalties may influence opinions.

11. In the course of their empirical analysis Przeworski and Sprague (1986: 167) state that "the numerical relations between class position and voting behavior remain remarkably stable." Their theoretical conclusions, however, seem to assume that the association between class and vote has declined.

12. Through 1981, the surveys asked about "skilled workers—such as carpenters, plumbers, electricians." In 1985 and 1990, the final phrase was dropped. Consequently, it is no longer clear that people understood the question as referring to skilled *manual* workers.

References

Alford, Robert R. 1963. *Party and Society*. Chicago: Rand McNally.

Anderson, Benedict. 1983. *Imagined Communities: Reflections on the Origin and Spread of Nationalism*. London: Verso.

Anderson, Margo. 1988. "The Language of Class in Twentieth-Century America." *Social Science History* 12: 349–375.

Berelson, Bernard, Paul F. Lazarsfeld, and William N. McPhee. 1954. *Voting*. Chicago: University of Chicago Press.

Brustein, William. 1988. *The Social Origins of Political Regionalism in France, 1849–1981*. Berkeley: University of California Press.

Campbell, Angus, Gerald Gurin, and Warren E. Miller, 1954. *The Voter Decides*. Evanston, Ill.: Row, Peterson.

Campbell, Angus, Philip E. Converse, Warren E. Miller, and Donald E. Stokes. 1960. *The American Voter*. New York: Wiley.

Castells, Manuel. 1997. *The Power of Identity*. Malden, Mass.: Blackwell.

Clark, Terry Nichols, Seymour Martin Lipset, and Michael Rempel. 1993. "The Declining Political Significance of Social Class." *International Sociology* 8: 293–316.

Converse, Philip E. 1958. "The Shifting Role of Class in Political Attitudes and Behavior." In E. E. Maccoby, T. M. Newcomb, and E. L. Hartley, eds. *Readings in Social Psychology*, 3d ed., 388–399. New York: Holt.

Erikson, Robert, and John H. Goldthrope. 1992. *The Constant Flux*. Cambridge: Cambridge University Press.

Franklin, Mark N., Thomas T. Mackie, and Henry Valen. 1992. *Electron Change: Responses to Evolving Social and Attitudinal Structures in Western Countries*. Cambridge: Cambridge University Press.

Goldthorpe, John 1999. "Modelling the Course of Class Voting in Britain." In Geoffrey Evans, ed., *The End of Class Politics?* 59–82. Oxford: Oxford University Press.

Hamilton, Richard F. 1972. *Class and Politics in the United States.* New York: Wiley.

Harrop, Martin, and William L. Miller. 1987. *Elections and Voters: A Comparative Introduction.* New York: New Amsterdam.

Heath, Anthony, and Roger Jowell. 1994. "Labour's Policy Review." In A. Heath, R. Jowell, and J. Curtice, eds., *Labour's Last Chance?* 191–209. Aldershot: Dartmouth.

Heath, Anthony, Roger Jowell, and John Curtice. 1985. *How Britain Votes.* Oxford: Pergamon.

Hout, Michael, Clem Brooks, and Jeff Manza. 1993. "The Persistence of Classes in Post-Industrial Societies." *International Sociology* 8: 259–277.

Hout, Michael, Clem Brooks, and Jeff Manza. 1995. "The Democratic Class Struggle in the United States, 1948–92." *American Sociological Review* 60: 805–828.

Inglehart, Ronald. 1990. *Culture Shift in Advanced Industrial Society.* Princeton: Princeton University Press.

Lijphart, Arend. 1979. "Religious vs. Linguistic vs. Class Voting." *American Political Science Review* 73: 442–458.

Lipset, Seymour Martin. 1968. *Revolution and Counterrevolution.* New York: Basic.

Lipset, Seymour Martin. 1981. *Political Man.* Expanded ed. Baltimore: Johns Hopkins University Press.

Lipset, Seymour Martin. 1991. "No Third Way: A Comparative Perspective on the Left." In Daniel Chirot, ed., *The Crisis of Leninism and the Decline of the Left,* 183–232. Seattle: University of Washington Press.

Lipset, Seymour Martin, and Stein Rokkan. 1967. "Cleavage Structures, Party Systems, and Voter Alignments." In Seymour Martin Lipset and Stein Rokkan, eds., *Party Systems and Voter Alignments,* 1–67. New York: Free Press.

Lipset, Seymour Martin, Paul F. Lazarsfeld, Allen H. Barton, and Juan Linz. 1954. "The Psychology of Voting: An Analysis of Political Behavior." In G. Lindzey, ed., *Handbook of Social Psychology,* 1124–1176. Cambridge, Mass: Addison-Wesley.

Maine, Henry Sumner. 1886. *Popular Government.* London: J. Murray.

Mariza, Jeff, and Clem Brooks. 1997. "The Religious Factor in U. S. Presidential Elections, 1960–92." *American Journal of Sociology* 103: 38–81.

Manza, Jeff, Michael Hout, and Clem Brooks. 1995. "Class Voting in Capitalist Democracies since World War II." *Annual Review of Sociology* 21: 137–162.

Mill, John Stuart. [1861] 1962. *Considerations on Representative Government.* South Bend, Ind.: Gateway.

Nieuwbeerta, Paul. 1995. *The Democratic Class Struggle in Twenty Countries, 1945–1990.* Amsterdam: Thesis Publishers.

Pakulski, Jan. 1993. "The Dying of Class or Marxist Class Theory?" *International Sociology* 8: 279–292.

Parkin, Frank. 1979. *Marxism and Class Analysis: A Bourgeois Critique.* New York: Columbia University Press.

Przeworski, Adam. 1985. *Capitalism and Social Democracy.* Cambridge: Cambridge University Press.

Przeworski, Adam, and John Sprague. 1986. *Paper Stones: A History of Electoral Socialism.* Chicago: University of Chicago Press.

Rosenberg, Morris. 1953. "Perceptual Obstacles to Class Consciousness." *Social Forces* 32: 22–27.

Sartori, Giovanni. 1969. "From the Sociology of Politics to Political Sociology." In S. M. Lispet, ed., *Politics and the Social Sciences,* 65–100. New York: Oxford University Press.

Sombart, Werner. [1906] 1976. *Why Is There No Socialism in the United States?* Translated by Patricia M. Harding and C. T. Husbands. Edited by C. T. Husbands. New York: Macmillan.

Weakliem, David L. 1997. "Race Versus Class? Racial Composition and Class Voting, 1936–92." *Social Forces* 75: 939–956.

Weakliem, David L., and Anthony Heath. 1995. "Regional Differences in Class Dealignment: A Comment on Johnston and Pattie." *Political Geography* 14: 643–652.

Weakliem, David L., and Anthony Heath. 1999. "The Secret Life of Class Voting." In Geoffrey Evans, ed., *The Decline of Class Voting?* 97–136. Oxford: Oxford University Press.

Weakliem, David L., and Mark Western. 1999. "Class Voting, Social Change, and the Left in Australia, 1943–96." *British Journal of Sociology* 50: 607–628.

Young, Iris Marion. 1990. *Justice and the Politics of Difference.* Princeton: Princeton University Press.

10

Upper-Middle-Class Politics and Policy Outcomes

Does Class Identity Matter?*

HERMAN L. BOSCHKEN

Political influence in American policymaking has been a longstanding theme in urban politics. For years, Lasswell's original query "Who gets what, when and how?" (1936) has inspired generations of scholars in interest group theory, community power, intergovernmental relations, and public organization theory. The research response has left political scientists well stocked with answers to the query, but the results remain incomplete from a larger social science perspective. Aimed at discovering the influence of actors *engaged in the political process,* most urban policy research (except that of a few like Dahl [1961] generally overlooks the *indirect* influence of anonymous social genre. The question raised by this book, then, may not be Does class matter? but In what form does it matter?

Typically, we assume that symbolic "actors," or identities, are not of organized groups and hence lack specific interest and the direct political force necessary to sway public policymaking. The result is that such influ-

---

*An earlier draft of this chapter was presented at the Research Symposium on Class and Politics at the Woodrow Wilson International Center for Scholars, April 1996, Washington, D.C.

ence on policy outcomes is not usually considered. The oversight may be especially symptomatic in the study of social class. This chapter examines a little-acknowledged thesis about an upper-middle-class (UMC) genre skewing a public agency's outcomes in ways that favor some interests at the expense of others. The thesis argues that policy outcomes are indirectly influenced by the "systemic power" (Stone 1980) of a UMC *genre* apart from the influence of political activities of UMC *persons*.

Given the qualitative nature of this relationship, the research offers a modest empirical test that links multivariate analysis with inferential reasoning. This includes developing (1) a multiple-perspectives framework of policy outcomes (the dependent variables), (2) a demographic profile of the UMC (the independent variable), and (3) three hypotheses linking the UMC with policy outcomes. Hypotheses are tested using controls for rival theses in a regression analysis of a nationwide sample of urban transit agencies.

Policy Outcomes from Multiple Perspectives

Before we propose connections between a UMC and policymaking, we first must ask about the meaning of "policy outcomes." In a plural society, institutional theory envisions the public agency "as a going concern, taking account of relevant stakeholders, attending to long-run interests, being sensitive to the operative structure of authority" (Selznick 1996: 272). Analyzing the agency's policy outcomes therefore involves a *multiple-perspectives* approach. However, with differences in perspective come disagreements over the benefits of outcomes, making this approach even more essential to policy analysis when "political actors . . . have significantly different expectations about bureaucratic performance"(Gruber 1987: 142).

Since a determination of "goodness" in agency results varies according to the interests of different stakeholders, the study measures policy results from a comparative perspective involving both administration-centered and external political-centered outcomes (Boschken 1992, 1994; Bozeman 1988). The analytical structure imparts an ability to compare policymakers' priorities in choosing who gets what (Levy et al. 1974) and reveals patterns of policy outcomes skewed to favor some stakeholders more than others. The framework therefore differs from single-norm analysis found in most studies of efficiency (e.g., Downs and Larkey 1986), effectiveness (e.g., Chubb and Moe 1990), and innovation (e.g., Clark 1994b).

The framework's analytical focus is on *outcome skewness* and consists of indexes (the dependent variables) representing different types of agency performance. A condition of skewness exists when an agency exhibits *outcome emphasis and deemphasis*, which combined form an asymmetrical pattern of performance. The key assumption is that with limited resources, an agency will not and cannot emphasize all legitimate outcomes. For example, when caught in a paradox, one agency might skew outcomes to favor bureaucratic efficiency, while another skews outcomes to emphasize social-program effectiveness.

Possible skewed patterns in this comparative framework are composed empirically of three types of agency outcomes, each fostered by different stakeholder perspectives. The first and second types, labeled outcomes of *strategic organizational effectiveness* and outcomes of *operational efficiency*, are preferred by the agency's administrative constituencies located at different levels within the agency. The third perspective, labeled outcomes of *social-program effectiveness*, is the principal interest of nonmarket "user" constituencies.

The first of these, strategic organizational effectiveness, is most often associated with a senior management focused on the vitality of the organization *as a whole*. With its substantial professional stake in agency prominence, this constituency promotes its economic status and overall budgetary growth (Niskanen 1971). Moreover, senior management is charged "with identifying new strategies and new projects that will add to the organization's overall strength" (Doig and Mitchell 1992: 21). Measures of this outcome fit a standard of organizational effectiveness because they show "the ability of an organization to exploit its environment to obtain resources, while maintaining an autonomous bargaining position" (Mindlin and Aldrich 1975: 382).

The second outcome category is operational efficiency, which is the domain of management charged with controlling resources in daily matters. Operational outcomes are about "efficient ways of bringing services to the public" (Doig and Mitchell 1992: 21) and represent goodness in terms of minimizing cost per unit by "adherence to engineering standards, accounting rules" (Doig and Mitchell 1992: 25). Included in this are the costs of administration, service delivery, and facilities maintenance and replacement.

Both administration-centered outcomes differ from one another in managerial function and motivation, and both are contrasted with the third outcome category of social-program effectiveness. Bozeman's (1988) distinctions between "economic" and "political" sources of agency

legitimacy offer a way to contrast this third outcome. From an extramar-
ket perspective, social programs provide results that seldom would arise
from market transactions. Natural market demand fails to result because either those who want such outcomes do not have the means to pay, or the
costs and benefits of such service outcomes cannot be meaningfully related
to each other by a market transaction.

Since not all political demands are legitimate and worthy of governmental response, criteria for social-program effectiveness usually are determined by legislative mandates and interagency agreements. Examples of
legitimated public demands range from transit services provided to the
handicapped under the Americans for Disabilities Act to broader programs
promoting economic development and mobility for the urban poor.

By threading together the above three policy-outcome categories
(henceforth called outcome I, II and III, respectively) into a multiple-perspectives framework, we make possible a comparison of government policymaking according to different patterns of outcome emphasis and deemphasis. This forms the basis on which to ask why such variance in skewed
patterns occurs across localities.

The Upper-Middle-Class Thesis

The upper middle class in American society is a permeable socioeconomic
status (SES) grouping, consisting of individuals whose status is defined
mostly by modern and postmodern institutions formed from the industrial
and information revolutions of the twentieth century. Its influence on politics has drawn a large social science following even though many disagree
over the existence and meaning of "class" in America. To contemporary
policymakers and scholars studying a UMC, this class genre exhibits certain central tendencies that are distinct, albeit empirically elusive. Robert
Reich, for example, summarizes the UMC as "the glass-tower people"—
those institutionally influential types who are *economically ascendant, college educated and professionally employed* (in Farney 1994: 1). Stone (1980)
theorizes about a similarly defined "upper stratum" that holds an indirect
and impersonal influence on policymakers through systemic power. Clark
(1994a) benchmarks a compatible profile (but adds age) that aspires to a
"New Political Culture." Brint (1994) outlines activities of a "matrix" of
educated professionals defined by their employment situation.

Over the twentieth century, writings reinforced a continuity in these
contemporary visions of an upper middle class. With regard to *high and ris-*

ing income, Riesman saw fiscal resources taking on increased social meaning as society moved away from a "scarcity psychology" toward an "abundance psychology" (1961: 19; 1964). Maslow (1954) predicted that as basic wants are met, surplus resources free individuals to "self-actualize" and pursue symbolic goals. Veblen (1948) saw as far back as the 1920s a "leisure class" engaging in "conspicuous consumption."

A *college-educated* UMC is seen as equally persistent, especially after World War II. As the repository of institutionalism, the contemporary university setting provides a particular instruction that prepares a person simultaneously in functional expertise and institutional protocol (Waldo 1948; Kerr 1963; Scott and Hart 1979). Nourished by this conceptual knowledge of institutions and science, members of the UMC acquire a common language, set of referent symbols, code of conduct, and awareness of institutional processes not shared for the most part by non-UMC individuals.

As *professionals,* UMC persons are characterized as society's "general staff" (Veblen 1948: 440), whose principal role is to apply their education to inventing new appliances continually and to managing organizational resources (Whyte 1956; Pfeffer and Salancik 1979; Brint 1994). To accomplish these roles, they are granted titles, positions, and other symbols of distinction suitable for those in charge of organizational methods and technologies (Veblen 1948; Whyte 1956; Reisman 1961: Scott and Hart 1979).

This socioeconomic profile is seen connected to the intensity with which UMC persons (1) exhibit "other-directedness" (Riesman 1961) toward each other rather than emulating other social groupings and (2) seek "associational position" (Stone 1980) by belonging to an *organized influential* social genre (Ashforth and Mael 1989). Why should such membership matter? Riesman says, without aristocratic ancestry or a psychological "gyroscope" to establish influential position, behavior protocol, or community connection, UMC persons must acquire status and approval through continual "responsive contact" with each other (1961: 23). All people seek social group identity, but the UMC is set apart by a preoccupation with "the process of striving itself" (21).

Why, then, is a UMC genre not more distinct empirically? Partly, it may be that striving to appear influential does not require *verbal* contact. Social psychology research shows that individuals "interact" with others in a similar social position even when they have no direct communications (Lazer 1995; Burt 1987). Using non-verbal cues, the formation of anonymous groupings is based on the exhibition of *structural equivalence* in socioeconomic status.

The term *structural equivalence* defines "a measure of an individual's status, where individuals are sensitive to what other individuals of similar status are doing, believing, etc." (Lazer 1995: 4). This involves prior consensus on "prototypical characteristics abstracted from the grouping" (Turner 1985). The UMC's economic ascendancy, university education, and professional status are convenient for determining structural equivalence because they are openly displayed without reliance on verbal communications. These symbols of institutional achievement demonstrate equivalence in *influential* position rather than *material* "look-alikes."

For the most part, the writings talk about these SES characteristics as interlaced dimensions of a *core profile* that empirically distinguishes a UMC from a non-UMC person (e.g., Verba et al. 1995). At various times, other attributes have been prominent as well, including ethnicity and religion (i.e., WASP), mobility, consumption patterns, and age. But, their lack of empirical salience over time in defining structural equivalence makes them peripheral to the core profile defined here.

What, then, is the connection of a UMC genre to policy outcomes? Stone (1980) theorizes that the UMC exercises an indirect influence that "is completely impersonal and deeply embedded in the social structure." (981). The mere presence of the UMC genre in a "diamond-shaped distribution" (983) of socioeconomic status may be sufficient as a systemic power to affect policy outcomes. Therefore, the proportion of UMC individuals in an agency's service population should approximate the visibility of the UMC's nonverbal display of influential position. The following hypotheses associate this proportion with emphasis on the three different policy outcomes:

Strategic Organizational Effectiveness (Outcome I)

Why the UMC genre promotes emphasis on organizational vitality in public agencies involves a two-step logic. First, UMC motives are defined by organizational values that promote administrative processes as a way of life (Whyte 1956). As "a vast complex of interlocking management systems, sharing a common set of values" (Scott and Hart 1979: 5), organizations offer "a distinctive *employment situation* for the majority of professionals" (Brint 1994: 12) and provide an arena in common for expressing "associational position" (Stone 1980: 982) and measuring structural equivalence.

Second, *public* organizations in this "interlocking" allocation system represent an extension of the field of business (Wilson 1941) and play an instrumental role in a UMC lifestyle. "Free markets thrive, not in splendid isolation, but in a context of large and productive business and government organizations," the latter of which provides "effectiveness of infrastructure and public goods" (Simon 1995: 404). Although the UMC's posture toward government may seem clouded by current antigovernment sentiment of the median voter, being against healthy public organizations is inconsistent with the faith and investment the UMC has made in the trappings of organizational culture: higher education, administrative protocol, and professional competence.

Hence, we deduce from these arguments:

Hypothesis 1: *The greater the proportion of UMC individuals in an agency's service area population, the greater the emphasis an agency will place on performance stressing strategic organizational effectiveness.*

Operational Efficiency (Outcome II)

The UMC is painted as having subordinate concern for efficiency by virtue of the group's achieved material security and fiscal abundance. While seemingly counter to happenings in the Progressive Era, this pre–World War II period is characterized by Reisman's "scarcity psychology" (1961), where a professional UMC had not yet replaced the robber barons and other nouveaux riches as influentials in American institutions. With the spreading of affluence after World War II, Riesman characterizes UMC ambience as driven by an "abundance psychology," where respect for the proficiency of work is subdued by a "cult of effortlessness." Other works as well sketch a psychology involving a worthiness in sacrificing efficiency for "higher order" symbolics. These include Clark and Goetz's New Political Culture influence on urban growth (1994); Brint's post–World War II rise of the educated professional (1994); Maslow's hierarchical pursuit of self-actualization (1954); and Veblen's conspicuous waste by a leisure class (1948).

Hence, we deduce from this:

Hypothesis 2: *The greater the proportion of UMC individuals in an agency's service area population, the more likely the agency will deemphasize operations efficiency in favor of strategic (higher order) outcomes.*

Social-Program Effectiveness (Outcome III)

Social-program effectiveness raises a perplexing question: Why should welfare programs matter to the UMC except from fiscal and employment standpoints? With few exceptions, the UMC is seldom very cognizant of its "use" of or dependence on most specific services like transit. Although traditional class theory might argue that UMC members are "social trustees" (Brint 1994) who accept "noblesse oblige," a more plausible answer is that UMC's urban habitat serves as another nonverbal means to calculate the structural equivalence of social position in interurban comparisons. Hummon, for example, points to the UMC's metropolis as "nonverbal medium for the communication of moral reputation, social rank, and other significant qualities of self" (1992: 258).

Because of this, the UMC becomes more concerned about the overall quality and character of the urban area, which taxes support (Clark 1994b: 27). Urban planning research shows that symbolic considerations including public accoutrements (prominent airport, arts and entertainment, reputable schools, modern mass transit) are more important than economic issues in UMC voting (Hahn and Kamieniecki 1987). Gottdiener supports this connection, saying that "the urban image must be read . . . as an outcome of a class society propelled by powerful forces of development and change" (1986: 216). Social programs that address UMC quality of life matter because living in a formidable "world class" urban area adds stature in the quest for positional influence and structural equivalence.

Hence, we deduce from this logic:

Hypothesis 3: *The greater the proportion of UMC individuals in an agency's service population, the more likely the agency will emphasize social-program effectiveness.*

The three hypotheses compose a thesis that UMC influence occurring as an anonymous agent causes a *skewed or asymmetrical pattern of outcomes* consisting of emphasis on strategic organizational effectiveness (outcome I) and social-program effectiveness (outcome III) and a deemphasis on operational efficiency (outcome II).

Rival Theses

Implying that class does not matter, research on urban policy outcomes seldom includes a UMC genre as an independent determinant (e.g.,

Pagano and Bowman 1995; Feiock and West 1993). If represented at all, the UMC is treated either as issue-defined political actors directly involved (e.g., political entrepreneurs, interest groups) or as demographic variables randomized with others describing the agency's surrounding social and physical environment. Hence, a central question is, Does the UMC genre operate independently of variables used in past research? To examine the UMC thesis in this context, four rival theses are incorporated into the model.

The most central is the "political actor" thesis, which targets the direct influence of high-status individuals and interest groups (Verba et al. 1995; Clark and Ferguson 1983; Lowi 1969), community conflict and power structure (Stone 1989; Peterson 1981), political competition and entrepreneurship of elected officials (Clark and Goetz 1994; Doig and Hargrove 1987; Feiock and Clingermayer 1986), and intergovernmental exchange (Boschken 1998; Shepsle and Bonchek 1997; Agranoff and McGuire 1993).

While predicted outcomes vary by type of actor investigated, the common denominator for all is *direct use of political power* as the causal agent of policy outcomes. For example, when the locus of power lies outside the agency (i.e., in mayors, dominant community group, or interagency network), the agency will be less likely to emphasize its bureaucratic prominence (outcome I). The thesis is a central rival because it argues that, since UMC *persons* are politically more active than others (Verba et al. 1995), UMC influence is most likely to be from individuals and not an anonymous source.

Other rival theses speak of urban structure determinants describing physical form and general social makeup of a city as *preconditions* in policymaking. Although not involving identifiable actors, urban structure presents agencies with "nonnegotiable" opportunities and limitations on policymaking. What these preconditions predict as policy outcomes, however, varies by rival thesis.

One is the "underclass" thesis (Clark 1994a; Lineberry 1977), which argues that policy outcomes are distributed according to class distinctions typically measured by race or ethnicity. Describing a "double standard," the thesis assumes a zero-sum allocation where "them that has, gets" (Lineberry 1977: 61). For government, this is likely to result in white preferences for lower taxes and reduced spending on programs that benefit the city's underclass. Focused on the powerlessness of lower classes, the thesis operationalizes the underclass determinant as a politically passive precondition of poverty demographics.

A second urban structure rival is the "resource availability" thesis, which has two components: native wealth of the urban area and intergovernmental funding opportunities (Dye 1992: 315–316; Schneider 1989; Clark and Ferguson 1983). The thesis holds that public agencies spend money to emphasize outcomes I and III according to the level of economic resources made available from local tax receipts or intergovernmental sources.

The third structural rival is the "urban spatial form" thesis (Boschken 2000; Cervero 1991; Timms 1971; Burgess and Bogue 1967). It argues that physical configuration of urban activities determines the level and proficiency of public expenditures. Contrasting configurations range along a scale from a monocentric pattern of urban activity (center-peripheral) to a polycentric (sprawl) pattern. The thesis holds that a monocentric pattern facilitates emphasis on organizational effectiveness (outcome I) and operational efficiencies (outcome II) because high densities allow an agency to achieve deeper market penetration, more concentrated use, and economies of scale.

Methodology

The research was designed to test the hypotheses with data from standard nationwide reporting systmes. It employed a cross-sectional sample of 42 urban transit agencies operating transit systems in large metropolitan areas (i.e., with at least 500,000 population). They were identified from the Federal Transportation Administration's directory of transit agencies (UMTA 1988). These agencies were selected because most are statutory public enterprises that pursue multiple policy outcomes and because transit is a visible infrastructure component of the urban environment. Data are specific to each transit agency and the population within its jurisdiction and are from the U.S. Census and the annual Section 15 reporting system compiled by U.S. Department of Transportation's Federal Transportation Administration (FTA). Section 15 reporting is mandated for federal funding and contains uniform self-reported data on agency finances, costs, and service levels.

As components of outcome skewness, three continuum-scaled *dependent variables* operationalize the agency performances contained in the policy-outcomes framework. Each variable is an *index* consisting of multiple measures commonly used in transit and is calculated from FTA data (see note to table 10.1 for detail). Since any one year is subject to unrepresentative distortions, five years of data (1987–1991) were averaged for individual measures. This procedure, however, does not eliminate the possibility that the averages are atypical of longer time frames.

Descriptive statistics and intercorrelations of the three outcome indexes are provided in table 10.1. The indexes have significant associations, indicating that the skewness pattern is composed of interrelated components. The two inversely (negative) related associations represent tradeoffs by the industry *as a whole* in emphasizing different performance outcomes. The most significant tradeoff is between strategic organizational effectiveness and operations efficiency ($r = -.56$). While an agency could try to emphasize strategic organizational effectiveness (outcome I) by striving to be efficient (outcome II), the correlations show a tradeoff as the industrywide rule. The other tradeoff is between social program effectiveness and oper-

Table 10.1

The Dependent Variables of Performance Skewness: Descriptive Statistics and Intercorrelations

Variable	Mean	s.d.	1	2	3
Outcome I	10.99	2.27	—		
Outcome II	13.01	2.74	$-.56^{**}$	—	
Outcome III	12.29	2.53	$.48^{*}$	$-.38^{*}$	—

N = 42

Two-tailed significance: * = .01; ** = .001

NOTE: Each outcome is an index of individual measures that meet criteria for that outcome "cell." Values for each measure are residuals of a bivariate regression controlling for size. The technique was used because (1) little disagreement is found over size as the most significant factor determining urban agency outcomes, and (2) regression residuals are more appropriate than ratio data, since regression produces the best overall linear estimator of variance. Residuals for each measure within an outcome cell were then studentized to make them additive to an outcome index.

The indexes consist of the following measures along with their legitimating stakeholders: Outcome I (administration-centered, strategic effectiveness): Market penetration (passenger trips/district population) shows domain dominance preferred by senior management; load factor (passenger miles/vehicle miles) shows user-validated service superiority preferred by senior management; and institutional growth (1990 revenue/1980 revenue, all sources) shows negative entropy preferred by senior management.

Outcome II (administration-centered, operational efficiency): Operations efficiency (operating expense/vehicle miles) shows cost control proficiency of production management; maintenance efficiency (maintenance expense/vehicle hours) shows cost control proficiency of maintenance management; and system efficiency (operations assets/vehicle revenue miles) shows use of capital proficiency of financial and engineering managements.

Outcome III (political-centered social-program effectiveness): Mobility for transit dependent (passenger miles/service area in square miles) measures access convenience to urban economic activities desired by dependent commuters (handicapped, working poor); noncommute service (off-peak vehicle miles/total vehicle miles) measures access convenience to social activities and welfare services needed by nonworking handicapped, poor, and elderly; and economic development contribution (annual capital investment/district population) measures economic development impact potential for the regional population.

ations efficiency ($r = -.38$). Together, they give a basis for asking whether the UMC genre matters in explaining this pattern.

As the *independent variable,* the UMC genre is operationalized by a factor consisting of four discriminant SES components. Choice of a factor fits the thesis that policy outcomes are influenced by the *whole* UMC profile and not individual components. It is supported statistically by a principal components analysis, which determined a *single* factor (eigenvalue of 3.14, accounting for 80 percent of the four-component variance). The four components were operationalized using 1990 Census data corresponding to agency jurisdictions. The components are (1) *high income (percentage of households with a 1989 income above $75,000—a figure more than twice the national mean)*, (2) income change (percentage of change in household income between 1979 and 1989, which captures upward economic mobility), (3) *college education (percentage of individuals with four or more years of higher education)*, and (4) professional status (percentage of individuals having careers in professional or managerial positions).

Control variables were included in regressions to represent rival theses. For the political actor thesis, past research includes numerous variables. As an alternative to arbitrary selection among actor-specific variables, a surrogate strategy was chosen that held the potential for estimating direct power for most types of political actors. However, the imprecise nature of surrogates may lead to underestimates of political power relative to the more specific UMC factor. To reduce the potential effect of random measurement error in assessing the political actor thesis, the strategy called for two surrogate forms.

In the first, agencies were assumed to be influenced by powerful political entrepreneurs when operating in a partisan arena of limited competition. Pressman (1972) characterized prerequisites of mayoral power that include strong one party-dominance. Feiock and Clingermayer (1986) found that strong political entrepreneurs emerge when elections persistently reflect a dominant party. Consistent with this research, the political actor thesis is represented in part by a variable called *party dominance.*

Party dominance is measured by a three-point scale dummied from 1988 and 1922 presidential election results. The scale was determined by whether a party won both elections and by how much. For example, a condition of dominance required that a party win both elections by more than 55 percent. The variable is not a perfect surrogate because, although political entrepreneurs seldom emerge as strong political actors when interparty competition is high, the dominance of one party enables, but does not assure, the emergence of strong entrepreneurs (Grimshaw 1996).

Hence, the dummy variable should be read as less likely/more likely to involve a powerful political entrepreneur.

For the second form, most uses of political power were assumed to be channeled through an intergovernmental (IG) process (Boschken 1998; Agrnoff and McGuire 1993; Schneider 1989). "In the public realm, federalism and separation of powers imply a plurality of targets for political activity" (Verba et al. 1995: 7), where politicians, bureaucrats, and interest groups interact to couple their individual preferences with focal-agency policymaking. Hence, the thesis is represented by IG surrogates measuring a focal agency's fiscal and statutory *autonomy* in an intergovernmental arena.

Effects of IG autonomy on policy should be inverse to political actor power because the greater the focal agency's autonomy, the higher the barrier of access for external actors (Feiock and West, 1993; Sharp 1991). A restated political actor thesis, for example, predicts that when the focal agency holds high IG autonomy, it will extend its political reach and regional prominence (Benson 1975: 232; Niskanen 1971).

Three IG variables are used as proxies of political actor power. The first, called *revenue autonomy,* is the percentage of agency revenues generated from user fees or dedicated sources (e.g., a permanent transit tax). Both sources provide high budgetary discretion to the agency. The second, called *capital autonomy,* is the percentage of an agency's capital funding sourced in a like manner and not dependent on annual legislation or IG negotiation. The third, called *IG interaction,* operationalizes Niskanen's "bureaucratic autonomy" (1971). It is the product of two measures: scope (number of IG actors involved in focal-agency policymaking) and intensity (percentage of those having veto authority over focal-agency policymaking). Data for the first two IG variables are from FTA Section 15 reports. Data for the third are from a survey of transit agency officials and records.

Three controls were included to represent the urban structure theses. Based on 1990 Census data extracted for transit district populations, they are *race* ("percentage of white persons" in the population), *average income* (1989 mean household income), and *cross-commuting* (percentage of workers commuting between a residence and a workplace, neither of which is located in the urban core). Cross-commuting reflects variance from a center-peripheral (monocentric) pattern of urban activities.

Table 10.2 reports descriptive statistics and correlations for all variables. The UMC factor is significantly intercorrelated with average income and marginally associated with cross-commuting (collinearity diagnostics for the models show a condition index of 39). The UMC's association with

Table 10.2

*UMC Genre and Control Variables: Descriptive Statistics and
Intercorrelations*

Variable	Mean	s.d.	1	2	3	4	5	6	7
UMC factor	0.00	1.00							
Political actor									
Party dominance	2.02	0.78	.32	—					
Revenue autonomy	76.72	22.38	.14	.06	—				
Capital autonomy	26.70	18.43	.37	.11	.37	—			
IG interaction	5.37	3.62	.32	.04	−.02	−.03	—		
Urban structure									
Race (% white)	68.57	15.00	−.03	.05	−.06	.03	−.20	—	
1989 avg. income	33.70	6.56	.85**	.28	.24	.36	.25	.01	—
Cross-commuting	44.25	17.17	.40*	.15	.34	.23	.06	.13	.57**

N = 42
Two-tailed significance: * = .01; ** = .001

average income is probably due to the high income component of the
UMC factor. The UMC's association with cross-commuting is probably
due to most of the UMC living in suburbs, greater proportions of which
are found in nonparametric urban areas (Cervero 1991). Except for average income and cross-commuting, which are associated (r = .57), none of
the other controls are intercorrelated at the .01 level. Collinearity is examined further in the discussion section.

Results

Table 10.3 reports results of ordinary least squares regressions for the three
UMC hypotheses. Each model, identified as outcome I, II, or III includes
the UMC factor and seven control variables. Regression statistics support
hypothesis I, which argues that a UMC genre encourages emphasis on
strategic organizational effectiveness. The UMC factor is the most significant variable in the model (signif. t = .005) and is in the predicted direction (beta = 0.81, t = 3.0). IG revenue autonomy is also significant (signif.
t = .02), but three others are, at best, only near significance: party dominance, intergovernmental interaction, and average income (signif. t = .17,
.13, and .11, respectively).

Regression statistics do not support hypothesis 2, regarding deemphasis
in operations efficiency (outcome II). The UMC factor is unstable (signif.
t = .43) but could be interpreted as UMC indifference to efficiency. Full-

Table 10.3

Upper-Middle-Class Genre and Performance Skewness: (OLS Regressions)
Urban Public Transit (42 Agencies, 1987–1991)

| | Dependent Variables | | | | | | | | |
| | Outcome I | | | Outcome II | | | Outcome III | | |
Independent Variables	beta	t	signif.	beta	t	signif.	beta	t	signif.
UMC factor	0.81	3.0	.005	−0.22	−0.8	.43	0.64	2.4	.02
Political actor									
Party dominance	−0.19	−1.4	.17	0.06	0.4	.67	0.13	1.0	.35
IG revenue autonomy	−0.35	−2.4	.02	0.62	4.0	.0003	−0.21	−1.5	.16
IG capital autonomy	0.09	0.6	.54	−0.29	−1.9	.07	0.30	2.0	.05
IG interaction	0.22	1.6	.13	−0.01	−0.1	.94	0.11	0.8	.45
Urban structure									
Race (% white)	0.03	0.2	.83	−0.02	−0.2	.87	−0.34	−2.5	.02
Avg. income (1989)	−0.46	−1.6	.11	−0.03	−0.1	.93	−0.51	−1.8	.08
Cross-commuting	0.02	0.1	.90	−0.12	−0.7	.50	0.21	1.3	.21
R^2			.46			.41			.46
Adj R^2			.33			.26			.33
F			3.5			2.8			3.6
Signif. F			.005			.02			.004

model significance is due instead to IG fiscal variables: revenue autonomy (beta = 0.62, t = 4.0, signif. t = .0003) and capital autonomy (beta = -0.29, t= −1.9, signif. t = .07).

Regression statistics provide strong support for hypothesis 3, dealing with emphasis on social-program effectiveness. The UMC factor is significant (signif. t = .02) and is in the direction predicted by the hypothesis (beta = 0.64, t = 2.4). Most controls are significant or near significance as well. Race (percentage of whites) is equally significant to the UMC factor (signif. t = .02) and consistent with the underclass thesis. Capital autonomy is significant (beta = 0.30, t = 2.0, signif. t = .05) but contradicts the political actor thesis. Average income is near significance (signif. t = .08) but contradicts the wealth thesis. Revenue autonomy and cross-commuting are not significant for social programs (signif. t = .16 and .21, respectively).

Discussion

Alongside its better-known rivals, the UMC thesis appears to matter a great deal and in accordance with the literature. Especially when compared with political power variables, the UMC factor is more significant in explaining variance in two out of the three policy outcomes composing the skewed pattern. Only for outcome II (operations efficiency) is direct use of political power more significant. Although the research did not include a great number of variables subsumed under urban structure, of those considered, the influence of race in deemphasizing outcome III (social-program effectiveness) and average income in deemphasizing outcomes I and III are the only ones of comparable significance to the UMC factor.

Although the evidence seems to support the importance of an independent UMC thesis, this conclusion might not be shared by advocates of more traditional arguments. Since the UMC factor seems to be intercorrelated with some control variables (i.e., average income and cross-commuting), a question remains about whether the rival theses have indirectly accounted for the influence of the UMC genre. For this to be true, two conditions must exist. First, a control variable with which the UMC is statistically associated must significantly affect a policy outcome. Second, that control must operate as a route of UMC influence on the outcome.

Applying the first condition, the UMC factor is intercorrelated only with household income ($r = .85$) and cross-commuting ($r = .40$). Of these two, neither is significant as a determinant of policy outcomes, although income is near significance for social-program effectiveness. Ordinarily, one could leave the discussion with these results if it were not for the possible effects of model collinearity caused by the intercorrelation of the UMC factor and income. Given this, the wealth thesis would argue that the UMC is accounted for in the simpler proposition that local personal income generates tax receipts for public expenditures. Since UMC influence is accounted for by its association with income, the desire for parsimony would side with the wealth thesis because it offers the more direct explanation of policymakers counting tax revenues.

However, the results cast doubt on average income as a route of determination for the UMC for two reasons. First, even though the UMC factor has a strong bivariate association with outcome I ($r = .42$) and outcome III ($r = .46$), average income has no association with any of the performance outcomes at the .01 level. Second, in regression models, average income is only very marginally significant in outcomes I and III (signif. $t = .11$ and .08, respectively) but has a negative influence, opposite that of the wealth thesis and the UMC factor.

The inclination, then, is to see income's significance as a fluke of collinearity. To examine this issue, regressions for outcomes I and III were rerun, first without average income and then with income but without the

UMC factor. When income is removed, the UMC factor diminishes only slightly in significance for outcome I from .005 in the original model (see table 10.2) to .009. In outcome III, the decline in significance is greater (signif. t moves from .02 in the original model to .13). On the other hand, when the UMC factor is removed, average income (which was near significance in the original outcome I and III models) becomes insignificant (signif. t = .29 and .92 respectively). This leads one to suspect the UMC factor is important in explaining variance in policy outcomes (especially for organizational effectiveness) with or without average income, but average income is not essential when the model contains the UMC factor. Moreover, as a weaker variable orbiting the UMC's influence, income's negative influence on outcomes I and III can be explained as an artifact of collinearity.

These results therefore leave advocates of urban structure theses hard-pressed for arguing against the UMC factor's independent significance. Statistics aside, though, one might still expect proponents of the political actor thesis to argue that UMC influence is reflected in political research because its effect on policy outcomes must be associated with individuals making direct use of political power. But, does the UMC genre act through *individuals* to affect outcomes, or does it indirectly influence as an *impersonal anonymous* agent? Could there be a connection between the two?

A case could be made for a connection between the UMC and political entrepreneurs and could be understood in one of two ways. In the instance of direct visible action, we know UMC individuals engage in political activity more than others and that UMC participation is principally limited to making political contributions and contacting government officials (Verba et al. 1995). This would suggest that the impact of elected officials on policy outcomes is mostly a UMC phenomenon of direct and visible proportions.

The second interpretation accepts the casual route as an indirect manifestation of UMC presence but also requires involvement of direct political activity. Stone (1980) implies that the UMC influences a city's politics and cultural image by its systemic power. Pagano and Bowman (1995) add that elected leaders crystallize a vision for world class status that "is tied to the city's image" (xiv). Hence, if we combine these interpretations, elected political entrepreneurs would adopt a vision consistent with the UMC, at least where one-party dominance provides an unobstructed opportunity for "credit claiming" (Feiock and Clingermayer 1986). This argument does not hold up well under the results, however. A strong correlation does not exist between the UMC and party dominance (r = .32), and the latter is not near significance for any policy outcome.

Another connection could involve interest groups and concurring governmental actors. This study did not consider interest group variables as UMC proxies because they are distinguished by their issue-specific nature (e.g., environmentalism, handicap access, abortion rights), and few could be characterized as representing the UMC *qua monolithic UMC* (as the UMC factor does). Nevertheless, assuming that a UMC could exist as a distinct, forceful, and *single*-interest group or entrepreneurial voice, two conditions probably would have to prevail.

First, to operationalize a set of monolithic UMC interests, its membership would want to act on its professional organizational norms by seeking influence through an institutional intergovernmental process. In a few key instances, the process might involve direct relations with only the focal agency. But, to manage its influence effectively across a wide urban policy landscape, the UMC would want to capture a few agencies with broad intergovernmental authority, such as the Environmental Protection Agency, rather than numerous specialized operators. Second, for these UMC "sentry" agencies to be powerful intergovernmental actors in focal-agency policymaking, the transit agency would have to possess limited autonomy.

In this scenario, analysis of the IG autonomy variables shows two results. First, in a principal components analysis, the UMC factor is orthogonal to all IG variables, thus indicating no casual route. Second, while the UMC factor is very significant in regressions, it does not show corresponding influence through the IG surrogates for political-actor power (i.e., the IG variables are either less significant than the UMC factor or have an effect opposite the UMC's influence). Hence, even though UMC *individuals* certainly operate through interest groups and politicians for specific interests, Stone seems to be correct: the influence of a UMC *genre* is "completely impersonal" and manifested as "systemic power [that] is not a general form of upper strata dominance through agenda control" (1980: 989).

Inferences

If we return to the book's original query, it would appear from the results here that social class is not in decline, at least with regard to skewing public policy outcomes. The presence of a UMC seems to influence urban public agencies in being more effective in achieving organizational stature in their service areas and in providing more robust social programs. Moreover, given the UMC's preference for living in world-class urban areas, it would seem the genre might also act as a suitable surrogate for identifying the emergence of global cities (Boschken, forthcoming, chap. 8). Certainly their respective attributes describing professionalized institutions central to the global economy, the presence of many university research centers, and disproportionally rising standards of living point to the same phenomena of globalization.

Nevertheless, despite the statistical appearance of social class influence, one issue remains. Although the results indicate that an anonymous UMC matters in skewing outcomes, they do not map how one could more precisely infer the power of the upper middle class. As an old issue in urban research, class power yields no easy or definitive answers. Nevertheless, pointing to socioeconomic stratification, Stone (1980) sees an indirect and anonymous route involving the UMC's systemic power: "Because the [UMC] are strategically advantaged, their extraordinary influence is not so much exercised as it is selectively manifested in the predispositions and behavior of public officials" (990). But, if influence is the central feature of the UMC ambience, how does the cuing process happen on the basis of nonverbal exchange?

One plausible extension to Stone's sketch is a process involving the *social construction* of the UMC by policymakers. The theory "refers to the cultural characterizations or popular images of persons or groups" (Schneider and Ingram 1993: 334) and stems from cognitive psychology (e.g., Tajfel and Turner 1986). With Stone's descriptions of political influence (1980: 980), social construction points to policymakers' designing agency outcomes to fit what they anticipate stereotypical target populations want (Schneider and Ingram 1993).

To Berger and Luckmann, however, two kinds of social constructs result in policy deliberations: images derived from the "face-to-face situation" with political actors and ones from "remoter forms of interaction" where cognition of individuals or organized groups is not apparent (1966: 30) . In this latter instance, they say cognition is of anonymous characterizations of a category (i.e., the UMC genre) rather than of individually known actors with which the agency interacts. "[A]nonymity may become near-total with certain typifications that are not intended ever to become individualized" (33).

What remains dim is how the UMC as an impersonal abstract is reified to the point that it matters in policymaking. Part of the answer may lie in Stone's belief that policymakers favor UMC interests over others because this genre is perceived to hold a disproportionate share of society's "diamond-shaped distribution of opportunities and resources" (1980: 982).

"Though they are the least numerous segment of the population, members of the upper strata possess resources strategically important to public officials [in furthering careers and agency growth]" (984).

Stone contends, then, that the UMC's influence on policymaking "flows more from the position they occupy than from the covert action they take" (1980: 984). Just perceiving UMC presence and social position may be sufficient to create the unspoken influence of referent power. In concert, Berger and Luckmann conclude, "Power in society includes the power to determine decisive socialization processes and, therefore, the power to *produce* reality" (1966: 119).

This raises a final point about the impact on policymaker perceptions. The powerful results for the UMC suggest it is a widely recognized genre, perhaps representing a predictable set of determinant public expectations. As a constant in a metropolitan milieu otherwise seen as a chaotic state, this class genre may provide a stabilizing influence on those urban governments where UMC individuals are a significant proportion of the metropolitan population. The genre offers a reliable context for policymaking, reducing uncertainty about political consequences for public officials having to make difficult policy choices.

If this stabilizing phenomenon exists, further research needs to delve into the social psychological origins of a UMC genre *within the agency.* Do bureaucratic structures and processes pose barriers to direct representation and foster more reliance on anonymous identities as political considerations? Is the "general public interest" derived from the UMC's systemic power or from the median voter? Is this reinforced by bureaucrats who are mostly UMC and aspiring to fulfill their own interests? Since living the UMC lifestyle gives policymakers knowledge about nuances, Lieberman believes the casual route more appropriately involves "political construction [that] asks not only how group identities arise in a political setting but also how and why they become politically relevant . . ." (1995: 440). In short, pursuing this line of inquiry reopens issues about the role of class structure and bureaucratic decision making.

References

Agranoff, Robert, and Michael McGuire. 1993. "Theoretical and Empirical Concerns for Intergovernmental Management and Policy Design." Paper presented at the 1993 meeting of the American Political Science Association, Washington, D.C. August 31–September 2.

Ashforth, Blake E., and Fred Mael. 1989. "Social Identity Theory and the Organization." *Academy of Management Review* 14: 20–39.

Benson, Kenneth J. 1975. "The Interorganizational Network as a Political Economy." *Administrative Science Quarterly* 20: 229–249.

Berger, Peter L., and Thomas Luckmann. 1966. *The Social Construction of Reality.* New York: Doubleday.

Boschken, Herman L. 1992. "Analyzing Performance Skewness in Public Agencies." *Journal of Public Administration Research and Theory* 2: 265–288.

Boschken, Herman L. 1994. "Organizational Performance and Multiple Constituencies." *Public Administration Review* 54: 308–312.

Boschken, Herman L. 1998. "Institutionalism: Intergovernmental Exchange, Administration-Centered Behavior, and Policy Outcomes in Urban Agencies." *Journal of Public Administration Research and Theory* 8: 585–614.

Boschken, Herman L. 2000. "Urban Spatial Form and Policy Outcomes in Public Agencies." *Urban Affairs Review* 36: 61–83.

Boschken, Herman L. Forthcoming. Social Class, Politics, and Urban Markets: The Makings of Bias in Policy Outcomes. (Book manuscript under review).

Bozeman, Barry. 1988. *All Organizations Are Public.* San Francisco: Jossey-Bass.

Brint, Steven. 1994. *In an Age of Experts.* Princeton: Princeton University Press.

Burgess, Ernest W., and Donald J. Bogue, eds. 1967. *Urban Sociology.* Chicago: University of Chicago Press.

Burt, Ronald. 1987. "Social Contagion and Innovation, Cohesion versus Structural Equivalence." *American Journal of Sociology* 92: 1287–1335.

Cervero, Robert. 1991. "Suburbanization of Jobs and the Journey to Work." Working Paper #3. Berkeley: University of California Transportation Center.

Chubb, John E., and Terry M. Moe. 1990. *Politics, Markets and America's Schools.* Washington, D.C.: Brookings Institution Press.

Clark, Terry N. 1994a. "Race and Class Culture: The New Political Culture." In Terry N. Clark, ed., *Urban Innovation.* Thousand Oaks, Calif.: Sage Publications.

Clark, Terry N., ed. 1994b. *Urban Innovation.* Thousand Oaks, Calif.: Sage Publications.

Clark, Terry N., and Lorna Crowley Ferguson. 1983. *City Money.* New York: Columbia University Press.

Clark, Terry N., and Edward G. Goetz. 1994. "The Antigrowth Machine." In Terry N. Clark, ed. *Urban Innovation.* Thousand Oaks, Calif.: Sage Publications.

Dahl, Robert. 1961. *Who Governs?* New Haven: Yale University Press.

Doig, Jameson W., and Erwin C. Hargrove, eds. 1987. *Leadership and Innovation.* Baltimore: Johns Hopkins University Press.

Doig, Jameson W., and Jerry Mitchell. 1992. "Expertise, Democracy, and the Public Authority Model." In Jerry Mitchell, ed., *Public Authorities and Public Policy.* New York: Greenwood Press.

Downs, George W., and Patrick D. Larkey. 1986. *The Search for Government Efficiency.* New York: Random House.

Dye, Thomas R. 1992. *Understanding Public Policy.* Englewood Cliffs, N.J.: Prentice Hall.

Farney, Dennis. 1994. "Elite Theory: Have Liberals Ignored Have-Less Whites at Their Own Peril?" *Wall Street Journal,* December 14.

Feiock, Richard C., and James Clingermayer. 1986. "Municipal Representation, Executive Power and Economic Development Policy Adoption." *Policy Studies Journal* 15: 211–230.

Feiock, Richard C., and Jonathan P. West. 1993. "Testing Competing Explanations for Policy Adoption." *Political Research Quarterly* 46: 399–419.

Gottdiener, M. 1986. "Culture, Ideology, and the Sign of the City." In M. Gottdiener and Alexandros Ph. Lagopoulos, eds., *The City and the Sign: Introduction to Urban Semiotics.* New York: Columbia University Press.

Grimshaw, William J. 1996. "Revisiting the Urban Classics." *Policy Studies Journal* 24: 230–244.

Gruber, Judith. 1987. *Controlling Bureaucracy.* Berkeley: University of California Press.

Hahn, Harlan, and Sheldon Kamieniecki. 1987. *Referendum Voting: Social Status and Policy Preferences.* New York: Greenwood.

Hummon, David M. 1992. "Community Attachment." In I. Altman and S. Low, *Place Attachment.* New York: Plenum Press.

Kerr, Clark. 1963. *The Uses of the University.* Cambridge, Mass.: Harvard University Press.

Lasswell, Harold. 1936. *Politics: Who Gets What, When, and How?* New York: McGraw-Hill.

Lazer, David. 1995. "Social Network Methods in the Study of Political Influence." Paper presented at the 1995 meeting of the American Political Science Association, Chicago, August 31–September 2.

Levy, Frank S., Arnold J. Meltsner, and Aaron Wildavsky. 1974. *Urban Outcomes.* Berkeley: University of California Press.

Lieberman, Robert C. 1995. "Social Construction (continued): Comment." *American Political Science Review* 89: 437–441.

Lineberry, Robert L. 1977. *Equality and Urban Policy.* Beverley Hills: Sage.

Lowi, Theodore J. 1969. *The End of Liberalism.* New York: W. W. Norton.

Maslow, Abraham. 1954. *Motivation and Personality.* New York: Harper.

Mindlin, Sergio, and Howard Aldrich. 1975. "Interorganizational Dependency." *Administrative Science Quarterly* 20: 382–392.

Niskanen, William A. 1971. *Bureaucracy and Representative Government.* Chicago: Aldine-Atherton.

Pagano, Michael A., and Ann O'M. Bowman. 1995. *Cityscapes and Capital.* Baltimore: Johns Hopkins University Press.

Peterson, Paul E. 1981. *City Limits.* Chicago: University of Chicago Press.

Pfeffer, Jeffrey, and Gerald Salancik. 1979. *The External Control of Organizations.* New York: Harper and Row.

Pressman, Jeffrey. 1972. "The Preconditions for Mayoral Power." *American Political Science Review* 66: 511–524.

Riesman, David. 1961. *The Lonely Crowd.* New Haven: Yale University Press.

Riesman, David. 1964. *Abundance for What?* Garden City, N.Y.: Doubleday.

Schneider, Anne, and Helen Ingram. 1993. "Social Construction of Target Populations." *American Political Science Review* 87: 334–347.

Schneider, Mark. 1989. *The Competitive City.* Pittsburgh: University of Pittsburgh Press.

Scott, William G., and David K. Hart. 1979. *Organizational America.* Boston: Houghton-Mifflin.

Selznick, Philip. 1996. "Institutionalism 'Old' and 'New'." *Administrative Science Quarterly.* 41: 270–277.

Sharp, Elaine B. 1991. "Institutional Manifestations of Accessibility and Urban Economic Development Policy." *Western Political Quarterly* 44: 129–147.

Shepsle, Kenneth A., and Mark S. Bonchek. 1997. *Analyzing Politics: Rationality, Behavior and Institutions.* New York: W.W. Norton.

Simon, Herbert. 1995. "Guest Editorial: Upon Acceptance of the Dwight Waldo Award." *Public Administration Review* 55: 404–405.

Stone, Clarence N. 1980. "Systemic Power in Community Decision Making." *American Political Science Review* 74: 978–990.

Stone, Clarence N. 1989. *Regime Politics.* Lawrence: University of Kansas Press.

Tajfel, H., and J. C. Turner. 1986. "The Social Identity Theory of Intergroup Behavior." In S. Worchel and W. G. Austin, eds., *Psychology of Intergroup Relations.* Chicago: Nelson-Hall.

Timms, D. W. G. 1971. *The Urban Mosaic.* Cambridge: Cambridge University Press.

Turner, J. C. 1985. "Social Categorization and the Self-Concept: A Social Cognitive Theory of Group Behavior." In Edward J. Lawler, ed., *Advances in Group Processes,* vol. 2, 77–122. Greenwich, Conn.: JAI Press.

UMTA. 1988. *A Directory of Urban Public Transportation Services.* Washington, D.C.: Urban Mass Transportation Administration.

Veblen, Thorstein. 1948. *The Portable Veblen.* New York: Viking.

Verba, Sidney, Kay Lehman Schlozman, and Henry E. Brady. 1995. *Voice and Equality.* Cambridge, Mass.: Harvard University Press.

Waldo, Dwight. 1948. *The Administrative State.* New York: Ronald Press.

Whyte, William. 1956. *Organization Man.* New York: Anchor.

Wilson, Woodrow. 1941. "The Study of Administration." *Political Science Quarterly* 56: 494 (originally published in 1887).

11

The Decline of Class Ideologies
The End of Political Exceptionalism?

SEYMOUR MARTIN LIPSET

> *No one any longer has any alternatives to capitalism—the arguments that re-main concern how far and in what ways capitalism should be governed and regulated.*
> —Anthony Giddens, *The Third Way*

The United States, as noted by Alexis de Tocqueville and Friedrich Engels, among many other visitors to America, is an "exceptional" country, one uniquely different in its organizing principles and social class structure from the more traditional status-bound postfeudal nations of the Old World (Tocqueville 1, 1948: 36–37).[1] The term *American exceptionalism,* first formulated by Tocqueville in the 1830s and since used in general comparative analyses, became widely applied after World War I in efforts to account for the weakness of working-class radicalism and class awareness in the United States. I dealt with the first usage in the book *American Exceptionalism* (Lipset 1996: 32–35, 77–109). In this chapter and a new book, *It Didn't Happen Here,* I discuss the second (Lipset and Marks 2000). And I conclude that the once-rigid social class structure and consequent political cleavages in the affluent industrially developed postfeudal countries are becoming more like the weaker and looser status structure of the never-feudal United States.

Political Exceptionalism

For students and practitioners of radicalism, "American exceptionalism" has meant a specific question: Why did the United States, alone among industrial societies, lack a significant socialist movement or a labor party (Flacks 1988: 104–105; Klehr 1971; Voss 1993; Halpern and Morris 1997)?[2] This issue has bedeviled socialist theorists from the late nineteenth century on. Friedrich Engels tries to answer it in the last decade of his life (Marx and Engels 1938; Engels 1953: 239; Engels 1942).[3] The German socialist and sociologist Werner Sombart dealt with it in a major book originally published in his native language in 1906, published in translation as *Why Is There No Socialism in the United States?* (1976). The question was also addressed by the Fabian Society member H. G. Wells in *The Future in America,* which came out the same year. Both Lenin and Trotsky were deeply concerned with the phenomenon, for it questioned the inner logic of Marxist historical materialism, as expressed by Marx himself, in the preface to *Das Kapital* where he stated that "the country that is more developed [economically] shows to the less developed the image of their future" (Sombart 1976; Wells 1906; Marx 1958: 8–9).[4] And there is no questioning that, from the last quarter of the nineteenth century on, the most developed country has been the United States. The Communist International had a special commission to deal with "the American question," attended by Joseph Stalin himself.

Given Marx's assumption, leading pre–World War I Marxists believed, as Engels noted in reiterating Marx's dictum in 1893, that the most industrialized capitalist country would lead the world into socialism (Sombart 1976: 15; Bell 1996). Sombart also emphasized this proposition: "If . . . modern socialism follows as a necessary reaction to capitalism, the country with the most advanced capitalist development, namely the United States, would at the same time be the one providing the classic case of socialism, and its working class would be supporters of the most radical of Socialist movements" (quoted in Quint 1953: 380).

This position became entrenched in orthodox Marxism. While still a Marxist, before he became the most influential revisionist of Marxist ideas, Edward Bernstein noted, "We see modern socialism enter and take root in the United States in direct relation to the spreading of capitalism and the appearance of a modern proletariat" (quoted in Moore 1970: 70). Karl Kautsky, considered the leading theoretician in the German Social Democratic Party, enunciated in 1902, "America shows us our future, in so far as one country can reveal it at all to another." He elaborated this view in

1910, anticipating the "overdue sharpening of class conflict" developing "more strongly" there than anywhere else (quoted in Moore 1970: 58, 102).

August Bebel, the political leader of the German Social Democrats, stated unequivocally in 1907: "Americans will be the first to usher in a Socialist republic." This belief, at a time when the German party was already a mass movement with many elected members of the Reichstag and when the American Socialist Party had secured less than 2 percent of the vote, was based on the United States being "far ahead of Germany in industrial development."

Bebel reiterated this opinion in 1912, when the discrepancy in the strength of the two movements was even greater, saying that America will "be the first nation to declare a Cooperative Commonwealth" (quoted in Moore 1970: 77). The French socialist Paul Lefargue, Marx's son-in-law, paraphrased his father-in-law on the flyleaf of his book on America: "The most industrially advanced country shows to those who follow it on the industrial ladder the image of their own future" (quoted in Moore 1970: 91). Many other Marxists, such as H. M. Hyndman in England, Maksim Gorky in Russia, and Daniel De Leon in the United States, also stressed the point.

The continued inability of socialists to create a viable movement in the United States was a major embarrassment to Marxist theorists, who assumed that the superstructure of a society, which encompasses political behavior, is a function of the underlying economic and technological systems. Many late nineteenth- and early twentieth-century Marxists understood their theory required them to believe that "the United States, of all the countries in the world, [was] most ripe for socialism" (De Leon 1904: 133). Max Beer, whose 50-year career in international socialism included participation in the Austrian, German, and British parties and who worked for the Socialist International, described the anxiety among European Marxist leaders created by the weakness of socialism in America, which they voiced in private discussions. They knew that it was a "living contradiction of . . . Marxian theory" and that it raised questions about the validity of Marxism itself (Beer 1935: 109–110).

Leon Trotsky took cognizance of Marx's statement in a 1939 publication intended for a popular American audience. He reprinted the sentence from *Das Kapital,* quoted above, and then simply dismissed it with the comment, "Under no circumstances can this . . . be taken literally" (1939: 38–39). Trotsky, of course, knew his Marxism and was well aware that the theory demanded the United States should have been the first on the path toward socialism. His comment suggests that the contradiction was much on his mind. His effort to dismiss it as a figurative statement indicates that he had no answer to the conundrum it posed.

In spite of the sorry record of organized socialism in America, it may, however, be argued that Karl Marx was right, that the most developed country "shows to the less developed the image of their future." Applying this generalization to the United States simply means that American culture, including politics, as it actually developed, not as Marxists hoped it would, reflects the logic of an economically and technologically advanced society. The never-feudal United States has been the prototype of a bourgeois society. As Max Weber understood, it could become the most productive economy precisely because its culture thoroughly encompassed capitalist values. The ideal-typical capitalist man was an American, Benjamin Franklin. For Weber, "the spirit of capitalism" was best contained in the Pennsylvanian's writings (1958: 64–65).

The argument that American nonsocialist politics would prove to be the model for the European Left was presented in full flower in 1940 by Lewis Corey, an early leader of the American Communist Party, as Louis Fraina, in a series of articles in *Workers Age,* the organ of a neo-Communist sect, the Lovestoneites. As summarized by *Harvey Klehr,* Corey foresaw in prescient terms that,

> Rather than being an exception, America was actually the model for capitalist countries. Only the positions in the race had been changed; European socialist could see in America the image of their own unhappy future. Far from being a unique or even only slightly different case, America was the prototype for capitalism. In a curious reversal of roles, it was now the European socialists who could look across the ocean to see the future of their own movement. American development was not different than Europe's; it was merely at a more advanced stage. (1971: 130).[5]

The Changing Left

As Louis Corey anticipated, the Lefts of the other Western democracies have increasingly become like the American nonsocialist Left. To a greater or lesser degree, they all reject statist economies and accept competitive markets as the way to grow and raise standards of living. The Social Democratic and Labor parties are now socially and ideologically pluralistic. Leaders of European social democratic governments—Blair, Jospin, Schroeder, and others—are trying to reconstitute the Socialist International into a new grouping of progressive left parties, The Third Way, in which the Democratic Party represents the United States.

The change in the character of the European parties reflects in large part a transformation of economic and class structures, one which moves their countries in a direction that makes them resemble the United States, as described by Tocqueville and pre–World War I Marxists. The emphasis on *Stände,* fixed, explicitly hierarchical, social classes derived from a feudal and monarchical past, has declined greatly. The growth in the economies, with a resultant considerable increase in consumption goods and more equitable allocation of education has greatly reduced the differences in style of life, including accents and dress, among the social classes. The distribution of income and occupational skills has changed from a pyramidal shape, ▲, enlarging toward the bottom, which characterized the late nineteenth and early twentieth centuries, to one that resembles a diamond, ◆, bulging in the middle. Left political parties now seek to appeal more to the growing middle strata, than to the industrial workers and the impoverished, who are declining proportionately. In the United States, the prototype of structural developments in industrialized societies, the proportion of those employed in nonmanual pursuits has increased from 43 percent in 1960 to 58 percent at the end of the century. Workers in manufacturing have fallen from 26 percent to 16. Corresponding drop-offs for the United Kingdom are from 36 percent to 19; in Sweden, from 32 to 19; for the Netherlands, from 30 to 19; for Australia, from 26 to 13.5. The declines have been less dramatic but definite for France, 28 to 20, and for Germany, 34 to 29 (Bureau of Labor Statistics 1981 and 1998).

The American system has always placed a lesser emphasis on class awareness and organization than the Old World societies have; in any case, these have been declining on both sides of the Atlantic. Union membership, the predominant base of the left parties, has fallen in proportionate terms in four-fifths of the 92 countries surveyed by the ILO (International Labor Organization 1997). Between 1985 and 1995, density declined by 21 percent in the United States. As of 2000, only 14 percent of employed American workers were union members, fewer than 10 percent in private employment. The losses in density in France and Britain have been even greater, 37 percent for France and 28 for the United Kindgom, while Germany fell off by 18 percent (International Labor Organization 1997). The European and Australasian Social Democratic parties have become like the Democrats, more socially heterogeneous in membership and support. The correlations between class (economic) position and vote choice, lower in

the United States than elsewhere in the industrialized world, have been declining in most developed nations in recent decades, as the distribution of
economic classes and consumption levels have changed.

Some of the underlying forces giving rise to these developments have
been specified by a number of neo-Marxist social scientists in discussing
the emergence of "post-industrial society," "post-materialism," and the
"scientific-technological revolution." Daniel Bell, a lifelong social democrat, has been the central figure in conceptualizing these changes in the
West (Bell 1978). Radovon Richta and his associates (1969) in the
Czechoslovakian Academy of Sciences projected similar developments in
Eastern Europe and the Soviet Union.

The consequent changes in class and political relations within industrially developed societies, much like the shifts in the politics of the Left between the United States and Europe, may be analyzed within the framework of an apolitical Marxism, that is, accepting the proposition that
technological structures and the distribution of economic classes determine the political and cultural superstructures, without assuming that socialism will succeed capitalism. Many of the trends anticipated by Marx—
a steady increase in the industrial proletariat, a decline in self-employment,
incumbent in the growth of factories—have ended. Tertiary technological
and service occupations rather than production jobs have been increasing
rapidly. The number of students in higher education and of university
graduates has grown many times. Alain Touraine, a leading French sociologist and left intellectual, suggests that the basis of power has changed as
a result of these developments: "If property was the criterion of membership in the former dominant class, the new dominant class is defined by
knowledge and a certain level of education" (Touraine 1971).

The neo-Marxists and technological determinist scholars have stressed
the extent to which theoretical and scientific knowledge have become the
principal source of social and economic change, altering social structures,
values, and mores in ways that have given considerable prestige and power
to the scientific technological elites. The emerging strata of post-industrialism—whose roots are in the university, the scientific and technological
worlds, heavily represented in the industries spawned by computers, the
public sectors, and the professions—have developed their own distinctive
values.

Ronald Inglehart, the most important empirical analyst of post-industrialism, points out that beyond the impact of technological innovations,
the "post-materialist" value changes and the decline of class conflict are
also functions of the growing climate of affluence in the last half century.

The generations that came of age during the second half of the twentieth century hold different values from previous cohorts, who were reared in an atmosphere of economic scarcity and experienced severe economic depressions. Survey data gathered by Inglehart over the past quarter of a century have shown clear generational effects as well as links to the massive growth in educational attainments, which have made the expansion in high tech and scientific pursuits possible (Inglehart 1971; Inglehart 1997).[6]

These developments have profoundly affected the political scene in the industrially advanced (post-industrial) North American, European, Australian, and Japanese societies. Post-industrial politics has been marked by a decline in ideological conflict over the role of the state, accompanying the growth of market power in economic arena. A better-educated citizenry has resulted in increasing concern with noneconomic or social issues—the environment, health, the quality of education, the culture, greater equality for women and minorities, the extension of democratization and freedom at home and abroad, and last, but far from least, a highly controversial, more permissive morality, particularly as affecting familial affairs and sexual behavior. In some polities environmental reformers have taken the lead in creating new Green parties generally allied in coalition with the new Third Way social democrats, as in France and Germany, or operating within them as in the United States and Britain.

It is notable that, much as the United States set a model for less statist, more market-oriented polities, more recently it has been in the forefront of a post-materialist New Politics, which has traveled, so to speak, from Berkeley and Madison to Paris and Berlin. The French political analyst Jean-François Revel, writing in the early 1970s, noted that the "revolutionary stirrings have had their origin in the United States." The newer forms of movement protest, whether in Europe or elsewhere, are "imitations of the American prototype, or extensions of, and subsequent to it; European dissenters . . . are the disciples of the American movements" (Revel 1971: 6–7).[7]

Many political analysts, while recognizing major reformulations on the left within their own country, do not realize the extent to which these changes reflect common developments throughout the economically advanced democracies, that they cannot be explained by specific national developments or leaders. To point up the magnitude and congruences of these events, I will summarize the ways in which left politics in country after country have taken an "American" path. This, of course, does not mean that parties and ideologies are the same cross-nationally. Necessarily, there are important variations reflecting diverse historical backgrounds, the varying nature of political cleavages, and the structural and demographic patterns that underlie them. But the similarities among the polities, as Tony Blair has stressed, are considerable. And he notes, "It's a perfectly healthy thing if we realize there are common developments the whole world over" (Harris and Barbash 1977: A27). The record suggests that the United States has become less exceptional politically, as the European socialists and social democrats begin to resemble American Democrats.

The Third Way Social Democrats

Following a meeting of European social democratic leaders with Bill Clinton in New York on September 24, 1998, Tony Blair proclaimed their new progressive Third Way doctrine:

> In the economy, our approach is neither laissez-faire nor one of the state interference. The government's role is to promote macroeconomic stability; develop tax and welfare policies that encourage independence, not dependence; to equip people for work by improving education and infrastructure; and to promote enterprise. We are proud to be supported by the business leaders as well as trade unions . . .
> In welfare and employment policy, the Third Way means reforming welfare to make it a pathway into work where possible. It promotes fair standards at work while making work pay by reducing the taxes and penalties that discourage work and the creation of jobs. (Blair 1998)

The 1997 British election, won overwhelmingly by the Labour Party after it had rejected its historical emphasis on public ownership, basically put an end to a century of socialist efforts to reduce sharply or eliminate private ownership of the economy.[9] Labour's leader, Tony Blair, has been deliberately stressing his agreement with the free-market, smaller-government policies of Bill Clinton. Even before Clinton, Blair proclaimed: "The era of big government is over." He promised to "govern from the center." Blair reformulated his party's image, as New Labour, as a nonsocialist party that is not committed to working with the trade unions. He emphasized that he wants unions to cooperate "with management to make sure British industry is competitive." Peter Mendelson, the ideologist of the Blairites, proudly asserted that Labour is now "a market capitalist party" (Will 1997).

Even more notable is Blair's advice to labor organizations in a 1994 article in the *New Statesman:* "It is in the unions' best interest not to be as-sociated with one political party." He argued that unions "should be able to thrive with any change of government or no change in government." (Blair 1994). All of this by the leader of a party largely founded by the unions and subsidized by them for all of its history. In effect, Blair said that the arguments against commitment to a party put forth by Samuel Gom-pers, the founding president of the American Federation of Labor, were right. During the 1997 campaign, the Labour Party released a special man-ifesto for business that promised that a Blair government would retain the "main elements" of Margaret Thatcher's restrictions on unions and would resist unreasonable economic demands. Blair noted in an interview that his administration will "leave British [labor] law the most restrictive on trade unionism in the Western world" (Druhan 1997).

The manifesto proclaimed: "Tax and spend is being replaced by save and invest." While the general election platform stated that "healthy profits are an essential motor of a dynamic market economy," it also emphasized that the goal of low inflation requires that wage gains be held down (Baldwin 1997; see also Harris and Barbash 1997). It is not surprising that Baroness Thatcher, at the start of the 1997 campaign, in an interview with Paul Johnson in the *Daily Mail* (London), said, "Britain will be safe in the hands of Mr. Blair." And speaking to a meeting of the Socialist Interna-tional, Prime Minister Blair returned the compliment, saying, "There were certain things the 1980s got right—an emphasis on enterprise, more flex-ible labor markets" (Harris and Barbash 1997: A28). One of Blair's first actions after taking office was to shift the power to control monetary pol-icy and interest rates from the Treasury to the Bank of England. Another, launched after his first meeting with Bill Clinton on May 31, 1997, was welfare reform designed to reduce sharply the number on the dole by pressing single mothers to take paying jobs. He stated he would "be tough on the long-term unemployed who refuse jobs" (Prescott 1997). At this meeting, Clinton and Blair asserted that the "progressive parties of today are the parties of fiscal responsibility and prudence" (Mitchell 1997; Har-ris and Barbash 1997). The two leaders called for partnership with business to create jobs, replacing the "old battles between state and market" (Wig-ton 1997).

As Tony Blair has emphasized, the same pattern is evident the world over. During the 1980s, the Labor governments of Australia and New Zealand cut income taxes, pursued economic deregulation, and privatized various industries. The Australian party made an "accord" with trade unions that resulted, as then Labor prime minister Robert Hawke emphasized, in reducing real wages by at least 1 percent in each of the eight years that he was head of the government. He stressed that "the move in the share of the national income from wages towards profits . . . has enabled us to grow" (see Lipset 1991: 184). The New Zealand story is similar. Returning to power in 1984, the Labour Party, in office until October 1990, ended "the tradition of taxation according to ability to pay," dismantled the welfare state, and privatized many state enterprises. According to a report in a social democratic magazine, Prime Minister David Lange argued that "social democrats must accept the existence of economic inequality because it is the engine which drives the economy" (see Lipset 1991: 185).[9]

The story can be reiterated for the left parties outside the English-speaking world. The Swedish Social Democrats, who held office from the early 1930s on, with brief interludes out of power between 1976 and 1982 and again between 1994 and 1998, reversed their previous wage growth, high income tax, and strong welfare state orientations and undertook several privatization measures as well. The late American socialist leader Michael Harrington reported critically that the government under Prime Minister Olaf Palme reduced the real income of those with a job while increasing employment, much as Hawke did in Australia (Harrington 1987: 130–131).

In Spain, before he left office, three-term Socialist prime minister Felipe Gonzalez converted his party—Marxist in its initial post-Franco phase—to support privatization, the free market, and NATO. He once noted in a near-Churchillian formulation that a competitive free market economy is marked by greed, corruption, and the exploitation of the weak by the strong, but that "capitalism is the least-bad economic system in existence" (Gallagher and Williams 1989: 3). His economic policies were described by the *Economist* as having made his government "look somewhat to the right of Mrs. Thatcher's" (*Economist* 1989).

The first major Marxist party in the world, the Social Democrats of Germany (SPD), rejected Marxism at their Bad Godesberg conference in 1959. American political scientist Russell Dalton commented on their program: "Karl Marx would have been surprised to . . . learn that free economic competition was one of the essential conditions of a social democratic economic policy." Speaking in 1976, Social Democratic chancellor Helmut Schmidt was a precursor of Australian Labor prime minister Robert Hawke in arguing that the interests of the workers required expanding profits, noting, "The profits of enterprises today are the investments of tomorrow, and the investments of tomorrow are the employment of the day after." The SPD's 1990 program noted in classical liberal fashion that within a "democratically established setting, the market and competition are indispensable" (Lipset 1991).

In 1995, the then SPD candidate for chancellor and currently the minister of defense in Berlin, Rudolph Scharping, emphasized that his party's historical assumptions have proven "wrong": "We Social Democrats created an overly regulated, overly bureaucratic, and overly professionalized welfare state." Among other problematic policies, he pointed to social security, noting, "The intergenerational contract in its current form, whereby the present generation pays for current pensions and at the same time commits the next generation to pay for its pensions . . . can not stand . . . . I think putting an end to the wasting of public money is highly moral because such waste always occurs at the expense of third parties" (Scharping 1996: 53, 54–55).

The chancellor elected in 1998, Gerhard Schroeder, continues in this tradition. He sees the SPD as part of a "New Middle" rather than the Left (Apple 1998). John Vinocur of the *International Herald-Tribune* notes that the New Middle "is a place where words like 'risk,' 'entrepreneurial spirit,' and 'flexible labor markets' coincide with expressions of allegiance to social justice and fair income distribution" (Vinocur 1998: 11–12). Schroeder promised to improve the German economy, reducing its high pre-election 11 percent unemployment rate by lowering its "prohibitive labor costs" and "providing incentive for new capital investment." He noted in the election campaign that the SPD is "breaking with . . . . statist social democratic attitudes. . . . [W]e've understood that the omnipotent and interventionist state doesn't have its place in the current circumstances" (Vinocur 1998: 24). Commenting on the 1998 election, the editors of *Die Zeit* and *Die Welt* noted that the contest was "about nuances" rather than fundamental differences (Andrews 1998).

In his inaugural speech after being inducted as chancellor on November 10, 1998, Schroeder stressed continuity with the previous Kohl government, saying, "We do not want to do everything differently, but many things better." To help reduce unemployment, he proposed to lower corporate taxes from the maximum rate of 47 percent under Kohl to 35 and called for business and unions to cooperate in a formal "alliance for jobs" (*This Week in Germany* 1998a; Drozdizk 1998; Cohen 1998). In office he has fostered private pension schemes, to encourage personal responsibility, and seeks to concentrate state subsidies and spending on the "truly needy"

while, in the words of the *Financial Times*, linking "fiscal policy with supply side measures, including deregulation and the opening of markets"
(Atkins 1998).

In the past, Socialist parties created extensive welfare states that required
a steadily increasing proportion of the gross domestic product to go to the
government, in some cases reaching over one-half. Today, however, the
same parties recognize that they simply cannot compete on the world market unless they reduce government expenditures. Their electoral situation
forces them to press for the voter support of the middle-class and affluent
skilled workers and high tech employees. Hence like Clinton, Blair and
Schroeder, they seek to lower taxes, reduce welfare entitlements, and balance their budgets but also to press for post-materialist reforms, cleaning
up the physical, social, and economic environments. And the prototypical
social democratic polity, Sweden, has sped up its efforts to restore the
economy by privatizing 25 more enterprises in 1999 (Burt 1999a). Finland and Denmark are pursuing similar policies under Social Democratic
leadership (Burt 1999b).

The only current exceptions to the move away from state intervention
among Socialist parties are in Norway and to some extent in France, both
favoring extensive welfare policies but, it should be noted, not nationalization of industry. Norway can retain a belief in "old-fashioned socialism"
because of its abundant oil resources, which pay for its welfare state. The
French Left operates within a society in which *dirigisme*, a strong direct-
ing state, has been as much a part of their culture's organizing principles
as antistatism has been of the American (Lichfield 1997).[10]

French uniqueness may be seen as the counterpoint to American exceptionalism. Both the Right and the Left in France have approved of a powerful state, an emphasis going back to the monarchy, the empire, and the
Revolution. The statist orientation of the Socialists is a necessary reaction
to the policies of the Right. As the journalist Roger Cohen (1997) notes,
"The Gaullist attachment to the state and rejection of market reform encouraged the Socialists to keep further to the left, to distinguish themselves." Or as an academic authority on French politics, Ezra Suleiman,
emphasizes: "The right can't let go of the state, so the left stays left" (Cohen 1997).

Yet, in an interview with *Le Nouvel Observateur* a month before the
1997 elections, Lionel Jospin, shortly to be prime minister, sounded like
other European socialists in saying he favored a move away from "statism,"
with more decentralization and growth in individual initiative. He praised
the extensive privatization measures carried through by François Mitter-

rand during his 14 years as president. Nevertheless, the French Socialists won in 1997, promising to deal with massive unemployment by creating 200,000 new jobs for young people, 25 percent of whom lacked work, and to protect the country's elaborate welfare state from budget cuts. Such policies could meet with approval in a country where the majority of the population told pollsters in 1997 that they feel good about "public service" (72 percent), respond favorably to "the state" (56 percent), and to the word *bureaucrat* (60 percent). Under the previous conservative cabinet, France had "the heaviest tax burden and the largest public pay roll in Europe."[11] In office, the Socialists have, however, reversed a number of policies, particularly seeking to cap welfare payments and control the budget deficit (Swardson 1998a).

Lionel Jospin has taken to emphasizing the need to emulate the American economy. In 1998, he criticized leftist disdain for the level of U.S. job growth saying, "Contrary to what we have claimed and indeed believed, the jobs being created in the United States are not only, or even mainly, low-paid, dead-end jobs, but skilled ones in the service and high-tech industries." The *Economist* reports that he stressed that the French "could learn much about America's economic dynamism, the vitality of its research and innovation, its competitive spirit and capacity for renewal" (*Economist* 1998: 50). [12]

Curiously, the model European country at the end of the century, frequently cited as such by the European social democrats and others, is the Netherlands. With an unemployment rate of 6.5 percent in 1997, far below the major continental economies, and a growth rate higher than in Britain, France, and Germany, the Dutch under a government headed by a former union leader, Wim Kok of the Labor Party, have kept down "wages, inflation and interest rates, and . . . [eased] the rules for hiring and firing and for opening new businesses." Unemployment benefits have been cut, and the rules for sick and disability pay have been tightened. Thomas Friedman of the *New York Times* describes the policy as "U.S. style downsizing, privatizing, and loosening up of labor rules" (Friedman 1997: A35).

In a "social pact" negotiated between the unions, then led by Kok, and the employers, a pact comparable to the Australian "accord," labor agreed to limit wage increases to 2 percent a year. Whether produced by these policies or not, the subsequent near-full employment economy in a "more competitive [Dutch] market" has led to an increase in income inequality, much as in the United States and other industrialized countries (Simons 1997: A6). The better educated and highly skilled are much more in demand in high tech economies than industrial workers and the less skilled are. They are relatively much better paid while the others have been de-clining proportionately in income terms, although not in consumption standards.

Far from the politically "backward" United States following the lead of the more "progressive" Europe, the Old World Left is now becoming more like the American, as Corey anticipated. Hence, it may be reiterated that in political terms the United States has shown Europe the image of its future. This reflects the trend that as the latter countries reached new heights of affluence and mass consumption, they began, as Antonio Gram-sci anticipated, to resemble the United States, socially less stratified, less status bound, and much better educated. Consequently, their less-privi-leged strata are much less class conscious than earlier.

The United States, therefore, is no longer as exceptional politically. Like other developed countries, it is divided among socially more conservative or traditional groupings, libertarian or classical liberal forces, religion-based factions, environmentalist and other post-materialist tendencies, and anti-elitist populist segments. The strength and organizational forms of the last group vary from country to country, but none of them is socialist or seriously class oriented. The now nonsocialist "progressive" left parties seek, as Adam Przeworski notes, to make capitalism more humane and more efficient (Przeworski 1985: 206). Or as the advisor of François Mit-terrand, Regis Debray, points out, the objective of European Socialist leader is "to carry out the politics of the Right, but more intelligently and in a more rational manner" (Debray 1990: 27).

Still an Outlier

America, it should be recognized, still remains an outlier at one end of many international indexes of behavior and values. It has higher rates of mobility into elite positions than any other nation; a larger proportion of its young people attend university, particularly graduate and professional schools, than elsewhere, making such upward movement possible. The economy is not just the most productive; it is also the greatest job producer by far in the developed world. From the end of World War II to the pre-sent, the American economy has created many more new jobs than the en-tirety of Europe and Japan, and as Jospin notes, most of them have been "good" ones, that is, requiring skill and education and being relatively well paid (Andrews 1998).

The comparative picture is not as positive for the United States in other dimensions. American exceptionalism is double-edged. The country leads in the proportion not voting in national elections. Its prison population is greater in per capita terms than elsewhere in the developed world, as its rates of violence are. The nation is among the leaders in the unequal distribution of monetary income. The gap between that received by its upper 1–5 percent income group and the lowest 5–20 percent is greater than in most Europe and Japan, though the gap has been growing in those countries too. This development is largely a result of the shift from factory to high tech jobs, which reward educated labor, while depreciating the level of the wages of less-skilled manual and service workers, many of whom in the United States are Latino and Asian immigrants or African Americans, and in much of Europe are immigrants from the south. Functional illiteracy is higher in the United States than in Europe and Japan.

Many of these cross-national differences parallel variations in public attitudes. Americans, traditionally most favorable to motivating the lowly to try to "win," to encourage upward mobility, are more disposed to provide high incomes for important positions than Europeans and Japanese. Americans are more prone than others to believe there should be "greater incentives for individual effort," rather than incomes should be made more equal, while proportionately fewer Americans (56 percent) agree that "income differences are too large," as compared with Europeans (66–86 percent) (Smith 1990: 22). Americans are more likely than Europeans to agree that "large income differences are needed for the country's prosperity." Nearly one-third of Americans surveyed justify inequality this way as compared with an average of 23 percent for seven European countries (Great Britain, Austria, the former West Germany, Italy, Hungary, Switzerland, and the Netherlands) (Kolosi 1987: 33). A review of American public opinion data over 50 years reports: "Surveys since the 1930s have shown that the explicit idea of income redistributing elicits very limited enthusiasm among the American public. . . . Redistributive fervor was not much apparent even in [the] depression era. Most Americans appear content with the distributional effects of private markets" (Page and Shapiro 1992: 300).

Not surprisingly, the World Values Surveys conducted in 1980 and 1990, like other polls, reveal that social democratic values are still much stronger in Europe and Canada than in America. They report, for example, that when asked to choose between the importance of "equality of income or the freedom to live and develop without hindrance," Americans are more favorable to the latter option; 71 percent felt this way compared with an average of 59 percent in Europe in 1990 (Inglehart 1990).

Americans are also more likely than Europeans to say that taxes are too high for middle-income individuals. In spite of the shifts toward approval of a free market by European leftists, government remains much less intrusive in society and economy in the United States. These national variations have a long history. The major European countries provided important social services long before the United States, which did not enact pensions, unemployment, or industrial accident insurance until the 1930s.

Americans are more prone to believe they live in a meritocracy. The greater American commitment to opportunity is also reflected in the findings that citizens in the United States have been more disposed than Europeans to favor sizable expenditures for education. "In fact, education has long been an area in which most Americans want government to spend more money" (Page and Shapiro 1992: 133). As Robert Shapiro and John Young note, these attitudes stem from "Americans views and values concerning individualism and the equality of opportunity, as opposed to equality of outcomes for individuals" (Shapiro and Young 1989: 59–89). Yet American students in elementary and high school test lower in international comparisons than their compeers in other developed societies.

Contemporary America is the outcome of processes that began with an egalitarian (meritocratic) and individualistic revolution (Lipset 1990: 8–13, 22–36). The United States remained through the nineteenth and early twentieth centuries the closest example of a classically liberal society that rejected the assumptions of ascriptive elitism, of statism, of Tory noblesse oblige à la Bismarck and Disraeli.

The major societal variables that reduced the potential for socialism and class consciousness in pre–World War II America were the antistatist value system, the socially more egalitarian social class structure, and the individualistic Protestant sectarian orientation. The emphasis on egalitarian social relations, the absence of a demand that those lower in the social order give overt deference to their social or economic superiors, and the stress on meritocracy, on equal opportunity for all to rise economically and socially, stem from an exceptional past and present. The country is characterized by the absence of hereditary privilege, an ascriptively legitimated upper class and fixed lower classes derivative from feudalism, and by its formation as a new settler society as well as by the elaboration of the Revolution-born libertarian and egalitarian ideology. Tocqueville noted these elements in the 1830s. He was, of course, aware of enormous variations in income and power and of a strong emphasis on the attainment of wealth (Tocqueville 1, 1948: 51). But he stressed that, regardless of steep economic inequalities, Americans did not require the lower strata to acknowledge their inferiority, to bow to their betters.

Society and politics, of course, have changed greatly in America as in Europe. The 1930s produced a qualitative difference from previous eras. As historian Richard Hofstadter wrote, that decade introduced a "social democratic tinge" into the United States for the first time in its history (1972: 308). The Great Depression resulted in a strong emphasis on planning, on the welfare state, on the role of the government as a major regulatory actor, and even on income redistribution.

The 1930s led to a kind of Europeanization of American politics as well as of its labor organizations. Class factors became more important in differentiating party support (Lubell 1965: 55–68). The conservatives, increasingly concentrated among the Republicans, remained antistatist and pro-laissez-faire, although many of them accepted an activist role for the state in response to the depression and war. Statist proclivities, however, gradually declined after World War II as a result of long-term prosperity that helped to refurbish traditional values.

A consequence of these developments has been a reemergence of the classical liberal ideology, that is, what Americans call conservatism. The class tensions, enhanced by the Depression, lessened as reflected in a great decline in union membership since the mid-1950s and lower correlations between class position and vote choices. Even before Ronald Reagan entered the White House, the United States had a lower rate of taxation, a smaller budget deficit, a less-developed welfare state, and many fewer government-owned industries than other industrialized nations.

To what extent is it still possible to speak of American exceptionalism? It is obvious that the United States and the rest of the Western world have changed dramatically over the past two centuries. They have all become more productive, industrialized, urbanized, and better educated. The central state has become more powerful. As noted, the postfeudal elements that existed in many European countries have declined enormously. In social structural terms, the latter are becoming more like America. To reiterate, their left parties have given up socialism.

The changes that have occurred, obviously, still leave many differences. The United States, Canada and Europe continue to vary along lines that flow from their distinctive national traditions. And the United States remains the least statist Western nation (Rose 1985).

Conclusion

The political divisions of modern democracy, conceptualized since the French Revolution as between the Left and the Right, remain. The Democrats and Republicans, the Social Democrats and Conservatives, still provide choices on the ballot, although their ideological bearings and internal factions are changing (Furet 1988).

Cleavages linked to stratification, of course, are no longer the main correlates of left or right positions. Issues revolving around morality, abortion, family values, civil rights, gender equality, multiculturalism, immigration, crime and punishment, foreign policy, and supranational communities move individuals and groups in directions different from those linked to stratification position. But basically most of these matters can be related to social ideology, which in turn correlates with religion and education.

There can be little doubt about the prospects for the continuation of the 200-year-old American political system. The Democrats, founded under Jefferson, have existed since 1976 with a base among the "out" groups, the less privileged, the status deprived, and the less religious. The intelligentsia have been founded in the nonbusiness-linked party ever since Jefferson's Democratic-Republicans. The more socially conservative, more business-oriented parties have had different incarnations, Federalist-Whig-Republican, with similar more privileged "in" group constituencies in each format. The Republicans, today, draw on libertarians and social and religious conservatives, as well as on economic conservatives comprehending classical Hayekian liberals. (The major exception to these generalizations occurred around the slavery and race issues).

The meanings of the terms left and right are changing. As we have seen, the parties of the Left, still self-identifying as social democrats or socialists, have reconstituted themselves as liberals in the American sense (not the European). To that should be added their emphasis on post-materialism, environmentalism, equality for women, minorities, and gays, and cultural freedoms. The Right has moved in varying degrees toward classical liberalism or libertarianism. One stresses group equality and economic security; the other, equality of opportunity and the weakening of state power. Logically, the Right should also support personal freedom, along the lines favored by nineteenth-century liberals. The links, however, between the new economic conservatism and religious traditionalism have fostered cultural conservatism with respect to sex, the family, and style of life. Given the

complex variations in the political cleavage structure, it is difficult to specify a consistent pattern differentiating the Left and the Right.

The confusion in linking ideological concepts to policy is illustrated by
the different meanings attached to *neoconservatism,* a term which arose in
the United States that is applied in a very different way outside the country's borders. In America, the label was formulated by some leftist intellectuals to discredit a group of hardline anti-Communists who were on the
left on domestic issues, for example, social democrats, Trotskyists, and liberals. Most were originally Democrats, and many still are. They identified
with Hubert Humphrey–Henry Jackson–Pat Moynihan Democrats,
George Meany–Lane Kirkland trade unionists, and the Social Democrats
U.S.A. led by Sidney Hook and Bayard Rustin. The Republicans tried to
win over those labeled neoconservatives, but those they did win over were
invariably used in foreign or defense policy positions or in education and
intellectual policy realms. They were kept out of economic and welfare policy, since most remained somewhat more to the left in these matters.[13] Not
surprisingly, in 2000, most Republican neoconservatives supported re-
former John McCain rather than George W. Bush for the presidential
nomination. But in Europe, where this background somehow is largely
unknown, the assumption exists that neoconservatives are new libertarian
conservatives because they reject the Tory statist emphases that have defined traditional conservatism, that they are Reagan-Thatcher conservatives, but most are not.

No major tendency, left or right, retains a belief in a utopia, in a solu-
tion for all major problems by dramatically reconstructing society and
polity. These post–cold war conditions bode well for democratic stablility
and for international peace. It has become a truism that democracies do
not wage war against each other, and most of the world is now democratic
(Rummel 1997). While extremist movements and parties exist, all of them
are relatively weak, at least in the West. The strongest are the Freedom
Party in Austria, with 27 percent of the vote, and Le Pen's National Front
in France, supported by 15 percent of the electorate. No other is close to
these levels. There are no charismatic leaders; there is also little political enthusiasm. Youth, as Aristole wrote, "have exalted notions . . . would rather
do noble things than useful ones . . . doing things excessively and vehe-
mently," and so are necessarily frustrated (Aristotle 1941: 1404).

Will this situation change? Of course it will, since economies, and consequently societies, never remain in a steady state. The inner dynamics of
market systems produce reverses in the business cycle. Such possibilities

and Russia's political instability once more threaten the West. The Japanese collapse has replaced the Japanese miracle. France's move to the left in 1997 and Le Pen's support on the right have not only been facilitated by the country's statist values; they also constitute a response to an unemployment rate of 12 percent. Demographic variations (e.g., the growth in the proportion of the aged, the decline in the number of the young, and the increase in single motherhood) affect the financial underpinnings of social security and medical systems. The rise of new major players in the international arena, such as China, can and will result in new trade disequilibriums. But all these prospects and more are for the future.

The little-anticipated end of the cold war seemingly gave America and its ideology an almost total victory (Lipset and Bence 1994). The country is now the *only* superpower. As noted, its economy is the most productive. As Revel emphasizes, the recent major successful movements for egalitarian social change and for improving the quality of life—feminism, environmentalism, civil rights for minorities, and gay rights—diffused from America, much like the democratic revolutions of the nineteenth century. The developed world has been more successful than ever in satisfying the consumption desires of mass society, including manual workers and the intellectual strata.

All this should make for more conservative and smug societies. Yet the standards by which Western countries now judge themselves are derived from the French, American, and Marxist revolutionary creeds. These proclaim: "All men . . . [now 'people'] are created equal" and agree with the goal of "life, liberty, and the pursuit of happiness." But all polities, even the classically liberal ones, must fail to live up to the utopian objectives, libertarianism and egalitarianism. Americans still lean more to the libertarian side, Europeans to the egalitarian. Both tendencies favor freedom for all and strong juridical restraints on state power. Americans prefer a meritocratic, libertarian society with an effective but weak government. They will not attain these objectives in any absolute sense, but they will keep trying. It may be noted that socialists from Marx Engels to Gramsci, Crosland, and Harrington acknowledge that socially, though obviously not economically, the United States was closer to their ideological goal of socially classless and weak state society than any other system they knew in their lifetime. Leon Samson, a left-wing American Marxist, concluded in the early 1930s that American radicals were unable to sell socialism to a people who believed they already lived in a society that operationally, though not terminologically, was committed to egalitarian objectives, property relations apart. Americans and Europeans must deal with racism, sexism, severe income inequality, corruption, dirty environments, and downturns in the business cycle.

America still has an ideological vision, the American Creed, with which to motivate its young to challenge reality. And Europeans are increasingly committed to a similar social vision, derivative in large measure from the French Revolution and social democracy. Both accept the competitive market as the means to increase productivity, with a resultant decrease of differences in consumption styles linked to class. Both are enlarging the scope of higher education with a consequent growth of mobility into the elite. And emphases on status differences in Europe, derivative from feudal estates, are declining. Economic inequality, of course, is still great, even increasing during periods of technological innovation, such as the present, because new skills are in much greater demand than old ones. But since patterns of deference, of social class inferiority, are declining while communications mechanisms open to the many are increasing with the spread of the Internet, power becomes more dispersed.

Notes

1. For evidence of the applicability of the concept, see Lipset 1996: 32–35, 77–109.
2. For other efforts to deal with "socialist exceptionalism," see also Robert J. Fitrakis 1993 and Mike Davis 1988: 3–51.
3. For a review of the literature by Marxists and others, see Lipset 1977: 31–149 and 346–363 (notes).
4. For Lenin's writings see Harvey Klehr 1976.
5. The full discussion of Fraina/Corey is in Klehr 1971: 126–130.
6. For further discussion see also Inglehart 1997.
7. See also Lipset 1985: 195–205.
8. For a detailed description and analysis of the changes, see Giddens 1998.
9. For Australian and New Zealand references, see Lipset 1991: 184–185.
10. On the shift to the right under Mitterrand, see Lipset 1991: 188.
11. These discussions of the sources of French statism are largely derived from Swardon 1998b.
12. Jospin's comments on the nature of new jobs in the United States coincide with reports from various studies of the Bureau of Labor Statistics.
13. For a more detailed discussion and documentation, see Lipset 1990: 193–202.

References

Andrews, Edmund L. 1998. "Rivals Have Found Little to Fight over in the German Election," *New York Times*, September 26, A6.
Apple, R. W., Jr. 1998. "A German Socialist Plunges toward the Center," *New York Times*, September 4, A1 and A10.

Aristotle. 1941. *Rhetoric*. In Richard McKeon, ed., *The Basic Works of Aristotle*. New York: Random House.

Atkins, Ralph. 1998. "Schröder Pledges Strict Financial Control." *Financial Times*, November 11, 2.

Baldwin, Tom. 1997. "New Labour Manifesto Steals Old Tory Slogans." *Sunday Telegraph*, March 30, 1.

Beer, Max. 1935. *Fifty Years of International Socialism*. London: George Allen and Unwin.

Bell, Daniel. 1952. "Marxian Socialism in America." In Donald G. Egbert and Stow Persons, eds., *Socialism and American Life*. Princeton: Princeton University Press.

Bell, Daniel. 1978. *The Coming of Post-Industrial Society*. New York: Basic Books.

Bell, Daniel. 1996. *Marxian Socialism in the United States*. Ithaca: Cornell University Press.

Blair, Tony. 1994. "No Favours." *New Statesman and Society*, November 28, 33.

Blair, Tony. 1998. "Third Way, Better Way." *Washington Post*, September 27, C7.

Bureau of Labor Statistics. 1981 and 1998. Calculated from *Statistical Abstracts of the United States 1981*, U.S. Department of Commerce, 1981, p. 401, available from ftp:/ftp.bls.gov/pub/special.requests/ForeignLabor/flslforc.txt; and calculated from *Employment and Earnings*, Bureau of Labor Statistics, January 1998, available from ftp://ftp.bls.gov/pub/special.requests/lf/aat.10.txt and from http://stats.bls.gov/webapps/legacy/cpsatab4.htm.

Burt, Tim. 1999a. "Sweden Plans State Company Overhaul." *Financial Times*, January 29, 2.

Burt, Tim. 1999b. "Nordic Governments Set Out on Path to Privatization." *Financial Times*, January 29, 3.

Chirot, Daniel, ed. 1991. *The Crisis of Leninism and the Decline of the Left*. Seattle: University of Washington Press.

Cohen, Roger. 1997. "France's Old Soldier Fades Away." *New York Times*, June 8, E5.

Cohen, Roger. 1998. "In Inaugural Speech, Schröder Stresses Jobs and Environment." *New York Times*, November 11, A4.

Dahrendorf, Ralf. 1990. "Mostly about the Strange Death of Socialism and the Mirage of a Third Way." In his *Reflections on the Revolution in Europe*, 77. New York: Times Books.

Davis, Mike. 1988. *Prisoners of the American Dream: Politics and Economy in the History of the U.S. Working Class*. New York: Verso.

De Leon, Daniel. 1904. *Flashlights of the Amsterdam Congress*. New York: New York Labor News Co.

Debray, Regis. 1990. "What's Left of the Left?" *New Perspectives Quarterly* (spring): 27.

Drozdizk, William. 1988. "Schröder Calls for Europe-wide Initiative to Fight Joblessness." *Washington Post*, November 11, A22.

Druhan, Madaline, 1997. "Union Reforms Stay, Labour Leader Says." *Globe & Mail*, April 1.

Economist. 1989. "As Gonzalez Glides Rightward." March 11, Spain Survey.

Economist. 1998. "Jospin Discovers America." June 27–July 3: 50.

Engels, Friedrich. 1942. Letter to Sorge, November 29, 1886. In Karl Marx and Friedrich Engels, *Selected Correspondence, 1846–1895*, 449. New York: International Publishers.

Engels, Friedrich. 1953. Letter to Weydemeyer, August 7, 1851. In Karl Marx and Friedrich Engels, *Letters to Americans 1848–1895*, 25–26. New York: International Publishers.

Fitrakis, Robert J. 1993. *The Idea of Democratic Socialism in American and the Decline of the Socialist Party*. New York: Garland Publishers.

Flacks, Richard. 1988. *Making History: The Radical Tradition in American Life*. New York: Columbia University Press.

Friedman, Thomas L. 1997. "The Real G-7's," *New York Times*, June 19, A35.

Furet, François. 1988. "Democracy and Utopia." *Journal of Democracy* 9, no. 1: 79.

Gallagher, Tom, and Allan M. Williams. 1989. "Introduction." In Tom Gallagher and Allan M. Williams, eds, *Southern European Socialism*, 3. Manchester: Manchester University Press.

Giddens, Anthony. 1998. *The Third Way: The Renewal of Social Democracy*. Oxford: Polity Press.

Halpern, Rick, and Jonathan Morris, eds. 1997. *American Exceptionalism: U.S. Working Class Formation in International Context.* New York: St. Martin's Press.

Harrington, Michael. 1987. *The Next Left: The History of a Future.* New York: Holt.

Harris, John F., and Fred Barbash. 1997. "Blair Savours Colleague Clinton's Arm on His Shoulder." *Washington Post,* May 30, A27–28.

Hofstadter, Richard. 1972. *The Age of Reform: From Bryan to F.D.R.* New York: Alfred P. Knopf.

Ibrahim, Yousef M. 1997. "Blair Gains Tax Cut for Business, But the Rest of Britain Must Wait." *New York Times,* July 1, 1.

Inglehart, Ronald. 1971. "The Silent Revolution in Europe: Intergenerational Change in Post-Industrial Societies." *American Political Science Review* 65: 991–1017.

Inglehart, Ronald. 1977. *The Silent Revolution: Changing Values and Political Styles among Western Publics.* Princeton: Princeton University Press.

Inglehart, Ronald. 1990. *1990 World Values Survey.* Ann Arbor: Institute for Social Research.

Inglehart, Ronald. 1997. *Modernization and Postmodernization.* Princeton: Princeton University Press.

International Labor Organizations. 1997. "ILO Highlights Global Challenges to Trade Unions." *ILO News,* November 4.

Klehr, Harvey. 1971. "The Theory of American Exceptionalism." Ph.D. dissertation, Department of History, University of North Carolina, Chapel Hill.

Klehr, Harvey. 1976. "Leninist Theory in Search of America." *Polity* 9: 81–96.

Kolosi, Thomas. 1987. "Beliefs about Inequality in Cross-National Perspective." Paper prepared for conference on the Welfare State in Transition.

Lichfield, John. 1997. "French Left Goes in Search of a New Ideology: Like Blair's Labour the Socialists Have Moved Right." *Independent* (London), April 25.

Lipset, Seymour Martin. 1977. "Why No Socialism in the United States?" In Seweryn Bialer and Sophia Sluzar, eds., *Sources of Contemporary Radicalism,* 31–149. Boulder, Colo: Westview Press.

Lipset, Seymour Martin. 1985. *Consensus and Conflict: Essays in Political Sociology.* New Brunswick, N.J.: Transaction Books.

Lipset, Seymour Martin. 1990. *Continental Divide: The Values and Institutions of the United States and Canada.* New York: Routledge.

Lipset, Seymour Martin. 1991. "No Third Way: A Comparative Perspective on the Left." In Daniel Chirot, ed., *The Crisis of Leninism and the Decline of the Left,* 182–232. Seattle: University of Washington Press.

Lipset, Seymour Martin, 1996. *American Exceptionalism: A Double-Edged Sword.* New York: W. W. Norton.

Lipset, Seymour Martin, and Gyorgy Bence. 1994. "Anticipations of the Failure of Communism." *Theory and Society* 23 (April): 169–210.

Lipset, Seymour Martin, and Gary Marks. 2000. *It Didn't Happen Here: Why Socialism Failed in the United States.* New York: W. W. Norton.

Lubell, Samuel. 1965. *The Future of American Politics.* 3d ed. New York: Harper and Row.

Marx, Karl. 1958. *Capital.* Vol. 1. Moscow: Foreign Languages Publishing House.

Marx, Karl, and Friedrich Engels. 1938. "Unpublished Letters of Karl Marx and Friedrich Engels to Americans." *Science and Society* 2 (1938): 368.

Mitchell, Alison. 1997. "2 Baby Boomers Who Share a Single View of Democracy." *New York Times,* May 30, 1, 3.

Moore, R. Laurence. 1970. *European Socialists and the American Promised Land.* New York: Oxford University Press.

Page, Benjamin I., and Robert Y. Shapiro. 1992. *The Rational Public: Fifty Years of Trends in America's Policy Preference.* Chicago: University of Chicago Press.

Prescott, Michael. 1997. "Labour Assault on Single Mothers." *Sunday Times,* June 1.

Przeworski, Adam. 1985. *Capitalism and Social Democracy.* Cambridge: Cambridge University Press.

Quint, Howard W. 1953. *The Forging of American Socialism: Origins of the Modern Movement.* Indianapolis: Bobbs-Merrill Co.

Revel, Jean-François. 1971. *Without Marx or Jesus.* Garden City, N.Y.: Doubleday.

Richta, Radovon, et al. 1969. *Civilizations at the Crossroads.* White Plains, N.Y.: International Arts and Sciences Press.

Rose, Richard. 1985. *How Exceptional Is American Government?* Studies in Public Policy 150. Glasgow: Centre for the Study of Public Policy, University of Strathclyde.

Rummel, R. J. 1997. *Power Kills: Democracy as a Method of Nonviolence.* New Brunswick, N.J.: Transaction Books.

Scharping, Rudolf. 1996. "Freedom, Solidarity, Individual Responsibilty: Reflections on the Relationship between Politics, Money and Morality." *Responsive Community* 6: 53, 54–55.

Shapiro, Robert Y., and John T. Young. 1989. "Public Opinion and the Welfare State: The United States in Comparative Perspective." *Political Science Quarterly* 104 (spring): 59–89.

Simons, Marlene. 1997. "Dutch Take 'Third Way' to Prosperity." *New York Times,* June 16, A6.

Smith, Tom W. 1990. "Social Inequalities in Cross-National Perspective." In J. W. Becker et al., eds., *Attitudes to Inequality and the Role of Government.* Rijswijk: Social and Cultural Bureau.

Sombart, Werner. 1976. *Why Is There No Socialism in the United States?* White Plains, N.Y.: International Arts and Sciences Press. (First published in Germany in 1906).

Swardson, Anne. 1998a. "French Electorate Results Tend to Decrease Role of Government." *Washington Post,* January 22, A24.

Swardson, Anne. 1998b. "Jospin Takes a New Stand on Austerity." *Washington Post,* January 22, A24.

This Week in Germany. 1998a. "Schröder Outlines His Vision of the 'New Center' before the Bundestag." November 12, 1–2.

This Week in Germany. 1998b. "Lafontaine Finds Common Ground on Economic Policy during U.S. Visit." December 11, 4.

Tocqueville, Alexis de. 1948. *Democracy in America.* Vols. 1 and 2. New York: Alfred A. Knopf.

Touraine, Alain. 1971. *The Post-Industrial Society: Tomorrow's Social History.* New York: Random House.

Trotsky, Leon. 1939. *The Living Thoughts of Karl Marx.* New York: Longmans, Green and Co.

Vinocur, John. 1998. "Downsizing German Politics." *Foreign Affairs* (September/October): 11–12.

Voss, Kim. 1993. *The Making of American Exceptionalism: The Knights of Labor and Class Formation in the Nineteenth Century.* Ithaca: Cornell University Press.

Weber, Max. 1958. *The Protestant Ethic and the Spirit of Capitalism.* New York: Charles Scribner's Sons.

Wells, H. G. 1906. *The Future in America.* New York: Harper and Brothers.

Wigton, David. 1997. "Job Creation: Clinton and Blair in Joint Initiative." *Financial Times,* May 30.

Will, George. 1997. "Last Rite for Socialism." *Washington Post,* December 21, C7.

12

The Debate over "Are Social Classes Dying?"[*]

TERRY NICHOLS CLARK

In 1991 Seymour Martin Lipset and I published "Are Social Classes Dying?" (Clark and Lipset 1991). It sparked an exchange in the journal *International Sociology* (see Pakulsi 1993; Hout et al. 1993; Clark et al. 1993), which continued in sessions at the American Sociological Association, in Bielefeld at the International Sociological Association (e.g., Goldthorpe 1999), a conference at Oxford (organized by Goeff Evans), and several books (e.g., Nieuwbeerta 1995; Lee and Turner 1996; Evans 1999; and this volume). Some key issues deserve elaboration in this rapidly changing field.

Once upon a time, class was everything, or so it seemed. Class was and often is the master concept guiding many subfields of social science, from social mobility to voting. Arthur Stinchcombe even suggested that class was sociology's only concept.[1] As this debate emerged, I read and spoke to colleagues about different subfields of sociology. I asked them: How important is social class in your field today? And has it changed over the past 30 years? Subfields vary dramatically.

[*]Presented at the annual conference of the American Sociological Association, Chicago, August 1999. This is research report #361b. I am grateful for assistance in data preparation from Dennis Merritt and Jerzy Bartkowski. Some material in this chapter was first used in papers presented to the American Sociological Association in Washington, D.C., August 1995, the Social Science History Association, Chicago, November 1995, and the Woodrow Wilson International Center for Scholars, Washington, D.C., April 19–20, 1996.

Consider two extremes: social mobility and crime research. Class remains central for social mobility. A recent volume bears the title *Persistent Inequality* (Shavit and Blossfeld 1993). The book's title echoes in its conclusion: "In most industrialized countries inequalities in educational opportunity among students from different social strata have been remarkably stable since the early twentieth century." A second volume on social mobility reports similar conclusions (Erikson and Goldthorpe 1992). Contrast this with crime research. For several decades crime and deviance studies drew on class-inspired models, especially the Mertonian version. But in the last two decades, research has largely stressed age and other nonclass factors.[2]

In other subfields of sociology, one finds mixtures of many traditions. In much historical sociology, class-inspired analyses were superseded in the 1980s by culture- and language-inspired models and by post-modernist conceptualizations.[3]

How about social stratification? David Grusky's reader *Social Stratification* (1994) suggests in its introduction and many of its chapters that, despite cosmetic changes, stratification is just as powerful and persistent as ever, even if specific meanings and measures of class have shifted. Sociologists' work on political parties and voting seems strongly dominated by class, while political scientists seem less sensitive to class concerns.

To interpret such differences in class across subfields is a challenge. First, some conceptual differences reflect empirical differences; yet this demands codification. Why should there be such variation across different sectors of the same society in the same time period? Second, some differences flow from researchers' broader theoretical and normative commitments. The legendary position of Marx probably helps sociologists see class in many social phenomena. A third variable is the degree of impact of nonsociological participants in the field. Perhaps participants like judges and criminologists make criminology research less dominated by sociologists, for instance, and less concerned with class.

How can we clarify such diversity? A first step is to look at what class means in different subfields. Competing views can be partly reconciled just by clarifying a range of definitions:

1. First there is Marx's classical definition.
2. A broader definition stretches Marx away from just the means of production. Dahrendorf stretched the concept of class to include "conflict groups generated by the differential distribution of authority in impera-

tively coordinated associations" (Dahrendorf 1959: 204). Anthony Griddens (1980: 108–112) identified a variety of workplace differences but retained the term *class,* as did Erik Wright (1985: 64–104), who even specified a 12-category "typology of class location in capitalist society," which combined ownership, skill level, and managerial responsibility.

3. A third, still broader, definition of class/stratification is any group treated differently, which in some sense violates the norm of equality. Women and ethnic minorities became salient in the 1960s and 1970s. In the 1990s, concerns expanded beyond national income distributions to include cross-national violations of equality. And among the ecologically inspired, equality applies to wildlife as well as to humans; hence animals, trees, and other endangered species become exploited classes of concern.

It is consistent with much past work to consider that class politics includes five core elements:

1. Political cleavages derive from occupational cleavages, especially between white- and blue-collar workers; blue-collar workers and the economically disadvantaged oppose parties they identify as supporting persons higher in occupation and income.

2. Labor unions and socialist political parties express the society's class cleavages and appeal to blue-collar workers. Membership in such groups similarly follows occupational cleavages.

3. Political issues tend to be oriented toward work and production (salaries, working conditions, health insurance, etc.).

4 Social issues (e.g., abortion, ecology, women's roles) are less salient than economic issues or are addressed by linking them to economic issues (e.g., by stressing economic implications of social issues and using terms like *exploitation).*

5. Parties and voters can be classified from left to right.[4]

Interpreting these conceptual differences involves strategic choices of *operational measures;* these can have huge implications for results. Consider a central example in the recent exchanges. The methodology from Robert Mare and others for social mobility applies logistic regression to specific social transitions. The conclusion of the book *Persistent Inequality* flows from its logistic method and corresponding attention to select portions of the overall stratification process. That is, in analyzing effects of parents on children's educational attainment, one might consider five points.

Two imply particularism and persistent inequality:

1. the effect of parents' education and occupation on the child's entry into the first level of education, i.e., grade school
2. continuing effects of parents' background on subsequent transitions by the child

These first two are analyzed in great detail in *Persistent Inequality.* But three other processes suggest universalism:

3. expansion of the overall educational system
4. effects on nonparental factors on the student's movement from one level to the next
5. the average number of years of schooling completed by the entire population

I could not find a systematic treatment of these last three (but see De Graff and Ganzeboom 1993, and appendix 1 below), although some interactions among effects are carefully analyzed, such as in Treiman and Yamaguchi (1993). This was surprising, since the contributors to the *Persistent Inequality* volume are talented people, and the contributions convey very little sense of normative ideology; most read like quite dry and serious science. (Contributors include Michael Hout, Adrian Raftery, Harry Ganzeboom, Don Treiman, Kazuo Yamaguchi, Robert Mare, and more.)

Still, to assess the relative importance of class persistence versus universalism, it would help to report something like how much variance is explained by both the particularistic and the universalistic subprocesses; but the setup in this tradition either ignores or does not directly measure enough key processes to permit an overall assessment. These methodological blinders similarly constrain recent work on class politics. Methods similar to those in social mobility were imported and applied to class politics by Anthony Heath et al. (1985), Mike Hout et al. (1995), and John Goldthorpe (1999). They and others adapt the logistic methods, using some seven occupational categories as independent variables and the party vote as the dependent variable. Most studies are of one or two countries over the last 20 years or so, using sample surveys of individual citizens. They generally report conclusions similar to those of the social mobility studies, which they label trendless fluctuation. That is, they suggest class has not declined in its impact on party voting, especially in Britain and the United States.

Proponents of the logistic methodology suggest that it improves on past work, like the Alford Index, by being unaffected by marginal distributions, such as the size of each social class or votes for each party. The log-odds-ratio indicates instead a slopelike relationship between each occupational category and vote for each party. Analysts such as Hout, Brooks, and Manza (1995) use the bic statistic as a measure of the explanatory power of all the independent variables, a sort of R^2 for their whole model, and find it relatively constant over time. This is a key indicator for their conclusions of constant class impact.

What does this method assume, implicitly or explicitly, to generate the reported trendless fluctuation? Consider just three assumptions: (1) No change in party ideology occurs over time. Implicitly, Democrats in 1964 are the same as Democrats in 1990. (2) Changes in magnitude or even direction of voting by members of an *individual* occupational category are insignificant, since most attention is on the impact of *all* occupations combined. This glosses over major changes in key occupations like the professions. (3) Other potentially important causal variables are often omitted, like income, education, race, religion, age and gender. Later work sometimes improves this.

These three assumptions indicate major potential spuriousness. Because so much current work proceeds with little explicit attention to these assumptions, I offer some evidence of how each may be operating in critical ways to bias the reported trendless fluctuation. (Methodological issues raised by logistic models are pursed in appendix 2.)

In an early draft of this chapter (Clark 1995), I suggested the need for and outlined a simple framework of key variables that many researchers might analyze in a properly specified model. It includes occupation as an indicator of class along with other key variables that often affect party politics and voting. Most researchers in this exchange recognize the potential importance of such variables as occupation, education, age, race, and so on, but few of the recent log-linear studies consistently use them in their work. This is a classic source of statistical bias, exaggerating effects of occupation.

These three assumptions sometimes flow from a too simplistic conceptualization, such as the question Is class significant over time? rather than testing alternative models, such as How important is class politics versus post-industrial politics? Post-industrial politics is the main candidate that Inglehart, Lipset, I, and others have specified as an alternative to class politics. Many empirical political systems have elements of both. We need to identify, measure, and compare specific components of political systems to assess the importance of class and other cleavages. How?

If class still operates in some manner in affecting politics, one must be cautious about concluding that this is evidence for a class-dominated society. We find feudal residues in post-industrial societies today, especially racial cleavages from slavery, which remain often the deepest cleavages in America. Should we conclude that this makes America a feudal society?

In contrast with class politics, here are some key elements of a version of post-industrial politics that I have termed the New Political Culture (or NPC):

1. Social and fiscal /economic issues are explicitly distinguished.
2. Social issues and consumption issues have risen in salience relative to fiscal/economic and production issues.
3. Issue politics and broader citizen participation have risen; hierarchical political organizations have declined.
4. These NPC views are more pervasive among younger, more educated, and more affluent individuals and societies.

Class politics issues classically concern salaries, workplace conditions, and other occupation-related matters. The NPC does not suggest that occupation is unimportant but that new social and other nonwork issues, often concerning consumption and lifestyle, are added to the political agenda.

In other publications I and others develop a body of propositions specifying conditions that heighten or suppress class politics versus the NPC. For instance, the higher the income, the less strong the class politics (Clark and Lipset 1991; Clark 1994; Clark and Hoffmann-Martinot 1998; Clark and Rempel 1997). But for now, consider how we may test such competing interpretations.

A Framework for Class Politics Analysis

Disparate results derive in part from incompletely specified models. To help identify critical variables that bias results when omitted, a framework of key causal relations is helpful. Even if each researcher does not incorporate all variables in each study, one can still (1) remain sensitive in making interpretations, at least to bias introduced by omitting variables from a simple two-variable model like "class affects vote," or (2) in some cases, introduce estimated coefficients from other studies to build a more comprehensive model.

One way of listing elements for a framework is to write two simple equations:

$$V = f(P, O, D, A)$$

$$LP = f(V, P)$$

where:

V = voting by citizens for political leaders (and occasional referenda)
LP = leaders' (esp. elected officials) policy preferences
P = party programs and political candidates' backgrounds and views
O = occupation and workforce participation, social class, and more
D = demographic characteristics of voters, including income, education, etc.
A = attitudes of citizens on politically significant issues

Each variable deserves some attention. Below I comment on them briefly and review why and how each can contribute to analyzing the impact of class.

Parties, Programs, and Voting

Parties and their programs have changed successively in such periods as social welfare reconstruction after 1945, radical social movements after 1968, and with new conservative leaders like Ronald Reagan and Margaret Thatcher in the 1980s. Such changes in party agenda transform the whole meaning of "class" and "voting." Consider a manual worker voting for the Communist Party in 1960 and 1990. The party stressed a proletarian revolution in 1960 but recycling garbage in 1990 (e.g., the Italian Communist Party). What does it mean to report that workers vote Communist in both years? As elaborated below, the mere party name is low in meaning content. The researcher who assumes that Party X is *constant* in meaning over time should make this explicit and support it empirically. Or if both class and party change, as for instance Heath et al. (1991) detail for Britain, how do such changes affect the meaning of the class-party linkage? This is one major analytical hole, but one that many of the creative researchers participating in these exchanges can readily fill and indeed have reported the data and tools to do so in overlapping studies.

The meaning of "class voting" shifts substantially if one considers the transformations that parties have undergone in the last two decades. Two dramatic, worldwide shifts are: (1) Socialist and Communist parties have tended to abandon central state planning and move toward more market-oriented solutions. (Lipset 1991 shows this in a country-by-country review for dozens of countries.) (2) Many parties have embraced "new social issues," such as those of women, ethnic minorities, the handicapped, gays, and ecological issues. In some cases, like the 1972 U.S. presidential election, these programmatic shifts powerfully alienate some voters while attracting others.

How can we model or interpret such changes? The options are:

1. Add ideological items to the model, ideally to match policy preferences of citizens and candidates, in the manner of a "loss function" in the public choice tradition from Anthony Downs (1957) and others. Heath et al. (1991) are close to this in some of their chapters, as are Weakliem and Heath (1994). For historical and cross-national work, Klingemann, Hofferbert, and Budge (1994) provide systematic data on changes in party programs, based on content analyses of every significant party for each year from about 1945 to the present in 28 countries. This could be inserted into historical studies of class voting.

2. Interpret key shifts, using data such as those in Klingemann et al. 1994 as well as other richer sources on specifics. Confronting a huge blip in an econometric time series, many economists do not feel unprofessional in seeking to interpret it. Why can't we interpret major shifts in party programs and elections rather than just labeling them trendless? Related literatures that do interpret series include work on election cycles, such as spending more just before and raising taxes just after an election (Kramer, 1971), and hiring more staff to do campaign work just before an election, then letting them go afterward (Fuchs 1992). Indeed, Fuchs (1992) comments (briefly) on each mayoral election in New York and Chicago for over half a century to interpret her time series. Cycles of reform- and machine-based political leadership alternate, as citizens seek to "throw the bums out," targeting those who have not only been in office too long but have grown "arrogant" as well. Margaret Thatcher in her last years is a classic case. Data on such matters are available in many surveys.

Consider just one U.S. example that led the Alford Index to plunge to zero, the lowest score for any of five countries from 1945 to the near-present (see the Alford Index in Clark and Lipset 1991). This "blip" recurs in Hout et al.'s (1995) series but is largely ignored by them. What happened? The classic union/Democratic Party leaders, led by Mayor Richard Daley in Chicago in 1968, had excluded new social movement activists and then used the police to beat them up at the Democratic presidential convention. This energized anti-Vietnam demonstrators, feminists, and ecologists. They mobilized behind George McGovern, who embraced the new social issues, and four years later he won the Democratic Party presidential nomination. The party then took strong positions on new social issues in its official program. This in turn alienated many union leaders and traditional Democrats, like Richard Daley. For the first time in their lives, millions of blue-collar workers voted Republican in 1972—for Richard Nixon, who won by a landslide. While this result blips in the Hout et al. series, this "baby" is thrown out with the bath water, because certain subsequent Democratic candidates for president embraced new social movement issues less strongly, and in some elections blue-collar voters returned to the Democratic Party. Is this trendless fluctuation? Not at all. Just underinterpreted findings with too few data on key substantive variables.

Is the magnitude of the 1972 U.S. election unique? By no means. Many other parties saw dramatic shifts in the last decade or two, as analyzed in recent research: among them were the Socialist parties reviewed by Lipset (1991). The British Labor Party moved in a radical direction in the early 1960s which appears as the high left blip in the Klingemann, Hofferbert, and Budge (1994) study. Communist parties around the word transformed themselves.

Interpreting such changes in ideology is harder for cross-national work over many years, but for single-country studies of a decade or two, especially in highly researched countries like the United States and the United Kingdom, it is reasonable to expect researchers to rise slightly above their unique data set and interpret major shifts.[5]

But a theory that suggests overall directions of such changes and how and why they interact with the class-party linkage is critical. One candidate for this theory is the propositions in Clark et al. (1993). These identify explicitly how some key variables affect citizen voting and how they may change, such as through leaders' and citizens' shifts in ideology.

Class and Occupational Classifications

What is class? The Alford Index, following a tradition from Marx and others, used the categories blue and white collar to define class. Research on the workplace, social mobility and other topics led to refining occupational classifications, such as Goldthorpe's (1999) seven-category measure (professionals not separate). Hout, Brooks, and Manza (1995) use six occupational categories (with professionals separate) and multinomial logistic regression (MLR). But both Goldthorpe and Hout et al. analyze relations between occupation and party voting, omitting from their empirical work other critical variables identified in our framework. They report trendless fluctuations from the 1950s to the 1980s for Britain and the United States in the sense that occupation explains "total voting" with roughly the same explanatory power over these decades. Their refinements by using six or seven separate occupational categories and logistic regression capture impacts of a wider diversity of occupational statuses on voting than blue versus white collar does. These approaches also control for the size of each occupational category.

But what does this mean substantively? This empirical work lacks an analytical framework to suggest "critical experiments." Hout et al. (1995) report specifics for each occupational category. These are fun for readers to reinterpret, as I have. Yet they do not explore some of their most critical results: Professionals voted Republican in the 1950s but Democratic in the 1980s. Skilled blue-collar workers, conversely, shifted from Democratic to Republican, although fluctuated by election. Why gloss over the substantive meaning of these findings? Do they lack data on two key intervening variables: party and candidate ideologies? These are critical since the Democratic Party changed. While individual candidates vary, Democratic programs have generally shifted away from traditional class issues of wages and workplace conditions to embrace a range of social issues. The Democratic Party itself has added active caucuses for women, blacks, ecology and so on. (So have many other left parties around the world, including the Italian Communists.) These shifts in ideology help explain the rise in left voting by professionals and the loss of blue-collar voters. This is part of the "two Lefts" argument, referring to (1) labor and (2) new social-issue voters. But even if one finds that the overall association (e.g., Hout et al.'s "total voting") is constant over time, the meaning of Democratic voting has changed. A left vote in many countries now often represents a shift away from workplace issues to consumption and lifestyle issues. This shift is not "trendless"; rather it illustrates the "realignment" pattern stressed by Clark and Lipset (1991) and others in identifying some major factors weakening traditional class politics.

Goldthorpe (1999) and others using his occupational classifications (e.g., Nieuwbeerta and De Graaf 1999; Ringdal and Hines 1999) that do not separate out professionals may not observe such dramatic shifts as Hout et al. Might analysis by separate occupation reveal changes similar to those of Hout et al.? Maybe elsewhere but not in Britain, per Heath and Savage (n.d.), who considered 113 occupations. They show professionals are rather consistently Conservative. Second, Weakliem and Heath (1999) contrast the United States and Britain and explicitly reach conclusions close to ours. They have nicely calculated a two-dimensional factor analysis of occupations, the second of which loads heavily on professionals. They write: "The rise of a new dimension representing middle-class, especially professional, support for the left is much more apparent in the United States. In Britain the evidence for this development is inconclusive" (26).

Nevertheless, our general point holds: neither Goldthorpe (1999), nor Hout et al. (1995), nor many other studies included ideological measures to help capture why British and American professionals might differ in their politics. In many countries , our theory suggests, professionals are moving toward the New Political Culture, but parties are only weakly crystallizing along these lines. Still, these differ considerably by country, time, and, in noncentralized party systems (clearly Switzerland and the United States) by region and locality.

Other Variables? Gender? Race? Region?

Such matters are considered in some recent publications on class politics. Evans (1993a) explored women's issues, mainly attitudes concerning women in the workplace (equal pay for equal work, etc.). These correlated highly with more traditional left-right patterns for Britain and four other countries using ISSP (International Social Survey Program) citizen data. But his results were surely affected by selecting the workplace issues rather than abortion or family lifestyle, for example, which are probably less closely linked to workplace and class views. Studying these issues can reveal both class politics and the New Political Culture, if one looks. For instance, in some countries (e.g., France), where we expect strong class politics, we found it: support for abortion there is strongly structured by party. But in other contexts (e.g., the United States), abortion support is unrelated to party; it is driven by gender and education (Clark and Inglehart 1988). Heath et al. (1991) nicely contrast issues such as economic and social and find that class and economic variables drive the economic attitudes, while education, religion, age, and gender tend to drive the social attitudes. They explore a number of interesting changes in issue support, which they often link to distinct subgroups. For instance, they do not just discuss *the issue* of the environment; they pose nine items that fall into five separate subissues, with their distinct supporters (Heath et al. 1991: 186ff.). Younger, working-class women favor nuclear disarmament, but older, more educated non-conformists support countryside beautification. Issue politics has risen in import and parents' party has declined in explaining party identification in the past 30 years for British citizens. Many findings show persistent class politics, but others provide clear support for NPC tendencies in Britain over the past 30 years, like the differentiated subtlety of environmental politics.

Income

Money is important. Is money class? Not as measured, for instance, by Hout et al. (1995) and Goldthorpe (1999); nor is it considered by them even as a control. We do not argue that income is class but rather a critical related element, so much so that many casual as well as sophisticated accounts of how "class" works stress money, even when denying its role—like the classic exchange written by Ernest Hemingway: "The rich are different" . . . "Yes, they have more money" (from *The Snows of Kilimanjaro*). Can we afford to omit money altogether? How highly associated with occupation is it? Some white-collar professionals are poor, and blue-collar workers rich, which may affect their voting on issues like health insurance and weaken the occupation-party voting relation. Money facilitates interaction. It should drive toward the NPC.

More generally, what might one expect in two societies (or cities) with identical occupational structures and parties, but in one of which income inequality is steep and in the other all occupations are *identical* in income? Are such patterns of income inequality worth study? Income is key in several Clark-Lipset-Rempel propositions. Increases in income inequality are politically divisive. Alternatively, if income grows for all, such prosperity should lower social dependence on family and state and weaken support for central government programs and planning. Income can thus serve as both an individual and a system characteristic that should shift from class politics to the NPC.

One graphic illuminating income-occupation relations shows both means and variance of income for separate occupational categories (figure 1). We should consider more such measures in political analyses. This is an area where the master of Nuffield is a world expert (Atkinson 1975). Computing four Atkinson inequality indexes for U.S. cities for income, education, occupation, and national origin, I found them so important that they even suppressed the effects of race.

Is "income" (1) cash in the bank (what accountants call a stock), or (2) a cash stream for one year (an accountant's flow), or (3) an expected flow for many years into the future (presumably more important for college students, whose cash in the bank and annual flows are even lower than those for social welfare recipients in some countries)? Evans (1993b) comes close to addressing these points. He finds, as hypothesized, that younger persons shift coefficients of multicausal models toward voting more conservatively. But he does not model actual attitudes toward time.

Pushing this one step further for our research agenda, one might analyze the time perspective of different subgroups rather than assuming it is uniform for the entire population or cross-nationally, following the old adage: The rich plan for generations; the poor plan for Saturday night. Or as Milton Friedman's "permanent income hypothesis" put it, only very long-term income provides a sense of security and shifts specific consumption patterns. He even suggested that several generations of higher income might be necessary before blacks in the United States would abandon low-income-driven consumption patterns and more closely approximate those of whites.

What is the actual empirically based time frame for political assessments by citizens that affect their vote? Many politicians feel it is last week. Surely it varies for subgroups of voters and probably interacts with occupational categories; the topic deserves modeling. Still if "parent's party" has some effect (Heath et al. 1991), that effect is longer than "last week." Empirical details on time budgets by Szalai (1973) or more complex modeling of time allocations by Fox (1974) illustrate approaches to consider for political analyses.

Figure 12.1
Income differences vary substantially within as well as across occupational categories.

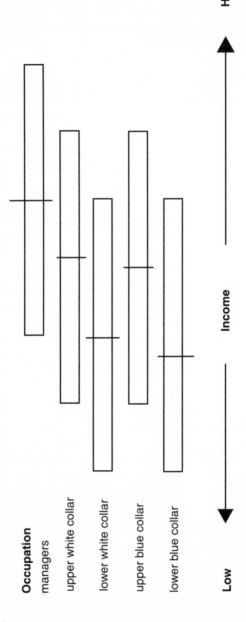

Occupation

managers

upper white collar

lower white collar

upper blue collar

lower blue collar

Low   Income   High

Note: This figure uses a simple method to show how much income varies by occupation. For each occupation three data points appear as a bar. In the center of each bar is the mean or average income (a vertical line) for all persons working in that occupational category. If we compare just the means, we see the normal story: persons in "higher" occupations earn more. But the story changes if we look at the other two data points, the right and left ends of each bar, calculated as the first and third quartiles of income of all persons in that occupational category. Here, occupation looks far less deterministic of income. For instance, a manager at the 25th percentile of income for all managers (at the left end of the top bar) earns less than many persons in "lower" occupational categories. If people's politics are influenced by both their occupation and their income, it is important to include both in modeling voting

Source: Adapted freely from data and methods reported for France and other countries by Henri Mendras and colleagues in their reports, such as Chauvel 1995.

Testing Class and NPC Models

The three assumptions used by many class theorists (discussed at the beginning of this chapter) suggest quite different patterns from the NPC propositions. What evidence can we consider to test the reasonableness of each? In this chapter I address these more general issues through two simple questions that have emerged as central in the class politics exchange: (1) Are parties changing; do they show more attention to social issues and less to fiscal issues? (2) How distinct are fiscal and social issues from one another, and are their associations changing?

Class politics and the NPC posit distinct differences on these two points. Parties have been referred to by some class theorists as black boxes. We must open them, especially because some have changed so substantially. If party agendas shift toward NPC issues, even a constant logistic coefficient over time for the effect of occupation on party does not indicate "trendless fluctuation."

The critical linkage role of parties in this exchange led me to acquire data on party programs from the Party Manifestos Project (of Ian Budge, Richard Hofferbert, and Hans-Peter Klingemann; see appendix 2). The Manifestos Project coded the platforms of 250 parties in 28 countries for most national elections from 1945 to 1988. Each idea or "quasi sentence" was assigned to a theme. The percentage of total space devoted to each theme was then calculated. These data permit us to monitor the shifting salience of themes across a rich set of countries and parties. For each party I tabulated five themes that differentiate class politics from the New Political Culture. The hypothesized changes are in table 12.1. For instance, the first line shows that we hypothesize that environmental protection issues will be stressed more by parties that lean more toward the New Political Culture than toward class politics.

Table 12.1's hypotheses were tested, first, using all 250 parties and, second, country by country. Two time periods were used—1945–1972 and 1972–1988—since I expected NPC themes to rise after the early 1970s because of the many new social movements that emerged then. The first period was compared with the second to see if themes had changed, pooling results from all parties in all countries. This simple method for testing the hypotheses is consistent with the form of the data. Results: four of the five hypotheses were supported for the 250 parties. That is, the 250 parties showed increased attention over time to the two NPC themes (environmental protection and government and administrative efficiency) and less attention to two of the three class politics themes. The exception was

Table 12.1

Hypotheses Concerning Five Themes

| Theme | Hypotheses: Relative Emphasis on Each Theme by | |
	Class Politics	New Political Culture
Environmental protection	less	more
Government and administrative efficiency	less	more
Traditional morality: positive	more	less
Labor groups: positive	more	less
Welfare state expansion	more	les

traditional morality, which did not decline. Second, I similarly calculated t-tests for all parties in each country separately, and report results for five major countries in table 12.2. These country-specific results for the five individual countries are weaker than those of all 28 countries combined. This is partly a function of the low number of cases, such that while one country may appear "trendless," combining cases can generate a trend. One can observe the detailed patterns in Figures 12.2 through 12.7; which show results for the largest left and right parties in major countries. The U.S. parties changed least of all five countries toward NPC themes—only by mentioning labor less (table 12.2) The United States also differed from three of the four other countries on traditional morality; it rose for the United States in total (table 12.2); it was stressed more often by Republicans in the Reagan and Bush years (but not by the Democratic party) (figure 12.2). Nevertheless traditional morality did decline in Germany, France, and Italy (see table 12.2), suggesting movement toward the NPC by parties in these countries. However on labor, the four European countries did not show the decreased emphasis found in the combined 28 countries. More detail on the Manifesto data and analyses are in appendix 3.

This simple evidence provides such compelling support for key points about the rise of the NPC that it seems best to report in this direct manner. One might probe (as Geoff Evans did), asking if such party thematic differences matter to citizens in terms of their own preferences or in their perceptions of where parties stand. There is considerable evidence in such works as the two Heath et al. volumes (1985, 1991) documenting the salience of several of these very themes among citizens, as well as the impact of such themes in explaining citizens' differential attachments to parties.

Table 12.2

Results from Content Analysis of Party Programs

	Average Space on Theme	Results for 250 Parties in 28 Countries Significance of change	Results for Five Individual Countries Significance of Change				
			United States	Germany	France	Italy	Great Britain
Environmental protection							
After 1973	3.69						
Before 1973	0.92	0.00	0.96	0.01	0.00	0.04	0.05
Gov. admin efficiency							
After 1973	2.70						
Before 1973	1.90	0.00	0.69	0.07[a]	0.68	0.08	0.15
Traditional morality							
After 1973	2.54						
Before 1973	2.31	0.59	0.15[b]	0.10	0.13	0.07	0.99
Labor +							
After 1973	2.16						
Before 1973	2.76	0.01	0.00	0.82	0.49	0.42	0.57
Welfare+							
After 1973	5.64						
Before 1973	6.40	0.02	0.72	0.09	0.08	0.44	0.33

Note: The mean percentage of space devoted to each theme was compared in the two periods, and a t-test was computed to indicate significance of the change. Results for all 250 parties in 28 countries showed significant shifts toward the NPC on four of the five themes. Details: The first row shows that 3.69 was the average percentage of total space devoted to environmental protection themes by 250 parties after 1973. The second row shows that before 1973 just under 1 percent was devoted to environmental protection. This change from 0.92 to 3.69 after 1973 was significant at the .00 level. The probability that the change for traditional morality was significant was just .59, which is insignificant. The individual country scores are for the significance of the change. Example: The first row shows that there was not a significant change in space on environmental protection in the United States (since .96 is way below the .10 level of significance), but the change was significant in the four other countries. The direction of all changes matched the hypotheses in table 12.1, except for government and administrative efficiency in Germany, which parties mentioned less after 1973, and traditional morality in the United States, although this last change was only at the .15 significance level.
[a] down
[b] weakly up

A second finding comes from our Fiscal Austerity and Urban Innovation Project, underway since 1982 in some 35 countries. We arrayed the parties on a general left-right scale from 1 to 100 using survey data (see appendix 1). How important are fiscal compared with social issues in driving this left-right party location? Many class politics analysts posit one dimension, largely fiscal. The New Political Culture stresses issue differentiation. We can test these competing hypotheses by regressing the left-right party

Figure 12.2
Changes of themes in U.S. Democratic Party programs

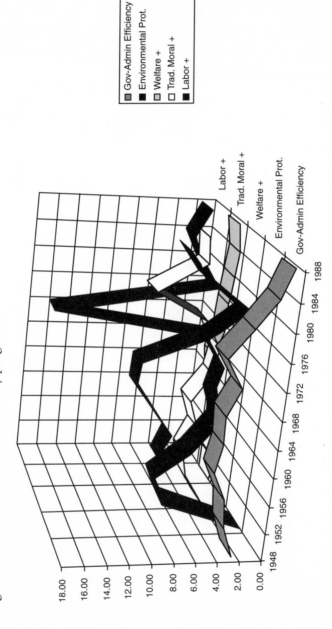

Note: The vertical axis shows the percentage of total space devoted to each of the five themes in the chart. The categories are explained in appendix 2. Items like welfare were coded as positive and negative; only positive is shown. This applies to figures 12.3 through 12.7 as well.

Figure 12.3
Changes of themes in U.S. Republican Party programs

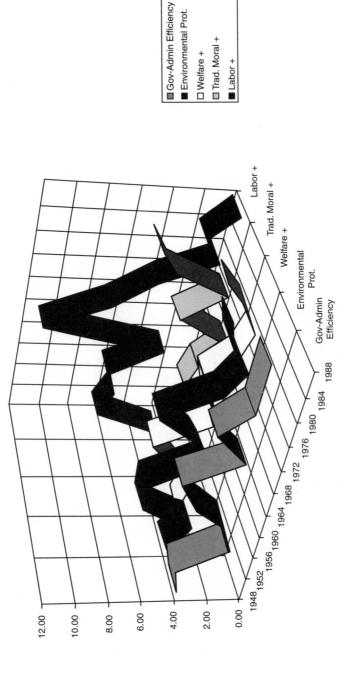

Figure 12.4
Changes of themes in German Social Democratic Party programs

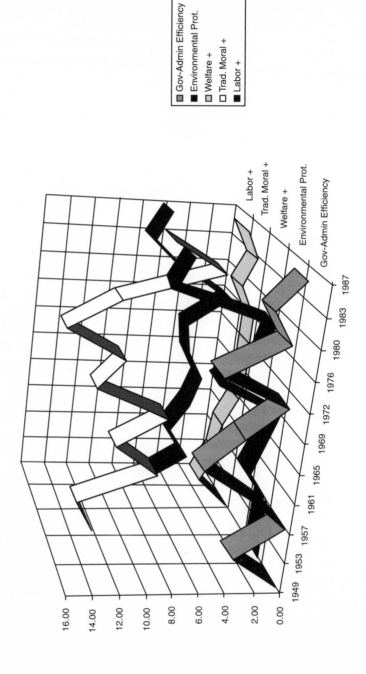

Figure 12.5
Changes of themes in French Socialist Party programs

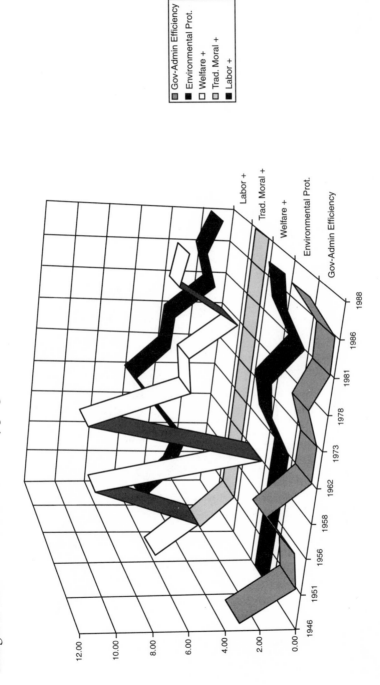

Figure 12.6
Changes of themes in British Labour Party programs

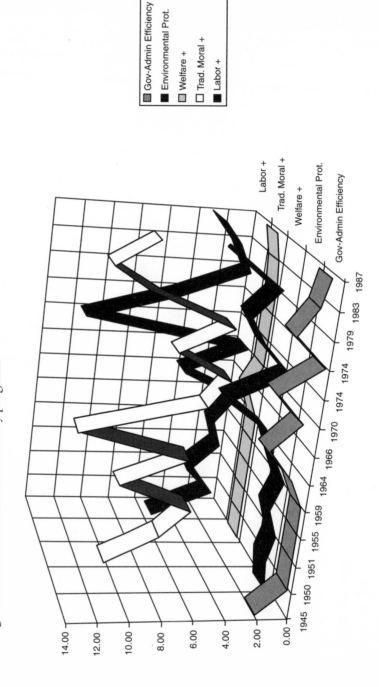

Figure 12.7
Changes of themes in Italian Christian Democratic Party programs

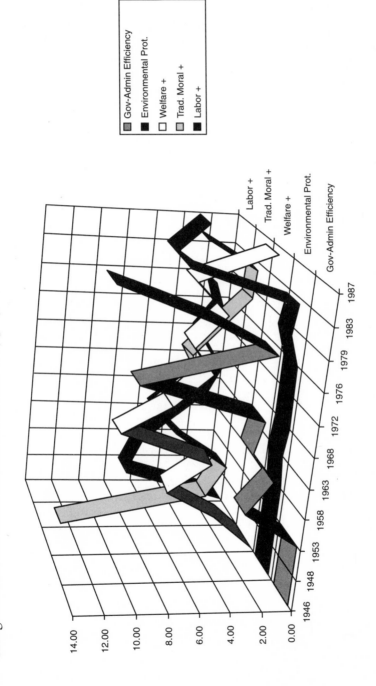

score on two ideology scales for each mayor: fiscal liberalism (preferring more or less spending) and social liberalism (supporting abortion and sex education). (See appendix 1 for definitions.) Results are illuminating. The regression weights for the fiscal and social indexes are almost equal in the pooled sample of 700 mayors from all countries. Repeating the analysis country by country, we find that in several countries social issues drive the relationship more than fiscal issues, but in most countries both variables are important. That is, one does not find that social issues are insignificant or spurious, as a strong class politics approach might suggest. Rather than economic or fiscal issues dominating party differences, we find that both

Table 12.3

Party Ideology Tightness by Country: Fiscal vs. Social Components

	Party Tightness[a] (Adjusted R^2)	Impact of Fiscal Policy On Party: All Areas	Impact of Social Conservatism on Party: All Areas	Number of Cases
All Countries	.09	-0.28^{***}	0.05	905
United States	.01	-0.12^{**}	0.01 ns	272
Canada	−.03	−0.16(n.s.)	−0.27 ns	19
France	.18	-0.42^{***}	−0.16 ns	80
Finland	.01	−0.12(n.s.)		175
Japan	.01	-0.19^{*}	0.05 ns	89
Norway	.07	-0.27^{***}		368
Australia	.33	$-.49^{**}$	0.28*	33
Belgium	−.01	−.19(n.s.)		24
Argentina	−.04	−.01(n.s.)		24
Czech Republic	.00	0.02(n.s.)	−0.12 ns	115
Hungary	−.01		0.03 ns	75
Slovakia	.04	.06(n.s.)	0.28**	51
Germany	.07	$-.27^{***}$		137
Italy	.80[b]	−0.03(n.s.)	0.89***	50
Britain	.31	$-.55^{***}$	0.05 ns	200
Poland, 1981	.00	−0.08(n.s.)		102
Israel	−.01	.11(n.s.)		49

[a] We measure party tightness by the adjusted R^2 of the regression of the left-right party measure of the mayor (IPARTY as dependent variable) on fiscal policy preferences (PRFAVG) and social conservatism (SOCCONS6).

[b] The impact measure is a beta statistic from the regression, computed by country. Italy has by far the tightest party system. Its tightness comes mainly from social, not fiscal, policy issues.

n.s. = not significant; *sig. < .10; **sig. <.05; ***sig < .01

social and fiscal issues are independently important in their association with political parties. However, in some countries like Italy and Britain, parties are highly crystallized along these ideological issues and show high R^2s, while in the United States parties are far weaker, issues are often specific to each mayor rather than defined by his or her party, and R^2s are low (table 12.3.) This documents at least point 1 (at the beginning of this section) concerning the New Political Culture: social and fiscal issues are separate.

With more time I would pursue several points but for now just flag some results concerning the second and third methodological assumptions of trendless fluctuation. The second assumption is that individual occupations do not change. Here I mention work by Steven Brint (1994) and Jeff Manza and Clem Brooks (1997). They find that professionals in the United States were often traditional conservatives in the 1940s but shifted dramatically by the 1980s, voting more often Democratic. In a careful analysis of why they shifted, Brooks and Manza test four theories—about the New Class, cumulative trends, the service class, and social issues. Conclusion: social issues drove changes most powerfully. This joins my results about the importance of social issues with specific occupational dynamics.

On the third point—what variables drive policies?—one main result is that context matters. Findings differ substantially across political systems. Class politics is still strong in some cities and countries. In France and Finland, having a large blue-collar population is the strongest predictor of having a left mayor. (See figure 12.8.) Similarly, inside the United States, class and race are dominant cleavages in cities with high proportions of nonwhite residents. By contrast, cities with high proportions of professional and technical workers, college educated, and few nonwhites have more post-industrial politics and New Political Culture, as measured by greater salience of social issues as reported by their mayors and council members, Sierra Club membership, antigrowth movements, recycling, and similar results (e.g., Clark 1994).

Interpreting Historical Changes and System Effects: Cross-National and Other Approaches

As Durkheim reminded us, science begins with comparison. Who cares if the occupation-voting relation is constant or changes in one country over a few decades? Journalists and politicians, of course. But for most social scientists to "care," such results must be located in a theory interpreting them; for analytical meaning, a pattern must be demonstrated that tran-

Figure 12.8
Why do mayors support higher spending? International Contrasts

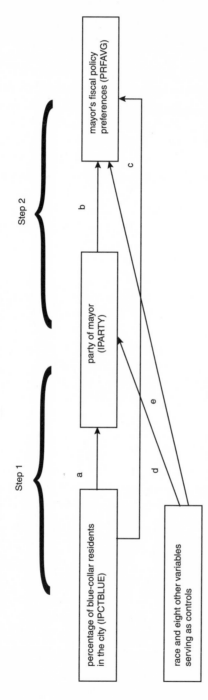

Note: Class politics is measured by the strength of paths a, b, and c above, using data for mayors and their cities in seven countries. Three patterns emerge:

 1. Strong class politics in France and Finland.
Blue-collar residents elect left-party mayors (strong path a), and left-party mayors prefer more spending (strong path b).
Blue-collar mainly operates via paths a and b but may have some direct effect on spending preference (path c).
 2. Weak class but some party politics in Norway, Canada, Japan, and Australia.
Insignificant a's and c's, mixed b's.

3. Race acts like class in the United States.

Insignificant a, b, and c but strong d and e paths from percentage of nonwhite residents to party and policy preferences.

This figure summarizes multiple regressions to explain support by mayors for increased spending on an index of up to 13 municipal spending areas, PRFAVG. The same basic model was used in each country:

Dependent variable: PRFAVG—average spending preference of mayor on 13 FAUI items

Independent variables:

LIPOPT—log of city population

IMEANEDU—mean level of education for the city's population

IPCINCT—mean level of income for the city's population

IPCTSEC—percentage of the population in manufacturing

IPOP3544—percentage of the population 35–44 years old

IPCTBLUE—percentage of the population who are blue-collar workers

IPARTY—mayor's party position on 0–100 scale of left-right party ideology (low = left)

IV144—age of mayor

CATHMY—dummy variable for Catholic mayors (1 = Catholic, 0 = not)

MAYED—years of education for the mayor

MAYYRS—years as mayor

FEMMAY—dummy variable for female mayors (1 = female, 0 = male)

FORNSTK—Percentage of the population who are foreigners and/or immigrants

Source: Fiscal Austerity and Urban Innovation Project surveys in each country. Data available for about 100 mayors in most countries. Details is in table A1.

scends description of one or two cases. Enough solid research has been conducted in this area to permit such accumulation of findings and the building of more systematic interpretations. The field practically cries for codification. What kind of theory, and thus what kinds of comparisons, can help? Comparing individuals suffices for many social psychological hypotheses, such as the role of party identification versus socialization for voting. But for more socially oriented political scientists and most sociologists, a good theory should include some more structural characteristics. Obvious candidates are class and party, but how and why are they interrelated in a manner that involves structural characteristics? Answers are too often lacking in recent research. Comparing multiple social units is key for most such structural theories. Nieuwbeerta and De Graaf (1999) include striking cross-national findings. Related work that seeks to explain the changing role of class-party linkages across units includes Przeworski and Sprague 1988, Inglehart 1990, and Franklin et al. 1992. All these report substantial differences over time and across countries. They reinforce Durkheim's admonition, which as restated by Przeworski and Teune (1970), called for researchers to formulate propositions and test them with cross-system data in such a manner that country names would disappear because they were analytically transcended. The statement, for instance, that class voting declines in the United States but not in Denmark should be replaced by an effort to specify what analytical characteristics differentiate the United States from Denmark, such as the strength of the unions and coherence of parties. Then the two-country difference can be reformulated: in political systems where unions and parties are more coherent, class voting is more likely to persist. Several such propositions are in the Clark, Lipset, and Rempel *International Sociology* papers (Clark and Lipset 1991; Clark et al. 1993). These more general propositions can be tested in cross-system analyses. Good examples of system propositions in nearby research include Budge and Kemen (1990), which elaborates a very clear set of deductive propositions about where and why different sets of parties join coalitions and shift policies. While stated as X causes Y-type propositions, they are tested with data for 20 national states. Similarly, Klingemann, Hofferbert, and Budge (1994) use several general models to analyze how specific party programs and coalition participation shift policy effects.

What kind of work on class politics moves in this direction? The first kind is studies using more countries, like Nieuwbeerta and De Graaf (1999). The second compares relations across other units, such as cities or regions, as well as across countries. Heath, Yang, and Goldstein (Und.)

and Weakliem and Heath (1999) are two papers that explore regional and local variations in class-party effects within Britain. Both pursue provocative system-type propositions. If they do not find support across the regions, they do find some interesting results about local differences: "Individuals from the same social class had very different propensities to vote Conservative in different constituencies . . . constituencies seemed to vary in their level of class polarization" (p. 14). This dovetails with the *International Sociology* propositions and some related local work.

Since 1982, I have coordinated the Fiscal Austerity and Urban Innovation Project, which has grown into the most extensive study of local government in the world. Why local government? Because it is a better fruit fly. Nations, by comparison, are prima donna elephants. Any good scientist should prefer fruit flies! We can advance theory better by studying 7,000 cities than by studying just 1 or even 15 nations. These should be generally compelling arguments to most participants in the recent class politics exchanges, whose quantitative sophistication is high. Surely as a reader I wince at the low degrees of freedom in some key analyses; the authors must be even more frustrated in trying to link their findings to some theory, especially in studies of only one or two countries. Historical changes and time series are a methodological option, but for periods as short as 20 years with only one or two inflection points, the substantive yield is meager.

Still, many types of research—purely descriptive, purely methodological, or purely theoretical—have contributed to this dynamic and rapidly changing subfield. My concern here is thus to call for more attention to (1) joining findings with more general structural propositions, (2) trying to eliminate country (or region or city) names, (3) joining results from several levels of research to bolster consistent patterns, fill in "exogenous" assumptions, or replicate findings. The last point demands elaboration: One powerful finding from our Fiscal Austerity and Urban Innovation (FAUI) Project is that class impacts on party vary enormously by country and by city within countries. In comparing seven countries, we find three distinct patterns linking class and party. These transcend country names. Results are summarized in figure 12.8, detail is in table A1 (see appendix 1).

Our FAUI surveys included comparable items to mayors analyzed here for seven countries. One question asked if the mayor would prefer more, the same, or less spending in 13 areas, which we summed in an index of fiscal liberalism (in the American, not Manchester, sense of liberalism, i.e., liberals favor more government). To explain fiscal liberalism, we analyzed characteristics of mayors and their cities in each country. We model the

strength of class politics in two key steps, shown in figure 12.8. Step 1
shows the impact of the percentage of blue-collar residents on mayor and
council member party affiliation (more blue-collar workers should increase
the number of left council members); step 2 shows the impact of party affiliation and blue-collar residents on the mayor's fiscal liberalism index.
The strength of class politics patterns is shown by the regression coefficients (betas) for these key variables (details in table A1). Additional variables are included as controls. We find three main patterns: (1) strong class
politics in Finland and France, (2) weak class politics in Canada, Japan,
Norway, and Australia, in that blue collar has little impact, but party does
affect mayor's ideology (in Japan and Australia only), and (3) the power of
race in the United States but the insignificance of class and party there. Although policy preferences in France and Finland are driven by parties and
percentage of blue-collar residents, party is insignificant in the United
States. Consistent with our propositions about race hierarchy in Clark
1994, the most powerful factor explaining American mayors' policy positions is the percentage of nonwhite residents; mayors with more nonwhite
residents favor more government spending. Race is the American version
of a class-based party; that is, race crystallizes majors' policy preferences in
America the way that class and party do in other countries with stronger
parties. But take methodological note: we would have found no structure
for the United States if we had used only party; this underlines the value of
including policy preferences along with party in such analyses.

These results come from ordinary least squares (OLS) regression and
use blue and white collar to measure class. OLS is appropriate because we
measure party in a manner others might consider to facilitate cross-
national research. The basic idea is to assign each party an IPARTY (I for
international) left-right score from 0 to 100, based on (1) expert rankings,
(2) citizen surveys, and (3) coding party programs. These three ranking
methods intercorrelate highly. Analogous methods can be used for measuring changes over time in one country. We have also estimated key relations for individual parties as dependent variables in logistic regressions,
calculated in two ways following the same methods as Heath et al. (1985)
and Hout et al. (1995). The basic results match those for OLS. The national differences are so large that they usually do not change with other
methods.

What is it about the three sets of countries that make some illustrate
strong class politics and others far less? One possible answer is "hierarchy."
That is, national societies and local units, which are more hierarchical, generate more antihierarchical politics to oppose hierarchy. This is our level-

ing principle. But as hierarchy declines, so do political reactions against it. We are measuring hierarchy in several ways, especially using indexes created with the methods developed by Atkinson (1975). Results for 20 countries are in Clark and Hoffmann-Martinot 1998, chapter 4.

Conclusion

In sum, across the many subsections above, we find considerable support for both class politics and the NPC in recent research on class-party relations. But because researchers in most studies have asked a narrower question—often, Is social class significant?—they have not usually observed how they cumulatively add considerable support for shifts toward an NPC (especially over the past 30 years in Britain, as studied by many). We are not in a zero-sum game; both class politics and elements of the New Political Culture are all around us. Rather than ignoring one or the other, should we not seek to illuminate both and explore contextual propositions about where each may grow or decline? A slight increase in conceptual sensitivity could make this happen.

Appendix 1. Modeling Class-Party Impacts in the Fiscal Austerity and Urban Innovation (FAUI) Project

The international FAUI surveys used a core set of items in all countries, supplemented with country-specific items. We use common survey items in table A1, socioeconomic variables assembled by our FAUI Project participants in each country and by several years of data analysis and interpretation by researchers in Chicago. Items in table A1 not explained above include:

PRFAVG represents the average spending preference of mayors on 13 FAUI items. The key FAUI spending item was Mayor Q4: Please indicate your own preferences about spending. Circle one of the six answers for each of the 13 policy areas: (1) spend a lot less on services provided by the city, (2) spend somewhat less, (3) spend the same as is now spent, (4) spend somewhat more, (5) spend a lot more, (DK) don't know/not applicable. Policy areas: all areas of city government, primary and secondary education, social welfare, streets and parking, mass transit, public health and hospitals, parks and recreation, low-income housing, police protection, fire protection, capital stock (e.g., roads, sewers, etc.), number of municipal employees, salaries of municipal employees.

SOCCONS6 summed two social liberalism/conservatism items:

Q19 (V131): Would you be for or against sex education in public schools? Circle one number: (1) for, (2) against, (3) don't know/not applicable.

Q20 (V132): Do you think abortion should be legal under any circumstance, legal only under certain circumstances, or never legal under any circumstances? Circle one number: (1) under any circumstances, (2) under certain circumstances, (3) never legal, (4) don't know/not applicable.

Source: Fiscal Austerity and Urban Innovation Project surveys, detailed further in Clark 1994.

FORNSTK = Foreign born: the proportion of persons in a city born outside the country. Data are not fully comparable in each country, but we are at the mercy of each national census for such items.

Table A1

Why Do Mayors Support Higher Spending? International Contrasts

A. Traditional class politics in France and Finland
B. Less class influence in Norway, Canada, Japan, and Australia
C. Race acts like class in the United States
Two-step process: Step 1—Percentage of blue-collar residents leads to traditional left-right party politics
Step 2—Percentage of blue-collar residents and left-right parties influence mayor's spending preferences

A—Step 1. Two countries illustrate traditional class politics: Blue-collar residents vote left, betas are significant.
Dependent variable: IPARTY

	France (N = 80)	Finland (N = 73)
Multiple R	.41	.35
R^2	.17	.13
Adj. R^2	.06	.06

Variable	Beta	Sig. t	Variable	Beta	Sig. t
IPCTBLUE	**-0.39**	**.01**[***]	**IPCTBLUE**	**-0.24**	**.04**[**]
MAYED	0.13	.27	IPOP3544	-0.17	.14
FEMMAY	-0.16	.16	MAYED	-0.15	.20
IV144	0.17	.19	IV144	0.10	.41
FORNSTK	0.17	.24	FEMMAY	0.00	.97
IPOP3544	-0.12	.44			
MAYYRS	-0.02	.88			
IPCINCT	0.23	.09			
LIPOPT	-0.04	.77			

A—Step 2. Traditional class-party politics: Party drives mayor's preferences, betas are strong.
Dependent variable: PRFAVG

	France (N = 80)			Finland (N = 73)	
Multiple R	.51			.50	
R²	.23			.25	
Adj. R²	.15			.17	

Variable	Beta	Sig. t	Variable	Beta	Sig. t.
IPARTY	**−0.42**	**.00*****	**IPARTY**	**−0.50**	**.00******
FEMMAY	0.03	.79	**IPCTBLUE**	**−0.29**	**.04**
IV144	0.18	.15	IMEANEDU	−0.26	.06*
MAYYRS	−0.12	.29	IV144	0.18	.14
MAYED	−0.11	.35	IPOP3544	0.12	.30
IPOP3544	0.11	.42	MAYED	−0.08	.49
LIPOPT	0.08	.50	FEMMAY	−0.03	.81
FORNSTIK	0.11	.42			
IPCTBLUE	**−0.01**	**.92**			
IPCINCT	0.09	.50			

IPCTBLUE = Percentage of blue-collar. For the United States, this includes the proportion of city residents whose occupations are listed as the following: private household services; protective service occupations; farming, forest, and fishing occupations; precision production, craft, and repair occupations; machine operators, assemblers, and inspectors; transportation and material-moving occupations; and handlers, equipment cleaners, helpers, and laborers. Other countries use similar measures, except for Canada, where the proportion of those in manufacturing is used.

IPARTY: We devised this measure to permit comparisons of each party in each country, as in table A1. This is an internationally comparable measure of left-right party ideology on a 0–100 scale, not distinguishing fiscal from social liberalism (low score is left). Scores came from one of two main sources. First was Castles and Mair (1984), who used experts to rank political parties on a left-right scale in many countries. Second, for countries not in Castles and Mair (1984), we used a survey where citizens affiliated with each party placed themselves on a general left-right scale (Sani and Sartori 1983). For France, party scores from past expert rankings (e.g., by Castles and Mair and others) were adapted by our French FAUI participant Vincent Hoffmann-Martinot to incorporate recent developments. The third source we compared against was Klingemann et al. (1994),

B—Step 1. Four countries illustrate weak class politics: betas are insignificant or reversed for blue collar. Dependent variable: IPARTY

	Norway (N = 364)			Canada (N = 67)			Japan (N = 70)			Australia (N = 37)[*]		
Multiple R	.34			.38			.45			.46		
R²	.11			.15			.20			.21		
Adj R²	.10			.03			.15			.05		

Variable	Beta	Sig. t	Variable	Beta	Sig. t	Variable	Beta	Sig. t	Variable	Beta	Sig. t
MAYED	0.27	.00***	CATHMY	-0.26	.06*	**IPCTBLUE**	**0.45***	**.00***	IPCINCT	0.24	.25
IPCINCT	0.22	.00***	IPOP3544	0.24	.06*	MAYYRS	0.13	.28	FORNSTK	-0.19	.29
IPCTBLUE	**0.05**	**.48**	FEMMAY	0.19	.13	MAYED	0.07	.56	MAYED	-0.19	.31
LIPOPT	0.02	-.77	IV144	0.18	.18	IV144	0.01	.91	LIPOP	-0.17	.35
IV144	0.06	-.22	MAYYRS	0.16	.22				**IPCTBLUE**	**-0.18**	**.38**
FEMMAY	0.06	.20	FORNST	0.12	.38				IV144	0.09	.63
			IPCTSEC	**0.03**	**.84**						
			MAYED	0.02	.87						

B—Step 2. Four countries illustrate less class influence on spending preferences: low or insignificant beta coefficients for blue collar variable, although party is strong in Norway, Japan, and Australia. Dependent variable: PRFAVG

Norway (N = 362)[b]

Multiple R	.34
R²	.11
Adj R²	.09

Variable	Beta	Sig. t
IPARTY	**-0.26**	**.00*****
FEMMAY	0.15	.00***
LIPOPT	-0.04	.53
IPCINCT	-0.12	.04
MAYED	0.00	.88
IV144	0.00	.99

Canada (N = 66)

Multiple R	.40
R²	.16
Adj R²	.02

Variable	Beta	Sig. t
FORNST	0.28	.04**
IPOP3544	0.18	.20
CATHMY	-0.15	.30
IPARTY	**0.09**	**.52**
MAYED	-0.07	.59
FEMMAY	0.06	.64
IPCTSEC	**-0.05**	**.69**
IV144	0.05	.72
MAYYRS	0.00	.98

Japan (N = 76)

Multiple R	.27
R²	.07
Adj R²	.02

Variable	Beta	Sig. t
IPARTY	**-0.21**	**.03****
IPCTBLUE	**0.21**	**.15**
MAYRS	0.18	.16
MAYED	0.03	.78
IV144	0.01	.91

Australia (N = 95 [37])[c]

Multiple R	.71
R²	.50
Adj R²	.36

Variable	Beta	Sig. t
IPARTY	**0.85**	**.00*****
IV144	0.27	.11
LIPOPT	-0.23	.14
FORNSTK	0.19	.24
IPCTBLUE	**-0.14**	**.46**
MAYED	-0.05	.76
IPCINCT	.05	.77

C—Step 1. For the United States percentage of nonwhite is strong; blue collar is insignificant.
Dependent variable: IPARTY

United States		(N = 239)
Multiple R	.35	
R²	.12	
Adj R²	.09	
Variable	Beta	Sig. t
CATHMY	−0.23	.00***
XNWH80U	**−0.15**	**.05****
MAYYRS	−0.10	.14
LIPOPT	−0.10	.15
MAYED	0.08	.23
IPCTBLUE	**−0.04**	**.54**
FEMMAY	−0.02	.70
FORNSTK	−0.01	.85
IV144	0.00	.96

C—Step 2. The United States falls in the middle: race performs like party and class in France, Finland, and Norway, but with less powerful effects.
Dependent variable: PRFAVG

United States		(N = 239)[b]
Multiple R	.27	
R²	.07	
Adj R²	.03	
Variable	Beta	Sig. t
XNWH80U	**0.18**	**.03****
IV144	−0.11	.11
IPARTY	**−0.07**	**.33**
FEMMAY	0.06	.34
FORNSTK	0.07	.36
MAYYRS	0.04	.57
CATHMY	0.02	.74
MAYED	−0.01	.85

Source: FAUI surveys of mayors in each country supplemented by census and similar data.

Notes: Table A1 shows the detailed results summarized in figure 12.8. Steps 1 and 2 refer to the paths in figure 12.1. There are multiple regressions to explain in step 1, IPARTY, mayor's party. Step 2 explains support by mayors for increased spending on an index of up to 13 municipal spending areas, PRFAVG. The multiple R, R², and adjusted R² are for equations containing all independent variables reported here. Similar models were utilized in each country; however, not all independent variables were completely identical; see discussion of each in text of appendix 1.

Key variables for class and race politics are bold throughout: percentage of blue collar, left-right partisanship, and the United States percentage of nonwhite.

Beta = standardized regression coefficient.

Sig. t = significance (probability) level for that independent variable.

Variables are ranked by the significance of the T statistic.

For Sig t: * = significant at .10 level; ** = significant at .05 level; *** = significant at .01 level.

[a] Blue collar is the "wrong" direction for Japan, indicating that blue-collar voters elect more conservative candidates. This is the opposite of "normal" class politics but consistent with Japanese voting research.

[b] Percentage of blue collar not included in this regression because of multicollinearity with IPARTY.

whose authors kindly provided the raw data. For those countries for which we had data from two or three sources, the intercorrelations of these three left-right rankings were nearly .9. We assigned the party of each mayor and council member in our survey an IPARTY score from these sources to permit analysis, for instance, of how strong the impact of blue-collar residents was on the mayor's party. Core analyses were replicated using individual parties as dummy variables and logistic regression.

Variables used in Table A1

PRFAVG—average spending preference of mayor on 13 FAUI items
LIPOPT—log of city population
IMEANEDU—mean level of education for the city's population
IPCINCT—mean level of income for the city's population
IPCTSEC—percentage of the population in manufacturing
IPOP3544—percentage of the population 35–44 years old
IPCTBLUE—percentage of the population who are blue-collar workers
IPARTY—mayor's party position on 0–100 scale of left-right party ideology (low = left)
IV144—age of mayor
CATHMY—dummy variable for Catholic mayors (1 = Catholic, 0 = not)
MAYED—years of education for the mayor
MAYYRS—years as mayor
FEMMAY—dummy variable for female mayors (1 = female, 0 = male)
FORNSTK—percentage of population who are foreigners and/or immigrants
XNWH80US—percentage of nonwhite residents in city (United States only)

Commentary on Table A1

Findings are robust for blue collar and party for the three countries illustrating type A traditional class politics. Type B is intermediary. Canada shows no effect of either blue collar or party in step 1 or 2, suggesting very little class politics. In the two other countries, differences in reported partisanship complicate interpretation. To simplify we have generally analyzed in this table only those mayors who reported party membership. But for Australia, this is just 37 of the 95 mayors; that is, most Australian mayors

are officially independent. In Japan even fewer mayors report party affiliation, but because Japanese councils are usually highly partisan, we assign
the mayor the average party affiliation of the council. In Australia and
Japan, step 1 indicates no significant impact of blue-collar residents on
mayor's party (or is reversed in sign. in Japan), but in step 2, party does affect mayor's ideology. We might thus refer to Australia and Japan as party-
politicized but not class-based. But party-politicized is only by comparison
with the United States and Canada, where similar methods (i.e., omitting
non-party affiliated mayors) generate no impact of either blue collar or
party in step 1 or 2. Still, party-politicized overstates the party effects for
Australian cities generally, since most mayors are nonpartisan. The United
States is unusual, first in that race (and Catholic affiliation) overwhelm blue
collar in explaining party affiliation of mayors in step 1. In step 2, party has
no impact on ideology, in sharp contrast with five of the six other countries, where party is the leading variable explaining ideology.

The same model was initially specified for steps 1 and 2 for all countries.
However, multicollinearity (r > .4) among some variables led us to omit
them. Specifically:

Country	Associated Variable	Variable Omitted
Finland	IPCTBLUE	IMEANEDU
Norway	IV144	MAYYRS
Norway	IPCTBLUE	IPOP3544
Japan	IPCTBLUE	IPCINCT
Japan	IPCTBLUE	IPOP3544
Japan	IPCTBLUE	IMEANEDU
United States	IPCTBLUE	IPCINCT

FEMMAY was omitted in Japan because there were no female mayors.

Appendix 2. Notes on How Methods Can Change Class Effects: A Critique of (Simplistic) Logistic Regression

Several points in the text about logistic regression deserve elaboration.
When logistic regression was first used by Heath et al. (1985) to analyze
class voting, the reported "trendless fluctuation" results brought an outcry
from many researchers (e.g., Crewe 1986; Heath et al. 1987; Dunleavy
1987). While most critics felt that logistic regression was somehow at fault,
no one to date seems to have traced the key assumptions and implications
of using logistic regression versus ordinary least squares (OLS) regression,
detailing how these methods specifically affect substantive results concern-

ing class voting. Most methodological writing is by logistic advocates and is largely a critique of OLS. It does not seek to clarify why results may change with these two methods or with variations in how they are applied. This note is a first step to encourage more such work.

How much does logistic regression "generate" class effects? This is the key question. As ever, it is largely not the method per se but how it is applied and interpreted. Logistic modeling flows often from a critique of just using the blue- versus white-collar classification of occupation and substitutes a larger number of occupations as independent variables. However, there is seldom an explicit rationale or set of hypotheses specifying why these several occupations should each generate specific political effects. There is a generally implicit assumption that more is better than less in operationalizing occupational categories. But is class really "just" occupation? This is a serious conceptual point glossed over in most recent research. The answer clearly depends on definitions of class and occupation, but redefining class by seven rather than two occupational census categories surely is open to criticism. It is not clear that Marx would endorse such analytical fragmentation, or more generally that current political leaders aim their programs or policies at such occupational subgroups, or that persons who work in the specific occupational categories used in this research have any sense of occupational distinctiveness that might have political consequences. Heath et al. (1985: 14ff.) reject the continuous measures (especially income) and social stratification rankings from Warner and Lunt (1941) (such as upper middle, lower middle class, etc.) as "appropriate for market researchers who are professionally concerned with such things as consumer purchases" (14) but not for politics; they propose instead that politics concerns conflict and that occupational groups are key measures of such cleavages. This clearly is a effort to focus on such conflicts as "politics" and explicitly denies that consumption issues are central to politics. If one might instead seek to test the appropriateness of this rather critical assumption and consider its implications for the hypotheses at stake, the results might be more compelling. Heath et al. use just five categories, salariat, routine nonmanual, petty bourgeoisie, foremen and technicians, and working class. Hout et al. (1995) are more explicitly inductive in simply using the available census measures of occupation.

Increasing the number of measures of occupation may indeed increase the possible impact that some combination of them statistically affects party choice, but if—as Hout et al. report—professionals vote Republican in the 1950s but Democratic in the 1990s, does this imply more, less, or no change in class voting? Their answer, "trendless fluctuation," derives not from inspecting the coefficients of individual occupations but from the bic statistic, a measure of the overall power of the model, analogous to an R^2 in multiple regression. This interpretation focusing on just one of several logistic statistics (the bic), of course, ignores the reversal of signs by professionals, a reversal that is anything but trendless. This point is stressed in Clark (1995), and Brooks and Manza (1997) subsequently completed two full papers exploring the political realignment by professionals, finally recognizing and addressing this critical shift.

Logistic regression in related research takes two basic forms. Several independent variables of occupation (and maybe more) are used to explain (1) a single dichotomous dependent variable (like voting Democratic vs. Republican) or (2) several discrete (noncontinuous) variables (like Labor, Liberal, Conservative). Either variation can truncate data. Consider a critical example: Are lower-status persons voting for left parties consistently over time? Logistic regression in recent work (e.g., Heath et al. 1985, 1991) suggests that the coefficient for manual workers is unchanged over time or varies trendlessly. But this result comes in part from ignoring the decline in numbers of manual workers and corresponding growth of new service jobs, including many lower-level office positions, which increasingly characterize Western societies, and from ignoring the corresponding change in the abilities and outlook of persons who today still have manual working jobs. They may be less able or ambitious than their counterparts 30 or 50 years ago, since the more able and ambitious are less likely to remain manual workers. This result can also be seen if one follows the logistic method of Heath et al. and many others; they dichotomize party into Labor and all others, rather than arraying several parties along a scale (as illustrated in the analysis in Clark 1995 and here using the IPARTY variable), or they employ some other multivariate statistical method (like OLS) that uses continuous variables rather than dichotomies or discrete variables. The result is (albeit not inevitably) to conflate the party continuum and ignore the votes going to new parties (like the Alliance in the United Kingdom) that won more votes over time. A key part of the postindustrial society argument is that (some) old parties change programs, and new parties emerge with new programs to respond to changing preferences. If one is to test competing theoretical models, one needs at least a method to look for such changes of party and program rather than assuming them away in the choice of method.

In social mobility research, logistic analyses are often applied to dichotomies to estimate "transition probabilities," such as going to high school or not, and then to college or not, rather than analyzing a continuous measure, such as total years of education completed. De Graff and Ganzeboom (1993) are an exception, stressing that Mare initially proposed such a total-education measure when he launched the logistic approach and focused on such transitions to the total. But if one shifts to this continuous measure of educational attainment and uses OLS, results often show continuous growth over recent decades in educational attainment by lower-status persons (see Treiman and Yamaguchi 1993: 237; and De Graff and Ganzeboom 1993)—the opposite of "persistent inequality." Other mobility analysts suggest that they seek to analyze the probability of a child of a manual laborer going to college, net of the effects of growth in higher education, and other such variables. They suggest that the logistic setup achieves this (Shavit and Blossfeld 1993). Still, one might ask, Why seek to eliminate the critical welfare state policy of expanding higher education? Or at least, could one not seek to measure what proportion of the overall mobility effect (or change in attainment) is due to this versus other factors?

It is no secret among stratification researchers that there is a huge ongoing debate involving Donald Treiman and Harry Ganzeboom versus Michael Hout and John Goldthorpe and others on methodological issues in social mobility research. They meet personally in Research Committee 28 of the International Sociological Association. Ganzeboom is skeptical of the "trendless fluctuation" results of the others, for some of the reasons listed above, among others. For instance, he suggests that in many studies the N is too low to isolate the interaction effects specified in logistic regressions, so they only appear trendless. Several of his papers are cited in De Graff and Ganzeboom 1993.

For politics and class voting analyses, however, if one occupational category, such as manual workers, has declined in size by half (which approximately has occurred in most Western countries in recent decades), yet its members continue to vote left in the same proportion as in the past (this is the coefficient stressed by most users), most logistic method users interpret this as implying no change or trendless fluctuation. Yet lower- and middle-level white-collar jobs have expanded in this same period. And, one critical point is that such white-collar workers vote left less often than manual workers do. In Britain, they vote more for the Alliance than manual laborers do. These huge shifts in size of occupational categories are ignored in reporting trendless fluctuation.

If one would instead create a measure of, say, the lower third of the population in terms of occupational prestige or income and analyze its voting over time, it would probably show a decline in "class voting" in most countries, especially if one uses a continuous party measure including new parties.

The great attention to trends in recent work also leads to ignoring the major differences that persist across countries (and localities) in the degree of class voting. We should observe Durkheim's comment that "science begins with comparison." If our methods only generate trendless fluctuation, this does not help explain how social dynamics work. Class voting and education attainment rates very considerably across countries, regions, and cities. To explain why, we should look for, measure, and analyze differences and their covariates. Then propositions about why social classes rise or decline in importance (as in Clark and Lipset 1991) can be seriously confronted.

Appendix 3: Notes on Party Manifestos Project

Data set CMPr3 [author A. Volkens], Comparative Manifestos Project, Science Center Berlin, Research Unit Institutions and Social Change [Director H.-P. Klingemann] in cooperation with the Manifestos Research Group [Chairman I. Budge]

These data come from coding the party "manifestos" or programs for national parties, often issued for nation elections. Programs were coded in a large international project for 250 parties in 28 countries from 1945 to present (the project continues). Each distinct idea was considered a "quasi sentence" and classified into one of 56 categories. Many categories involved national or international issues (foreign policy, peace) or did not fall clearly into more traditional left-right or New Political Culture themes. We selected nine themes that seemed to differentiate traditional left-right versus the NPC reasonably clearly. But the number of mentions for four of these was so low that they were deleted: Marxist analysis, nationalization, free enterprise, antigrowth economy. Five were retained, defined as follows:

> *Environmental protection:* preservation of countryside, forests, etc.; general preservation of natural resources against selfish interests; proper use of national parks; soil banks, etc.; environmental improvement.
> *Government and administrative efficiency:* need for efficiency and economy in government and administration; reduction of civil service; improvement of governmental procedures; general appeal to make the process of government and administration cheaper and more effective.

Traditional morality: positive: favorable mentions of traditional moral value; prohibition; censorship and suppression of immorality and unseemly behavior; maintenance and stability of family; religion.

Labor groups: positive: favorable references to labor groups, working class, unemployed; support for trade unions; good treatment of manual and other employees.

Welfare +: welfare state expansion: favorable mentions of need to introduce, maintain, or expand any social service or social security scheme; support for social services such as health services or social housing. Note: This category excludes education.

The units reported on the Y (vertical) axis of figures 12.2 through 12.7 are the percentages of quasi sentences that the manifesto devoted to each theme. Given the form of these data, the simple hypothesis that was tested was that there was an increase in NPC themes over the post–World War II period. Thus two subperiods were compared: 1945–1973 and 1974–1988 (the last year currently available). The mean percentage of space devoted to each theme was then compared in the two periods, and a t-test computed to indicate significance of the change. Results for all 250 parties in 28 countries showed significant shifts toward the NPC on four of the five themes; the exception was traditional morality, which showed no change.

Notes

1. Stinchcombe's comment is discussed in note 1 of chapter 1 of this volume.

2. As reported by my colleague Robert Sampson (pers. comm.), the tradition of class, at least as mediated by R. K. Merton (1995) was superseded by others.

3. My main informant here is my colleague Roger Gould.

4. Many analysts follow Dahrendorf in preserving the rhetoric of class despite empirical changes. This permits continued application of normative labels like "exploitation," "oppression," and "domination" and the corresponding need to organize and protest to move toward an alternative ideal, such as more equality. John Meyer refers to this tendency among stratification researchers: "The issues involved here infuse the stratification literature as well as modern social discussion with much normative excitement. Minor details of the distribution of income or education become salient, and analyses of mobility give great attention to causal pathways distinguishable according to their justice and efficiency" (1994: 733).

5. The possibilities for such dramatic shifts in ideology are illustrated by perhaps the most important internationally shared plank of the New Political Culture: environmental politics: The starkest shift in environmental rhetoric came in September 1988, when Prime Minister Margaret Thatcher addressed the Royal Society. Before that date she had shown very little public interest in environmental issues and had led a government that had become infamous for resisting even modest action on sometimes life-threatening global problems. Yet in her 1988 speech, Thatcher staked out the environmental high ground with great vigor and called for united efforts to preserve global environmental catastrophes.

This was followed a few weeks later by an address to the Conservative Party conference, in which she staked out the environment as an important issue and called Conservatives "not merely friends of the Earth, but its guardians and trustees for generations to come."

This was followed by a more official adoption of environmental programs by the Conservative Party, white papers adding specifics, continuation by Prime Minister John Major, and adoption of new domestic policy laws including a comprehensive Environmental Protection Act submitted to Parliament in January 1990 and adopted November 1990. It includes "stricter standards for air pollution emissions, waste disposal, and other environmental hazards," plus a comprehensive industrial pollution policy to avoid merely shifting pollution across regions (Levy 1991: 2, 3).

References

Atkinson, A. B. 1975. *The Economics of Inequality*. London: Oxford University Press.

Bell, Daniel. 1973. *The Coming of Post-Industrial Society*. New York: Basic Books.

Brint, Steven, 1994. *In An Age of Experts*. Princeton: Princeton University Press.

Brooks, Clem, and Jeff Manza. 1997. "The Social and Ideological Bases of Middle Class Realignment in the United States, 1972–1992." *American Sociological Review* 62: 191–208.

Budge, Ian, and Hans Keman. 1990. *Parties and Democracy*. Oxford: Oxford University Press.

Castles, F., and P. Mair. 1984. "Left-Right Political Scales: Some 'Expert' Judgments." *European Journal of Political Research* 12: 73–88.

Chauvel, Louis. 1995. "Inégalités singulieres et plurielles." *Revue de l'Observatoire Français des Conjonctures Economiques* 55 (October): 211-240.

Clark, Terry Nichols. 1995. "Who Cares if Social Class Is Dying, or Not? Being an Effort to Articulate a Framework to Deepen the Meaning of Such Questions." Prepared as background for conference on social class at Nuffield College, Oxford, February 1995.

Clark, Terry Nichols. 1994. "Program for a New Public Choice." In James L. Chan, ed., *Governmental Accounting and Public Choice*, Vol. 8, *Governmental and Nonprofit Accounting*, 3–28. Greenwich, Conn: JAI Press. (See also Aussie June Pallet, "Commentary on Terry Nichols Clark," same volume, pp. 29–38.)

Clark, Terry Nichols, ed. 1994. *Urban Innovation: Creative Strategies in Turbulent Times*. London, Newbury Park, New Delhi: Sage Publications.

Clark, T. N., and R. Inglehart. 1988. "The New Political Culture." Paper presented at the annual meeting of American Political Science Association, Atlanta, Georgia. (Revised version appears as chap. 2 of Clark and Hoffmann-Martinot 1998.)

Clark, Terry Nichols, and Seymour Martin Lipset. 1991. "Are Social Classes Dying?" *International Sociology* 6 (December): 397–410.

Clark, T. N., and V. Hoffmann-Martinot, eds. 1998. *The New Political Culture*. Boulder: Westview.

Clark, T. N., and M. Rempel, eds. 1997. *Citizen Politics in Post-Industrial Societies*. Boulder: Westview.

Clark, Terry Nichols, Seymour Martin Lipset, and Mike Rempel. 1993. "The Declining Political Significance of Social Class." *International Sociology* 8, no. 3 (September): 293–316.

Coleman, R. P., and L. Rainwater, with K. A. McClelland. 1978. *Social Standing in America*. New York: Basic Books.

Crewe, Ivor. 1986. "On the Death and Resurrection of Class Voting: Some Comments on 'How Britain Votes." *Political Studies* 34: 620–638.

Dahrendorf, R. 1959. *Class and Class Conflict in Industrial Society*. Stanford: Stanford University Press.

De Graff, Paul M., and Harry B. G. Ganzeboom. 1993. "Family Background and Educational Attainment in the Netherlands for the 1891–1960 Birth Cohorts." In Y. Shavit and H. -P. Blossfeld, eds., *Persistent Inequality,* 75–100. Boulder: Westview.

Downs, Anthony. 1957. *An Economic Theory of Democracy.* New York.

Dunleavy, Patrick. 1987. "Class Dealignment in Britain Revisited." *West European Politics.* 10: 400–419.

Dunleavy, Patrick, and C. Husbands. 1985. *British Democracy at the Crossroads.* London: Allen and Unwin.

Erikson, Robert, and John Goldthorpe. 1992. *The Constant Flux.* Oxford: Clarendon Press.

Erikson, R., J. H. Goldthorpe, and L. Portocarero. 1979. "Intergenerational Class Mobility in Three West European Societies." *British Journal of Sociology* 30: 415–441.

Evans, Geoffrey. 1993a. "Is Gender on the 'New Agenda'?" *European Journal of Political Research* 24: 135–158.

Evans, Geoffrey. 1993b. "Class, Prospects, and the Life-Cycle." *Acta Sociologica* 36: 263–276.

Evans, Geoffrey, ed. 1999. *The End of Class Politics?* Oxford: Oxford University Press.

Evans, Mariah D, and Edward O. Laumann. 1983. "Professional Commitment: Myth or Reality." In Donald J. Treiman and Robert B. Robinson, eds., *Research in Stratification and Mobility.* 3–40. Greenwich, Conn.: JAI Press.

Fox, Karl A. 1974. *Social Indicators and Social Theory.* New York: Wiley-Interscience.

Franklin, Mark, Thomas T. Mackie, and Henry Valen, et al. 1992. *Electoral Change: Responses to Evolving Social and Attitudinal Structures in Western Countries.* New York: Cambridge University Press.

Fuchs, Ester. 1992. *Mayors and Money.* Chicago: University of Chicago Press.

Giddens, Anthony. 1980. *The Class Structure of the Advanced Societies.* New York: Harper and Row.

Goldthorpe, John H. 1999. "Modelling the Pattern of Class Voting in British Elections, 1964–1992." In Geoffrey Evans, ed., *The End of Class Politics?* 59–82. Oxford: Oxford University Press.

Grusky, David, ed. 1994. *Social Stratification.* Boulder, Colo.: Westview Press.

Heath, Anthony, and Mike Savage. N.d. "Middle Class Politics." In *British Social Attitudes,* chap. 6, 61–74.

Heath, Anthony, Robert Jowell, and John Curtice. 1985. *How Britain Votes.* Oxford: Pergamon Press.

Heath, A., R. Jowell, and J. Curtice. 1987. "Trendless Fluctuation: A Reply to Crewe." *Political Studies* 35, no. 2: 256–277.

Heath, A., M. Yang, and H. Goldstein. N.d. "Multilevel Analysis of the Changing Relationship between Class and Party in Britain 1964–1992." Draft. Nuffield College.

Heath, Anthony, et al. 1991. *Understanding Political Change: The British Voter 1964–1987.* Oxford: Pergamon Press.

Hout, M., C. Brooks, and J. Manza. 1993. "The Persistence of Classes in Post-Industrial Societies." *International Sociology* 8, no. 3: 259–277.

Hout, Michael, Clem Brooks, and Jeff Manza. 1995. "The Democratic Class Struggle in the United States, 1948–1992." *American Sociological Review* 60, no. 6 (December): 805–828.

Inglehart, Ronald. 1990. *Culture Shift in Advanced Industrial Society.* Princeton, N.J.: Princeton University Press.

Klingemann, Hans-Dieter, Richard I. Hofferbert, and Ian Budge. 1994. *Parties, Politics, and Democracy.* Boulder: Westview.

Kristol, Irving. 1978. *Two Cheers for Capitalism.* New York: Basic Books.

Kramer, Gerald. 1971. "Short-Term Fluctuations in U.S. Voting Behavior, 1896–1964." *American Political Science Review* 65 (March): 131–143.

Lee, David J., and Brian S. Turner, eds. 1996. *Conflicts about Class*. London: Longman.

Leighley, Jan E. and Jonathan Naglet. 1992. "Socioeconomic Class and Bias in Turnout, 1964–1988: The Voters Remain the Same." *American Political Science Review* 86: 725–736.

Levy, Marc. 1991. "The Greening of the United Kingdom." Paper presented to annual meeting of the American Political Science Association, Washington, D.C. Available from Center for International Affairs, Harvard University, 1737 Cambridge St., Cambridge, Mass. 02138.

Lipset, Seymour Martin. 1981. *Political Man: The Social Bases of Politics*. Baltimore: Johns Hopkins University Press.

Lipset, Seymour Martin. 1991. "No Third Way: A Comparative Perspective on the Left." In Daniel Chirot, ed., *The Crisis of Leninism and the Decline of the Left*, 183–232. Seattle: University of Washington Press.

Manza, Jeff, and Clem Brooks. 1995. "Explaining Partisan Trends among Professionals and Managers in the United States since the 1960s." In Terry Nichols Clark and Michael Rempel, eds., *Citizen Politics in Post-Industrial Societies*. Boulder: Westview.

Manza, Jeff, Michael Hout, and Clem Brooks. 1995. "Class Voting in Capitalist Democracies since WWII." *Annual Review of Sociology* 21: 137–163.

Merton, Robert K. 1995. "Opportunity Structure: The Emergence, Diffusion, and Differentiation of a Sociological Concept, 1930s–1950s." In Freda Adler and William S. Laufer, eds., *The Legacy of Anomie Theory: Advances in Criminological Theory*, vol. 6, 3–78. New Brunswick, N.J.: Transaction Publications.

Meyer, John. 1994. "The Evolution of Modern Stratification Systems." In David B. Grusky, ed., *Social Stratification*, 730–737. Boulder: Westview.

Nieuwbeerta, Paul. 1995. *The Democratic Class Struggle*. Amsterdam: Thesis Publishers.

Nieuwbeerta, Paul, and Nan Dirk De Graaf. 1999. "Traditional Class Voting in Twenty Postwar Societies." In Geoffrey Evans, ed., *The End of Class Politics?* 23–58. Oxford: Oxford University Press.

Pakulski, Jan. 1993. "The Dying of Class or Marxist Class Theory." *International Sociology* 8, no. 3 (September): 279–292.

Przeworski, Adam, and John Sprague. 1988. *Paper Stones*. Chicago: University of Chicago Press.

Przeworski, Adam, and Henry Teune. 1970. *The Logic of Comparative Social Inquiry*. New York: Wiley-Interscience.

Ringdal, Kristen, and Kjell Hines. 1999. "Changes in Class Voting in Norway." In Geoffrey Evans, ed., *The End of Class Politics?* 181–202. Oxford: Oxford University Press.

Sani, G., and G. Sartori. 1983. "Polarization, Fragmentation, and Competition in Western Democracies." In H. Daalder and P. Mair, eds., *Western European Party Systems*, 307–340. Beverly Hills: Sage.

Shavit, Yossi, and Hans-Peter Blossfeld, eds., 1993. *Persistent Inequality*. Boulder: Westview.

Svallfors, Stefan. 1999. "The Class Politics of Swedish Welfare Policies." In Geoffrey Evans, ed., *The End of Class Politics?* 203–230. Oxford: Oxford University Press.

Szalai, Alexander, ed. (with Philip Converse, Pierre Feldheim, Erwin K. Scheuch, and Philip J. Stone). 1973. *The Use of Time*. The Hague: Mouton.

Treiman, Donald J. and Kazuo Yamaguchi. 1993. "Trends in Educational Attainment in Japan." In Y. Shavit and H.-P. Blossfeld, *Persistent Inequality*, 229–250. Boulder: Westview.

Vanneman, R., and L. Weber. 1987. *The American Perception of Class*. Philadelphia: Temple University Press.

Verba, S., N. H. Nie. 1972. *Participation in America*. New York: Harper and Row.

Warner, W. Lloyd, and Paul S. Lunt. 1941. *The Social Life of a Modern Community*. New Haven, Conn.: Yale University Press.

Weakliem, David. 1991. "The Two Lefts? Occupation and Party Choice in France, Italy and the Netherlands." *American Journal of Sociology* 96 (May): 1327–1361.

Weakliem, David. 1995. "Two Models of Class Voting. "*British Journal of Political Science* 25: 254–270.

Weakliem, David. 1997. "Race Versus Class? Racial Composition and Class Voting, 1936–92." *Social Forces* 75: 939–956.

Weakliem, David L. and Anthony Heath. 1994. "Rational Choice and Class Voting." *Rationality and Society* 6, no. 2: 243–270.

Weakliem, David, and Anthony Heath. 1995. "Regional Differences in Class Dealignment: A Comment on Johnston and Pattie." *Political Geography* 14: 643–631.

Weakliem, David L., and Anthony F. Heath. 1999. "Resolving Disputes about Class Voting in Britain and the United States." In Geoffrey Evans, ed., *The End of Class Politics?* 281–307. Oxford: Oxford University Press.

Wright, Erik Olin. 1985. *Classes.* London: Verso.

Wright, Erik Olin. 1996. *Class Counts.* New York: Cambridge University Press.

Contributors

Herman L. Boschken teaches at San Jose State University. He holds a B.S. from the University of California, Berkeley, and a Ph.D. from the University of Washington, Seattle, in urban affairs, public policy, and administrative theory. His publications in these fields include two dozen scholarly articles and five books, one of which is forthcoming under the title *Social Class, Politics and Urban Markets: The Makings of Bias in Policy Outcomes*. He has lectured widely in the United States, Europe, South Africa, and China and has had two Fulbright awards, the most recent a Fulbright Distinguished European Chair. For his work related to social class, he has also received the Herbert Kaufman Award presented by the American Political Science Association. He was the founding editor of *Intermodal Fare*, published by the transportation section of the American Society for Public Administration, and was a past associate editor of the *Political Research Quarterly.*.

Clem Brooks is associate professor of sociology at Indiana University, Bloomington. His research interests are electoral politics, values and public opinion, social change, and quantitative methods. Guided by theories of partisan realignment and political culture, he is investigating long-term sources of political change in the United States since the 1960s and probing the interrelationship of stratification and political behavior.

Terry Nichols Clark is professor of sociology at the University of Chicago. His books include *Prophets and Patrons: The French University and the Emergence of the Social Sciences, City Money and Research in Urban Policy* (8 volumes published to date, JAI Press), and *The New Political Culture*. He is president of Research Committee 03 of the International Sociological Association, which launched the Fiscal Austerity and Urban Innovation (FAUI) Project in 1982. He is coordinator of the FAUI Project, a survey of all US cities with populations over 25,000, and parallel surveys in 35 other countries. He holds M.A. and Ph.D. degrees from Columbia University, and has taught at Columbia, Harvard, Yale, the Sorbonne, UCLA, and the University of Florence.

322   *Contributors*

John H. Goldthorpe is an official fellow of Nuffield College, Oxford, a fellow of the British Academy, and a member of the Academia Europaea. His publications in the field of social stratification and mobility include (with David Lockwood et al.) *The Affluent Worker,* 3 vols., 1968–1996; *Social Mobility and Class Structure in Modern Britain,* 2nd ed., 1987; and (with Robert Erikson) *The Constant Flux: A Study of Class Mobility in Industrial Societies,* 1992. A collection of his recent essays, entitled *On Sociology: Numbers, Narratives and the Integration of Research and Theory,* was published by Oxford University Press in 2000.

Mike Hout is Professor of Sociology and Director, Survey Research Center. University of California, Berkeley, where he has taught since 1985. He is the author of *Mobility Tables* (Sage, 1983) and *Following in Father's Footsteps: Social Mobility in Ireland* (Harvard, 1989) plus articles on social stratification in the United States, Ireland, and elsewhere. With Erik Wright he has recently completed fieldwork on comparative surveys of social stratification in Russia and the United States. He is a member of the ISA Research Committee on Stratification and Mobility (RC 28) executive board.

Dick Houtman is an assistant professor of sociology at Erasmus University, Rotterdam, the Netherlands, and a member of the Amsterdam School for Social Science Research (ASSR). After the completion of his Ph.D. dissertation, *Werkloosheid en sociale rechtvaardigheid: Oordelen over de rechten en plichten van werklozen* (Unemployment and social justice: Judgments on the rights and obligations of the unemployed) (Amsterdam: Boom, 1994), he conducted research in the United States in 1995, enabled by a TALENT fellowship, granted by the Netherlands Organization for Scientific Research (NWO). Since then, he has published mostly about unemployment and social justice and about the relationships among social stratification, modernity, and political values. On the last-mentioned topic he has recently published *Een blinde vlek voor cultuur: Sociologen over cultureel conservatisme, klassen en moderniteit* (A blind spot for culture: Sociologists on cultural conservatism, classes, and modernity) (Assen: Van Gorcum, 2000).

Seymour Martin Lipset is a Senior Scholar at the Woodrow Wilson Center, Senior Fellow at the Hoover Institution, Stanford University, and Hazel Professor of Public Policy and Professor of Sociology at George Mason University. His books include *Political Man; Class, Status and Party; Agrarian Socialism; The First New Nation; Revolution and Counterrevolu-*

tion; The Politics of Unreason; Continental Divide, and *It Didn't Happen Here: Why Socialism Failed in the United States.* He is co-editor of *The International Journal of Public Opinion.* He founded and served as president of the International Sociological Association's Research Committee on Political Sociology, which conducted several international comparisons of social stratification and its political consequences. He has been president of the American Sociological Association and of the American Political Science Association.

Jeff Manza is an associate professor of sociology at Northwestern University. He is the author (with Clem Brooks) of *Social Cleavages and Political Change: Voter Alignments and U.S. Party Coalitions* (Oxford University Press, 1999) and (with Christopher Uggen) a forthcoming study of the political consequences of felon disfranchisement laws in the United States (University of Chicago Press).

Paul Nieuwbeerta is a senior researcher at the Institute for the Study of Criminality and Law Enforcement in the Netherlands. He is the author of a number of articles on social cleavages and voting behavior, most recently (with Nan Dirk de Graff and Wout Ultee) "Effects of Class Mobility on Class Voting in Post-War Western Industrialized Countries," *European Sociological Review* (December 2000).

Jan Pakulski is Professor of sociology at the University of Tasmania. He writes on social class movements, elites, and social change. His more recent books include *Social Movements,* Postmodernization (with S. Crook and M. Waters) and *The Death of Class* (with M. Waters).

Michael Rempel is a Ph.D. candidate in sociology at the University of Chicago with interests in political sociology and stratification.

David L. Weakliem is associate professor of sociology at the University of Connecticut. He is the author of a number of articles on class and politics, including "Class Voting, Social Change, and the Left in Australia, 1943–96," in the *British Journal of Sociology* (December 1999).

Index